CONTESTED KNOWLEDGE

Social Theory in the Postmodern Era

Steven Seidman

BLACKWELL
Oxford UK & Cambridge USA

First published 1994

Blackwell Publishers
238 Main Street
Cambridge, Massachusetts 02142
USA

108 Cowley Road
Oxford OX4 1JF
UK

Library of Congress Cataloging-in-Publication Data
Seidman, Steven
    Contested Knowledge: Social Theory in the Postmodern Era/Steven
  Seidman.
      p. cm.
    Includes bibliographical references and index.
    ISBN 1-55786-507-8. – ISBN 1-55786-508-6 (pbk.)
    1. Sociology–Methodology. 2. Postmodernism–social aspects.
I. Title.
HM24.S382 1994
301'.01–dc20   93-42087
                                                  CIP

British Library Cataloguing in Publication Data
A CIP catalogue record for this book is available from the British Library.

Typeset in 11 on 13pt Garamond by TecSet Ltd, Wallington, Surrey.
Printed in Great Britain by Hartnolls Ltd, Bodmin.
This book is printed on acid free paper.

CONTESTED KNOWLEDGE

in memory of Aaron Roth

Contents

PART 3
DISLODGING THE CANON: THE REASSERTION OF A MORAL VISION OF THE HUMAN SCIENCES

Preface

I am very much a child of the sixties. I dropped out of school, took drugs, looked to my body as a source of pleasure and rebellion, and marched to change the world. I imagined the social sphere as a field of enormous possibilities for self and collective renewal. As the sixties dead-ended in drugs, violence, and either political extremism or liberal accommodation, I followed the hordes of the middle class into graduate school. I took my Ph.D. in sociology in 1980. I figured sociology to be a discipline that would help me to make sense of myself, envision different futures, and enact change.

I recall the bitter disillusionment of my first few years as a sociologist. I expected my colleagues to share my moral vision of sociology. The reality was sobering. My colleagues hardly read anything outside of their specialty areas; few of them talked about ideas of broad public significance; the culture of sociology seemed a parochial world where "scientific" talk and status anxieties produced an insulated expert world. I was aghast at the wreckage of professionalization: smart, well-intentioned individuals with good values, whose intellect was stunted by a disciplinary culture that was largely ignorant of history, different cultures, and that lacked strong ties to a public world of social conflict and moral debate.

I rebelled. I turned to the roots of modern social thought in order to call sociology to task for abandoning its moral promise. I undertook a study of the Enlightenment origins of European social theory. The passion that previously went into personal and social rebellion was now channeled into a quest to reform sociology. I hoped to find in the original inspiration of modern social theory a warrant for approaching sociology as a moral and political practice. I found what I was looking for: The *philosophes* and the classics viewed social analysis as a vehicle of social critique and change.

As the memories of the sixties faded, my own writings became obscure. In the apolitical spirit of the "me generation" of the 1980s, I was absorbing the disciplinary culture of sociology. I started thinking of myself as a "theorist," as if theory had its own problems and value apart from social analysis and critique. I was losing myself in "theory" discussions. My work was starting to feel sterile and pointless. I felt alienated from my original moral and political motives for becoming a sociologist.

The AIDS crisis jolted me. It was 1981. I remember reading of the mysterious disease that was taking the lives of gay men. I recall the media hysteria, the homophobic public response, and the governmental neglect. I was living in New Mexico trying to finish my book on the classical social theorists. As I was preoccupied with Marx's *Capital* or Durkheim's *Suicide*, the fatalities from AIDS seemed to be growing exponentially. The AIDS epidemic fed into a backlash against the social rebellions of the sixties. America, once again, seemed in the throes of a major political and cultural war. As a leftist and gay man, my whole life felt raw and vulnerable. The progressive culture that I valued was under attack. AIDS was an enemy killing off my friends and threatening me personally. In the midst of this social and personal upheaval, my work on classical sociology felt more and more pointless, as did the field of sociology in general.

In a manner of speaking, I took leave of sociology in the early 1980s. I finished my book on classical social theory. But my focus had definitely shifted. AIDS and the backlash against the progressive movements of the sixties gripped me. I began clipping out everything that appeared in the press on AIDS and the social backlash. I stopped reading sociology and sociological theory. As the politics of the body, sexuality, gender, and knowledge moved to the center of my life, I found myself absorbed in the texts of feminism, gay and lesbian studies, race theory, poststructuralism, and cultural studies. In the course of reading and writing in these areas, I became a part of a community of intellectuals who shared common values and a broad moral and political vision of social knowledge. I had for all practical purposes ceased being part of the sociological community.

And yet, I have returned to, or at least made peace with, sociology. I write *Contested Knowledge*, in part, as a sociologist. Why?

Perhaps I was drawn back to the discipline the way a young adult, having struggled for independence and attained security in his or her individuality, returns to his or her original family with a newfound sense of belonging. Sociology was the community that originally nourished me and provided me with new ways of thinking about myself and the social world. I have learned that, as much as I hate sociology, I also love it. I have realized that this discipline, which has claimed Marx, Weber, Durkheim, and C.W. Mills, but also George Homans, Peter Blau, and James Coleman, is a home for me. I like to think of sociology as a sort of extended family or, better yet, a church. We quarrel with passion and sometimes fury, because many of our deepest beliefs and values are attached to our social ideas and because we care dearly about each other, if not always in an intimate way, then as individuals who share a similar disciplinary history and culture.

I have returned to sociology, but I am not quite the same person that I was. Like any traveler who spends considerable time in the alien culture, I have come to see my native land as just one among many cultures. I have relativized the premises, concepts, and knowledges of sociology. In particular, I have come to see the theory debates among postwar sociologists as simply one tradition of debate about "the social." Sociological theorists have wrongly imagined that their central problems, for example, the logic of social action and order, the dispute over the validity of conflict versus order paradigms, or the question of the relation between the micro–macro levels of analysis, pertain to the very nature of "the social." The presumption is that if anyone, at anytime, were to think seriously about the social he or she would end up centering reflection on these issues. This is, as anthropologists would say, an example of ethnocentrism, a practice that claims universality and validity for the particular values and ideas of one group. For example, postwar Western feminists have not defined these theory problems as central. Instead, feminist debate has revolved around questions of the natural and social aspects of gender, the concept of gender as a master category of social explanation, the origins of male dominance, the relation between the private and public realm, the nature of identity and difference, and the multiple character of domination and resistance. Relativizing sociological theory does not mean denying its importance. There is much in sociological theory that is valuable and worth defending, in particular, its social understanding of the self, its rich conceptual languages for understanding institutions and whole societies, its stories of social development, order, and crisis, and its tradition of cultural social studies. And yet, sociological theory has all too often, especially in the last two decades, become isolated from public life and has chased the idol of science to a point of its own obscurity. Much sociological theory has abandoned a moral and political intention to engage the world as a medium of critical analysis and change.

I return to sociology as I initially came to the discipline, with the hope of finding a home where social analysis is valued because it is inspired by a will to make a better world. This does not mean giving up empirical analysis; nor does it mean abandoning analytical perspectives. However, I do believe that the purpose of sociology is not to accumulate knowledge, evolve a science of society, or build a system of sociology, but to be a part of the ongoing conversation and conflict over the present and future shape of the social world. The hope that has guided sociology and modern social theory for some 200 years is that knowledge can make a difference in our lives, that its chief value lies in the kinds of lives it imagines and helps to create. This hope is what inspired *Contested Knowledge*.

Acknowledgments

I t is a pleasure to recognize the many individuals (some anonymous) who commented on drafts of the chapters or otherwise contributed to the making of *Contested Knowledge*. Many thanks to Jeff Alexander, Pat Akard, Bob Antonio, Molefi Asante, Zygmunt Bauman, Robert Bellah, Roslyn Bologh, Judith Butler, Craig Calhoun, Patricia Clough, Edith Kurzweil, Richard Lachmann, Michelle Lamont, Charles Lemert, Barbara Laslett, Linda Nicholson, Dorothy Smith, Stephen Turner, Bryan Turner, David Wagner, and Jeffrey Weeks. A special thanks to Jeff Alexander and especially Linda Nicholson with whom I have had the good fortune to carry on a conversation about these matters for many years. We should all be blessed with editors who have the integrity and intelligence of Simon Prosser. The making of this book would have suffered greatly without the wonderful secretarial support of Eileen Pellegrino and Sharon Baumgardner. As this book reached its end, I had hoped to bring to termination a different sort of examined life. This has not yet come to pass, but the days are decidedly more cheery due to my loving acquaintance with Bob Cutler.

Introduction

Modern social theory announced its arrival with an extraordinary promise: to help deliver humanity from oppression to freedom through the vehicle of scientifc knowledge. By conceiving of the human condition as a social fact, the human sciences anticipated the possibility of humanity rationally fashioning its own destiny. If social customs and institutions were products of human actions, not natural or divine law, could they not be designed to benefit all of humanity?

The faith that science could contribute to the making of a better world lay at the heart of modern social theory. The social scientist stepped forward as a public educator and advocate whose chief task was public enlightenment. Social scientists attempted to furnish knowledge illuminating the dangers to freedom and the prospects for social progress. The pioneers of the human sciences, Montesquieu, Condorcet, Marx, Comte, Weber, Charlotte Perkins Gilman, and W.E.B. Dubois, proposed imaginative understandings of the origin and meaning of their social worlds. Their ideas addressed matters of public moral and political significance, for example, the origins of inequality, the bureaucratic threat to freedom, the state of the Negro in society, and the exploitation of women. For the founding figures of the human sciences, knowledge was valued as a means of public enlightenment and social progress.

Contemporary sociological theory has not abandoned this social mission. Sociologists continue to provide critical perspectives on the present age that attempt to enlighten a broad public. Yet sociological theory, and sociology in general, has become more and more isolated from public life, to the detriment of both sociology and public life. As sociological theorists retreat from their role as public educators and advocates, their ideas lose social relevance. Moreover, the general public suffers from sociology's diminishing social authority. Sociology has been a catalyst of public debate and an important source of social perspectives on the self, society, and history. As sociologists have drifted into parochial disciplinary concerns, public officials, activists, policy makers, journalists, and media commentators have assumed the chief role of public intellectuals. Unfortunately, these groups are typically focused narrowly on specific issues or political events (e.g., gays in the military or Bosnian Serb aggression); they are pressured to meet commercial deadlines and standards. Accordingly, their social ideas often lack a level of conceptual and historical depth that has characterized the human sciences. A vigorous democratic public culture is nourished, I believe, by the critical social mappings that have been crafted in the human sciences.

What happened to sociological theory? Many theorists still aspire to the role of public critic or educator, but they are isolated from the public. The culture of sociological theory is more and more removed from a general public culture. Sociology continues to produce theorists of impressive talent and imagination, but their ideas are typically addressed to other members of this expert culture. The growing insularity of sociological theory reflects, in part, the fact that theorists simply do not speak a broad public language; the conventions and concerns of this disciplinary culture render their ideas either inaccessible to a general public or irrelevant to the ways in which the moral and political issues of the day are discussed in everyday life. The sad truth is that sociological theory is hardly read today outside of its own enclave.

Sociological theory is in crisis. One chief reason is the scientization of sociology. Since at least the postwar period, theorists have relentlessly pursued the idol of a scientific theory. Many theorists believe that only if their social ideas are truly objective and scientific can sociology secure its public authority and deliver on its promise of social enlightenment. Unfortunately, sociologists have been unable to achieve anything approaching consensus about the core premises, concepts, and explanatory models that would provide the foundations of a science of society. Sociology's claim to science is increasingly met with suspicion by the public and by its practitioners. Moreover, sociology's drive to be scientific has engendered a preoccupation with arcane conceptual and methodological debates among sociologists, especially theorists. Sociological theorists are relinquishing their role as public educators.

The drfit of sociological theory into social insularity is paralleled by the growing shrillness of public discourse. Sociology must recover its role as public educator. I urge a recentering of sociological theory in public debates and conflicts. Instead of sociological discourses being driven by disciplinary conventions and disputes, theorists should take their problems, themes, and language of argumentation from a public world of social and political conflict. Sociologists need to recover the moral impulse of their role, to see themselves less as scientists and more as public educators engaging the issues of the day. I imagine a sociology that can sustain its rich tradition of conceptual and empirical analysis while recovering its public role and authority. If we abandon the false promise of science to achieve objective and universal knowledge, if we accept our role as story-tellers or social critics, we can revitalize sociology and contribute to the strengthening of a democratic public culture. I call for a sociology that is not afraid of moral advocacy, that is inspired by its original promise of a human studies in the service of making a better world. I envision a sociology that is fully engaged in the very making of society. This is a sociology that assumes responsibility for the world that it is partly responsible for creating.

The lost promise: sociological theory in crisis

In 1989, the American Sociological Association held its annual meetings in San Francisco. Thousands of sociologists gathered, as we do each year, to present papers, exchange ideas, network with publishers and colleagues, interview for jobs, and renew old friendships. At every annual meeting, there is a guiding theme, around which panels and presentations are organized. The chief theme of the 1989 conference was "Macro and Micro Interrelationships." How does behavior at the individual level relate to behavior at the group or institutional level? How can we explain social life as both a product of individual actions and institutional dynamics?

In talking with my theory colleagues, I discovered that many of them believed that the focus of the conference on the "micro–macro link" was considered a major triumph for sociological theorists. This was so because it was sociological theorists, explained my colleagues, who initially brought attention to this problem as a central issue for all sociologists. In their view, making the micro–macro link the chief theme of the conference signaled the mainstreaming of sociological theory, its movement from a specialty area to its rightful place at the center of the discipline. For some theorists, a euphoric sense of triumph was in the air. Perhaps sociology was entering a new era defined by a close connection between theory and research and by the central role of theory.

I was unable to share in my colleagues' sense of triumph. Featuring the theme of the micro–macro link at the conference struck me as a sign of what I considered to be wrong with sociology and sociological theory. This was 1989, I thought, and we were in San Francisco, the very center of perhaps the most pressing national crisis since the Vietnam War. The AIDS crisis had already taken tens of thousands of lives, with estimates of fatal-ities over the course of the epidemic in the millions. AIDS was a major social event. Beyond the tragic loss of lives and the urgent public health concerns stemming from AIDS, it brought communities, ideologies, and institutions into collision. Not only were specific populations such as gay men and ethnic minorities thrown into social upheaval, but medical, economic, and governmental institutions at the local, state, and federal levels were challenged by the AIDS epidemic. In the midst of this social crisis, in San Francisco where the human turmoil marking AIDS was everywhere apparent, thousands of sociologists gathered to discuss the theme of the micro–macro link. Rather than focusing the conference on the social crisis of AIDS, on the urgent, sometimes fatal, relationship between individuals, HIV, and institutions, instead of analyzing the sometimes heroic, sometimes reprehensible, response of individuals, communities, and institutions to the AIDS crisis, sociologists marched into San Francisco to clarify, through innumerable panels and presentations, the story of the micro–macro link!

Reviewing the presentations to be given by sociological theorists was, well, distressing. In a major thematic session organized under the rubric of "From Exchange to Structure," the presentations included titles such as "The Micro Foundations of Social Structure" and "Rational Organization." Another panel entitled "Action and Structure in Social Theory" featured essays entitled "Action, Interaction, and the Interaction Order," "Power and Agency: A Critique of Giddens' Structuration Theory," and "Structure and Agency in Marxist Theory." In still another major panel entitled "Contemporary Sociological Theory: Micro–Macro Linkages" there were papers with titles such as "Macro–Micro Linkage: Community and Society," "Micro–Macro Linkage in Sociological Theory," and "Structural Psychology and Micro–Macro Linkages." Other panels included a range of presentations with similar titles: "Theoretical Modeling through Expert Systems," "Contradictions or Maximization: Theories and an Affective Structuralist Alternative," and "Emile Durkheim and Carl Jung." There were, to be fair, papers and panels aimed at engaging current issues of politics, nation building, and social crisis. However, I did not come across one, *not one*, panel, not even one presentation, on AIDS-related themes at any of the theory sessions!

I thought to myself, "How is it possible that so many sociological theorists gathered together at the site of a major national crisis can be so blind to what was happening right before their eyes!" Had sociological theorists become so insulated that they were unaware of their growing public irrelevance?

How had sociological theory gotten sidetracked into a preoccupation with a series of highly abstract, socially remote issues such as the micro–macro link, the interrelationship between agency and structure, action and order, and structure and culture? What made questions about the nature of social action, the consensual versus conflict-based character of social order, or the rationality of action or the materiality of social institutions so compelling to sociological theorists? I do not wish to wholly discount the value of these questions; however, theorists' preoccupation with these metatheoretical or philosophical issues has superseded their engagement of the social and political issues of the day.

Current sociological theory is not all of one stripe. Although much of sociological theory has been captured by these philosophical questions, there are counterstrains that need to be recognized to get at the whole picture. Some theorists have renounced this sort of philosophical theorizing but have substituted the equally illusory and insulating project of creating a natural science of society. They aim to explain the social laws of the universe or to reduce society to a set of general principles that, like physics, can be formulated in mathematical equations and formulas. Ironically, although these scientific theorists are in rebellion against the obscurity of the philosophical theorists, their work ends up being equally remote and socially pointless. The general principles they enunciate are either so broadly formulated as to be trite, or they propose to capture dense social dynamics through complicated explanatory models, with innumerable variables causally intersecting in mind-boggling ways, that render their theories so obscure as to be useless to researchers and inaccessible to most theorists.

Sociology is not completely lost in a futile quest for philosophical foundations or scientific purity. Theorists have not forgotten their social role as public intellectuals. There are theorists who have not surrendered to the quest for a unified, coherent image of society. They interpret sociology less as a science aspiring to uncover the essential meaning and laws of social behavior than as critical and interpretive enterprise. They align sociology closer to the humanities than to the sciences. Theory in this "moral" mode is an evaluative, socially committed practice. Theorists engage the issues of the day from the standpoint of ordinary citizens. Their aim is moral advocacy and social change.

Social theory as moral inquiry often assumes the form of storytelling. Theorists craft social narratives of the origin, meaning, and possible future outcomes of the present. They alert us to potential social dangers and to the possible remedies and prospects for social progress. There are stories of class conflict, male dominance, the decline of religious faith, the crisis of solidarity, and the bureaucratization of society. The aim of this sociology is to educate the public in order to prompt or guide social and political action. Twentieth-century sociological theorists have provided compelling and imaginative stories of social development. I think, for example, of Talcott Parsons's grand social evolutionary account of Western liberal civilization [1], Peter Berger's powerful mapping of Western cultural secularization [2], Immanuel Wallerstein's dramatic account of the evolution of a world system pitting First World societies against Third World nations [3], Norbet Elias's sketch of the evolution of everyday mores and manners [4], and Daniel Bell's narrative of the cultural crisis of Western capitalism [5]. Sociological theorists continue to serve as public educators and advocates, but their voices are being drowned out by the chorus cheering on the project of a scientific sociology.

I have identified three prominent styles of theory: philosophical, scientific, and moral. In fact, most theorists combine these three styles of social analysis. A theorist, for example, whose dominant style is "scientific" may at some point "go philosophical" and may imbue his or her theory with moral hope. To the extent that theorists make use of different theoretical styles, we can expect their writings to exhibit tensions and strains. For example, a sociologist who views theory as a scientific enterprise may, from time to time, wish to justify this enterprise in a philosophical way, thus providing a kind of legitimacy to philosophical theorizing.

In this book, I examine a vital tension that goes to the heart of modern social theory between a "scientific" and a "moral" vision of human studies. This conflict has been at the center of social theory from its beginnings in the Enlightenment through the classical period and into the present. My chief aim is to bring back into the center of social theory a vision of social science as a moral public practice.

The vital tension in social theory

Sociological theory has been divided between a "scientific" and a "moral" vision of the social sciences. The scientific approach views the social sciences – e.g., sociology, anthropology, political science – as the only method capable of achieving true social knowledge. Whereas our commonsense, everyday social ideas, as well as the social understandings of poets and novelists, journalists and social commentators, are said to reflect personal prejudices and opinions, the social sciences tell us what is real and true. The ideas of the social sciences mirror the world in contrast to the ideas of ordinary folk which mirror the interests and subjective experiences of the individual.

From the standpoint of a scientific vision of the social sciences, the task of theory is twofold: to unify and to justify social knowledge. Scientific theorists aim to provide an integrated image of social behavior. Their goal is to bring together into a unified body of knowledge the massive quantity of empirical findings accumulated by researchers. As is true of all disciplines today, sociology is divided into specialties (e.g., crime, organization, gender, urban, demography). Sociologists are trained to become experts in one field, often one area of a field. Thus, sociologists who specialize in crime may stake out areas of specialty in, say, the sociology of prisons, punishment, or criminal law. While research specialization may encourage imaginative and productive perspectives on some narrow range of social experience, it also threatens to create a state of empirical incoherence and intellectual chaos as data, research results, and concepts pile up without any apparent order. The "scientific" theorist steps forward to produce conceptual and empirical coherence within specialty areas and across the discipline by discovering unifying principles, general laws, or creating theoretical integration.

Theorists not only aim to give unity and coherence to social knowledge but wish to serve as a kind of final court of appeal for a discipline racked by conflict. Sociology has not been blessed with a great deal of agreement on, well, just about anything. We disagree about facts, methods, research findings, explanations, and conceptual approaches. As in a family, conflict may allow for individual dissent, but it threatens to undermine social unity. Unlike in families, pervasive intellectual discord among sociologists poses an additional risk, that of sociology losing its status as a science. If sociologists are unable to agree on the very basics of their discipline – for example, the nature of social facts, methodological premises, research aims, core concepts, and explanatory models, in what sense is sociology different from everyday social disagreements or political conflict? If sociology can be described as an extension of our private and public conversations about society, does it really deserve the current level of public support? In the face of divisions that indeed threaten to diminish its public credibility, sociological theorists have stepped forward to claim the role of the arbiters of sociological truth.

How does the theorist intend to adjudicate between the empirical and conceptual disputes among sociologists? In principle, the theorist aims to clarify the standards that should guide practicing social scientists in deciding between alternative research and conceptual choices. I say "in principle" because to date there is no agreement among theorists as to what criteria might be suitable and how such a consensus might be accomplished. For example, standards of validity as varied as objectivity, comprehensiveness, conceptual economy, empirical adequacy, predictability, empirical richness, methodological reliability, moral rightness, and social change have been advanced, but with little consensus. The idea, though, is that standards will emerge through a prolonged ordeal of critical intellectual exchange that revolves around analyzing basic assumptions about society and social knowledge. In effect, theorists become experts in conceptual and textual analysis, just as social researchers become experts in empirical analysis. Whereas researchers are supposed to tell us about the social world, theorists examine the texts of the researchers to determine if their statements mirror the world "out there" or their private world. Theorists intend to pass judgment as to what counts as knowledge. In a discipline as divided as sociology, the role of adjudicating conflicts by declaring what counts as knowledge confers a great deal of prestige on theorists.

As we will see in the story I tell, theorists' good intentions have led them astray. In their quest to unify and justify social knowledge, theorists have gotten lost in the thickets of conceptual and textual analysis; we have created an insular world where only other sociological theorists can, and would care to, enter. For the past two decades, many sociological theorists have been preoccupied with a series of philosophical problems that have little relevance to practicing researchers or to a public starved for compelling social perspectives on their lives. Even when the writings of sociological theorists show extraordinary brilliance, their work is typically pitched in a language obscure to anyone but a fellow theorist. This leaves their work more or less irrelevant from the standpoint of researcher and public citizen alike.

It would, however, be premature to dismiss sociological theory as lacking contemporary value. Although I am distressed that many theorists have surrendered to the illusory search for philosophical foundations or scientific coherence, others continue to fashion innovative stories of social development and crisis and critical perspectives intended to promote public enlightenment and action. A moral approach to human studies, one which links empirical social analysis to public conflicts and intends to shape the outcome of these conflicts, remains a part of the contemporary sociological tradition. The reassertion of a moral vision of sociology is the guiding critical impulse of this book.

As much as theorists have navigated into a series of dead ends in pursuit of a true science of society, most theorists have not relinquished a moral hope for their efforts, a wish that theory might make the world a better place to live. Most, if not all, sociological theorists would still, if push comes to shove, concede that social science finds its ultimate rationale in whatever good for humanity comes of it. The tribe of theorists and social scientists are, by and large, a good lot, who care about people and believe that science is socially beneficial. Yet the sad truth is that this moral hope that is so powerfully felt by many social scientists is not acknowledged as an important criterion in judging the worth of social research and theory. It is, for most social scientists, simply a hope, a heartfelt hope, but one that should not influence decisions about methods, concepts, explanations, and scientific aims. This does not mean that the values and moral vision of the social scientist do not find a prominent place in social research. No matter how much a social scientist may wish to expunge moral commitments from his or her work, they remain. Unfortunately, though, while moral commitments linger, they are not acknowledged or integrated as a deliberate part of the work of social scientists.

There are, however, social scientists for whom the moral commitments of their work are explicitly acknowledged as central. I think of C. Wright Mills, Robert Bellah, or Dorothy Smith [6]. These social scientists' values, social interests and, at times, explicit political or policy aims guide their conceptual and empirical decisions. For example, a sociologist may do research on gender for the purpose of abolishing discrimination against women and promoting gender equality. Not all theorists who are committed to a moral vision of social science wish to abandon claims of scientific validity. For example, Marx, and more recently Habermas, propose a synthesis: a critical social science. Other theorists, as we will see, have repudiated the link between human studies and a scientific vision. They imagine a postscientific type of human studies whose value lies in its role as a medium of public education and moral advocacy. A major problem for proponents of a moral vision of social science is to reconcile their moral advocacy with their claims to knowledge. Even strong advocates of a moral vision of human studies must concede, moreover, that the very effectiveness of their ideas may depend on their public authority, an authority that may be weakened by their moralism. The vital tension between a scientific and a moral vision will be examined as we analyze the meaning and comtemporary role of social science.

Overview of *Contested Knowledge*

Let me be clear about the aims and scope of *Contested Knowledge*. I do not offer a new history of social theory. The historian would have to be attentive to the diversity of social thinking, the struggles between different languages of social analysis (e.g., religious, poetic, novelistic, scientific, narrative) and the precise social and institutional forces that shaped the formation of social theory. I do not do this. However, I do proceed in an historical way. In parts 1 and 2, I outline a fairly conventional history of modern social theory. I begin with the Enlightenment and proceed to trace a line of development through classical sociology to the rise of disciplinary sociological theory in this century.

Why tell an historical story while disclaiming to rewrite the history of social theory? I have two reasons. First, I think that social ideas should be placed in their historical context. Ideas should be seen as part of the culture and institutional life of a particular society at a specific time. Approaching social theory as embroiled in particular social struggles around, say, nation building or class and gender dominance is necessary in order to challenge the still dominant view of social theory as part of an ongoing, universal dialogue about the general nature of "the social." I approach human studies as a response to historically unique conditions and conflicts. Theory is a social practice, an effort to do certain things. Theorists have specific goals they want to achieve. I rely on a contextual, pragmatic understanding of human studies. Second, I take over, at least provisionally, the standard interpretive sketch of the development of modern social theory in order to raise doubts about it. I could have unsettled the conventional history by crafting a new history. However, I can achieve the same end by simply disrupting the standard story. In any event, this is what I intend. In part 3, I sketch the outlines of what an alternative story of contemporary social theory might look like.

In part 1, I trace the beginnings of modern social theory in the Enlightenment and the "classical" tradition. In the European and Anglo-American countries of the eighteenth century, the social scientific disciplines, as we know them today, did not exist. There were, however, figures such as Voltaire, Hume, Ferguson, Condorcet, Mary Wollstonecraft, and Montesquieu who wrote, not only in the areas of philosophy, literature, science, and history, but who also developed social explanations of human behavior that their successors recognize as marking the beginnings of modern social science. The very terms "science of man" or "social science" were first coined by the figures of the Enlightenment (henceforth to be called the "Enlighteners"). Although the Enlighteners claimed objective and universal knowledge for their social ideas, I argue that at the heart of their ideas were particular moral commitments (social values and ideals) and an interest in promoting social change. To be more precise, the forging of a social science in the Age of Enlightenment was part of a struggle by new social and cultural elites to undermine aspects of the religious culture that underpinned the institutions of the church, monarchy, and the ruling aristocratic elite. The idea of a social science was deployed in the service of modernization and for the benefit of a new social elite trying to establish their own social legitimacy.

The first successor generation to the Enlightenment inherited many of their social values and ideas. Comte in France and Marx in Germany stand out as among the most influential heirs to the Enlightenment. In very different ways, they echo their predecessors' grand vision of social science. They narrate sweeping stories of humanity achieving social progress through overcoming barriers of our own making. Comte and Marx would like us to believe that their social values and ideals represent the actual course of history. It is as if science and morality meld together; science reveals the laws of history – humanity's origin, development, and future – and, therewith, sets out the right social norms and principles. However, the grand sweep of their social vision, raises suspicions regarding the credibility of their claims to scientific validity.

By the second half of the nineteenth century, social science was assuming the role of *the* authoritative language of social truth. Religious, philosophical, or everyday social ideas were perceived as unreliable or merely "subjective." The dichotomy between social science and ideology (subjective or class-based social beliefs) was assuming prominence. To gain public authority for social ideas required a claim to their scientific status; social ideas that were labeled ideological lost considerable public credibility. The nineteenth century witnessed the proliferation of social perspectives, each claiming scientific status and each attacked as ideology by their competitors.

Many current historians and sociological theorists consider Max Weber and Emile Durkheim to be the two greatest social thinkers of the late nineteenth century. Indeed, some historians say that these two figures pioneered a breakthrough in the history of social science. Although Comte and Marx are said to have employed a rhetoric of science, their social theories were still tied to the philosophical and moral ideas of the Enlightenment. Weber and Durkheim were thought to have achieved a genuine breakthrough to a science of society. They substituted for the utopian visions and grand interpretations of the meaning of history of their predecessors, a commitment to objective, value-neutral, and empirically controlled social explanations. I do not agree. It is no doubt true that the social and intellectual conditions of the human sciences changed between the early and late nineteenth century, e.g., the social sciences achieved an institutional footing in universities and there was a heightened attention to concerns of methodology and problem-oriented empirical studies. Nevertheless, the ideas of Weber and Durkheim are no less inspired and informed by moral and political commitments; they were both, as I show in chapter 2, responding to national crises. Their social scientific efforts were intended to shape the course of historical events. Like Marx and Comte before them, Weber and Durkheim buried their moral commitments in the language of empirical science; their values and social interests are revealed, however, in their conceptual and empirical statements about society.

I observe a growing tension in the classical tradition between a "scientific" and "moral" vision. As the claim to science enhanced the authority of ideas, nineteenth century theorists framed their ideas in the language of science. At the same time, the desire to shape national events through their scientific theories gave to their ideas moral and political character.

The social pressure to legitimate ideas as scientific contributed to the increasing social remoteness of theory. To the extent that claiming

scientific status for social ideas was thought to give them and their supporters public authority, it was inevitable that conflicts between theorists and
their ideas would ensue. An effective strategy for discrediting intellectual
and social rivals was to accuse them of being ideological. "Theory" came to
be thought of as that practice which authorized or discredited claims to
scientific status; it evolved into a philosophical and expert practice.
Although I detect in the classical tradition the beginnings of "theory" split-
ting off from public moral and political concerns, the great turning point
was the making of a sociological theory canon in this century that was
anchored in the claims of the autonomy of theory.

In part 2, I turn to twentieth century social theory. I chart the making
of an American sociological theory canon. The pivotal figure is Talcott
Parsons. His influential interpretation of the classical tradition has proved
central to the development of sociological theory. Parsons viewed the
classics as moving towards a unified theoretical framework that would
mark a breakthrough in the social sciences analogous to Darwinian evolutionism or Einsteinian relativity theory. His own grand synthesis, his
so-called voluntaristic theory of action, later elaborated into structural-
functionalism, was intended to establish the foundations for a general
social science. Parsons framed theory as an autonomous practice aimed
at identifying and justifying the basic concepts of social science and
elaborating them into an overarching conceptual framework that would
provide a synthetic image of society.

Parsons's grand synthesis met with much criticism in the 1960s and
1970s. Nevertheless, he succeeded in establishing the terms of the debate. His critics at the time, for example, Ralf Dahrendorf and Peter
Berger, took issue with functionalist sociology. They did not, however,
contest Parsons's scientific vision of human studies, nor his view of theory
as an autonomous expert practice whose task is to create conceptual
unity and justifications for analytical and empirical decision-making.

By the 1970s, a scientific vision of the social sciences had become
orthodoxy in mainstream sociological theory. Henceforth, the chief
debates centered on disagreements over conceptual strategies, justifications, general categories, or explanatory models. Thus, "theory" was
focused on questions regarding the relative merits of a "conflict" versus
"order" paradigm or an "individualistic" versus a "holistic" approach to
sociological explanation or a "functional" versus a "deductive" model of
causality. The social turmoil of the sixties prevented theorists from becoming too socially insular. However, with the decline of social activism and
the heightened emphasis on self-fulfillment through career building and
lifestyle design in the 1980s, sociological theory turned more completely
away from public life. Textual analysis replaced social analysis; building

synthetic theories took precedence over engaged social criticism. The retreat of theory into a textuality in which texts comment and criticize one another in a spiral of printed passion has rendered much current sociological theory obscure and socially irrelevant.

The sociological theory canon has not gone uncontested. In part 3, I review various efforts to dislodge the canon. I turn to theorists who reassert the centrality of a moral vision of the human studies.

Central to contesting the sociological mainstream has been a vision of a critical social science. If Parsons can be said to be the crucial figure in the making of the sociological canon, C. Wright Mills may serve as a pivotal counterfigure. Mills sought to reconfigure sociology into a morally and politically engaged social discourse. He was not alone in advocating a critical social studies. Mills was preceded by sociological critics such as Thorstein Veblen, W.E.B. Du Bois, Charlotte Perkins Gilman, and Robert Lynd [7]. Mills shared an ideal of a public sociology with colleagues such as David Riesman and successors such as Erving Goffman, Alvin Gouldner, and Daniel Bell [8].

Paralleling this indigenous American critical sociological tradition was a German school of critical social theory. Immigrating to America in the 1930s, the so-called Frankfurt School of Critical Theory (Theodor Adorno, Max Horkheimer, Herbert Marcuse, Franz Newmann, Leo Lowenthal) issued a major challenge to the evolving sociological canon by defending a value-committed, politically engaged human studies. From the early 1960s through the 1980s, the German philosopher and sociologist Jürgen Habermas has been perhaps the most influential figure in making the case for a critical social science. Habermas has challenged sociological orthodoxy by insisting on the moral meaning of sociology.

Mills and Habermas were somewhat equivocal in their critical attitude towards the sociological canon. They did not fully relinquish a vision of a scientific sociology. Paralleling the critical sociology of Mills and Habermas were new movements of social and political thinking that were less ambivalent with regard to surrendering a vision of a science of society.

The sixties and early seventies were a period of enormous success in the institutionalization of sociology. Student enrollments soared, and sociology departments grew more prestigious. And while a younger generation may have been congratulating themselves for slaying the specter of functionalism, the spirit of Parsonian theory triumphed. Sociology was not, though, fated to ease into a smug complacency. The sixties witnessed radical social movements that challenged society and sociology. In France, the political rebellions of May 1968 were paralleled by "poststructuralist" critiques of disciplinary knowledges. In chapter 6, I argue that French poststructuralism has fashioned alternative proposals for human studies to the dominant

Enlightenment paradigm of knowledge and society. Perhaps the major challenge to the scientific vision was issued by the liberation movements of the 1970s. They produced new agents of social knowledge, for example, feminists, lesbians and gay men, African-Americans and Latinos. This social and cultural ferment gave birth to new ways of thinking about human behavior and society, for example, feminism, lesbian and gay theory, and Afrocentrism. These are reviewed in chapter 7.

By the mid-1980s, these postdisciplinary social discourses began to be absorbed into the disciplines. In chapter 8, I provide an overview of three efforts to refashion human studies that are inspired by post-Enlightenment paradigms of knowledge and society: Robert Bellah's social science as public philosophy, Zygmunt Bauman's postmodern sociology, and Dorothy Smith's materialist feminist sociology.

The current period is one of enormous turmoil and unrest in the human sciences. Old orthodoxies, standard conventions, and established canons are being contested; local skirmishes quickly escalate into full-scale disciplinary warfare. Disciplinary boundaries are being crossed as easily as are national borders. The shape of social knowledge in the very near future is likely to be quite different from what it is presently. What will come from this war of world views and interests is, as yet, very unclear. I am convinced that this collision of minds is necessary in order to disrupt the spiraling insularity of much sociological theory. *Contested Knowledge* remains inspired by the promise that social knowledge can contribute to making a better world.

References

1. Talcott Parsons, *Societies: Evolutionary and Comparative Perspectives* (Englewood Cliffs, NJ: Prentice-Hall, 1966).
2. Peter Berger, *The Sacred Canopy: Elements of a Sociological Theory of Religion* (Garden City, NY: Doubleday, 1967).
3. Immanuel Wallerstein, *The Modern World-System*, 3 vols. (New York: Academic Press, 1974–1989).
4. Norbert Elias, *The Civilizing Process*, 2 vols. (Oxford: Basil Blackwell, 1978–1983).
5. Daniel Bell, *The Cultural Contradictions of Capitalism* (New York: Basic Books, 1976).
6. See chapters 5 and 8.
7. Thorstein Veblen, *The Theory of the Leisure Class* (New York: Macmillan, 1899); Charlotte Perkins Gilman, *Women and Economics* (New York: Harper, 1966 [1898]); W.E.B. Dubois, *The Philadelphia Negro: A Social Study*

(New York: Benjamin Blom, 1967 [1899]); Robert Lynd, *Knowledge For What?* (Princeton: Princeton University Press, 1939).

8. David Riesman et al., *The Lonely Crowd* (New Haven: Yale University Press, 1950); Erving Goffman, *Asylums* (Garden City, New York: Doubleday, 1961); Alvin Gouldner, *The Future of Intellectuals and The Rise of the New Class* (New York: Oxford University Press, 1979); Daniel Bell, *The Cultural Contradictions of Capitalism.*

PART 1

THE ENLIGHTENMENT AND THE CLASSICAL TRADITION: THE DREAM OF REASON

1

GRAND VISIONS:
Auguste Comte and Karl Marx

ll societies appear to develop their own understandings of human
behavior. Perhaps this is inherent in the language-using character
of humankind. In any event, we find that human association is
accompanied by ideas about human motivation, social interaction, and
social order. However, not all societies have produced "social thought,"
defined as a deliberate, systematic approach to social ideas. Similarly, not
all societies have created social institutions (e.g., universities, publishing
companies, journals) and social roles (e.g., professors, social critics and
commentators) whose purpose is to analyze and debate social ideas to
determine their truth.

It is impossible to locate the origins of social thought. In many of the so-
called "ancient" civilizations (China, Egypt, Greco-Roman), we observe
diverse traditions of social thought. For example, in ancient Greece,
Plato, Aristotle, and Thucyidides crafted social analyses of war, the origins
of the family and the state, and the relation between religion and the
government. Aristotle's *Politics* offers a rich social account of the formation
of different political systems and analyzes the interconnections between the
individual, family, culture, and politics. Although thinkers like Plato and
Aristotle were insightful about humanity and society, most historians do
not credit them as founding figures of the social sciences.

What makes the social thought of premodern times different from social
science? One account suggests that the social sciences hold to different
assumptions about the world and about social knowledge than do the
traditions of premodern social thought. Ancient and Christian social
thought often viewed the universe as a static hierarchical order in
which all beings, human and otherwise, have a more or less fixed and
proper place and purpose. Premodern social thought approached human
behavior in relation to a conception of the overall natural and moral
structure of the universe. For example, Aristotle's social thought was
less concerned with explaining social dynamics than with prescribing
an ideal society in the context of a comprehensive philosophy of life.

Social science has abandoned the static, hierarchical world view of its Greek and Christian predecessors. Modern social scientists have, in the main, abandoned the effort to craft a comprehensive philosophy of life. Social science, it would seem, focuses on a different world of ideas from premodern social thought.

In this chapter, we take our first glance at the world of modern social science. Eighteenth and early nineteenth century Europe was the principal home for the birth of social science. Beginning with the figures of the Englightenment and then turning to two of its great heirs, Auguste Comte and Karl Marx, we explore the tension between a scientific and a moral vision of human studies.

The Enlightenment

To the extent that we can date the beginnings of social science, the so-called Age of Enlightenment is generally agreed upon as a reasonable one. In eighteenth century Europe, we find a remarkable gathering of thinkers such as Voltaire, Hume, Adam Ferguson, Condorcet, Montesquieu, Adam Smith, and Mary Wollstonecraft. Although they wrote widely on philosophy, natural science, and literature, they produced an impressive body of social ideas. Of particular importance, Enlightenment social thinkers (Enlighteners) imagined themselves as breaking away from the Greco-Roman and Christian traditions of social thought. They claimed to have pioneered a new science of society.

Although the Enlighteners took up the cause of science with the enthusiasm of crusaders, they were not its original creators. The great breakthroughs to a scientific world view occurred from the fifteenth through the seventeenth centuries, the result of the efforts of Copernicus, Kepler, Galileo, and Newton. From the perspective of that period, the commitment to science amounted to a serious challenge to the prevailing Aristotelian-Christian world view. In early modern Europe, the universe was seen as a hierarchical order in which every being (human, animal, plant, spiritual) had a rightful place and purpose in a divinely created and ordered universe. The natural and social worlds were viewed as spiritually infused with value, meaning, and purpose. By contrast, the scientific revolution conceived of the universe as a mechanical system composed of matter in motion that obeyed natural laws. Both divine purpose and human will became peripheral, indeed unnecessary, features of the scientific world view.

If the Enlighteners were not the creators of the scientific revolution, they were its great popularizers and propagandists. Through their writing and speeches, they proved indispensable in spreading the word of science to

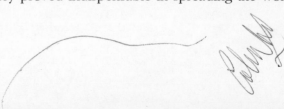

educated Europeans[Moreover, they were themselves innovators, less in
their efforts in the natural sciences than in the study of humanity. They
dismissed all previous social thought as based on prejudice, opinion, revelation, philosophical reasoning, and tradition; true knowledge, they
asserted, can only rest on the solid ground of fact and scientific method.
They ridiculed premodern social thought, with its concept of a fixed,
religiously based social order. Departing from what they described as the
illusions of their predecessors, the Enlighteners perceived society as a
sphere of individual interaction responsive to human intentions. The
Enlighteners created a social world view that has become dominant in
the modern West. At its core is the notion that humans create society; we
form a world of institutions which in turn shapes us; the interplay between
individuals and the social system pattern the history and future of humanity.
Finally, since humanity creates itself through its action, but within the
constraints of human nature, history exhibits a predictability that makes
social engineering possible.]

[The Enlighteners championed the scientific world view but only after
they altered it to suit their own purpose. Like many educated men and
women of the time, they saw in the scientific world view a triumph of
reason over prejudice. However, they were troubled by this revolution in
thinking to the extent that science imagined the universe as a purely
materialistic, mechanical place with no room for freedom and morality. It
was perhaps the genius of Montesquieu, Adam Smith, and Condorcet that
they were able to wed science to a liberal humanistic world view. This was
achieved by conceiving human history as an act of freedom exhibiting
immense social variation. Yet history obeyed laws that were anchored in
human nature, and therefore unfolded in an orderly manner.] Thus, in his
great work, *The Spirit of the Laws*, Montesquieu traced the variations in
political systems to somewhat arbitrary factors such as geography, religion,
or climate while claiming to demonstrate that this variation was limited by
the constraints of human nature [1]. Similarly, in his grand vision of history
as the march of human progress, Condorcet invoked freedom to explain the
varied rates of social progress among different societies, while underscoring
the laws of humanity by pointing to the uniform, linear progressive movement of history [2]. The Enlighteners sought to press science in the service
of promoting liberal humanistic social values.

[The Enlighteners' aim to deploy science to benefit humanity raises suspicions about their "scientific vision" of human studies. How can science be
both a morally neutral instrument of knowledge and a vehicle of social
progress? Many Enlighteners believed that the link between science and
progress was not contradictory. For example, in a *Sketch for a Historical
Picture of the Progress of the Human Mind*, Condorcet asserted that the

very nature of science – its reliance upon facts and observation, its open-ness to criticism and revision – inevitably promotes individualism, toler-ance, equality, and democracy. Hence, the progress of science automatically translates into social progress. Today, in the aftermath of Nazism, Hiroshima, widespread revelations about scientific torture and control through medicine and psychiatry, we would surely want to ques-tion whether science is *intrinsically* wedded to liberal humanistic values. Is it not possible that the Enlighteners read their own liberal values into science? Many Enlighteners held that, by discerning the laws of history, social science would have insight into the correct social norms and social policies. But how do we guard against the possibility that the so-called "objective" laws of history "uncovered" by scientists might, in fact, be colored by the social values and interests of the scientist? If social knowl-edge is to guide social affairs, we need to be certain that these ideas truly mirror the objective, not the subjective, world of the scientist. But how can we be certain?

The social motivation of the Enlighteners raises further suspicions that their scientific vision was not innocent of moral and political meanings. The figures of the Enlightenment lived in a period of social turmoil. European societies were divided between social forces that defended social hierarchy and the status quo (the church and landed aristocracy) and forces of change (from a new strata of commercial enterpreneurs to oppressed peasants and laborers), who struggled for more freedom, equality, and democracy. The Enlighteners were mostly from socially privileged backgrounds (sons of nobility or parliamentarians) but were typically not members of the ruling church and aristocratic elite. Their livelihood was neither guaranteed by the ruling elite nor by an independent university system of the kind that devel-oped in the twentieth century. As educated men with few social privileges, their sympathies generally were with the party of change.

The Enlighteners were participants in the social struggles of the time. Their activities as polemicists and social critics carried serious risk, from fines and economic insecurity, to exile, imprisonment, even execution. Indeed, many of them wrote under assumed names or penned essays whose critical message was carefully camouflaged by humor or parody. Since they were typically not landowners or members of the parliament, their battle site was culture. They fought against the beliefs and social norms that upheld a society organized around social hierarchy, intoler-ance, and inequality. In eighteenth century France, the struggle was pri-marily against the Christian culture and Catholic hierarchy. At one level, they fought for freedoms relating to public expression, free speech, and tolerance of dissent. At another level, their battles were centered on the very issue of which beliefs, values, and social norms should prevail in

✓ conclusion

society. In other words, the Enlighteners challenged the very basis of the landed aristocracy and church hierarchy by disputing the legitimacy of a society organized on the basis of a Christian religious culture. In this regard, they took up the cause of science as a key part of their struggle to shape the future of France and Europe.

In light of the breakthroughs to a scientific world view by their predecessors, it is hardly surprising that the Enlighteners seized on science as the vehicle to challenge the Christian culture. Through the persecution of Galileo and other innovators of science for heresy, the public associated science with social rebellion. Moreover, the scientific world view was interpreted by both the church and its detractors as a grave threat to the Christian cosmology. In a universe that functioned wholly according to mechanical laws, God was rendered as little more than a peripheral, detached observer. As the role of God in natural and human affairs was reduced to a spectator, the social role of the church would diminish accordingly.

The cosmology of science challenged the public authority of the church. Science projected a universe in which all beings were reducible to matter in motion, the only differences that counted were those related to shape, force, mass, or velocity. Fundamental Christian beliefs about the existence of spiritual beings and actions (e.g., angels or divine incarnations) and about the very notion of a human soul differentiating us from animals were placed in doubt. Similarly, to the extent that science assumed that true knowledge is based on observations, facts, and scientific method, Christian knowledge founded upon revelation, tradition, and the authority of the church was discredited. Finally, we should not fail to notice the close tie between the social values built into modern Western science and those of the Enlighteners. For example, the Newtonian universe placed all beings on an equal footing; scientific knowledge itself was not an inherited right or gift but a product of education and effort; natural laws apply to all beings in the universe. In short, the scientific revolution seemed in tune with modern liberal values and the social agenda of the forces of change. It was not, however, the generation of Galileo or Newton that translated the scientific cosmology into a social world view; it was the Enlighteners.

Whereas the first phase of the scientific revolution (from the fifteenth to the seventeenth centuries) still left God and the church in charge, in the second phase, initiated by the Enlighteners, God was a matter of personal belief and the church, a human institution deserving of no special public authority. The Enlighteners directly contested the social power of the church and the landed aristocracy by criticizing religion as the source of knowledge, social norms, and public values. If true knowledge is based on observation and fact, then religion, which is based on revelation or tradition, is mere opinion or an illusion. Indeed, many Enlighteners accused the church of inventing Christianity in order to gain social privileges by keeping the masses in a state of awe, fear, and ignorance. The existing social order, with its alliance of the church hierarchy, monarch, and landed aristocracy, was viewed as a fragile artifice resting upon rather shaky religious foundations.

By trumpeting the cause of science, the Enlighteners were able to mount a frontal assault upon the social status quo. Yet the very style of their criticism can just as easily be turned against them. If the church forged a world view that masked their desire for social power, is not the same true for the Enlighteners? Were they not simply intending to replace religion with science and priests with scientists? Is the claim that only science ensures true knowledge and guarantees social progress not merely another ruse on the part of a rising social elite wishing to legitimate their own aspirations for privilege and power?

Our suspicions gain credibility when we note that, for all their rhetoric of science as based on facts, observations, and method, they ignore the point that science, just like religion, rests upon a series of assumptions that cannot be scientifically proven. For example, the claims that humans are natural beings, that nature is uniform and lawlike, that observations yield knowledge, and that history is a patterned and purposeful realm cannot be proven by science. Moreover, despite reassurances that their social explanations rested upon a bedrock of fact, their comtemporaries and successive generations have raised grave doubts. For example, insisting on his scientific approach, Montesquieu declared "I have not drawn my principles [of social organization] from my prejudices, but from the nature of things [3]. But did "the nature of things" reveal unambiguously that climate, as Montesquieu believed, rather than religion or social class, is the main determinant of political systems? When Montesquieu proposed that cold climates produce individuals who are courageous, generous, and insensitive to pain, when he explained the "Englishmen's love of liberty" by the impatience produced by cold weather, was he simply giving voice to "the nature of things" or to his prejudices? Perhaps even more telling of the moral patterning of Enlightenment social thought are their grand stories of the march of human progress and the triumph of reason over superstition. These narratives look suspiciously like secular versions of Christian millennialism. We are, in short, left with the impression that Enlightenment science is as weak a guarantor of truth as religion. The cultural clash between the backers of religion and the proponents of science appears to be a battle over the shape of society and the right to legislate social norms and ideals.

For all their celebration of science as a medium of truth, the Enlighteners deployed science as a powerful instrument of social change. I do not doubt the sincerity of their belief in science as the path to true knowledge. They accepted the equation that science equals Truth precisely the way their predecessors professed Christianity – as a faith. Beliefs harden into a faith when they become the commonsense understandings of large segments of society. By the mid-to-late eighteenth century, science was already a central part of a secular humanistic world view that was valued by many educated Europeans. Moreover, many Europeans perceived science as both a symbol of a new enlightened era and a force of social progress. To champion science was to be in step with the march of human progress. Christianity may have been the object of the Enlightener's derision, but its faith that truth will bring salvation continued to animate even the enlightened mind.

The Age of Enlightenment may not have been the great turning point in human history that the Enlighteners and their successors believed, but it was a period of great turmoil and change. The outlines of a modern society were visible in the expansion of commerce, the formation of liberal political institutions, and the emerging class organization of European societies. For many individuals, especially in the West, these changes have represented genuine human progress. From this perspective, science stands as both its symbol and chief cause. These defenders of the Enlightenment have often rallied behind a "scientific vision" of human studies.

The champions of the Enlightenment had their detractors, critics who disputed the equation that science equals Truth and that the modern era clearly demonstrates linear human progress. The Enlightenment provoked a counter-Enlightenment. As in the former category, the latter exhibited a great deal of diversity. "Romantic" critics such as the English poets, Wordsworth and Coleridge, championed intuition and affect, spiritual longings and the unity of nature, humanity and God [4]. The great "conservative" social critics Edmund Burke and Joseph de Maistre insisted on a social ideal linked to the vitality of religion and tradition [5]. Revolutionary critics such as the French radicals, Gracchus Babeuf and Charles Fourier defended egalitarian values that were tied to a pastoral, agrarian social ideal [6]. Common to these multiple strains of the counter-Enlightenment was a deep hostility towards economic individualism, the secularization of culture, the scientization of knowledge, and the doctrine of social progress.

As the new era swept through Europe and the United States, the ideological conflicts among Enlighteners, and between them and proponents of the counter-Enlightenment, intensified and moved into the center of public life. The question of the meaning and social significance of science was at the heart of these cultural clashes.

Successors to the Enlightenment science of society inherited the Enlighteners' faith in science. They absorbed the great moral hopes that were attached to science. However, the heirs to the Enlightenment could hardly ignore the sobering realities of the excesses of the French Revolution or the many critics of Enlightenment secular humanism. As we move into the nineteenth century, it is the clash over images of science, history, and society that underlies the grand visions of two of its greatest social theorists, Auguste Comte and Karl Marx.

Auguste Comte

Comte lived in a period of extreme social upheaval in France. The high hopes attached to the French Revolution (1789) by many Europeans were dashed by its recourse to political terrorism and the failure to realize a new France. However, the ardent faith in liberty and progress inspired by the Age of Enlightenment did not disappear in the aftermath of the revolution. Comte shared in this Enlightenment faith. Like many of his contemporaries, he was dismayed by the restoration of monarchical rule in the early decades of the nineteenth century. Comte's social thought was formed in a France that was torn between Enlighteners and revolutionaries on the one side and supporters of empire and monarchy on the other.

Comte observed that France in the first half of the nineteenth century was in a state of social crisis. The Enlightenment and the French Revolution went a long way towards undermining the old France that was dominated by the church and wealthy, landed aristocracy. The revolution failed, however, to create a new France. The Enlighteners, especially the more radical elements that inspired the revolution (e.g., Rousseau and Robespierre) were right to attack the oppressive state of the peasants and laborers, and the corruption of the church and aristocracy. Unfortunately, their utopian social hopes could not be translated into a realistic agenda of social reform. It was no accident that, once the revolutionaries assumed power, their rule rapidly degenerated into fierce power struggles and resorted to violence and brutal repression. In this regard, Comte thought that the critics of the Enlightenment, mostly voices of conservative tradition and Catholic orthodoxy, were correct in assailing the Enlighteners for failing to understand that social change has to be anchored in custom and tradition. However, these conservative critics sounded only one option: to defend the status quo against the chaos they anticipated being unleashed by the reforms of the Enlighteners. Comte did not think that this position was credible in light of the far-reaching social changes that occurred in the past century. France was a nation on its way to becoming a modern industrial society; this was irreversible and a sign of social progress.

France was in a transitional social state. The old France was dying. Restoring the monarchy and the power of the church and aristocracy would only incite social chaos. The future of France lay with change. Yet the new France imagined by the revolutionaries – a society of universal rights, equality, mass democracy, and secular humanism – was no less an invitation to social disorder. Contrary to the faith of the Enlighteners, a new society could not be fashioned according to the dictates of a reason that legislates the laws and institutions of an ideal social order. Society is not a mere piece of clay that we can mould by our will. Comte was convinced that it was this rationalist faith of the Enlighteners that resulted in the failure of the French Revolution. Social change must be anchored in the living traditions of a nation's past and in an understanding of the principles of social order.

France was in a social crisis; it was polarized between Enlighteners who advocated change and defenders of a social order in decline. This made for a remarkably unstable social condition, as was manifest in the flip-flop in nineteenth century France between republic, empire, and monarchy. Comte himself lived through seven different political regimes, from short-lived republican governments to restored monarchs and a Napoleonic empire. The social unrest was not just political; France was undergoing intensive industrialization which created enormous social strains in a still largely agrarian society. The clerical and aristocratic ruling elite was being challenged by a powerful strata of industrialists and bankers who were, in turn, threatened by discontented peasants, laborers, and craftsmen.

Comte wished to find a way out of this social impasse. He proposed a program of social reform that offered a social vision of France marching to the tune of social progress. The vehicle for this social reformation was to be a new science of society which Comte called sociology.

Comte's scientific vision of sociology

Comte felt that the current era was a turning point in history. Whereas some Europeans interpreted the current social crisis as symbolizing social decline, Comte understood it as marking the birth pangs of a new era of unlimited human progress.

In essence, the current crisis was a cultural one. France, like all of Europe, was in the throes of a great cultural change that would shape the fate of humanity. Humanity was about to undergo a great transformation in its cultural foundations. The change involved a shift from a religious and metaphysical to a scientific world view. The cultural collision between the religious, metaphysical, and scientific world views had reached a climax in nineteenth century France. Underlying Comte's perspective on the cultural crisis of Europe was a grand vision of the evolution of the human mind.

Comte thought that he had discovered a law governing the progress of the human mind. According to the so-called Law of the Three Stages, the human mind passes through three stages of thought: the theological, metaphysical, and the positive. In the first stage, the theological, the human mind explains the origin and ultimate purpose of phenomena by reference to supernatural entities (e.g., spirits, divine beings, gods). A Christian world view would exemplify the theological stage. In the second stage, the metaphysical, human thought continues its search to uncover the first and final cause of things but appeals to essences or abstract forces (e.g., human reason or natural law). The philosophical systems of Descartes or Leibniz illustrate the metaphysical stage. The final stage, the positive, abandons the search for essences, first causes, and final purposes in favor of explaining the interconnection and succession of facts. Philosophical or religious speculation gives way to the discovery of natural and social laws. The positive stage represents the era of the modern sciences.

Comte is not simply sketching a series of changes, but a progressive development. The sciences represent not just a successor world view to religion and philosophy, but a breakthrough from speculation to truth. As an heir to the Enlightenment, Comte believed that the discovery of a language of truth is a turning point for humanity. Truth will liberate humankind from the web of ignorance, illusion, and error that has slowed, sometimes to a halt, the march of human progress.

Comte believed that each science passes through these three stages, but at varying rates depending on their degree of difficulty. To the extent that the most general and simple of the sciences precede those that are more concrete and complex, Comte proposed that mathematics and astronomy would reach the positive stage prior to physics, chemistry, biology and sociology. In other words, Comte thought that humankind would first be able to free itself from religious and metaphysical ideas in matters remote from human considerations (e.g., mathematics or astronomy or physics). Once our ideas about nature were freed from religious and metaphysical beliefs, it would be possible to apply a scientific approach to human affairs. Accordingly, sociology, as the study of humanity, is the last science to develop because it is the most complex and concrete.

Sociology is the queen of the sciences. Unlike the other sciences which analyze one narrow segment of life, sociology integrates all knowledge about humanity. Comte relied upon biology for his guiding social imagery and language. Society is visualized in organismic terms, as a system whose "needs" are met by the normal operation of its functionally interdependent parts. Like any organism, society grows in a slow, continuous, linear way, exhibiting a movement from simplicity to complexity and from potentiality to self-realization. Sociology was to be *the* science of society; its aim was to discover the universal laws that govern the organization and evolution of humanity.

Comte conceived of sociology as consisting of two parts: statics and dynamics. Social statics analyzes the structure and functioning of society; it describes the elementary parts of society, their functions and interconnections. Social dynamics investigates the evolution of humanity; it reveals the source of change and its stages and direction. Comte's aim was nothing less than to sketch the universal laws of social statics and dynamics, a project that he began in *The Course of Positive Philosophy* (1830–1842) and completed in the *System of Positive Polity* (1851–1854) [7].

Comte's sociology begins with the premise that every science has its own separate subject matter. Departing from the conventional wisdom of many Enlighteners, Comte thought that it was a mistake to conceive of society as a mere collection of individuals. He approached society as a realm of social interaction, social rules, and institutions that are independent of the psychology of individuals. Social statistics investigate the structure and functioning of this social realm. The chief problem is to explain social order, especially in modern societies. Given the strains towards individualism promoted by an industrializing society, how is self-interest curbed to permit social stability? Comte emphasized the role of the family, government, and religion in explaining social order. The family provides the initial and sustaining formative moral milieu for the individual; the idea of the self-sufficient, independent individual is a myth, as we are born and formed in families. Where the moral influence of the family comes up short, religion compensates. Religion furnishes a common creed which strengthens our social bonds and loyalties to social and political institutions.

Comte introduced the idea of social dynamics to explain the laws of social evolution. He elaborated a grand vision of the progression of humanity towards perfection. Basic to his theory of social evolution is the notion that insofar as human nature is everywhere the same (e.g., humans are motivated by common instincts and drives), the changes of particular societies can be understood as exhibiting the evolution of humanity. Comte envisioned humanity passing through fixed, invariable stages, each successive one representing a higher level of human development. Although all societies would pass through the same stages simultaneously if there were no interferences, accidents (e.g., natural disasters) result in social change proceeding at different rates. Thus, the differences among societies that we can observe across history are interpreted as exhibiting all of the successive stages of human evolution. From this perspective, we can locate all societies on a hierarchy of human development, from lower to higher social types.

Social change is viewed as a linear, directional progressive process. Humanity is moving towards the same goal or endpoint, even if at varying rates. Underlying social development is the evolution of the human mind. Changes in social and political institutions are correlated with cultural evolution. Thus, the theological stage is dominated by priests and military institutions. In the metaphysical stage, which corresponds roughly to the early modern period (1300–1700), it is lawyers and clergy who govern society. Finally, the positive stage, an era just coming into view in European societies, will evidence the growing social authority of industrialists and scientists. Comte held that all humanity evolves through these three social stages; history culminates in the positive age.

Comte believed that human evolution has reached a turning point. The crisis in France and Europe was at bottom the result of a great collision between these three social systems and world views. The Enlighteners represented a metaphysical stage, although some strains of Enlightenment thought were indicative of the positive era; their archenemies, the conservative defenders of the status quo, exemplified the theological stage. In the breakthroughs towards science in the past few centuries, Comte detected the ascending spirit of the positive stage. Comte's sociology was intended to provide a diagnosis of the contemporary crisis and to suggest a remedy: the consolidation of the positive/industrial/scientific order. According to the Law of the Three Stages, social evolution points irreversibly towards the positive era. In his opinion, the destiny of France was to serve as the midwife to the birth of the new world order. And, as we will see, Comte was equally convinced that it was to be the fate of sociology to show France its appointed historical role.

Comte's heavenly vision of sociology

There is a paradox at the heart of Comte's sociology. His scientific vision of sociology was animated by a moral passion that eventually came to dominate his work. Comte frankly admitted the moral motivations of his science. He wished to provide humankind with an understanding of the laws of humanity in order to provide moral guidelines for social reform. If sociology could reveal the underlying principles of social order and change, it could be used to guide social reforms.

Like many Enlightenment social thinkers, Comte thought that the role of science in producing objective, universally valid knowledge could be

:separated from its moral role. However, Comte himself failed to maintain the separation of science and morality.

Comte imagined sociology as resting on a firm bedrock of observation and facts, even though he held that facts are made coherent by a unifying perspective. Comte never clarified, though, the origins of these interpretive perspectives or their relation to "facts." If the theories that guide observation originate in a particular cultural world view, how can we be sure that they are not biased by the values and social interests of their social origin? If theories guide the selection and interconnection of facts, how can we avoid the suspicion that theorists select and interpret facts in ways that confirm the theory? An even cursory look at Comte's social thought heightens these suspicions. The guiding ideas of his sociology, for example, assumptions about the uniformity of human nature, the continuous, linear, directional process of history, and the progress of humanity, are little more than leaps of faith akin to a religious and philosophical cast of mind. What facts could possibly confirm or disconfirm a theory as grand as the Law of the Three Stages? How can we avoid the conclusion that Comte's evolutionary theory betrays the prejudices of a modern Western, largely secular man inspired by a faith in progress? The entire non-Western world is reduced by Comte to little more than a bit player in human history. Is this not the conceit of the modern West? Comte's vision of humanity is deeply millennial exhibiting standard Judeo-Christian themes, most impressively the anticipation of a period of world peace and human perfection.

In the end, Comte's moral vision bursts through his rhetoric of science. A central aim of Comte's sociology was to not only lay bare the principles of social order and change but provide a blueprint of the good society. Whereas his earlier major work, *The Course of Positive Philosophy*, intended to uncover the universal laws of social statics and dynamics, his later work, a *System of Positive Polity*, addressed the moral role of sociology. In the fully realized positive society, industrialists would share power with scientists. Whereas the former would have priority in the mundane sphere of institutional functioning, the latter would govern spiritual matters. The sciences would furnish the core beliefs of the new society. The creators of science such as Galileo, Newton, and Comte himself would be deified; cults would form around these sacred figures. In particular, to the extent that sociology provided a unifying social vision, sociologists would become the high priests of the positive society. Sociologists would reveal the moral guidelines of the positive society, specify the duties, obligations, and social roles that have to be fulfilled in order for social harmony to prevail.

Twentieth century sociologists inspired by the scientific vision have been embarrassed by Comte's wish to make science into a religion. They have tried to dismiss this prophetic, religious impulse as either a reflection of his gradual mental deterioration or at least as separable from his scientific achievements. I disagree. Comte was a visionary sociologist. His moral vision was built into the very heart of his sociology. Nor was he alone, as we turn to his contemporary, Karl Marx, a visionary no less than Comte.

Karl Marx

Marx never met Comte. His few belittling comments on his somewhat older contemporary suggest that he thought of Comte as a bit of a crank. In truth, though, Marx himself was reportedly quite quarrelsome and irascible, especially with intellectual competitors. And, in the first half of the nineteenth century, Comte had made a name for himself among educated Europeans, while Marx, for most of his life, labored in public obscurity. In fact, Comte and Marx had much in common, in particular, a hope that a new era was dawning that would liberate humanity. Like Comte, Marx ardently believed that science had a key role to play in creating this new age.

The unity of theory and practice

Comte developed his social ideas in the context of postrevolutionary France. France was a society divided between a tradition of Enlightenment imbued with millennial hopes of humankind's capacity to make the future according to its own will, and social forces that steadfastly defended the authority of the past. Underlying this clash of world views was a conflict between a nascent middle class and an established landed nobility and clerical elite. Comte's sociology forged a social vision that integrated these antagonistic elements by proclaiming that progress can be achieved only through gradual, orderly change that is respectful of the past. This was a message that had special appeal to the middle classes who feared both a restoration of the old regime and a revolution from below.

   Germany did not experience a revolution comparable to the revolutions in France or the American colonies. Moreover, whereas France was viewed by many educated Germans as a dynamic, even if intensely conflicted society, Germany seemed by comparison static and backward. Politically, Germany was divided into many independent states. German unification came in 1871 and only as a result of the military and economic power of Prussia and the diplomatic skill of Bismarck. Economically, Germany was largely agrarian, with spurts of industrialization frustrated by government regulation and an antibusiness religious culture. Socially, Germany was dominated by a highly conservative landed nobility that permitted little freedom and social innovation. Given this social backwardness in relation to France, it was not surprising that the German middle classes were politically weak and admiring of the martial, paternalistic spirit of the landed aristocracy.

Germany was, however, influenced by the new spirit of change in Europe. The ideas of the Enlightenment took hold in Germany, especially among educated circles. Many German cultural and political elites imbibed the Enlightenment spirit of progress. They did so, however, in a society where there were few real prospects of social change. Unlike in France and England, where the middle class played a crucial role in promoting liberal social change, the German middle classes aspired to imitate, rather than to overthrow, the aristocracy. Lacking an identifiable social group that could bring about social change, German Enlighteners assumed that the real forces of change were ideas and their producers, i.e., intellectuals. Instead of approaching society as an arena of social conflict, German intellectuals imagined the collision of world views as the real source of social change. History was rewritten as the story of the development of reason through the medium of the clash of ideas.

As a child of the Enlightenment, Marx came of age in a Germany largely hostile to change. There was no viable middle class movement motivated to challenge the social status quo. Discontent among peasants and laborers was unorganized in the first decades of the nineteenth century. In his early writings, Marx raised the following questions: What are the prospects for social change in Germany? What social forces are positioned to struggle for change? What role does science have in promoting social change? Finally, what kinds of changes are possible and desirable? In addressing these questions, Marx often went beyond a liberal Enlightenment vision of science and society towards a revolutionary perspective. In the remainder of this chapter, I will sketch Marx's ideas, beginning with his early writings, which focus closely on Germany, proceeding to his general concepts of science, theory, and modernity.

As he surveyed the German political scene, Marx noted two social groups that were interested in effecting social change: liberal reformers and idealist philosophers.

Liberals reformers believed that change required piecemeal administrative and legislative actions. Science might be useful in analyzing particular problems or supplying information about specific issues, but there was no need for a theory of society or history. Marx disagreed. He argued that, in order to effect change, it is necessary to understand the social forces – institutions, cultural traditions, social groups – that block it. This requires a social theoretical perspective. Moreover, Marx thought that German religious traditions that emphasize the sacredness of the past, social hierarchy, and submission to authority were a key factor obstructing change.

He argued that social change required that these cultural traditions be weakened to allow for new ideas and attitudes favoring social progress. Social criticism has a pivotal role to play in undermining the authority of these anti-Enlightenment traditions.

Marx's sympathy was with the idealist philosophers. In fact, the young Marx was a member of a group of brilliant theorists who were inspired by the German idealist tradition. They drew on the idealist philosophy of Kant and Hegel to articulate their own vision of enlightened change. Their aim was to change consciousness and replace German religious culture by a secular-humanistic culture that promoted broadly liberal ideas of individual autonomy, tolerance, and social change. The vehicle of cultural change was to be a critical theory that disputed the truth of the religious underpinnings of German national culture and substituted an alternative secular humanistic philosophy.

Marx may have been a member of the idealist circle, but he was impatient with the limits of their vision. The critical philosophers, Marx argued, were right to insist upon the importance of theory to change consciousness. They were naive, though, to think that simply appealing to the truth of their ideas would transform German culture. Marx proposed what was to become a controversial tenet of his thought: Individuals do not act on ideas primarily because they are true or have been "proven" correct but on the basis of their self-interest. Ideas may shape our actions, but our social interests determine which ideas we adopt. Moreover, our social interests are determined by our social position, in particular, our class status. It follows that, if ideas are rooted in social structural conditions, only by changing the latter can the former be changed. A critique of culture – the realm of ideas, values, meanings – is important, but it must be connected to a critical analysis of the social conditions that sustain cultural meanings. Marx was moving away from an idealist philosophy preoccupied with intellectual critique; he was gravitating toward a "materialist" perspective that viewed the real source of social change in the clash of social interests arising from the tensions and inequities of the social structure.

Marx also took issue with the way the idealists imagined that their critical ideas would change society. Idealists assumed that the power of reason to reveal the truth was sufficient to bring about change. Once the truth of idealism was demonstrated, the public would be converted to their ideas. Marx held that it is social interests, not abstract reasons or theories, that motivate behavior. People believe what their self-interest dictates. This does not mean that theory lacks a crucial role to play in promoting social change. Quite the contrary: Theory can become a force of change only if it appeals to individuals whose self-interest is to change social conditions. In other words, if theory expresses the social interests of individuals who are socially positioned as oppressed, it can become a force of change. To the extent that individuals take over a theoretical perspective as their own, to that extent they understand the world through the lens of that theory. "Theory . . . becomes a material force once it has gripped the masses" [8]. Theory can be transformative: It can help change a mass of isolated individuals who lack a common social and political identity into a group with a sharp political identity and agenda. To take a contemporary example, as women adopted a feminist perspective in the 1970s, their understanding of themselves, men, and society was dramatically altered; these women were transformed into a social and ideological bloc of feminists mobilized for political action.

Although Marx had high expectations for the role of theory as a political force, he did not believe that theory by itself could bring about change. Theory could be a force for change only if there existed individuals who, because of their social positioning, had an interest in changing society. It is this shared social positioning as, say, wage laborers, that created the potential for social discontent and an interest in changing social conditions. Theory by itself could not create the social conditions of discontent nor the interest in change. It could, however, give voice to social discontents and direct its political expression. If the social conditions conducive to change were absent, theory would be essentially impotent. Marx's point seems to be that, while it is individuals who make change, this occurs only when they are propelled by self-interest which, in turn, depends on underlying social conditions of inequality. As individuals are socially positioned to experience discontent, they will have an interest in social change. Theory cannot create the underlying conditions ripe for change or the interest in change, but it can make those individuals aware that their discontent is social in origin and can transform their images of self and society in a political way.

Marx saw few prospects for substantial social change in Germany's near future. However, he was aware of the big changes that were happening throughout Europe. While industrialization was slow in Germany, in France, England, America, Belgium, and Spain, the appearance of factories, the spread of commerce, and the emergence of new banking and financial institutions were transforming the social landscape. Moreover, accompanying industrialization were giant steps towards secularization (the separation of state and church) and democratization (e.g., the rise of political parties, constitutional governments, the extension of civil and political rights). Marx viewed these changes positively. While he believed that the middle classes were the main forces behind the initial phase of modernization, Marx was convinced that they would oppose continued social advancement. His stint as a journalist in the early 1840s and his subsequent stay in Paris from 1843 to 1845 exposed him to the ruthless treatment of peasants and laborers by capitalists who, fearing social rebellion from below, often aligned themselves with the old guard aristocracy. In Paris, he became aware of the centrality of the conflicts between capitalists and laborers as he read the new writings of the English and French political economists and met with socialists and radical workers. Gradually, Marx would see in the laboring class the vehicle to transform Germany, Europe, and indeed humanity.

Marx never gave up his Enlightenment faith in the coming of a new era. He did, though, abandon his youthful idealist philosophy with its faith in the power of reason and ideas to change the world. He gradually developed an original theoretical perspective whose aim was to provide an understanding of history and present-day society for the purpose of social revolution. The agents of change were not the middle classes, a group that was not only weak in Germany but that had already showed its true colors in its ruthless oppression of peasants and laborers. The true carriers of revolution were to be the working classes, the mass of laborers whose poverty, insecurity, and degradation would propel them to social rebellion. Marx intended to wed his new science of society – historical materialism – with the mass of laborers to create a revolutionary ferment powerful enough to liberate humanity.

Historical materialism: a revolutionary science

Marx's growing political radicalism went hand in hand with his turn to social theory. As we have seen, Marx insisted that an agenda for social change must rely upon a theoretical perspective that highlights the social sources of political conflict and the groups likely to enact change. Drawing on the writings of English and French political economists and historians, Marx had already come to the conclusion that the idealist philosophy needed to give way to a "materialist" social theory, i.e., a theory that analyzed the political economy of society. Throughout the 1840s, Marx sketched what a critical social theory anchored in political economy might look like.

In *The German Ideology*, a massive, erudite, somewhat pedantic two-volume work, Marx, along with his friend and collaborator, Friedrich Engels, had his final intellectual reckoning with the idealist philosophy [9]. Marx and Engels aimed to shift the focus of social criticism from the analysis of consciousness and the evolution of ideas to that of the development of social institutions and conflicts.

The German idealists held that what is unique about humans is that we have the capacity to reason and think. Although many idealists focused primarily on the nature of human consciousness or the structure of reason, they did outline a social perspective. Central to this was the notion that human thought produces beliefs, values, and norms. At a societal level, these symbolic products of individual thought form a cultural configuration. Every society is said to have its own unique cultural system, i.e., its own world views, values, standards of truth, rightness, beauty, and its own social ideals. The cultural realm was the dynamic core of society. At bottom, society was said to be a collective mind or the sum of its shared ideas. The cultural system shapes the structure of society and provides its source of dynamism and direction. The evolution of society reflects the evolution of its culture. It follows that the key to analyzing society lies in understanding its culture which, in turn, is interpreted as marking the level of development of human reason. The major social conflicts involve a clash of ideas. History was described as the evolution of the mind towards higher levels of rationality and human advancement.

Marx bought into more of idealism than he cared to admit. For example, he borrowed from idealists the view of society as a contradictory organic whole and their evolutionary view of history. Yet he was so intent on breaking from his intellectual family in order to stake out his own identity that he frequently stated his position in extreme antithetical terms, a strategy that made Marx an easy target of criticism.

Marx acknowledged that humans are "rational" thinking beings in that we form thoughts that have varying levels of coherence and consistency. However, it is a mistake to take our deliberate, reasoning capacities as the essence of what it means to be human. The idealist premise ignores one crucial fact: The human species is a part of nature. Our conscious, rational life presupposes our physical, material existence. Humans are capable of a conscious, reasoning life but only as we maintain ourselves as natural, embodied beings. Idealists mistakenly abstract our conscious, thinking life from our material life. Humans are a part of nature; our conscious lives reside in our bodies; material neediness and want is our destiny. Before we can be in a position to reason and create culture, we must maintain ourselves as natural beings. The reproduction of material life precedes the production of culture.

As natural beings whose material needs must be met in order to survive, and therefore to reason and create culture, we must maintain a commerce with our natural environment. Humankind is not self-maintaining as a physical entity; our bodies do not produce the resources they need to reproduce. The pristine natural environment, moreover, does not provide humans with what we need to live. Humans must not only look to the natural environment to survive but must alter it in order to satisfy our bodily needs. In other words, humans do not simply live off nature but transform it in order to survive. The activity by means of which we maintain this interchange with the natural environment Marx calls, somewhat ambiguously, labor or productive activity. Moreover, as we transform the natural environment to survive, we shape our own human nature. It is precisely the fact that humans make their own nature (e.g., our needs, wants, desires, and consciousness) through their laboring practices that Marx takes to be truly unique to humankind. It follows that human consciousness and its products – culture – should be grasped in relation to our material productive life.

Underlying Marx's concept of human nature is a powerful Enlightenment secular-humanistic vision. Humankind creates its own nature through its own actions. We alone have the potential to fashion our lives with purpose and reason. The fate of humanity is in our own hands, not in the will of God or the laws of nature. Marx believed, however, that history to the present does not tell a story of humankind's purposeful self-creation. Quite the contrary: the history of humanity relates a sad tale of humankind submitting to the control of the very forces it has created. As an Enlightener, Marx imagines the story of humanity taking a different, better turn in the current epoch. Indeed, Marx enlists science to provide humanity with the vision and the instrument to allow us to seize control of our destiny. The tale of human sorrow is about to turn into a story of hope and wonder, but, to understand Marx's prophetic role, we must grasp the rudiments of his science of society.

To the extent that Marx defines humanity in terms of our productive activity, the starting point of a social perspective should be to determine how the labor or productive activity of a society is organized. Assuming, as Marx seems to, that productive activity means economic labor or paid (in kind or money) labor, social analysis should initially explain the dominant means of economic production of a society. In other words, why does a particular society organize its economic labor or its means of production (land, raw material, technology, human labor power) the way it does? Marx discounts geographical and technological explanations since they are unable to account for social variations in socioeconomic systems. What makes Marx an important social theorist is his social explanation: Class dynamics shape the organization of socioeconomic systems which, in turn, determine the structure and direction of the whole society. This is, at bottom, the heart of historical materialism.

Marx proposed a class theory of society. As his classic "The Communist Manifesto" states: "The history of all hitherto existing society is the history of class struggles. Freeman and slave, patrician and plebeian, lord and serf, guildmaster and journeyman, in a word, oppressor and oppressed, stood in contrast opposition to one another" [10]. All societies, past and present, have been divided between individuals who own and control the "means of production" (i.e., raw materials, technology, and money or the resources to hire or buy labor) and individuals who own only their capacity to labor. In short, all societies have been stratified, roughly speaking, between a propertied and a laboring class. Except for periods of social revolution, the propertied class has had more power due to their economic resources. Accordingly, they have been able to determine the organization of labor, i.e., what is produced, how, and who does what. Most importantly, the propertied class has the power to control the distribution of wealth in society.

What makes the propertied class a key social force is that they are able to translate their immense economic power into control over political, cultural, and social institutions. For example, their wealth, available leisure time, organizational skills, education, and social connections give them the upper hand in struggles to control the government. These same resources allow the propertied class to take control over cultural institutions (e.g., schools, the church, and mass media) and therefore to shape what ideas circulate in society and have credibility. "The class which has the means of material production at its disposal, consequently, also controls the means of mental production, so that . . . the ruling ideas are nothing more than the ideal expression of the dominant [social class]"[11]. The economic, political, and cultural power of the propertied class is directed to promoting their social interests and protecting the basis of their power, i.e., private property. In a word, the propertied class becomes a ruling class shaping the whole society in its own image.

Marx was convinced that the power of the ruling class is never total, and its efforts to exert complete control over society fail. Not only are there divisions within the ruling class (e.g., different segments of the propertied class may clash) but, more importantly, the mass of laborers do not meekly submit to social rule from above. Despite efforts by the ruling class to impose a uniform culture and system of domination, segments of the working class develop their own culture which fosters social discontent and resistance to the status quo. There emerges a state of social conflict that reflects the antagonistic interests of the two classes. The propertied ruling class is interested in a cheap, insecure, docile labor force; they wish to preserve their social privileges and power by maintaining the social status quo. In contrast, the interests of the laborers is to raise their wages, improve their work and nonwork conditions, and enhance their control over society. Beneath the surface calm of all societies are deep contradictions that inevitably surface in battles over work and social conditions and at times erupt into open class warfare over the very fate of society. This signals a period of transition to a new society. Human history unfolds as a series of epochal changes driven by the suffering and hope that underlie class conflict.

Marx's vision of history has a definite Enlightenment cast. History is patterned and meaningful; the succession of individual societies that pass in and out of existence relate a story of the progress of humanity. Marx's stage theory of history begins with the "primitive tribal community" to be succeeded by the "ancient communal type," the "feudal type," and finally the "capitalist-bourgeois" society which is destined to give way to "communism." Underlying these stages is the progress of humanity from a state of simplicity and underdevelopment in which human affairs are governed by nonrational and unconscious forces (e.g., myth, religion, class conflict) to a state of complexity, individualism, and cultural development. In the communist stage, humanity will be governed by conscious choice and reason; freedom will coincide with moral order and social harmony. The vehicle to inaugurate this heavenly city was to be the working class. Inspired by the high ideals of liberal society, yet driven to revolt by their massive deprivation, the working class would smash the iron grip of capitalism while preserving its marvels of technological and social advance. Marx envisioned a cataclysmic revolution bringing forth a new era of communist freedom.

Das Kapital: *The logic of social revolution*

During his stay in Paris (1843–1845), Marx had arrived at the conclusion that the working class would be the agent of revolution in the era of modern capitalism. He was convinced that this revolution would be the last major historical change. It would bring to an end the succession of class-based revolutions that mark history. The working class, unlike the bourgeois-capitalist class, the patricians or feudal nobility before them, would not set itself up as a new ruling class. The working class would be the first class in history to truly represent the interests of all humanity. The conflict between the working class and capitalists was viewed as a struggle over the destiny of humanity; the triumph of the working class anticipated an era free of class division and exploitation.

In Marx's early writings, his vision of working class revolution was already presented as a conclusion of his science and society. Drawing on the writings of classical economists such as Adam Smith and David Ricardo, Marx pushed their liberal perspective on industrial capitalism in a radical direction. For example, in some notes that were posthumously published under the title of *The Economic and Philosophical Manuscripts of 1844*, Marx interpreted the division of labor as creating a class structured society, rather than, according to the liberal economists, as providing the engine of social productivity and progress [12]. The immense wealth produced under capitalism, Marx argued, simultaneously created a rich and privileged capitalist class and extreme poverty and deprivation for the mass of laborers. Marx thought that the material and spiritual impoverishment of the laborers, in the context of a rich society inspired by the ideals of human liberty and happiness, would eventually incite them to revolt. However, by the mid-1850s, it was clear, even to Marx, that a working class revolt was not imminent. Marx did not abandon his belief in social revolution. Rather, he assumed that social revolution would occur as a result of the very logic of capitalist development. Marx's humanistic vision of humanity rising up in revolt against social injustice gave way to a much more mechanistic view of social revolution. Marx's search for the logic of social revolution in the guise of a science of society lay at the very heart of his unfinished masterpiece, *Capital: A Critique of Political Economy* [13].

Marx sketches a picture of Western industrial capitalism whose very inner dynamics reveal a logic of social revolution. Guided by the premises of historical materialism, Marx found the key to Western societies in their economically based class structure.

Capital starts with an analysis of the commodity since, under capitalism, wealth assumes the form of a vast production and circulation of commodities. A commodity is a good produced for the purpose of exchange. Accordingly, it has both a "use value" or a value by virtue of satisfying a need and an "exchange value" or a value at which it is exchanged or, to simplify, a price. The source of exchange value and its magnitude is the amount of time it takes, on average, to produce a commodity. For example, assuming that one hour of labor produces a value of $5, then an eight-hour workday would produce a value of $40. The so-called "labor theory of value" explains why different commodities are exchanged in different proportions or at particular prices. If we pay $50 for shoes, it is because there is an equivalence of labor time represented in the $50 and in the shoes.

Capitalism is not the only commodity-producing society. It is, however, the only society that produces commodities for the primary end of making profit. Why else would an entrepreneur risk starting a business unless profit was anticipated? A central question for understanding capitalism is: Where does profit come from? Marx did not think it came from cheating the consumer by charging a higher price for the good than its actual value. Moreover, Marx rejected the liberal view that profit came from the risk-taking decisions of the capitalist. Marx proposed that profit originates from the exploitation of the laborer by the capitalist.

To grasp Marx's view of profit as exploitation, it is helpful to recall the standpoint of the capitalist. A business is started with the intention of realizing a profit. To go into business, the capitalist must purchase the necessary means of production. A series of exchanges occur between capitalists; our aspiring entrepreneur purchases raw materials and technology from other capitalists. The exchange is fair in that there is an equivalence between the value of the goods purchased and the money paid. A business does not operate on raw material and technology alone; capitalists need human labor power to set the work process in motion. Interestingly, says Marx, labor power is for sale just like any other commodity. Laborers sell their ability to labor or "labor power" as the only commodity that they own. Its price or exchange value is, like all commodities, equal to the amount of time that it takes, on average, to produce a living wage, i.e., to maintain human life from day to day. If it takes eight hours to produce a value of $50, which is sufficient to maintain the laborer for a day, then that is the cost of labor. Now, says Marx, when the capitalist and the laborer meet on the market, they enter into an ostensibly free and fair contractual agreement. The capitalist agrees to pay the laborer a wage equal to his/her exchange value for which, in return, the capitalist gets to use the laborer for an agreed-upon number of hours. Accordingly, our entrepreneur purchases not only raw materials and technology but enough labor power for the business to operate productively.

Viewed from the vantage point of these exchanges among capitalists and between them and laborers, capitalism seems to epitomize fairness and freedom. However, if we look at the exchange between the capitalist and the laborer from the latter's vantage point, its exploitive and unjust character is revealed. The laborer *must* sell his/her labor power in order to survive. It is true, though, that the capitalist pays the laborer a fair wage, i.e., a wage equal to the exchange value of labor power. In return for this wage, the laborer must work for the capitalist for the amount of time they agreed upon. What if the laborer produces a value for the capitalist in excess of the value paid to him or her in the form of a wage? This "discrepancy" or exploitation, as Marx calls it, is the origin of profit.

Let's say that a worker contracts with a capitalist to work 10 hours for a fair wage of $50. During this work time, the worker creates a value of $60. Who gets the extra $10? The wage contract states only that the capitalist agrees to pay the worker a wage equal to the exchange value of labor power, not a wage equal to the amount of value created by the worker. So long as the capitalist pays the laborer the agreed-upon wage, whatever value the laborer creates belongs to the capitalist. The extra $10 belongs, fair and square, according to the wage contract, to the capitalist. But, you ask, why doesn't the laborer protest this exploitation? From the laborer's point of view, it seems like he or she is getting paid for each hour worked. If the laborer works ten hours for a wage of $50, it appears that he or she is being paid $5 per hour. The laborer doesn't realize that, after eight hours, a value equal to her or his wage ($50) is created and that two additional hours is profit for the capitalist. The laborer doesn't perceive exploitation because this unpaid work time is obscured by the hourly wage system. Moreover, exploitation is concealed by the capitalist ideology which asserts that everyone gets paid for their work and that profit comes from the risks, hard work, and managerial skills of the capitalist. In contrast to the social surface of capitalist society with its apparent equal and just exchanges between free individuals, Marx argued that capitalism is founded upon the class inequality between capitalists and laborers and a system of exploitation.

Initially, the mass of laborers do not see their own exploitation; they do not pierce through the capitalist ideology of a society based on individual freedom, equality, and justice. Their social discontent is directed at machines that threaten to replace them or at other workers who compete for their jobs. Gradually, the mass of laborers are transformed into a working class political movement advocating the overthrow of capitalism. How does this social transformation of the workers, and of capitalism, transpire?

The nature of capitalism is to realize profit. Capitalists have no choice. If one starts a business, regardless of personal motives or values, a profit must be made. No profit, no livelihood. Profit making must, moreover, permit economic modernization. If capitalists don't make enough profit to reinvest and modernize the work process, they risk losing a share of the market to the competition. The logic of capitalism demands that individual entrepreneurs make profits and continuously modernize, under the threat of competition and failure. This same logic has grave social and political implications for workers. Economic modernization means not only devising new and better products, but making the labor process more efficient, keeping wages down, and maximizing worker productivity. In other words, just as the laborers must sell their capacity to labor to capitalists to survive, capitalists have little choice but to exploit and oppress laborers.

Marx does not criticize the capitalists for being greedy or lacking social conscience. The logic of capitalism forces them to make profit, modernize, and exploit labor. *Capital* is a story of a social system that controls the lives of individuals. Moreover, Marx is not saying that the system is without redeeming value. Quite the contrary: Marx had great admiration for the capacity of capitalism to produce wealth, stimulate technological, social, and cultural innovation, and create the conditions of political democracy. Capitalism brings into existence social conditions that make possible true human freedom, but, at the same time, it blocks that potential by channeling its immense social productivity to the benefit mostly of one small segment of society. The realization of the great human potential created by capitalism requires its transformation. Marx thought he saw the logic of social revolution in the very dynamics of capitalism.

Driven by competition, capitalists are compelled to modernize. While this permits the survival of individual entrepreneurs, it creates the conditions for the end of capitalism. Economic modernization contributes to transforming the mass of laborers into a politically aware working class. Rationalizing the workplace further disempowers workers; it often translates into relatively decreased wages, worker insecurity as machines replace workers, and extreme specialization which strips work of all its skill, imagination, and creativity. In a word, every effort by capitalists to increase profits intensifies worker degradation and alienation. The progress of capitalism and the immense social wealth and opportunities for individual development it creates are experienced by workers as social and spiritual impoverishment. Their work lives are materially and spiritually deadened; their families are often disrupted as both parents and children work; their communities are devastated by poverty and social instability. The growing visible disparity between the rich lives of capitalists and the deprivation of the laborers incites their political awakening. Initially, their struggles are focused on work conditions, the length of the workday, wages, or child labor laws. Gradually, they come to view the source of their discontent in the capitalist system itself, not in their personal defects or those of the capitalists.

Social revolution does not occur, however, until the system offers no other choice to workers. The stimulus to this ultimate act of revolt is a series of socioeconomic crises that escalate in intensity and rapidity. Regular periodic crises express the irrational nature of capitalism. Capitalists modernize to survive. This dynamic yields leaps in productivity but also recurring social crises. Consumption must expand to absorb the increased flow of goods. This spurs the internationalization of capitalism and the widening of the domestic market by commercializing hitherto noncommercial sectors (e.g. leisure, recreation, sports). Unfortunately, no matter how fast new markets are created, the rapid shifts in capital investment inevitably give rise to periodic gluts in the market, massive layoffs, and far-reaching social dislocations. For example, computer sales get hot; capital is poured into computer production without any idea of what the market will hold; at some point, production will exceed demand; computer production slows or halts; workers are laid off; families and communities are disturbed and stressed. Marx maintained that regular economic crises undermine worker's faith in the system as their lives and those of their families and friends are repeatedly debased despite their greatest efforts.

The mass of laborers become political agents in order to survive and preserve their human dignity. Because they work, live, and socialize together, and because they share similar outlooks, their discontents coalesce into a unified working class consciousness. Attacks against machinery and capitalist give way to union organizing and the formation of socialist or labor political parties. Inspired by a socialist ideology that expresses their social vantage point, the working class directs their political activity towards socializing the economy and democratizing social institutions. The socialist revolution, peacefully accomplished wherever the ballot box is accessible but violent if it is not, will signal a shift from a state where humanity is controlled by a system to a society under human control.

Tensions between a scientific and moral vision

Marx was clear that the chief aim of his theorizing was to change society. As he stated in his "Theses on Feuerbach," "philosophers have only interpreted the world, the point is to change it" [14]. Social change must, of course, be guided by moral values. Marx offered a radical Enlightenment vision. He took liberal ideals of individualism, liberty, and equality seriously; he was convinced that Western capitalist societies realized these ideals but in partial, incomplete ways. For example, capitalist society cherished individualism, but, as a class-based society, it extended real freedom only to the business class. Similarly, legal equality was an advance over a feudal system of legalized social hierarchy, but it left intact gross social inequalities. Marx wished to realize the moral hopes of liberalism; this required a great social transformation, the overthrow of capitalism. Marx championed the working class as carriers of this revolutionary moral will.

Social theory and social change went hand in hand. Science not only provided an understanding of society but could become an actual force in changing society. Marx believed that science could become a force of change if its social understandings were accepted by individuals and groups interested in change. A social scientific perspective might serve as the lens through which individuals viewed their personal and social reality. Scientific ideas could politicize people's identities and practices. This was the moral hope that informed *Capital*. Marx thought that the mass of laborers had an interest in change. He intended *Capital*, or some popularized version, to become the lens through which laborers would view themselves as an exploited, oppressed social class. *Capital* provided a social explanation of worker discontent that targeted the system of capitalism as its source and socialist political practice as the remedy. *Capital* was intended to be a part of the moral and political struggles of the time.

Although Marx never denied the moral impulse behind his social theorizing, from the mid-1840s, he began to see himself as a scientist. For example, in *The German Ideology*, Marx claimed that his perspective on history was a breakthrough to a true science of society. In contrast to social ideologists who offered biased, one-sided social ideas, Marx declared that historical materialism provided an objective understanding of social reality. Marx was persuaded that the premises, basic concepts, and explanations of his social perspective were valid. Yet nowhere did he clarify the standards of truth that guided his judgment. Marx did offer some rationales for his claims, but they are, by and large, rather feeble. For example, his claim that human nature is not uniform and fixed but that humans make and remake their nature through their actions is asserted, not demonstrated. We can just as easily counter Marx with the equally plausible claim that human nature is constant and uniform though humans change their beliefs and values. Assumptions about human nature as fixed or changeable or good or bad are akin to religious or metaphysical beliefs. Similarly, Marx's claim that economic productive activity is more important than culture in structuring society is little more than a statement of faith or, if you will, a rhetorical political claim. How could one possibly know which is causally prior? Indeed, it is not at all clear that Marx's claim is coherent. Can there be productive activity that is not symbolic, that does not include consciousness and moral regulation? Finally, exactly how are we supposed to distinguish productive, laboring activity from symbolic, religious, domestic, or reproductive practices?

Marx's premises appear to be little more than beliefs that carry less the authority of reason than that of shared cultural bias. This does not mean that his social ideas are illusionary or worthless. The usefulness of ideas and their truthfulness are not necessarily correlated. Ideas may be true but useless; they may be "wrong" but useful. If Marx intended to shape the political awareness of the laborers into a critical force through his social ideas, the "success" of his efforts should be judged by this practical standard, not by whether or not his ideas are true. Unfortunately, Marx aspired to justify his social ideas solely on the grounds of their correspondence to the world "out there." This is unfortunate, not only because it was unnecessary and probably impossible, but because it has undesirable consequences. By defending his social and political ideas solely on the basis of their empirical truth, Marx avoided having to advance serious arguments defending the moral and political values that inform his social perspective. Marx simply invoked the laws of history and society to authorize his social values (e.g., socialism, democracy, and individualism).

Marx's critical attitude towards Western industrial societies did not extend to his faith in science and its power to liberate humanity. No less than his ideological opponents, Marx was a captive of the Enlightenment dream of science revealing truths in the service of humanity. He saw himself as the Newton of social science. *Capital* was to be to the social sciences what Darwin's *On the Origin of Species* was to the natural sciences. Such grandiose claims have not been peculiar to Marx in the history of social science. Condorcet and Comte before Marx, and Spencer, Durkheim, and virtually every major twentieth century theorist from Parsons to Habermas have made similar auspicious announcements. The claim that a set of social ideas are scientific, rather than ideological, might appropriately be viewed as a strategy to confer public authority on these ideas. By the mid-nineteenth century, if not sooner, science carried authority; to speak in the name of science was to speak the language of truth. Science gave legitimacy to the social cause in whose name it spoke. Science conferred social status and power on social ideas and those who produced and supported them. From this perspective, Marx's claim to scientific status was a political strategy, an effort to impose a particular social and political world view.

Marx's vision of a science of society was powerful and surely drove his thinking. Yet, however much he wanted to wrap his ideas in the mantle of science, he was driven to offer majestic visions of history and the future. These images are aesthetically, morally, emotionally, and politically captivating, as the history of the twentieth century makes clear. As much as Marx may have wished to separate his values and social hopes from his science, they are built into his basic premises, concepts, and explanations. For example, assumptions regarding the changeable nature of humanity or the linear movement of history towards communism are directly wedded to his social agenda. Similarly, while *Capital* purports to offer an objective view of current Western societies, its basic assumptions, concepts, and explanations reflect a critical attitude. Profit equals exploitation only if one accepts the labor theory of value and rejects the value additive role of managerial, risk-taking behavior. Finally, his vision of history as a movement from simplicity to complexity, from the dominance of the group to individualism, from a social state controlled by unconscious forces to one directed by deliberate, reasoned action is akin to those of the great world religions.

The irony of Marx is that this great social visionary, a figure who truly rivals the Judeo-Christian prophets in fashioning a powerful moral vision aimed at redeeming humanity by a great transformation, could delude himself into believing that his social ideas were merely a revelation of scientific reason. How odd it is that great modern minds such as Comte and Marx, men of immense insight and observation, could be so unaware of how they offered beautiful and socially powerful moral and political visions in the name of science. Perhaps it is because, in Western societies, the belief in science as liberating humankind from myth and oppression is itself one of the chief illusions of our era.

Afterword

The formative years of modern social science comprised a period of enormous social turmoil. The seventeenth through the nineteenth centuries witnessed the formation of modern industrial societies. European societies were transformed by the development of capitalism, the modern bureaucratic state, constitutional democracy, the political party system, secularization, the nation-state, and a culture of science and individualism. The modern era was not the inevitable product of an evolutionary process; it wasn't predetermined by human nature, the laws of history, or God. Modernity was made by people – individuals and groups. It came into being in the throes of life-and-death struggles between proponents of modernization and their opponents and among modernizers whose values and visions clashed. From the ordinary individual to power elites, conflict ensued in every Western nation over what form the economy, government, and the family should assume, over the role of religion and the state, over who should have rights, vote, hold office, define truth, practice medicine, educate children, and pray.

Intellectuals were part of the struggle over the social formation of modernity. They had an important social role. They crafted stories of historical development and visions of the meaning of modernity that were used by the various parties to the struggles to authorize their social agendas. Intellectuals legitimated the social elites whose position was hardly secure. They provided maps of society, of what kind of society was developing and possible futures, which were in demand in this period of transition. In addition, the developing modern social system required technical information about everything from managing a centralized bureaucratic state to controlling the massive shifts of populations from the countryside to cities. The Enlighteners were embroiled in these struggles over the social organization of humanity. Like their fellow citizens, they had their own social values and political agendas. Many of them were directly politically engaged, for example, in struggles for tolerance, freedom of speech, the secularization of education and government, women's rights, social equality, or constitutional government. The Enlighteners were positioned, to varying degrees, against rigid social hierarchies and a religious culture defended by the church and landed aristocracy. Their social values and visions were advanced under the banner of advocating for secular knowledge, science, the unity and uniformity of humanity, and social progress.

Some critics have maintained that the Enlightenment and its idea of a science of society have had the effect of diminishing human freedom. They argue that, despite the humanitarian ideology of the Enlightenment, its true spirit and social consequence have been to enhance social control and domination. For example, the claim that science is the only valid form of knowledge has the effect of devaluing and marginalizing nonscientific ideas and whole societies that are organized around, say, a religious culture. Similarly, we might accept at face value the claim of the Enlighteners that the assumption of the identity and uniformity of humanity was intended to discredit social hierarchies that rested upon the idea of different races and rankings of humans. However, one social effect of this idea has been to promote a harsh intolerance towards human diversity and the assertion of social differences between individuals and groups. Some critics have concluded that the Enlightenment shaped a society hostile to individuality, social differences, non-Western cultures, and nonscientific ideas.

I think that there is considerable truth to this critique of the Enlightenment. The Enlighteners took for granted that Europe represented the high point of civilization, that individualism is the highest value, that men should rule, that science is the vehicle of enlightenment and progress. These ideas have played a key role in shaping a human order that makes Europe and the United States superior and that gives privileges to a social elite of men. For all their claims to reason, the figures of the Enlightenment were remarkably nonreflective about the social origins and possible prejudices of their own ideas. Key assumptions of the Enlightenment regarding the equality and unity of humanity, science as knowledge, social progress, and so on mask a constellation of social interests and values that they never examined and that have played a role in shaping history. Why didn't they become aware of the social forces shaping their own ideas? Perhaps the battles of the day made it politically difficult to see their own values and ideas as anything more than truths.

I do not think, however, that the Enlightenment has been only a social evil. I take issue with the view of the Enlightenment science of society as merely an instrument for the modern state and emerging power elite in need of legitimation and effective strategies of social control. I view the Enlightenment and the original idea of social science with great ambivalence. Enlightenment ideas have been carriers of liberal and democratic values and social hopes for a better society – a society tolerant of difference, protective of individual rights and privacy, committed to democracy and equality, insistent on secularization or the separation of the state and church. We should not dismiss the struggles of many Enlighteners for tolerance of social difference, women's rights, or social equality. While I agree with critics who fault the Enlightenment for its Eurocentrism and male-biased concepts of reason, I would also point out that figures such as Voltaire, Condorcet, Hume, Thomas Paine, Thomas Jefferson, and Kant created compelling images of humanity and stories of history that imagine a world of individual autonomy, equality, democracy, and tolerance. Can anyone read Voltaire's *The Age of Louis XIV* and not come away with a hatred of fanaticism and the evils of intolerance? In this regard, I remain impressed, indeed moved, by the moral vision of the Enlightenment.

At the core of the Enlightenment is a social view of humanity. The individual and human institutions are conceived of as social, not natural, creations. The role of social factors (e.g., economics, social class, religion, values, population) is emphasized in the Enlightenment stories of human development. Why is this important? It allows us to imagine the possibility of humans creating their own destiny. Instead of assuming that nature or God control the fate of humanity, the Enlightenment envisions the possibility of humans deliberately making their own future. I find a utopian impulse in the Enlightenment science of society that I do not want to surrender: the hope of humanity making itself guided by social knowledge.

Comte and Marx inherited this social hope. They assumed a social view of humanity. In this regard, Comte and Marx moved considerably beyond the Enlighteners, many of whom continued to assume a concept of human nature organized around a fixed set of biologically based needs and instincts. Comte, and especially Marx, articulate deeply social perspectives on humanity. Humans are social; we are made in society; individual motivations and needs are social. There is no opposition between the individual and society. Marx asserts: "Above all we must avoid postulating 'society' again as an abstraction vis-à-vis the individual. The individual is the social being" [15]. Defining humanity as a social creation requires that we explain the shape of humanity by referring to social and political factors. Moreover, it offers the possibility that knowledge can direct social change.

There have been many critics of this sort of social rationalism. No doubt it lends itself to extremes or to legitimating a knowledge elite controlling society. Ominous social images come to mind, especially in light of the history of communism, in invoking the idea of humankind willfully designing a society. This evil potential *is* present in this utopian social hope. Nevertheless, the excesses of communism are less the product of Marxism's vision of a society guided by social knowledge than by the Stalinist commitment to rapid industrialization in Russia. A distinction is crucial here. Comte seemed to envision a knowledge elite who would design a perfect society. Marx defended the more modest, and democratic, proposal that social knowledge could shape the history of humanity by becoming part of the culture of a society that could be drawn on to shape the future. I reject the Comtean utopian vision, as it justifies an authoritarian society. I share the Marxian social hope of a science of society whose knowledges find their chief value in their utility to citizens and social movements.

In my view, the chief legacy of Comte and Marx is their imaginative and powerful social perspectives on historical development. They furnished understandings of society, history, and modernity that have proved gripping in the way many of us have made sense of our lives and struggle to shape the future.

Comte's chief social perception rests on the claim of the centrality of religious moral beliefs and values in forging social coherence. Comte asserted that, without shared moral values or some kind of common culture, society is unstable and directionless. Even more than Marx, Comte challenged the dominant utilitarian individualistic social vision of the Enlightenment, a social picture that has come to dominate Western societies and the social sciences. Abandoning images of society as a collection of self-interested individuals, Comte thought of society as an organic order whose center was religiously based shared values. Departing from the utilitarian celebration of individualism and social progress in Adam Smith or Ben Franklin, Comte alerted us to the dangers of "social progress" to social unity and moral order. This social vision was elaborated by Durkheim and Parsons and has served as an important alternative to utilitarian concepts of society. While I do not agree with Comte's particular ideas about the religion of humanity and the positive stage of history and would strenuously object to his views about the family, gender, the role of scientific elites and the state, I value his view of the conceptual priority of society over the individual, his institutional approach to social behavior, the importance he places on the dynamics of social integration, moral order, and his vision of sociology as a transformative force in social change.

Marx shared with Comte this social approach to humanity. He was critical of a view of society as made up of a collection of individuals, whose impulses, interests, and needs produce institutions. Society was not, for Marx, an instrument for satisfying individual needs. However, as we have seen, Marx's critique of individualistic approaches to human studies focused on political and economic dynamics, not religion and culture. Marx proposed an alternative perspective to the individualism of many Enlightenment thinkers and to the idealism of Comte. Marx thought of society as organized around the clash of social interests anchored in the contradictory social class positioning of individuals. Drawing from a limited stock of categories (e.g., labor, mode of production, social class, ideology), he constructed a magnificent synthetic view of society and history. Marx related a social drama of epoch proportions that not only is useful in making sense of inequalities and social conflicts but authorizes a particular political agenda and vision. More than any other social thinker, Marx's vision has moved the world.

I recall my own romance with Marxism. It was in my junior year as an undergraduate. This was 1972. I was in a seminar on law and society. I knew little of Marx. The professor was pressing me to think about law in sociological terms. I remember arguing that law seemed to be a way for the rich to stay rich, that it was enacted by those who were already powerful and used for their benefit. This was not a surprising view for a young idealistic student who was at the time working as an intern at the Legal Aid Society in New York City. The professor described my position as Marxist. I was surprised. Like most Americans, I imagined Marxism to mean communism. I had not thought of Marxism as simply a sociological perspective. I began to read Marx; indeed, by the time I went to graduate school, I thought of myself as a Marxist. Marx's ideas struck me as brilliant and true. He explained social realities in a comprehensive fashion. I was deeply impressed by the way he linked economics, politics, law, and culture into a critical analysis of capitalist societies inspired by a vision of a full liberated individual. As a child of the student protests and counter-culture of the late 1960s, I found in Marxism a compelling world view animated by a beautiful vision of human potential.

I have since abandoned Marxism. Some of the reasons will be related in subsequent chapters. The gist of my disillusionment was that the very elegance and beauty of Marx's social vision was achieved at the price of suppressing tensions and conflicts (e.g., sexual and gender conflicts) that I came to believe were important. The wish to outline a synthetic, overarching, morally compelling image of society and history, to have the one, complete, right statement of social reality proved in the end to be shockingly ruthless, to exclude too much. Concerns that came to be crucial in the seventies for me, such as sexual and gender identity and the dynamics of solidarity and community, can not be addressed by Marxism in ways that I feel are necessary.

I find a sort of conceptual authoritarianism in both Comte and Marx. This is revealed less in their explicit values than in their insistence that they have the right social viewpoint, that their particular views of the self, social process, and history are basic and true. Marx would have us believe, for example, that labor is the formative act creating and recreating humanity. And on this basis, he erects a whole theoretical system. It is this certitude, a certainty wrapped in the language of science, justified by largely feeble arguments, that I find especially objectionable in Comte and Marx, and, I'm afraid, in much human studies that is inspired by a scientific vision.

References

1. Baron De Montesquieu, *The Spirit of the Laws* (New York: Hafner Press, 1975).
2. Marquis De Condorcet, *Sketch for a Historical Picture of the Progress of the Human Mind* (New York: Noonday Press, 1955).
3. Montesquieu, *The Spirit of the Laws*, p. lxvii.
4. Regarding the romantic critique of the Enlightenment, the reader should consult M.H. Abrams, *Natural Supernaturalism* (New York: Norton, 1971); Charles Taylor, *Hegel* (Cambridge: Cambridge University Press, 1979); and Alvin Gouldner, "Romanticism and Classicism: Deep Structures in Social Science," in *For Sociology* (New York: Basic Books, 1973).
5. For an overview of conservative social thought in this period, see Karl Mannheim, "Conservative Thought," in *From Karl Mannheim*, edited by Kurt Wolff (New York: Oxford University Press, 1971) and Robert Nisbet, *The Sociological Tradition* (New York: Basic Books, 1966).
6. Regarding the revolutionary critics of the Enlightenment, see G.H. Cole, *Socialist Thought* (New York: St. Martin's Press, 1962); J.L. Talmon, *The Rise of Totalitarian Democracy* (Boston: Beacon Press, 1952); and George Lichtheim, *The Origins of Socialism* (New York: Praeger, 1969).
7. Auguste Comte, *The Course of Positive Philosophy*, 3 vols. (London: George Bell and Sons, 1876 [1830–1842]); *System of Polity*, 4 vols. (New York: Burt Franklin, 1875, [1851–1854]).
8. Karl Marx, "A Contribution to the Critique of Hegel's Philosophy of Right. Introduction," in *Early Writings* (New York: Random House, 1975), p. 251.
9. Karl Marx and Friedrich Engels, *The German Ideology*, in *Collected Works*, Vol. 5 (New York: International, 1975).
10. Karl Marx, "The Communist Manifesto," *The Revolutions of 1848*, edited by David Fernbach (New York: Random House, 1974), pp. 67–68.
11. Marx and Engels, *The German Ideology*, in *Collected Works*, Vol. 5, p. 59.
12. Karl Marx, *The Economic and Philosophical Manuscripts of 1844* (New York: International Publishers, 1964).
13. Karl Marx, *Capital*. Vols. 1–3 (New York: International, 1967–1973).
14. Karl Marx, "Theses on Feuerbach," in Marx and Engels, *Collected Works*, Vol. 5, p. 5.
15. Marx and Engels, *The German Ideology*, in *Collected Works*, Vol. 5, p. 299.

2

THE PROMISE OF SOCIOLOGY:
Emile Durkheim and Max Weber

Many Enlightenment social thinkers took over the social hopes already attached to the science of nature. The power of science was thought to lie in its capacity to liberate humankind from material want, from illusions that mired us in fear and ignorance, and from a world that felt beyond human control. The Enlighteners imagined science as a vehicle of human progress.

In the context of eighteenth century Europe, science was enmeshed in a series of social conflicts. To speak on behalf of science threatened the authority of religion and the social power of aristocratic and clerical elites. Enlighteners rallied behind science as part of a struggle to change society and to legitimate their own world view and aspirations for secular authority.

The Enlightenment vision of society was, broadly speaking, modern and liberal. Against a religiously based, hierarchical, and elite-governed society, the Enlighteners struggled for a secular culture that was tolerant of diverse beliefs and values and a society that expanded individual liberties, social equality, and political democracy. The Enlighteners envisioned a freer, more open, and dynamic society. Under the banner of reason and social progress, they promoted a liberal social agenda.

The liberal social ideal of the Enlighteners received its most powerful theoretical formulation in the writings of the classical economists. For example, Adam Smith and John Stuart Mill helped pioneer a science of political economy [1]. They argued that the most important feature of modern societies was the freedom given to the individual to choose his or her work, lifestyle, and leaders. Individualism was the hallmark of modern capitalist society; it underpinned the division of economic labor which, in turn, engineered an economy of material abundance; the system of free economic exchanges allowed individuals to fashion a life according to their personal preferences and values. To the extent that the government confined itself to enforcing the law, protecting national security and civic peace, the reign of individual freedom would promote social prosperity and progress.

A liberal social agenda was supported by many entrepreneurs who wanted less government and church interference with business and more say in political decision making. In other words, the liberal world view of the political economists was a part of an ongoing social struggle between the middle classes and the existing ruling elite.

The liberal social ideology met with a great deal of opposition. In part, resistance came from the landed aristocracy and clerical hierarchy whose social authority was directly threatened by the strata of entrepreneurs and liberal intellectuals. Conservative spokesmen for the social status quo assailed liberalism; they highlighted the importance of religion, social hierarchy, and elite rule for maintaining social peace [2]. Opposition to liberalism also came from radicals for whom the hopes of the French Revolution were betrayed by a liberal agenda [3]. Radicals pushed the moderate hopes of liberals to the extreme, imagining a society free of all social hierarchy, inequality, and domination.

European societies in the late eighteenth and early decades of the nineteenth century were deeply divided. On the one hand, Enlighteners who fought for the emerging modern civilization were in conflict with critics who defended the status quo. On the other hand, there were disputes among Enlighteners who disagreed over the meaning and direction of modern society. This pervasive social and ideological strife was the setting for the social thought of Comte and Marx. They were both heirs to the Enlightenment who ardently defended individualism, secularism, and progress. Yet their social visions were antagonistic to individualistic liberalism. They disputed the notion that the individual lies at the heart of society, that capitalism inevitably promotes social progress, and that entrepreneurs and the educated classes are destined to be Europe's moral and social leaders. Comte attempted to temper his liberalism by introducing counter-Enlightenment conservative values stressing the role of a religiously based order, social hierarchy, and elite rule. Marx pushed the liberal vision in a radical direction, believing that true freedom and equality required the transformation of capitalism into socialism. In the end, Comte's initial notoriety was far overshadowed by Marx's success in shaping a European working class movement inspired by a socialist ideology.

Comte and Marx succeeded beyond their highest expectations in altering the discussion of modernity, science, and social reform. No social thinker coming of age in late nineteenth century Europe could avoid engaging their ideas. They represented the most important alternatives to both the narrow individualistic liberalism of the classical economists and the backward-looking vision of the counter-Enlightenment.

Emile Durkheim and Max Weber are considered by many current historians and social thinkers to be the greatest social theorists in the period between the late nineteenth century and World War I. They shaped in key ways the development of social theory in our century. Although they were bearers of the Enlightenment tradition, their ideas were filtered through the lens of Comte and Marx. Whereas it was Comte's communitarian social ideal that was central to Durkheim's sociology, the towering figure of Marx shaped Weber's ambivalent response to the Enlightenment.

As we move from Comte and Marx to Durkheim and Weber, we find ourselves in a substantially altered social environment. By the end of the nineteenth century, France and Germany had become preeminent modern nation-states and world powers. The broader social context of their ideas will be discussed shortly; I wish to call attention to their unique social positioning. Neither Comte nor Marx were university professors; though trained as academics, their lives and ideas were formed outside of the academe. In the end, they assumed prophetic roles as creators of social movements whose aim was to transform society. Like the great Judeo-Christian prophets, Comte and Marx fashioned grand visions of history and human freedom. By contrast, Durkheim and Weber were professors more or less throughout their lives. They were the first generation of social thinkers to assume chairs of sociology and to write as sociologists. Sociology was understood as a specialized discipline rather than as a general theory of humanity. Unlike Comte and Marx, Durkheim and Weber wrote research-oriented studies. Durkheim's study of suicide and Weber's analysis of Protestantism and capitalism are still considered models of scientific sociology by many social scientists. Nevertheless, neither Durkheim nor Weber abandoned the wish to craft a sweeping vision of history, nor did they abandon the moral hope that science could and should change society. Whereas Comte and Marx wore their moral commitments on their sleeves, Durkheim and Weber wove their moral vision into the very premises, concepts, and empirical explanations of their social studies.

Emile Durkheim

In the course of the nineteenth century, France had changed considerably. Through the first half of the century, France was largely an agrarian society of peasants, divided by language, social custom, and regional disputes. France was ruled by the Catholic Church, the landed nobility, and the monarchy. By the turn of the century, France was well on the way to becoming a modern, secular, industrial nation. Nevertheless, in one important respect, very little had changed: France remained socially and politically unstable. Just as Comte faced a nation polarized between the forces of revolution and reaction, Durkehim came of age in a period of similar social division. Durkheim aimed to legitimate a social liberal alternative to the ideological agendas of the Right and Left. Durkheim shared Comte's hope that sociology could serve as the vehicle for the ideological defense and reconstruction of a liberal France.

Durkheim came of age at a critical juncture in French history. The Third French Republic had established itself as the longest surviving liberal political regime in French history. Whatever optimism existed among supporters of the Republic, however, was tempered by the organized strident opposition of the conservative Right and the radical Left. Social modernization in France did not lead inexorably to a society unified by a liberal moral center. On the one hand, France remained a society tied to an agrarian, patriarchal, and Catholic culture; the church, landed aristocracy, and military elites resisted secularism, individualism, and the free market ideology of middle class liberals. On the other hand, modernization brought forth a new social force equally opposed to liberalism: a socialist Left rooted in the discontent of laborers and, to a lesser extent, a revolutionary feminism anchored in the disempowerment of women. Whereas the Right attacked liberalism for supposedly unleashing moral and social anarchy, the Left assailed liberalism for preserving social inequality and injustice. Turn-of-the-century France may have succeeded in fashioning a liberal social order, but its fate was very much in doubt.

Durkheim's sympathy lay with the Third Republic. He was, by all accounts, personally uncomfortable with radical change, whether forward looking or backward looking. He was not, though, a simple-minded apologist for the republic or for the business and professional strata for whom social liberalization often meant a social policy of unrestrained capitalism. Durkheim wished to preserve a republican France but only if it was inspired by the high ideals of the French Revolution – *liberté*, *equalité* and *fraternité*.

Durkheim's liberalism shared little with the English and American defense of an unbridled economic individualism. His liberalism fused the English and American respect for individualism with the European concern with moral order and civic virtue; it affirmed economic freedom but only if socially regulated; he defended individualism but only if the individual was firmly rooted in social institutions; he valued cultural pluralism but only in a society that had a clear moral center. In short, to end the bitter conflicts in France, Durkheim reached for a social vision that would integrate the spirit of liberalism (individualism), radicalism (social justice), and conservatism (moral order). Durkheim's liberal social values were not articulated in an explicitly philosophical and moral way but through his empirical sociology.

His moral vision is at the heart of two of his most important sociological studies: *The Division of Labor in Society* and *Suicide* [4].

Durkheim's liberal vision of history and modernity

In the course of the ninteenth century, science had become an important language of moral argumentation. Appeals to scientific facts, explanations, or principles justified moral preferences and social values. Thus, Comte invoked the Law of the Three Stages as proof of the inevitability and desirability of the positive society. Marx sought to justify his own social values by identifying them with the laws of history. If the laws of society require particular social norms or institutions, they are said to be objective rather than merely subjective or ideological. Durkheim likewise wished to give his moral preferences an objective authority by framing them in the language of science. He intended to show that his social liberal ideal was rooted in the very evolution of society.

In *The Division of Labor in Society*, Durkheim presented a social liberal ideal that took the form of an evolutionary theory of society. He set out to write a story of the development of humanity from our early "primitive" stage to the "advanced" modern era. It was a story, not only of how humankind evolved, but of the necessity of this development and of its direction and endpoint.

Durkheim's evolutionary theory is anchored in a social typology. He distinguishes two types of society: segmental or traditional societies that are unified by "mechanical solidarity" and organized or modern societies that feature "organic solidarity." The history of humanity is charted by positioning social development somewhere along this continuum of "primitive" segmental and "modern, organized" types of societies.

"Primitive" societies exhibit a fundamental simplicity and uniformity in thier social structure. Typically, they are composed of a series of kinship groupings whose structure and functioning are more or less identical. Each individual is born into a kin group that assigns specific statuses and social roles in the course of the individual's life cycle. The kin group defines and regulates the behavior of its members. There are minimal social exchanges between these groups as each is more or less socially self-sufficient. This lack of substantial social differentiation between kin units is what Durkheim means by a segmental social structure. The social units (kin groupings) replicate one another in terms of their organization.

If primitive societies feature a segmental social structure, what gives to these societies their sense of coherence or, to use Durkheim's phrase, "social solidarity"? If each kin group is self-sufficient, what social force knits them together into an identifiable, coherent social whole? Durkheim's answer is that primitive societies are unified by a religiously based common culture. Durkheim maintains that, in a society where individual experiences are wedged into a narrow range exhibiting a strong uniformity, kin units develop similar beliefs and values. Primitive culture is characterized by a large number of beliefs, values, and norms held in common. Moreover, because primitives are unable to understand the social and natural forces that shape their lives, they imagine a universe governed by supernatural forces; the core of primitive culture is religious. Primitives view the human order as a sacred order filled with gods, spirits, and supernatural beings. It is precisely this religious common culture that brings the disparate social segments together into a coherent social whole.

To the extent that primitive societies are unified by a common culture, we can expect them to be conservative. A primitive society cannot, according to Durkheim's social logic, tolerate individuals who deviate from shared beliefs or social norms. If it is a common culture that keeps society integrated, then any cultural transgression would be a threat to social unity. Accordingly, deviance is treated harshly; social and legal repression is the dominant logic of social control. Durkheim is proposing a sort of unconscious social logic: Individuals act as the unwitting vehicles of social forces. Primitives repress deviance because it is unconsciously felt as a threat to personal and social coherence. Like Comte and Marx, Durkheim believed that, in primitive societies, humankind is under the control of social forces that are not understood. As we will see, the story Durkheim relates is one of humanity evolving towards a condition of rational understanding and social control. Western modernity signals the key turning point in human evolution; science destroys the illusions of supernatural powers giving to humanity the potential to fashion its own destiny.

Societies organized in a segmental way are inherently unstable. Drawing from Darwinian biological theory, Durkheim reasons that the very social insularity and parochialism of primitive societies limits their capacity to respond effectively to changes in their natural and social environments. Social invasions, encounters with foreign civilizations, changes in natural resources, climate, or population compel primitive societies to change in order to survive. Social adaptation requires introducing more social complexity and differentiation. For example, kinship groups would evolve toward economic specialization, thereby permitting the emergence of a market system. However, once humanity starts down the path of social differentiation, social evolution will inevitably ensue. In other words, natural and social events set in motion an inexorable dynamic pushing humanity forward. The endpoint of social evolution is a modern type of society characterized by an "organized" social structure and "organic" type of solidarity.

Modern societies are the antithesis of primitive ones. Modernity is said to be characterized by a highly differentiated social structure. Whereas the basic social units of primitive societies reveal a high level of structural and functional uniformity, in modern societies, they are differentiated. Large encompassing multifunctional kin groups are replaced by a multitude of specialized social institutions (e.g., the economy, polity, family, welfare, military, educational), each regulating a sector of individual behavior. For example, primitive kin groups satisfied a range of political, emotional, economic, religious, and educational needs. The modern Western family specializes in attending to the emotional and psychological needs of the individual. Nonfamilial institutions have developed that specialize in economic, political, or educational functions. Social differentiation and specialization is internal to institutions as well. Thus, the production of knowledge becomes a specialized role of the educational system, but, within this sphere, a process of differentiation transpires. Knowledge is broken down into disciplines, specialties, and subspecialties.

The evolution of society towards increased social differentiation is paralleled by a dynamic of cultural pluralism. In a modern, differentiated society, individual experiences exhibit a wide variation depending on social class, nationality, religion, occupation, age, or regional location. As individuals are allowed more latitude in shaping their ideas, the range of culture held in common shrinks. Moreover, those beliefs and values held in common will be highly general and abstract. For example, moderns may share a general belief in the value of the individual but disagree about the meaning and social role of the individual. Indeed, Durkheim was convinced that, as modern culture becomes pluralistic, one of the few beliefs we share is individualism. Moderns make the individual sacred; individualism is our public religion. Despite the deification of the individual, modern culture undergoes a thorough process of secularization. The world of natural and human events is more clearly differentiated from the world of supernatural spirits and forces. Whereas the former sphere is, in principle, intelligible and accessible by science and reason, the latter sphere is a matter of private faith. Modern culture projects a human-centered world; institutions are judged by their value to the individual.

The evolution of humanity towards a modern society is accompanied by a process of individualism. Durkheim observes two powerful social forces promoting individualism. First, the advance in the division of labor requires that individuals be given more freedom to regulate their institutional behavior. In a differentiated society, neither the state nor the church has the capacity to impose social rules that can regulate institutions as varied as the economy, the state, family, school, and the military. Their regulation must be left in large part to individuals who occupy social roles

in those institutions. This institutional pressure to permit greater individualism is reinforced by cultural pluralism. If there are fewer common ideas in
modern societies, then society *must* rely more on individuals than on
institutional authorities such as the state or church to create social rules
and norms. The very survival of society depends upon permitting the
individual more freedom to make rules and regulate social affairs. To
translate this empirical proposition into moral terms, Durkheim is invoking
supposedly objective principles of social organization to justify modern
individualism and cultural pluralism.

A final question remains. Assuming that modernization entails social
differentiation, cultural pluralism, secularism, and individualism, how are
modern societies unified? What prevents such societies from being
wrenched apart by the centrifugal forces of modernization? Contrary to
some on the Left, Durkheim does not believe that the modern state can
impose moral order in a society where social rules and norms are decentralized and heterogenuous. Against conservatives, Durkheim argues that
any effort to impose a religious order will create disorder. Social order must
arise from the very organization of modern social and cultural structures.
How does this happen? In its routine, everyday functioning, institutional
differentiation and specialization (the social division of labor) create an
interdependent, socially integrated, and unified society.

Durkheim proposes that the division of labor functions not only as an
economic but as a moral force. Specialization and interdependence of
social roles and a corresponding system of moral rights, duties, and
exchanges create social bonds. Durkheim explains:

> Where society relies most completely upon the division of labor, it does not
> become a jumble of juxtaposed atoms. . . . Rather the members are united by
> ties which extend deeper and far beyond the short moments during which
> exchange is made. Each of the functions that they [individuals] excercise
> is . . . dependent upon others, and with them forms a solidary system . . . .
> Because we fill some . . . social function, we are involved in a complex of
> obligations. . . . There is, above all, . . . the state . . . [which] is entrusted with
> the duty of reminding us of the sentiment of common solidarity [5].

Modern social institutions – the family, economy, government, church,
educational system – are mutually dependent; they are locked into a network of exchanges that bind them together through functional interdependency, shared social norms, and the moral authority of the state into an
integrated system. For example, the economy depends upon the family to
socialize individuals who are disciplined and motivated by work and career
values. Similarly, the family depends upon the economy for its material

basis; in addition, an economic system functioning independently of the family makes it possible for individuals to establish households apart from their family of origin. The functional and moral interconnectedness of modern societies is, moreover, more stable and durable than the culturally enforced solidarity of primitive societies because they are more adaptable to environmental changes. Thus, contrary to critics on the Right and Left, Durkheim held that, in principle, modern societies successfully combine economic and cultural dynamism, individualism, and a stable, coherent social order.

Durkheim was aware that the actual state of social affairs in France and Europe did not mirror the social ideal he outlined. He perceived endemic social conflict, economic crises, and moral disarray across the continent. In fact, he wrote *The Division of Labor in Society* to provide a perspective on current social developments that would offer a different interpretation than that of socialists, conservatives, and individualistic liberals. Thus, whereas the socialist Left described economic crises as symptomatic of the inherent contradictions of capitalism, and therefore requiring a socialist transformation, Durkheim believed that such crises reflect the disruption of norms coordinating production and consumption that result from the rapidity of change. In other words, in the initial phases of economic modernization, especially as substantial spatial separation between producers and consumers is introduced, producers are unclear about market demand. Regular communication will allow producers to adjust levels of production to consumer need. Similarly, whereas conservatives denounced modern individualism and secularism for causing social chaos and, accordingly, called for a restoration of the power of religion, Durkheim viewed these social strains as transient or the birth pangs of a new order. In a modern social structure, a period of adjustment is needed in order to determine the appropriate set of social rules, norms, rights, and obligations, to fine-tune, as it were, institutional functioning.

Although Durkheim defended modern Western social developments against critics from the Left and Right, he was equally critical of liberal ideologues. English-styled liberals uncritically celebrated Western modernity. They defined individual freedom and creativity as the very essence of social modernization. They held that unrestrained freedom yields productivity, civic harmony, and the public welfare. They advocated a free market unencumbered by governmental regulation. Durkheim believed that they were blind to the realities of coercion, social domination, and the socially and personally destructive aspects of modernization. For example, these individualistic liberals championed the market system for unleashing individual freedom but did not consider the division of labor that compels individuals to exchange; they saw only individual opportunity but not the inequalities of social classes. Durkheim did. He did not, though, follow the Marxist view of class conflict. Rather, he believed that a rigid class system would disappear as modernity was democratized. Durkheim was convinced that social democratization, by which he meant equal opportunity for individual advancement in economic, political, and educational institutions, was an intrinsic aspect of modernization. He advocated reforms that would equalize social competition (e.g., abolishing inherited property) and promote a condition of social justice.

Durkheim sketched a broad social perspective for a liberal social regime that he intended to defend without becoming an apologist for a narrow economic liberalism. Unlike individualistic liberals, Durkheim acknowledged serious disturbances in current social developments. In particular, he was alarmed at the potential personal and social costs of individualism. Whereas, in *The Division of Labor*, his focus was on social structure and the problem of social order, subsequently, his attention shifted somewhat to the social and moral meaning of individualism. Durkheim never retreated from his commitment to individualism, but he wished to defend the individual as positioned in a stable moral and social framework. This rethinking of individualism, which was fundamental to Durkheim's social liberalism, is clarified in a major study, *Suicide*.

Suicide: *individualism and community revisited*

Durkheim disagreed with conservatives who criticized modern society for promoting individualism at the expense of moral and social values. In *The Division of Labor in Society*, Durkheim argued that social differentiation, cultural pluralism, and secularism stimulate individualism. Modern societies necessitate that individuals have more freedom to create the social rules that regulate their lives. Far from undermining social coherence, individual freedom makes it possible because social norms and values cannot be legislated by the state, church, or the family. Modern society creates the individual as a social agent, so to speak, because individualism is necessary for its ongoing social functioning.

The social importance of the individual in modern societies is symbolized by the reverance surrounding the individual. Durkheim argued that, when intense group feelings are attached to an idea or object, and these feelings are articulated in shared beliefs and social practices, we are witnessing what is in essence a religion. Despite the secularity of modernity, as evidenced in the separation of the church and state and in the decline of Judeo-Christian dogma, it evolves its own religion of humanity. The individual functions as a sacred object; laws, social institutions, and customs construct and protect the rights and dignity of the individual. Subsequent to *The Division of*

Labor, Durkheim emphasized the contribution of this religious culture of individualism to social coherence.

Durkheim distinguished his own defense of individualism from English-styled liberalism which celebrated individualism freed from virtually all institutional constraints. Unbridled individualism was supposed to guarantee social progress. For example, economic greed was said to promote the public welfare by producing more and better goods at a cheaper price for the consumer or by encouraging the virtues of hard work, self-sacrifice, and risk taking. Durkheim disagreed. Championing a form of individualism that resisted all social limits is personally and socially destructive. Individualism is a social good only when it occurs within a social and moral framework. This moral claim was what Durkheim intended to prove in the book that has been hailed as the first work of scientific sociology: *Suicide.*

Durkheim's decision to study suicide was a calculated, even if provocative, gesture. His reasons were twofold. First, Durkheim was struggling to legitimate sociology as a science. At the time, sociology was a fledgling field of study that had no academic status. In early twentieth century France, sociology was not a recognized science. Few sociology courses were taught, and professors advocating sociology were in a bitter struggle with their colleagues. Chief among the enemies of sociology were humanists (secular and religious) who believed that sociology denied free will and therefore undermined moral responsibility. Perhaps an even more formidable opponent were social scientists for whom society was reducible to individual psychology and behavior. To legitimate sociology as a science, Durkheim had to persuade his detractors that society is a reality irreducible to the psychology of the individual. What better way to make his case than to show that suicide, an act that seemed so obviously explainable by individual psychology, was a social fact. At the same time that a study of suicide could disarm critics of sociology, Durkheim could show the social dangers of unbridled individualism. *Suicide* would be an ideal vehicle for trumpeting his social liberal vision under the sign of science.

Durkheim does not deny that psychological distress prompts individuals to take their own lives knowingly. Rather, his chief claim is that social conditions produce this suicidal disposition. Durkheim's three basic types of suicide (egoistic, altruistic, anomic) mark different social conditions of integration and regulation. I intend to provide an overview of each type with an eye to spotlighting Durkheim's social liberal values.

In egoistic suicide, individuals take their lives because of the psychological distress that stems from their lack of social integration. "In this case the bond attaching man to life relaxes because that attaching him to society is itself slack. The incidents of private life which . . . are considered its [suicide's] determining causes are in reality only incidental causes. The individual yields to the slightest shock of circumstance because the state of society has made him a ready prey to suicide" [6]. Durkheim explores the dynamics of egoistic suicide through an empirical case study relating religion and suicide. He observes that statistical portraits of suicides in Western industrial nations consistently show that Protestants have higher suicide rates than do Catholics. There is no credible reason to assume any psychological difference between these two populations. There is little difference, moreover, in terms of doctrine; both denominations condemn suicide. However, Durkheim notes some key social differences. In particular, Protestantism is highly individualistic. Protestants arrive at their faith through an appeal to individual conscience. They share few common beliefs and practices; accordingly, they are less socially integrated into their religious community. By contrast, the centralized bureaucratic organization of Catholicism imposes a unified faith on its practitioners. Catholics share most of the same beliefs and practices; accordingly, they are strongly integrated into their religious social community.

Durkheim infers a general social principle: suicide rates increase as social integration decreases. Why? Because, lacking close social ties, the individual loses moral purpose and falls prey to ennui and a deadly melancholic isolation. "Social man necessarily presupposes a society which he expresses and serves. If this dissolves . . . we are bereft of reasons for existence. . . . In this sense it is true to say that our activity needs an object [social goal] transcending it" [7]. Translating this "scientific principle" into a more explicitly moral language, Durkheim is suggesting that lacking a stable social framework individualism is a social danger.

Although Durkheim's analysis of egoistic suicide voiced the message that unrestrained individualism is undesirable, he insisted that too much social integration is equally harmful. This empirical and moral position is sounded in his comments on altruistic suicide. Altruism is the flip side to egoism. It indicates a condition of excessive social integration in that the needs, interests, and identity of the group overwhelm and extinguish a separate individual existence. If the individual's life is so completely fused with the well-being of the group, any disturbances in this social fusion threaten individual well-being. Suicide is one symptom of this disruption. Given the pronounced individualism of modern societies, altruistic suicide is rare; it is almost exclusively confined to the military. War situations provide the clearest illustration. Inspired by the spirit of intense group identification and nationalism, individuals perform heroic acts of self-sacrifice for the sake of higher social principles. The moral message here is that too much group control is unhealthy, at least in modern societies.

Social integration represented one social axis of suicide; the other was social regulation. Anomic suicide illustrates a condition in which the individual lacks sufficient social direction. Durkheim assumed that society defines and directs individual wants, desires, and goals. Lacking adequate social regulation, individuals cannot organize and order their own lives in a stable and coherent way. Durkheim's example of anomic suicide is the rise in suicide rates during economic crises. He asserted that this social phenomenon is less the product of economic decline (since it affects upwardly and downwardly mobile individuals) than the result of the moral disorder that accompanies abrupt socioeconomic change. As individuals quickly shift their socioeconomic status (up or down), there occurs, at least temporarily, a disruption in expectations and goals as social opportunities are dramatically altered. Suicide is one expected outcome of the moral confusion and distress experienced in an anomic state. Interpreted from a moral perspective, Durkheim's analysis of anomic suicide contains an unpleasant message to English-styled liberals and to the socialist Left. Despite their good intentions to free the individual from repressive social controls, too much freedom may bring its opposite, suicide, as an escape from the tyranny of freedom. Durkheim concludes that individuals require a stable, intact social and moral framework to set limits, give direction and purpose to their behavior.

Durkheim insisted upon the scientific status of his analysis, but is it merely coincidental that the principles he claims to have discovered coincide precisely with his own social liberal values? *Suicide* served Durkheim as a medium through which to engage current public debates regarding the proper relation between the individual and the social community. Against conservatives, he insisted upon individualism as a condition of a healthy society. Against individualistic liberals and socialists, he maintained the necessity of social and moral regulation as a condition of a healthy individualism.

If Durkheim's social agenda is not entirely clear in the analysis of types of suicide, it is spelled out in the concluding section where he assumes the explicit role of social reformer. If suicide rates indicate a social disturbance in the relation of the individual to the group – a breakdown of social integration and regulation, the remedy must be social. Durkheim believed that neither the family, church, or state could function to offset currents of egoism and anomie in modern societies. For example, secularization has weakened the social role of the church; the loss of social functions has similarly weakened the family; the removal of the state from daily affairs has rendered it incapable of directing individual life. Durkheim imagined that, as the workplace becomes central to modern life, forms of community and moral regulation will crystallize, providing a kind of moral and social center for the individual. As in *The Division of Labor, Suicide* served Durkheim as a vehicle to imagine and recommend a society that combined individualism, moral coherence, and social justice.

Science, truth, and moral hope

Durkheim made it clear that science would have little value if it did not contribute to advancing human welfare. "We should judge our researches to have no worth at all if they were to have only a speculative interest. If we separate carefully the theoretical from the practical problems, it is not to the neglect of the latter; but, on the contrary, to be in a better position to solve them" [8]. In his sociological studies of the division of labor, suicide, the family, education, and religion, Durkheim never restricted social analysis to stating facts and proposing explanations and theories. This initial stage was followed by moral judgments and proposed social reforms. For example, in the first two major sections of *The Division of Labor in Society*, Durkheim sets out the social facts, as he sees them, pertaining to the evolution of humankind from a primitive to a modern society. He sketches an ideal of modern society that serves as a norm to judge current developments. In the third section of *Division* entitled, "Abnormal Forms," Durkheim tells us what is wrong in the current social division of labor and what reforms would be appropriate (in light of the "normal" evolutionary process) [9]. Thus, present economic crises are interpreted as temporary maladjustments to rapid social change, requiring expanded communication between producers and consumers, not the transformation of capitalism into socialism. For Durkheim, science, mortality, and social policy go hand in hand, though they remain distinct phases of social analysis.

Durkheim offered a justification for this sociological logic in *The Rules of the Sociological Method* [10]. He outlined the assumptions and the steps involved in sociological analysis. His strategy was, broadly speaking, to distinguish the establishment of scientific facts and explanations from ideology for the purpose of making moral and social policy recommendations.

Durkheim defines the subject matter of sociology as those shared institutions, cultural beliefs, and social conventions that are irreducible to individual psychology. He calls these phenomena "social facts." Their key feature is that, though produced by individuals, they exist, external to us and constrain our behaviour. For example, the division of labor is a social fact in that it constrains our behavior (e.g., we must specialize and buy and sell on the market), seemingly irrespective of our personal wishes.

Sociology studies social facts as if, in Durkheim's phrase, they were "things." Durkheim counsels that we view social facts dispassionately – without feelings or preconceptions. Our ideas of social facts should come from the world as it is, not from our individual biases. By immersing ourselves in the study of facts, we can avoid contaminating our socio- logical ideas with personal values. The sociologist aims to establish social facts, relate them to their appropriate societal type (e.g., primitive, feudal, or modernity), and offer historical, causal, and functional explanations. This allows sociology to ascertain the "normal" structure and functioning of social facts. Durkheim believed that the normality of social facts is a function of their being "general" to a given social type and useful or contributing to its stability. Thus, since individualism in a modern differ- entiated society is, according to Durkheim, both general and socially useful, it is normal. By contrast, individualism would be abnormal in a primitive society because it would be an isolated phenomenon and dys- functional.

Durkheim asserted that his methodological rules made it possible for science to produce universal truths about social facts. This would permit sociologists to make objective moral judgments. He was, I am convinced, badly mistaken.

His claim that sociologists can somehow set aside their prejudices and preconceptions in order to gain access to social reality "as it actually is" ignores the important role that human interests and values play in social knowledge. Contrary to Durkheim's recommendation that "all preconcep- tions must be eradicated" [11], our preconceptions guide our perceptions. They tell us what is important, how to relate perceptions to form concepts and frame relations between concepts, and make it possible to fashion disparate bits of information into a coherent social story or picture. Durkheim's thought that, if we could open ourselves to the world, it would impress its essential nature upon us. However, the world is always experienced as meaningful. We can never get around our preconceptions to get to a world that exists as raw experience. To the extent that our social perceptions are guided by our interests and preconceptions, our social ideas are saturated with particular social interests, values, and culturally biased assumptions. Consider Durkheim's social evolutionary theory. Durkheim's image of primitive society exhibits the standard Western stereo- types of the time, for example, primitive society as socially simple, cultu- rally homogeneous, mired in supernatural religousity, anti-individualistic, socially intolerant, and resistant to change. His concept of modernity is no less stereotyped, even if in an idealized way, for example, modernity as socially complex, secular, culturally pluralistic, individualistic, tolerant, and socially dynamic. If there is any doubt that this "typology" is little more than a thinly disguised story of human progress, the subtitle of *Division*, "A Study of the Organization of Superior Societies," betrays Durkheim's mod- ern, European, middle class viewpoint.

Durkheim imagined an intimate tie between scientific knowledge and morality. Science was not only to serve moral ends but was to give morality an objective status. Yet Durkheim wished to maintain the separation between science, morality, and politics. In the end, he did not succeed. For example, his retreat into a view that assumes an unambiguous separation between the scientist and society in order to justify a value-neutral, objective view of science is contradicted by Durkheim's insistence on the social formation of consciousness. If the culture of a society is shaped by its social structure, then doesn't this hold true for our social ideas? As we have seen, Durkheim's ideas about social knowledge, social evolution, and modernity look suspiciously like the social values and ideas of a modern, middle class, liberal Frenchman.

His moral vision bursts into center stage in his last great work, *The Elementary Forms of Religious Life* [12]. Durkheim attempted to explain the origin and nature of religion. His thesis, to simplify enormously, was that religious beliefs are really symbolic ways of understanding the power of society to fashion the individual; religious rituals are interpreted as socially integrating practices. Prior to the advent of the Enlightenment, humankind lacked the power of reason to grasp that the supernatural and spiritual forces that they assumed governed human affairs were social forces (e.g., the division of labor, cultural beliefs, law). Modern science destroys this illusion; science forces humanity to confront a reality governed by human and natural forces. In particular, sociology steps forward as the successor to religious social beliefs and ethics. The sociologist occupies the social role previously held by shamans, prophets, and priests. Clearly, there are strong echoes of Comte's fusion of sociology and religion. Durkheim seems to open up the possibility that, by uncovering the true reality of society as a transcendent power productive of human life in the sense of giving our lives coherence and purpose, sociology may become the centerpiece of a religious cult.

Durkheim inherited a dilemma: how to make science both a medium of pure truth and yet socially useful. A science of society too detached from social problems seemed pointless; a science too close to public conflicts was in danger of losing its moral authority by becoming a mere ideology. Durkheim was not alone in wrestling with this problem; his German counterpart, Max Weber, seemed at times preoccupied with the blurring of the lines between science, truth, and values.

Max Weber

Weber shared with his French contemporary the view that the period between 1890 and World War I was crucial in determining the fate of modern liberalism. In both France and Germany, industrialization, national unification and bureaucratization, the formation of a secular educational system, the establishment of constitutional government, and the rule of law marked the triumph of modernization. While Durkheim and Weber were convinced that social modernization promoted a liberal political society, they were aware of its illiberal potential. For example, a centralized bureaucratic state may be necessary for economic development and national security, but it threatens to become a new type of despotic rule.

In contrast to many liberals, Weber did not believe that economic modernization automatically translated into social and political liberalization. Whereas in England and the United States, a liberal political culture accompanied industrial capitalist development, German industrialization coexisted with a feudal-like social and political culture. Despite the phenomenal success of the German economy in the second half of the nineteenth century, social and political power remained in the hands of a feudal-styled class of Prussian landowners called the "Junkers."

Germany was unified as a result of the iron will of Bismarck who made the Prussian state into the dominant national force. Prussia was, moreover, ruled by the Junkers. They were a landed aristocracy who aggressively supported nationalistic and militaristic values. Unlike in France and England where capitalist development was paralleled by the economic and political decline of the landed aristocracy, the Junker class adapted by either becoming successful capitalists, or, where they lost economic power, they managed to retain their social and political authority. If the Junkers didn't dominate Germany in a directly political way, their social authority allowed them to imprint on society their bellicose nationalism, economic protectionism, support of church orthodoxy, and antilabor sentiment. The Prussian Junkers, with the support of a religious and a humanistic cultural elite deeply hostile to Enlightenment values, exercised considerable public authority in Germany through World War I.

Weber came of age in a Germany that was deeply divided. There were conflicts between the defenders of modernization and its detractors who nostalgically looked backward. Moreover, defenders of social modernization split into hostile camps. There were individualistic liberals who advocated a free market system, conservative nationalists who backed an activist state that could weave together economic development and military national strength, and revolutionary socialists who repudiated both capitalism and nationalism. These ideological divisions expressed deep-seated antagonisms between the middle class, the landed aristocracy, and the working class. The similarity with Durkheim's France is striking except – and this is a big exception – that there was no German counterpart to the Third French Republic. There was, in fact, no German counterpart to the French Revolution or to the English or American revolutions; there was no middle class revolution in Germany! Although the German middle class prospered, it did not challenge the social and political power of the Junkers. Instead of becoming a political force mobilized to overthrow Junker rule, the German middle classes aped their conservative, nationalistic values.

Whereas Marx, a generation earlier, surrendered any hope of the middle class becoming a progressive force in Germany, Weber did not. Weber was convinced that only the middle classes had the social authority and resources to deal the death blow to the Junkers. However, Weber did not imagine that middle class rule would bring about inexorable social progress. It is not that Weber put his social faith in the working class; he did not. Rather, Weber never fully bought into the social faith of the Enlightenment. Although he was committed to many Enlightenment values, Weber never abandoned some counter-Enlightenment ideas. Curiously, he held onto more of the conservative nationalism of the Junker class than he realized. Whatever hopes he harbored for human progress were tempered by a streak of pessimism and *Realpolitik* he imbibed from the Prussian, Lutheran culture that he otherwise detested. Lacking in Weber is the millennial hope we observed in the culture of the Enlightenment, from Voltaire to Marx and Durkheim. Weber's social vision blends a championing of individualism with an equally passionate commitment to nationalism.

Puritanism and the making of the middle class

The future of Germany was tied to the destiny of the middle class. Weber believed that only a strong, politically aggressive middle class could succeed in both modernizing the social structure of Germany and making this nation into a world power. He was not very hopeful. The German middle class had a history of retreating from political struggle. In his early writings, Weber wished to explain the political immaturity of the German middle class. In the process, he elaborated a vision of an heroic middle class fashioning the world in its own image in the hopes of politicizing the German bourgeoisie.

This moral and political motivation underlies Weber's first great work of sociology, *The Protestant Ethic and the Spirit of Capitalism* [13]. Although its chief theme revolves around the link between Protestantism and capitalism, the subtext is Weber's appeal to the disillusioned, hard-working, inner-directed Puritan as an ideal for the German middle class.

The Protestant Ethic explores the religious origins of the "spirit" or culture of capitalism. Weber believed that modern capitalism would not have developed without certain psychological attitudes and orientations. In order for individuals to risk the capital investment involved in starting up an enterprise, and in order for workers to accept the disciplined, specialized labor of industrial capitalism, there had to exist a culture that made this behavior meaningful and valuable. Why should an entrepreneur work hard and sacrifice in the present for a precarious hope of a future payoff? Of course, once capitalism was established, entrepreneurs would be compelled to accumulate wealth and reinvest profits in order to be competitive and survive. However, in the early stages of capitalist development, there was no market mechanism that enforced self-sacrificing, risk-taking behavior. Weber wished to explain why individuals would become entrepreneurs.

Weber thought he detected a cultural milieu in European societies that contributed to the rise of modern capitalism. This culture valued discipline, hard work, frugality, deferred gratification, the accumulation of wealth without ostentatious consumption, and a pride in economic success. Unlike many European liberals who maintained that humans are naturally competitive, hard working, greedy, and economically motivated, Weber argued that this behavior is culturally induced. And while Weber agreed with socialists that competition enforces entrepreneurial behavior once capitalism is established, they did not identify the social forces that initially encouraged this behavior.

Weber proposed what at first glance seemed like a far-fetched thesis: Protestantism formed the cultural origins of capitalism. Of course, Protestantism was not motivated by economic interests. Quite the contrary, the Protestant Reformation was a movement of spiritual renewal in revolt against the materialism and secularism of the Catholic church. Its salvationist doctrine, however, unintentionally propelled entrepreneurial activity. Weber's story is sadly ironic. The intense spiritual salvationist hopes that drove Protestantism unwittingly created a vast materialistic, secular civilization devoid of morally elevated aspirations and values.

In ascetic Protestant sects such as Calvinism, Pietism, Methodism, Baptism, and Congregationalism, Weber found a cultural world view that placed a high *religious* value upon entrepreneurial behavior. Weber's most famous example is Calvinism. Calvin enunciated the doctrine of predestination: God predetermined who was saved at the moment of creation. Moreover, priests were not privileged to act as the chief messengers of divine judgment. The clergy had no special insight into the purpose of creation nor into the calculus of salvation. Good works, charity, monetary contributions, or prayer did not guarantee salvation; each individual was alone with his or her own doubts about personal salvation. In response to the heightened feelings of anxiety that spread throughout the religious community, Calvinists appealed to external signs to interpret the fate of their souls. Economic success served as a chief marker of religious fate. Accordingly, economic behavior was imbued with transcendent religious significance. To work hard at an occupation and to signal success by a prosperous business or career achievement, rather than by conspicuous consumption, was perceived by the community as a clear indicator of a saved soul. The salvationist religious meanings attached to entrepreneurial behavior formed the cultural matrix for the rise of modern capitalism.

The full irony – and pathos – of Weber's tale is revealed in the finale of *The Protestant Ethic*. The very success of Protestantism in stimulating capitalism would result in its death knell. Once capitalism was established, competition would enforce entrepreneurial behavior; religious motivations would be replaced by secular, utilitarian ones. The Protestant work ethic would give way to motivations based on survival, status, and power.

Weber's perception of the emerging modern capitalist civilization shared little of the celebratory spirit of the Enlightenment. In contrast to liberals and socialists who championed industrial development for making possible a new era of individualism and social progress, Weber laments the decline of a culture of moral virtue and individualism. Inspired by religious values that emphasized actively engaging worldly affairs, the Protestant in the seventeenth and eighteenth centuries was a genuine individualist. His or her nineteenth and twentieth century heir is trapped in a capitalist, bureaucratic system, what Weber called an "iron cage" [14].

The Protestant Ethic did not offer an entirely pessimistic social vision. Although the full glory of Protestant individualism can never be recaptured, Weber hoped that the Puritan spirit of worldly activism might be an inspiration to the German middle classes. The self-made Puritan who struggled relentlessly to refashion the world in his or her own image was precisely what was lacking among Weber's contemporaries. The German middle class seemed to aspire to little more than staking out their own small share of Germany's wealth and prestige by accommodating to Prussian rule. *The Protestant Ethic* offered a partial explanation of this phenomenon. In Germany, it was not the worldly activist ethic of Calvinism that shaped its culture but a more traditional, other-worldly Lutheran spirit that was dominant. Lutheranism enjoined the individual to fulfill the duties of the occupation or social station one occupies; its spirit is one of world accommodation rather than transformation. Lutheranism shaped a culture that produced a placid, other-directed individual. The contrast between the inner-directed Puritan who struggles to refashion the world and the other-directed, socially accommodating Lutheran was intended to stimulate self-awareness and social activism on the part of the German middle classes.

Explaining Western modernity and the irony of history

The Protestant ethic thesis originally appeared as an essay in 1904. Subsequently, Weber pursued the theme of Western modernization in a series of comparative studies. Investigations of Greco-Roman and Mesopotamian civilizations, followed by studies of China, India, Ancient Judaism, Islam, and medieval Christian civilization analyzing the development of law, religion, cities, political structures, comprised his two master works, *Economy and Society* and the *Collected Essays in the Sociology of Religion* [15]. In each study, Weber asks, "why did modernization initially occur in the West and not in Eastern civilizations?". For example, why did modern science originate in the West? Why did a rational-legal system first develop in Roman civilization? Why did modern capitalism arise in the West? How to explain the Western political formation of constitutional government, the rule of law, parliamentary bodies, civil rights, and political parties?

Weber's sociology of modernity avoided naturalistic explanations that appealed to human nature, individual psychology, climate, or geography. He rejected explanations of social development that relied on one factor, for example, the economy, population, or ideas. Although Weber did not avoid an evolutionary story of humankind that posits change as patterned and meaningful, he did not assume a set of fixed stages humanity passes through towards a predetermined endpoint. Nor did Weber relate a story of the progress of humanity from a lowly beginning to a higher, liberated endpoint. Nevertheless, Weber's sociology of civilizations reveals a vision of the meaning of history that centers on the fatefulness of modernity. To illustrate Weber's sociology of modernity, I will consider his study of Chinese civilization, *The Religion of China* [16].

At various times in its history, social conditions in China were favorable to modernization. Despite the accumulation of economic wealth and the formation of trade companies and merchant associations in China, modern capitalism never developed. Despite its technological superiority over the West through the early modern period, modern science remained foreign to Chinese soil. Despite the formation of a political empire, Chinese bureaucracy remained highly traditionalistic. Weber intended to explain the absence of modernization in China.

Weber offered less a dynamic analysis than a static, almost snapshot picture of China. Chinese unification in 221 B.C. proved fateful. Rule by warring feudal lords was replaced by a bureaucratic empire ruled by an emperor and a cultural elite (mandarins) who administered the empire. The mandarins were the principal carriers of the state ideology: Confucianism. State and ideological social control from above was reinforced by control over the individual in daily village life by a rigid kinship system. Weber held that each of these pivotal social forces (the bureaucratic state, the Confucian ideology, the village kinship system) contributed to blocking Chinese modernization.

The emperor was the symbolic ruler of China. The class of mandarins who administered the bureaucratic state effectively ruled China for some 2,000 years. Weber distinguishes the "patrimonial" bureaucracy of China from the modern Western bureaucratic state by its essentially personalistic character. For example, the emperor, in principle, owns and has unlimited control over all bureaucratic offices, personnel, and resources; officials serve at the emperor's discretion; their loyalty is to the emperor, not to their office or to an ideal of bureaucratic professionalism. The Chinese patrimonial state avoided both "refeudalization" and modernization. By limiting terms of office, routinely circulating officials, implementing a system of surveillance, and instituting an examination system that fostered an identification of the mandarins with the imperial state, the emperor sought to avoid decentralizaton. On the other hand, political modernization was opposed by the mandarins since a modern bureaucratic ethic of expertise, specialization, and technical training would undermine their legitimacy. The mandarins were joined by the emperor for whom a modern bureaucratic order, with its notions of the rule of law, the authority of the office, and professionalism, would restrict imperial power.

The patrimonial bureaucratic state not only opposed political modernization, it impeded social and economic modernization. For example, Weber argues that the imperial state favored a more personalistic legal system that gave wide latitude to the decisions of the judge. By contrast, a modern legal code operates according to rules of evidence and precedent that greatly restrict the discretion of the judge. In the West, the development of a modern juridical code (e.g., in Rome) was made possible by the existence of an independent strata of jurists and lawyers. Imperial China opposed the rise of such a group as a restriction on the emperor's rule. Similarly, the imperial state favored state-financed and -controlled businesses over a free market because it feared the development of an independent merchant class. In Weber's view, the patrimonial Chinese state suppressed the very forces that could have been the vehicles of social modernization.

The only countervailing social force to the imperial state was the village clan. Despite the ambitions of the imperial state to exercise total control over society, the expanse and diversity of China made that impossible.

Village life was more or less free from state rule but was dominated by the local kinship system. Instead of creating space for social innovation, the clan reinforced Chinese traditionalism by exerting strict control over the individual and village social life. Anchored in a culture of ancestor worship and the rule of the elders that made tradition and social customs sacred, the village clan enforced social conservatism, for example, by greatly restricting occupational choice, individual mobility, and the accumulation of individual wealth.

Imperial rule was, ultimately, in the hands of the mandarins. This cultural elite administered the bureaucratic state on a daily basis; they shaped the political culture of China. It was the mandarins who made Confucianism into a state ideology.

From the perspective of the Judeo-Christian tradition, Confucianism appears less as a religion than as a cultural ideal. For example, Confucianism lacks a concept of a creator God with whom individuals have a personal relation. Confucianism imagines the universe as an ordered cosmos in which all beings have a fixed place and purpose in a hierarchal order. Cosmic harmony is to be maintained by the individuals establishing an equilibrium internally (psychologically) and externally (socially). The Confucian ethic enjoins an ethic of individual control over feelings and behavior as a way to maintain emotional and social balance. Its social ethic emphasizes family piety, literary cultivation, and public service. Private wealth and power are important but only if they are achieved through public office; private enterprise disturbs inner and outer poise. The Confucian ethic directs the individual to accommodate to the world as it is, to fulfill the duties of one's social station. Material comfort, familial honor and security, and a public office carrying status are the earthly rewards to be expected from following a Confucian ethic. Foreign to Confucianism is the Puritan struggle to refashion the world according to a moral vision.

As in his studies of India, ancient Judaism, or ancient Far Eastern civilizations, Weber's study of China purported to be a scientific analysis of the divergent paths of the West and the East. Weber catalogues the factors that stimulated the breakthrough to modernity in the West and obstructed modernization in the East. For example, the worldly activist ethic of Protestantism promoted modernization, whereas the Confucian ethic of world accommodation, in combination with the imperial bureaucracy and the village clan system, impeded modernization in China. As much as Weber tried to document his perspective on modernization by painstaking empirical comparisons and tentative causal sketches, his sociology discloses a moral vision of humankind enacting a tragic drama.

The standard Enlightenment historical narrative envisioned a progressive movement of humankind from a simple underdeveloped social state where the individual was dominated by the group, myth, and nature to a complex advanced society where, with the aid of science, the individual reigned supreme over nature and history. The perspectives of Comte, Marx, and Durkheim are variations on this story of social progress. It was not Weber's vision. His view of social evolution originates with the bureaucratic civilizations of the ancient Far Eastern and Roman civilizations. Although Weber admires their achievements of national unity and military prowess, this is bought at the price of individual freedom and social dynamism. Whether Weber is discussing the Imperial empires of ancient Rome, Egypt, or China, he underscores the bureaucratic stifling of social pluralism and individualism and, ultimately, their social paralysis and decline. Political liberalization and social modernization go hand in hand; where institutional pluralism and individualism are permitted, a prosperous and dynamic social state flourishes. For example, the overriding theme of Weber's sociology of China is that modernization failed, in large part, because the imperial bureaucracy suppressed countervailing social forces. By contrast, in the West, state bureaucracy had to contend with multiple power centers, e.g., the church, jurists, and lawyers, an independent merchant class, cities freed from centralized state authority where social and cultural innovations were encouraged. Weber's vision is decidedly liberal: Social pluralism and individualism promote an innovative, dynamic society.

Weber does not, however, fashion this liberal theme into a narrative of modernization as social progress. The story he tells is that of the movement of the West from bureaucratic empire to social liberalization to the present day where European nations are potentially returning to some form of bureaucratic empire. Modernization is described, so to speak, as consisting of two phases. The first phase, roughly from the sixteenth to the mid-nineteenth century, was the dynamic phase. Western societies created modern science, free-market capitalism, the inner-directed individualism exemplified by the Puritan and political democratic structures such as rule of law, constitutionalism, civil rights, and parliamentary government. Successive waves of social modernization threatened to undermine this liberal, individualistic society. In particular, the spread of bureaucracy and its utilitarian, status-oriented culture to all modern institutions fashioned a society of other-directed, spiritually bland, and apolitical individuals ruled by a soulless bureaucracy. In other words, Weber saw in China not simply the past from which Western modernization departed but the possible future of the West and humanity. The tragic irony of the present is that the future of humanity may be less the utopian visions of the Enlighteners than the dystopian reality of bureaucratic despotism. Distracted and dazed by modern utopian dreams, Enlighteners, tragically, are not even aware of the dystopian world that humankind is entering. Whether this blocked vision was the tragedy of Enlighteners or whether the tragedy was Weber's inability to see that he projected the worst features of Germany onto humanity's future is crucial in assessing his social vision.

Charisma and bureaucracy: the modern dream turned nightmare

Unlike his Enlightenment predecessors and contemporaries, Weber does not relate a story of humankind's continuous march forward. Weber imagines a perpetual conflict between the forces of order that threaten to squash individual freedom and those that support social innovation and change. If bureaucracy represents the exemplary force of order, then charisma is the power of change. Weber's social evolutionary perspective charts a movement from bureaucratic empires to social modernization in the West in which charismatic movements play a key role [17].

Weber puzzled over how to explain social change in the face of the conservative power exercised by bureaucratic empires. In the concept of charismatic movements, he identified a force whose collective intensity could offest extreme bureaucratic social paralysis. Charisma is the magical power that an individual claims to possess. The charismatic leader commands public authority by virtue of claiming to possess extraordinary powers. Between the charismatic leader and the disciple, there are powerful moral and emotional bonds; the leader enunciates a social mission that the discipline pledges to enact. Charismatic movements are potentially revolutionary social forces in that the personal loyalty that the disciple owes the leader is to be demonstrated by enacting a far-reaching social mission. Despite the fact that charismatic movements inevitably either dissipate or are routinized (i.e., evolve their own stable social life), Weber believed that they have been key forces in loosening or destroying the social strangulation of bureaucracy.

In another ironic twist, Weber believed that, while charismatic movements were pivotal in engendering modernization, the latter environment is hostile to charisma. For example, the secularity of modern culture diminishes the credibility of individual claims to possess magical powers. Similarly, capitalism fosters a utilitarian culture inimical to charismatic authority. Perhaps the most significant obstacle to charisma is modern bureaucracy which encourages individuals to value a secure and orderly social environment. In fact, Weber thought that the defining feature of Western modernity was the spread of bureaucracy, along with its conservative culture, to all social spheres. The bureaucratization of society anticipated a bleak future for humanity. To the extent that social modernization went hand in hand with bureaucratization, the advance of science, democracy, law, and so on promised to inaugurate a stultifying era of bureaucratic domination.

The very social forces that have brought forth a dynamic modern society have stimulated bureaucratization. For example, capitalism introduces a dynamic market system, but its need for a massive infrastructure of transportation and communication, and a legal administrative apparatus that ensures that contracts are enforced encourage the bureaucratization of the state. Similarly, market competition inevitably leads to the development of giant corporations which, with their high capital investment, coordination of massive resources, and planning, stimulates economic bureaucratization. Or, modernization entails political democratization (e.g., the spread of civil rights, political parties, representational political bodies) which, in turn, requires bureaucratic administrative structures to sustain mass democracy. Gradually, but inevitably, bureaucracy spreads to virtually every social sphere – the economy, government, political parties, church, welfare, military, education, and science.

Bureaucratization implies a unique administrative and social order; social institutions are organized according to a spirit of impersonality and professionalism. Bureaucratic institutions are divided into offices, each defined by a specific function and social role; offices are arranged in a hierarchical way so that there is a kind of top-down command system; individuals are assigned specific roles with clearly marked duties and authority. Bureaucratic business is carried out according to a set of impersonal rules and procedures that aim to exclude personal considerations and conflicts from interfering with institutional operations. Finally, bureaucracy creates a new type of worker, the official or white collar worker, who is a technically skilled, specialized professional hired on the basis of qualifications.

Weber maintained that bureaucracy's spirit of impersonality and professionalism makes it the most efficient mode of administration in modern societies. Its spread is inevitable and irreversible. For example, bureaucratization makes possible mass democracy and national social planning. Moreover, bureaucracy promotes social justice and equality, as individuals – as both clients and officials – are, in principle, treated equally and fairly. The same features that make bureaucracy efficient and socially beneficial, however, render it a truly ominous social force. Weber left little doubt that bureaucracy was the most powerful social force in modernity, one that threatened humanity with a bleak future.

Weber's views on bureaucracy have become conventional wisdom in Western societies. Bureaucracy is said to signal a substantial diminution of individual freedom. In a bureaucratic society, individuals lose control over the means to satisfy their needs. For example, in a bureaucratic economy, whether capitalist or socialist, most individuals do not control access to the means of production (technology, raw material, labor) which, given their sheer size, technical complexity, and cost, are either bureaucratically administered or beyond the resources of most individuals. We are dependent on economic institutions for our livelihood. Similarly, the bureaucratization of the means of scientific and scholarly research means that individuals gain access to research technology and textual materials only as members of universities or research centers. As these institutions own the means of scientific production, they exercise control over the form and content of science. Weber concluded that as institutions are bureaucratized, and individuals lose direct control over the means (e.g., economic, educational, military) to shape their own lives, they become dependent on bureaucracy to satisfy many of their needs. Bureaucratization fosters an experience of the self as dependent and powerless. It cultivates an other-directed type of individual who values cooperative and approval-seeking behavior, the very opposite of the inner-directed, Puritan self who sought to refashion the world.

Bureaucracy foreshadows a political calamity. As individuals become dependent on bureaucracy, they believe that their fate is sealed by it. Ironically, modern citizens lose interest in politics, even as they are empowered by the franchise, political parties, and parliamentary bodies. Moreover, politicians find themselves dependent on the technical knowledge and skills of bureaucracies in order to formulate and implement public policy. The reliance of policy makers on the technical knowledge of bureaucratic officials and their limited public accountability encourage high-level bureaucrats to appropriate the policy-making powers of politicians. The expanding political role of the bureaucracy is, according to Weber, unfortunate; democracy suffers because citizens lose power and political representation; the power interests of the nation suffer because bureaucrats are not leaders with political vision but pursue limited, parochial interests.

Weber paints a bleak picture of the development of modern Western modernity. The initial dynamic phase of modernization energizes widespread bureaucratization which threatens to thwart individuality, freedom, and democracy. In the face of the bureaucratization of society, the two dominant social ideologies become obsolete. Classical individualistic liberalism, with its championing of unrestrained individualism, a free market, and minimal government, is irrelevant since it ignores the social and political meaning of bureaucratization. The socialist promise of freedom through state economic regulation and mass democracy would unintentionally expedite the spread of bureaucratization and political authoritarianism.

What can be done? Like the Puritan that he so admired, Weber counsels that we face facts: The evil today is neither capitalism nor socialism but bureaucracy. Neither nostalgia for the past nor the utopian flight from the present are responsible reactions to *irreversible social bureaucratization.* "Where administration has been completely bureaucratized, the resulting system of domination is practically indestructible" [18]. Weber offers a sobering view of enlightened Westerners' social prospects. Bureaucracy is permanent, but, if we promote multiple, conflicting bureaucracies, some vestiges of social dynamism and freedom can be preserved. Thus, Weber defended capitalism against the socialist Left less because he disagreed with their critique of its class inequalities than because he believed that capitalism preserves the tension between state elites, business owners, and unions that promotes social dynamism and freedom. Weber was especially worried that the bureaucratization of politics would give rise to mediocre, conservative leaders who would be either guided by parochial social interests or ruled by the bureaucracy. In the context of the ongoing conflict among world powers, Weber feared that weak political leaders would diminish national power and pose a danger of political or economic colonization. He recommended a political arrangement that would encourage the rise of charismatic leaders to offset the bureaucratization of the state and the political parties. Toward the end of his life, he defended a political system in which political leaders would be selected directly by the citizens. Ignoring the potential for abuse, Weber hoped that this would permit the rise of charismatic leaders who would otherwise be repressed by bureaucratized political parties and interest groups.

Science, truth, and values

Weber was a theorist filled with contradictions and irony. He was an Enlightener who passionately believed in the power of reason and science. He was an ardent defender of modernity against its critics. Yet Weber's vision of modernity is bleak. He imagined advanced phases of modernization resembling the stultifying empires of the ancient East: authoritarian bureaucracies dominating public life and a retreat into cult movements and parochial utilitarian lifestyles in the private sphere.

Despite his dark vision of humankind's future, Weber never relinquished an Enlightenment faith in science. Unlike conservative or romanic critics of modernity who viewed science, like other aspects of modernity, as socially destructive, Weber's faith in science was never shaken. Even in the face of humanity's imminent descent into darkness, Weber imagined himself as remaining soberly engaged with the world as it is. Like the Puritans he so admired, Weber would not take flight in prophecy or ideological fancy. If science had to abandon its millennial dream of a resurrected humanity, it must not forsake its role of compelling us to take a sober, responsible look at ourselves.

To the extent that Weber preserved an Enlightenment faith in science, it was a sobering faith compared with that of many of his predecessors and contemporaries. For Condorcet and Comte or Marx and Durkheim, science was a catalyst of modernization and social progress. Science destroyed the myths and superstitions that constrained our lives and originated from ignorance, error, or priestly manipulation. Science freed us from prejudice to see reality as it is; it revealed humanity as the active agent in shaping the social world. Finally, science promised to uncover the principles of social organization and laws of history; it made possible a rational organization of society by providing moral and policy guidelines based on social knowledge.

Weber shared a belief in the disillusioning power of science. Science can force us to take responsibility for our behavior. By clarifying the social world as a sphere of individual actions, science compels individuals to grasp their own actions as socially consequential. Weber even imagines a "moral" role for science: By clarifying the personal and social implications of our values, science can exert pressure on us to act in a morally responsible way. Science cannot, though, illuminate the meaning and purpose of history; it cannot provide us with directives for social action since moral decisions are always subject to contention and ultimately are matters of conscience [19]. In this regard, Weber criticizes Enlighteners who wish to go beyond viewing science as a medium of social disillusionment to constructing new world views or myths. Efforts to replace a religious with a scientific world view (e.g., Comte or Marx) are doomed to failure because of their artificial, merely intellectual character. Moreover, Weber was insistent that science forfeit its credibility when it goes beyond interpreting facts to assigning meaning and value to social events.

Reacting to the tendency of many social scientists to blur the line between science and morality and to make science into a quasi religious world view, Weber advanced the doctrine of value neutrality. Social science should confine itself to establishing facts and causal relationships and proposing general models and sociological principles. Value judgments and proposals for social reform belong in the realm of private life and politics. Why? Because, while it is possible to have knowledge about social facts and their relations, judgments about their value or rightness are a matter of opinion or ideology. It is a matter of empirical science that capitalism involves private property and the production of commodities; it is a matter of ideological values as to whether capitalism is defended because it expands freedom or criticized because it creates inequalities. Science and ideology, factual knowledge, and moral judgment are, in Weber's view, separate intellectual spheres.

In Weber's more considered reflections on science, however, he is compelled by the logic of his own analysis to throw suspicion around this neat division between science and morality. This point deserves clarification.

The scientist, says Weber, never approaches reality with a blank mind. Reality is always filtered through a conceptual lens. We always know the world from a particular standpoint. A standpoint involves a series of assumptions about the nature of the world. For example, an image of the social world as a hierarchical purposeful order, a social organism, an aggregate of self-interested individuals, a dynamic contradictory system, or images of society as driven by economic or class dynamics, religious ideas, or nation-state conflicts, frame what we can know. These overarching, cohering frameworks are products of a specific social milieu and cannot be directly subject to empirical verification or proof. Yet their role is pivotal in scientific research. They guide our problem selection; they frame what we see, how we see the world, and the significance and role that "facts" or "events" play in social knowledge. These overarching frameworks are translated into a series of concepts, typologies, and causal models that make possible a scientific or empirical-analytical ordering of reality.

Our broad intellectual standpoint governs the major changes in scientific theories. As a standpoint shifts, so will its empirical and conceptual apparatus, including what problems are considered important, the underlying concepts, causal models, and so on. Weber makes it perfectly clear, moreover, that it is not specialized scientific research that drives these broad shifts in the standpoint and conceptual structure of science, but changes in the surrounding social context. Broad social changes alter our basic images of society and social values which, in turn, get translated into new areas of interest, problems to study, and new conceptual and empirical approaches.

> All research in the cultural [social] sciences in an age of specialization, once it is oriented towards a given subject matter through particular settings of problems and has established its methological principles, will consider the analysis of the data as an end in itself. . . . It will lose its awareness of its ultimate rootedness in value ideas in general. . . . But there comes a moment when the atmosphere changes. The significance of the unreflectively utilized viewpoints becomes uncertain. . . . The light of the great cultural problems moves on. Then science too prepares to change its standpoint and its analytical apparatus [20].

Is not Weber saying that it is social interests and values that structure science, that govern its problem selection, conceptual approaches, and transformation? It is this understanding of the social structuring of science that compelled Weber, despite his principled declaration of the separation of science and morality, to conclude that it is but a "hair-line that separates science from faith" [21]. Weber still hedged. He was convinced that values inform science in its problem selection, concept formation, methodological criteria (e.g., economy, precision, consistency), and interpretive function. Moreover, if broad social interests and values are the prime movers of social scientific change, perhaps Weber should have surmised, with his usual sober and disillusioning candor, that the idea of science as a pure sphere of knowledge is itself an illusion of the modern West!

Afterword

Some historians argue that the generation of social thinkers who came of age between the 1880s and World War I represent a breakthrough to a truly scientific study of society. They contend that, for all their brilliance, Comte and Marx were philosophers, moralists, and ideologues; they were more interested in changing the world than in knowing it. Durkheim and Weber are said to be the true founding figures of scientific sociology. They abandoned partisanship in favor of scholarship, philosophy for empirical research, ideology for science. I disagree. No less than their predecessors, Durkheim and Weber approached human studies with moral and sometimes specifically political purposes. Their sociology was formed in response to particular social developments with the aim of affecting their outcome. Despite their rhetoric of value-neutrality and objectivity, they constructed social visions that carried moral and political import. Moreover, is Durkheim's vision of historical evolution in the *Division of Labor in Society* or Weber's narrative of the social rationalization of the West any less grand or mythic than the social vision of Comte or Marx? I don't think so.

Durkheim and Weber are heirs to their predecessors in an additional way: They fully absorbed the concept of the social character of humanity. Against the conventional wisdom of their time, Durkheim and Weber insist on the social formation of the self and his or her embeddedness in institutions and webs of cultural meaning.

The social shaping of the self is a chief motif in Durkheim's sociology. For example, in *Suicide*, he argues that the act of self-destruction, an act often imagined as psychologically driven is explained by social conditions, for example, the degree to which an individual is socially integrated or regulated. Against the individualism of much social and political thinking of the time, Durkheim advances a compelling picture of social forces, not individual desires, as the dynamic force in history. Does Durkheim's sociology erase the individual as an agent of social life? I don't think so. In *The*

Division of Labor in Society, he proposes that individualism is a product of social forces. In industrial societies, the individual becomes a common cultural belief and value. This makes possible legal protections for the self and a wide latitude for subjective choice and expression. I consider Durkheim as an originator of a social liberal ideal. In contrast to the individualistic liberal social ideal that views society as the sum of self-interested, rationally calculating individuals, Durkheim approaches the individual as embedded in social institutions and emphasizes the importance of shared cultural beliefs and values as a condition of freedom and social unity.

Weber was no less an advocate of a social concept of the individual. In particular, Weber emphasized the cultural construction of the self. This was a key point in his *The Protestant Ethic and the Spirit of Capitalism*. In popular and scientific thinking in Weber's time, it was often assumed that individuals are naturally motivated to compete for economic goods and accumulate wealth. Capitalism was often regarded as an expression of human nature. In contrast, Weber held that capitalist economic behavior, which entailed work specialization, career success, accumulating wealth, and delayed gratification, is a result of social beliefs and values. Weber traced a "capitalistic" economic ethic to the Protestant Reformation. He arrived at the paradoxical conclusion that it wasn't human nature that produced capitalism but the spiritual longing of Puritans who assigned to capitalist behavior a religious, redemptive value. In other words, Weber asserted the cultural formation of individualistic economic behavior.

Weber was decidedly more individualistic in his sociological approach than Durkheim. In Weber's sociology, society is inseparable from the subjective meanings and actions of individuals. He had little patience with sociological concepts that did not refer to subjective meaning. The importance that he assigned to charismatic leaders in effecting social change highlights the dynamic role that Weber attributed to the individual in his sociology. I prefer Weber's way of thinking about self and society because it affirms the subjective making of social life as much as the social making of the self. Curiously, while Weber's broad sociological approach is quite congenial to a liberal social ideal, his political values edged into a nationalism that compromised his individualism. I have little sympathy for the chauvinistic nationalism that Weber shared with many of his German contemporaries.

In many key respects, Durkheim and Weber inherited the broad impulse and aims of Comte and Marx. Although I do not see a break between the two generations in terms of a movement from ideology to science, I detect a shift from thinking of society as an organic whole to a field of conflicting social forces and practices. Comte and Marx imagined society as an organic whole or integrated system; its parts were neatly interrelated, and the major axis of social formation and its direction of change could be easily identified. For example, Marx sketched a picture of a society organized around a "base" of property ownership and class social division upon which a "superstructure" of law, culture, and politics was erected. Property relations determined class division which determined the formation of the whole society and its mechanism (class conflict) and direction of change (socialism). Admittedly, Durkheim did not entirely abandon a view of society as an organic whole. Despite retaining the language of organicism, Durkheim considered the different parts of society (the state, economy, family, religion) as interrelated in complex, multicausal ways. Weber abandoned organic metaphors entirely. Society was framed as a field of social practices, meanings, conflicts, movements, and long-term trends. Thus, whereas Marx proceeds from property to class to social stratification, Weber speaks of multiple axes of stratification (class, status, party). Property and class are no longer the "social base" but one axis of social formation; culture and politics are no longer "superstructural" effects but parallel aspects of social organization. Against the current of nineteenth century organic thinking, Weber substituted an image of a "fractured" or "decentered" social field.

Durkheim, and especially Weber, have occupied a special place in my own intellectual biography. I was a Marxist by the time I finished my undergraduate degree. But even then I was a cautious Marxist, charmed yet suspicious of the completeness, neatness, and certitude of the Marxian system. I was seduced by the beauty of this social vision. Marxism resonated with my high-minded criticalness towards the United States; it furnished a sophisticated language of social criticism to substitute for my more individualistic folk language. Yet, even as an undergraduate I was uncomfortable with the absence of a language of self and subjectivity in Marx. I recall that my reading at the time was divided between Marx and the symbolic interactionism of George Mead and Herbert Blumer. I was enamored, as well, with the existentialist philosophy of Camus and Sartre which romanticized individual choice and rebellion.

I pursued my graduate studies at the New School for Social Research. I kept reading Marx and the history of Marxism. I was not alone. This was 1974. It seemed like all the passion that many of us channneled into social protest was directed into elaborating a Marxist social critique. Courses on Marxism were packed; reading groups focusing on a particular canonical Marxist text proliferated. At the same time, my doubts about Marx were growing. I was dissatisfied with his core categories of labor, property, and class. I was unhappy with his failure to incorporate a view of the self as an agent of history. In light of my experience in the protest movements of the sixties, I could not think of culture as superstructural. Social life seemed a great deal more messy and fluid than the Marxian picture would allow. I was searching for approaches to society that responded to these concerns. It turned out that the New School for Social Research was a haven for scholars of Weber. I quickly found myself fascinated by Weber. He spoke to my interests in a sociology that took the self and culture seriously. My experience in the counterculture and psychotherapy had underscored the importance of nonrational and symbolic sources of human behavior and social life. Weber seemed tuned in whereas Marx was deaf to the symbolic and affective aspects of the human condition. The rest of my graduate education was preoccupied with rehearsing a dialogue between Marxism and classical sociology.

In recent years, I have come to be far more critical of Durkheim and Weber. My reservations are both broadly intellectual and political. I was always uncomfortable ideologically with these classical sociologists. Their liberalism seemed compromised by the lack of a strong commitment to social and political democracy. Indeed, Weber's liberalism was discredited by his nationalism. I share none of his trust in a powerful state. Moreover, Weber's commitment to democracy, even political democracy, was at best weak, at worst cynical. Weber's nightmare image of the relentless bureaucratization of the modern world precluded a vision of democratic social change which was anathema to this child of the counterculture. In the end, Weber's sober, indeed somber, social outlook seemed at odds with the peculiar sense of social hope I shared with many Americans. If my unhappiness with Weber related, in part, to his pessimistic, nondemocratic world view, Durkheim seemed almost Polyannaish to me. Despite Durkheim's democratic social values, his sociology was bereft of a drama of domination and resistance. I learned to appreciate the dynamics of solidarity and moral regulation from Durkheim, in particular, his unorthodox view of modern societies as sacred, religious cultures. I was frustrated by his apparent deafness to the sounds of oppression and political struggle.

In recent years, I have come to see Marxism and classical sociology as very much products of their time. For all their criticalness towards the Enlightenment, Marx and Comte, Durkheim and Weber are very much the children of the Enlightenment. Marx never escaped the economism and utilitarianism of the classical economists he criticized so severely. Comte may have ridiculed the Enlightenment for its blind faith in reason, but he was no less inspired by a vision of human perfection that his own science of society would bring to fulfillment. Durkheim raged against the individualism of Enlightenment social science, but his own sociology made the individual into a sacred entity. And for all his animus against the naive social hopes of the Enlightenment, Weber never relinquished the Kantian hope that reason made autonomy and moral responsibility possible.

The classics were captives of the era of modernity. Their grand narratives of human history invariably began and ended in the West; scripted men as the primary actors; wrapped themselves in the mythic aura of science; marked out good and bad, evil and redemption, without ever owning their stories as moral tales. Today, we can appreciate that their faith in science, reason, individualism, progress, and the West were entangled in the making of modern nation-states and colonial empires, but also in producing powerful moral and political visions filled with social hope for a better world. How much more satisfying to see Comte and Marx, Durkheim and Weber as just smart, privileged, passionate men who were caught up in the struggles of the time, trying to speak to the public and shape history. I now see their legacy as noble but as marking an era that we in the West, or at least the United States, are perhaps leaving as we enter the postmodern age.

References

1. Adam Smith, *An Inquiry into the Nature and Causes of the Wealth of Nations* (New York: Dutton, 1912) and John Stuart Mill, *Principles of Political Economy* (London: Longmans, Green, 1909).
2. Joseph de Maistre, *Works,* edited by Jack Lively (New York: Schocken Books); Edmund Burke, *Reflections on the Revolution in France* (New York: Dutton, 1935).
3. The revolutionary Babeuf and the utopian critic Fourier were important critics of the Enlightenment. See Charles Fourier, *Design for Utopia* (New York: Schocken Books, 1971) and R.B. Rose, *Gracchus Babeuf* (Stanford, CA: Stanford University Press, 1978).
4. Emile Durkheim, *Suicide* (New York: Free Press, 1951); *The Division of Labor in Society* (New York: Free Press, 1933).
5. Durkheim, *The Division of Labor in Society*, p. 227.
6. Durkheim, *Suicide*, pp. 214–215.
7. Durkheim, *Suicide*, p. 213.
8. Durkheim, *The Division of Labor in Society*, p. 33.
9. Durkheim, *The Division of Labor in Society*, Book Three, "Abnormal Forms."
10. Emile Durkheim, *The Rules of Sociological Method* (New York: Free Press, 1966).
11. Durkheim, *The Rules of Sociological Method*, p. 31.
12. Emile Durkheim, *The Elementary Forms of Religious Life* (New York: Free Press, 1954).
13. Max Weber, *The Protestant Ethic and the Spirit of Capitalism* (New York: Free Press, 1958).
14. Weber, *The Protestant Ethic and the Spirit of Capitalism*, p. 181.

15. Max Weber, *Economy and Society*, Vols. 1–3 (New York: Bedminster Press, 1968); *Gesammelte Aufsätze zur Religionssoziologie*, Vols. 1–3 (Tubingen: 1920–1921).
16. Max Weber, *The Religion of China: Confucianism and Taoism* (New York: Free Press, 1951).
17. Max Weber, "Charisma and Its Transformation," in *Economy and Society*, Vol. 3.
18. Max Weber, "Bureaucracy," in *Economy and Society*, Vol. 3, p. 987.
19. Max Weber, "Science as a Vocation," in *From Max Weber: Essays in Sociology*, edited by Hans Gerth and C.W. Mills (New York: Oxford University Press, 1946).
20. Max Weber, "Objectivity in Social Science and Social Policy" in *The Methodology of the Social Sciences* (New York: Free Press, 1949), p. 112.
21. Weber, *The Methodology of the Social Sciences*, p. 110.

PART 2

DISCIPLINING THEORY: THE MAKING OF A SOCIOLOGICAL THEORY CANON

3

From European Social Theory to American Sociological Theory: Talcott Parsons and the Autonomy of Theory

C omte coined the term "sociology." Herbert Spencer and many other European intellectuals placed their work under the sign of sociology. Durkheim and Weber were pivotal in establishing sociology departments in French and German universities. Nevertheless, as a discipline, sociology did not prosper in Europe. Perhaps the rise of fascism and two world wars fought on the shores of Europe impeded the successful institutionalization of sociology. Incomplete institutionalization did not prevent Europe from producing arguably the most imaginative, influential sociologists in the twentieth century. As we will see, many of the pioneers of sociological theory in this century were European by birth, though many of them took positions in American universities.

The United States has been central to the development of sociological theory in the twentieth century. It is in America that sociological theory has evolved furthest as a distinct tradition of social theory. In the next two chapters, I will identify the outlines of a unique sociological theory canon. In the immediate postwar years, if not earlier, there emerged a loose consensus among sociological theorists about the meaning and role of theory, about what problems count as theoretical and which argumentative strategies are credible. The sociological canon includes celebrated founding figures and texts, dramatic historical turning points, and a grand narrative of the evolution of social theory.

Canons do not form without creating many exclusions and silences. In the sociological theory canon, certain figures, problems, conceptual approaches, and argumentative strategies were ignored, suppressed, or marginalized. In the history of sociological theory, notable exclusions include feminism, sex and gay theory, Black nationalism, and left cultural criticism. Canons are, if nothing else, strategies to maintain intellectual and social hierarchy by fixing boundaries.

Talcott Parsons was a pivotal figure in the making of a sociological theory canon. As we will see, Parsons inherited a logic of theoretical priorities from his predecessors and contemporaries. Yet Parsons effected a shift of major importance. He abandoned the close association of sociological scholarship and partisanship that prevailed in American sociology. By claiming that Durkheim and Weber pioneered a revolution in theoretical sociology, Parsons undermined the dominance of a Comtean and Spencerian American sociology. Moreover, departing from the moral vision of many early American sociologists, Parsons interpreted the European breakthrough as enjoining sociologists to abandon a moral advocacy role. Sociological theory was to be a strictly value-neutral, conceptual, or analytical exercise whose sole justification was its will to truth and its promise to provide foundations for a general social science. Parsons did not succeed in purging sociological theory of social interests and values. However, he defined moral advocacy as beyond the boundaries of scientific theory. Parsons's functionalism may have been defeated in the 1960s, but Parsonianism as a vision of the autonomy of theory and science has triumphed almost unscathed in mainstream sociology.

In defense of liberalism: the founding years of American sociological theory

Modern social theory originated in eighteenth century Europe. In particular, France and Scotland were centers for the proliferation of scientific theories of society. To be sure, there were Enlightenment figures of importance in the United States (e.g., Benjamin Franklin and Thomas Jefferson), Italy (Vico), and Germany (Herder and Kant), but the key pioneers of Enlightenment social thought, figures such as Hume, Montesquieu, Voltaire, Turgot, Condorcet, and Adam Smith, were either French or Scottish.

France continued as a major center for the development of social theory in the nineteenth century. Montesquieu, Turgot, and Condorcet made possible Saint Simon, Comte, and Durkheim. Similarly, England remained a key source of social theory. Adam Smith layed the foundations for the classical political economy of David Ricardo and John Stuart Mill in the nineteenth century. Moreover, if England did not have a Comte or Durkheim, it did nurture the likes of Herbert Spencer, perhaps the most widely known theorist in late nineteenth century Europe and the United States. Although France and England were centers of social theory throughout the century, Germany nourished perhaps the most brilliant traditions of social theory in the period: Marxism and the sociology of Max Weber.

Social theory in the classical age was dominated by Europe. Perhaps this reflects the political and economic world hegemony of Europe. As the self-appointed cultural center of the world, Europe made its own social and cultural creations into the finest fruits of civilization. Europe's preeminent cultural role, or at least its pretense to being the cultural crown jewel of history, was no doubt enhanced by the existence of a well-established, secular university system.

Describing Europe as the center of classical social theory in no way implies that modern social theory was absent in other nations or civilizations. Most impressively, the United States nurtured rich traditions of social theorizing. Indeed, long before books described as sociology appeared in Europe, they surfaced in America. As early as 1854, Henry Hughes published *A Treatise on Sociology*, and his southern contemporary, George Fitzhugh, wrote *Sociology for the South* [1]. By the turn of the century, major works in sociological theory were produced by the likes of William Graham Summer (*What Social Classes Owe to Each Other*), Albion Small (*General Sociology: An Exploration of the Main Developments in Sociological Theory from Spencer to Ratzenhofer*), Franklin Giddings (*The Principles of Sociology*), and Lester Ward (*Dynamic Sociology*) [2]. Yet much of nineteenth century American sociological theory derived from Comte and Spencer.

During the twentieth century, the social center of sociological, if not social, theory became the United States. From World War I through the 1980s, Europe continued to spawn major innovators in sociological theory. However, the United States was the center of its production, discussion, and worldwide dissemination. It was in the United States that sociological theory emerged as a unique tradition of social theory, i.e., with its own jargon, conceptual strategies, problems, paradigms, and audience.

Turn-of-the-century America provided an exceptionally favorable environment for the takeoff of sociology. Unlike in Europe, universities in the States were not well established; there were no entrenched academic traditions or hostile cultural elites to impede the development of sociology. The modern, research-oriented university did not appear in the United States until the end of the nineteenth century. With ample financial support from private, religious, and public institutions, American universities achieved a level of independence from both political and cultural elites that was absent in Europe.

The founding years of sociology coincided with the phenomenal expansion of the American university system. By the turn of the century, sociology courses were taught routinely. The first department of sociology was established at the University of Kansas in 1889, followed closely by the University of Chicago in 1892. By World War I, sociology was a recognized academic discipline, with its own departments, doctoral programs, professional associations, conferences, and journals.

The successful institutionalization of sociology was facilitated by the relatively broad-based liberal ideological consensus that characterized middle America at the time. In Europe, sociology emerged in societies sharply polarized between a socialist Left and a conservative Right. To the extent that sociology was identified with a liberal alternative, it was resisted by the ideological Left and Right. Although the United States was not as sharply divided ideologically as Europe, the founding years of sociology were a period of social upheaval and conflict. Many of these conflicts did not challenge a broadly liberal society and politics. For example, divisions around the outlawing or regulating of prostitution, the level of state regulation in social and economic affairs, municipal reform, the legitimation of divorce, and extension of the vote to women did not threaten a liberal consensus. However, this period witnessed the rise of movements and critical perspectives that did contest a liberal consensus. Sociology did not absorb these critical perspectives or themes; it resisted them. Indeed, sociology was enthusiastically supported by middle America, in part, because it defended the liberal center against these critical social impulses. Sociology was formed, then, through a series of defensive formations and exclusions. Let me briefly elaborate.

The founding years of sociology coincided with a series of movements that defied the liberal consensus. In particular, turn-of-the-century America was experiencing serious labor unrest. As in European nations, processes of commercialization and industrialization gave birth to heightened conflicts between capitalists and laborers. While entrepreneurs were investing huge sums of capital in mass-production factories and pressuring the government to protect their investment through legislation and military force, laborers were organizing into unions that were often inspired by socialist ideas. This was the heyday of socialism in America. The Socialist Party became a major social force. At its peak in 1912, the party had 118,000 members. Socialists held 1,200 offices in 340 cities, including 79 mayors in 24 states. The socialist presidential candidate, Eugene Debs, polled 6% of the popular vote in the 1912 election. Although the Socialist Party diminished considerably as a political force by the end of World War I, a socialist political culture sustained by newspapers, magazines, literature, and popular essays and lectures remained a prominent feature of America through the early 1930s.

Unlike the socialist movements in Europe, American socialism was less dogmatically tied to unionism and a narrow antibusiness agenda. Prior to World War I, socialism was part of a broader radical political culture. As one expression of a broad middle class reaction against a Victorian order that restricted women's role to the household, spiritualized women, sex, and marriage, and disapproved of the sensual, expressive, and impulsive aspects of personal and social experience, many socialists were committed to feminism and a politics of sexual and personal liberation. A socialist agenda of labor empowerment and economic change was often connected to sexual, gender, and broad cultural struggles. Moreover, although the Socialist Party assumed a peripheral presence in American politics, many radicals carried an influence beyond their narrow social circles. Radical social critics such as Max Eastman, Floyd Dell, Emma Goldman, and Margaret Sanger lectured and wrote for a broad-based American audience [3].

These currents of indigenous social criticism were not absorbed by an evolving sociological discipline. A case in point is the rise of Black nationalism. The race problem cut to the heart of American society. Blacks may have been emancipated from slavery, but they did not have equal civil, political, and social rights. By the turn of the century, a Black nationalist culture of dissent, including its own tradition of social criticism, had developed. One of its leading figures, W.E.B. Du Bois, was a sociologist. In many articles and books, Du Bois developed a perspective that sharply challenged public stereotypes of Blacks as different and inferior. Despite his pioneering sociological monograph, *The Philadelphia Negro*, his much-acclaimed collection, *The Souls of Black Folk*, and his establishing one of the earliest departments of sociology at Atlanta University, Du Bois was not recognized as a sociologist by the profession [4]. His African American understanding of Blacks fell on deaf ears as many sociologists continued to believe in the doctrine regarding the hierarchy of races.

Another example of sociology narrowing its liberal reform agenda is its neglect of the women's movement. Through World War I, women had neither the right to vote nor social equality at home or at work. The women's movement, which, at the time, was divided between liberals who campaigned for the vote and radicals who advocated for broad social change, gave rise to uniquely feminist social perspectives. Writers such as Charlotte Perkins Gilman (who called herself a sociologist and published in the *American Journal of Sociology*), Emma Goldman, and Margaret Sanger developed women-centered analyses describing the social forces that shaped women's lives, often rendering them socially subordinate [5]. Despite the social impact of the women's movement (the right to vote was won in 1920), a social perspective on gender that was attentive to dynamics of women's oppression remained largely foreign to American sociology.

American sociology was institutionalized as a White, male-biased, middle class discipline. This speaks to the dominant characteristics of the profession. It describes the points of view and values that shaped sociological theory and research. Blacks or women may have been topics of sociological thinking. However, the perspectives of sociology – its basic premises, concepts, and explanations – reflected the experience, social interests, and values of predominantly White, middle class men. To the extent that assumptions of the natural superiority of Whites and men – and assumptions regarding the natural separation of the races and sexes – were taken for granted in mainstream America, we would expect a racist and sexist coloring to sociology in this period. As disconcerting as it might be, I believe that the exclusion of an African-American and feminist perspective, if not a more explicit racism and sexism, made sociology more acceptable because it was more in line with the mainstream of liberal America. In other words, the relatively painless institutionalization of sociology was, in part, achieved by a narrowing of its social and intellectual standpoint to exclude those movements and perspectives that were threatening to middle America, e.g., feminism, Black nationalism, socialism, sexual radicalism.

Sociology came of age in a period of dramatic social change. The United States was shifting from a primarily agricultural economy anchored in small towns and controlled by a White, male, Protestant elite to an industrial, urban-centered, consumer-oriented, multiethnic, multiracial, society. Although a White, male, largely Protestant elite continued to rule, its power was contested by organized labor, Black nationalists, feminists, and the influx of Catholic immigrants. Moreover, divisions surfaced within the ruling elite between an older middle class whose lives were tied to the Victorian era of small business ownership and a culture of sobriety and respectability and a new middle class who were more likely to be professionals, urban, and sympathetic to changing sexual and gender styles. For the new middle classes, sociology was embraced as a vehicle to manage the myriad social problems of an urban, industrial liberal society. Advocacy for sociology was a way for the new middle classes to prove their superiority over older elites by showing their competency to solve social problems and to maintain America on the path of social progress. Animated by the spirit of liberal reform and social progress, sociology functioned as a secular expression of the Christian faith in the manifest destiny of America that was at the core of the American civil religion.

In these early years, American sociologists believed that the value of science lay in its social utility. Indeed, moral reform was at the heart of sociology. In the first sociology textbook to appear in the United States (1894), Albion Small and George Vincent expressed succinctly the conventional wisdom: "Sociology was born of the modern order to improve society" [6]. In the midst of labor unrest, feminism, mass immigration, and Black northern migration, rising divorce rates, and the visibility of pornography and prostitution, sociology was to replace religion in maintaining America on the road to earthly virtue and salvation. Its charge was to provide knowledge to solve social problems. Moreover, where its problem-solving capacities proved limited in the face of difficult social ills, sociologists would resort to general theories that reassured Americans that current social tensions would give way to civic harmony and social progress. The founding years of American sociology was a period of grand theorizing. Influenced heavily by Comte and Spencer, sociologists such as Lester Ward, William Sumner, Franklin Giddings, and Albion Small created evolutionary theories of historical change in which progress was guaranteed by the laws of survival and competition.

Despite the proliferation of general theories of social evolution in the founding years of sociology, it was specialized empirical research oriented towards problem solving that was the most conspicuous feature of American sociology. The mandate of sociology, so to speak, was to produce factual knowledge on narrow social problems. This research was vigorously supported by foundations, religious denominations, philanthropic organizations, and the government. This narrow, empirical focus became virtually definitive of the first major school of sociology, the Chicago school of sociology which had consolidated after World War I. Chicago-styled sociologists were trained to go out into the world and study a small slice of it in an objective, value-neutral way. Drawing from muckraking journalists such as Lincoln Steffens, Chicago-trained sociologists produced detailed, descriptive case studies of, say, the Negro, slum life, the ghetto, specific occupations (e.g., the taxicab driver or the factory worker), and immigrants. This was a bottom-up sociology, a sociology of the taken-for-granted everyday life that revealed and reveled in the patterned pluralism of American culture.

American sociology was polarized from the beginning between the development of systems of sociology and specialized, problem-oriented, empirical research. Through World War I, this tension was not especially troubling because Americans seemed to want both broad evolutionary theories that assured them of their manifest destiny and narrow fact-finding research responsive to social problems. Underlying the peaceful coexistence of theory and research was a liberal consensus that was unshaken in its faith in the manifest destiny of the United States.

In the post-World War I years, social events were troubling to the liberal consensus. The Russian Revolution disturbed the belief in the naturalness and inevitability of a liberal capitalist society. The Russian threat was heightened with the rise of American communism. The communist prophecy of the imminent decline of capitalism was made credible by the Great Depression, an event that stretched to the limits American's faith in manifest destiny. To many Americans in the 1930s, the rise of fascism and Nazism felt like the breaking point: History seemed on the verge of giving birth to a new world order in which the United States and liberal civilization itself were destined to decline. By the mid-1930s, a perception of a social crisis not only of the United States but of Western liberal civilization was widespread. A civilization that was unable to put its people to work and that sacrificed an unseemly number of its citizens in two unprecedented world wars in rapid succession could hardly defend its claim to being the high point of human progress.

In the face of a civilizational crisis of Western liberalism, neither the tradition of a problem-solving empiricism nor the grand theoretical systems that guaranteed social progress through revealing the natural laws of social evolution, were compelling. Many American liberals felt the need for a new social image, one that was general enough to provide a novel and affirmative perspective on the present, yet avoid the naive optimism and millennialism of the grand social evolutionary theories. What they sought was a new vision, a social liberal perspective that clarified the present crisis while restoring an unwavering faith in Western liberalism. Many social thinkers offered such visions, but the social liberal vision of one sociological theorist, Talcott Parsons, marked a turning point in American sociological theory.

Talcott Parsons

In its formative years, American sociology was deeply indebted to European social thought. The organic metaphor and the naturalistic evolutionary ideas of Comte and Spencer resonated with the broadly social Darwinian culture of early twentieth century American society. These influences were offset, to some extent, by a German impact. American academics looked to Germany as a model of a modern, research-oriented university; many socialists (e.g., Albion Small, William G. Sumner, E.A. Ross, W.I. Thomas, Robert Park) studied in Germany and were influenced by German historical and idealist culture. In the post-World War I period, Germany's intellectual prestige soared as major German intellectuals (e.g., Einstein) migrated to the United States; the works of German sociologists (e.g., Albert Schaeffle, Georg Simmel, Ferdinand Tönnies, Max Weber) became widely known. Undoubtedly, the intellectual prestige of German ideas motivated this diffusion. Perhaps the German emphasis on national historical uniqueness resonated with American exceptionalism and manifest destiny.

Like many of his predecessors and contemporaries, Talcott Parsons looked to Europe and, in particular, to Germany for theoretical direction. However, whereas other American sociologists drew from European ideas to build on an already existing American-centered sociology, Parsons turned to European social thought to effect a radical break from American sociology. He intended to alter the foundations of sociology by centering American sociology squarely in European traditions. Parsons hoped to take sociology beyond the split between the theoretical quest for a system of sociology inspired by Comte and Spencer and the social problem-centered research tradition of liberal reformism. He sought a radical shift in the elementary premises, concepts, and aims of American sociology. This was to be accomplished by centering sociology in a non-Comtean, non-Spencerian European tradition. Underlying this attempt to reorient sociology was a moral hope that a reconfigured sociology could contribute to resolving the current crisis of Western liberalism.

Moral discourse parading as theoretical foundations

After spending a year at the London School of Economics, Parsons took his doctorate from the University of Heidelberg, Germany. It was not, I think, fortuitous that his dissertation was on German perspectives on modern capitalism. The success of the Russian Revolution gave enhanced credibility to the Marxist critique of capitalism – and Western liberalism – as destined to decline. Parsons hoped to find in the German sociologists an alternative to the Marxist critique. In the next decade, Parsons' project would go beyond the defense of capitalism. In the face of the Great Depression and the rise of Nazism, Parsons hoped to create the intellectual resources to defend Western liberal civilization. He wished to discover in European sociology at the turn of the century a new foundation for a general theory of society and history. Neither Marxist, Comtean, nor Spencerian, this European-centered sociology would be less tied to defending capitalism than to legitimating a liberal civilization.

Parsons's strategy was bold. Instead of critically engaging American sociology and analyzing the flaws and limits of its basic premises and explanations, he largely ignored his American predecessors and contemporaries. He offered no sustained critiques of Albion Small, Robert Park, Charles Cooley, or contemporaries such as Howard Becker or Robert MacIver. Like his sociological predecessors and successors, however, Parsons aimed to carve out a sociology whose liberal commitments would exclude the themes and perspectives of radical critics and movements. Parsons's sociology was not formed through any serious engagement with socialists, feminists, Black nationalist thought, or American cultural critics. Parsons attempted a wholesale switch to a distinctively European-centered sociology. Comte and Spencer were to be replaced as the core of the classical tradition by Weber and Dukheim. This was the intention of his first major work, *The Structure of Social Action*, a book that was largely ignored by his contemporaries but that has since become a "classic" text in sociological theory – a measure indeed of Parsons's success in achieving a recentering of sociology [7].

The Structure of Social Action may strike us as a rather odd book to write in the 1930s. In the face of a devastating economic depression, a communist revolution in Russia, the rise of fascism and Nazism, Parsons delivers a massive 800-page book whose primary question is: "What is the general, indeed universal, structure of social action?" Why would Parsons choose to engage in a seemingly philosophical investigation of the nature of social action as the world was reeling from cataclysmic, epoch-shaping social changes? Parsons's study is studiously academic; it is composed of painstakingly detailed textual analyses of European thinkers with an eye not to their perspectives on capitalism or politics but to their most general ideas about the self, social action, and society.

Is this the case of an academic retreating into the calm civility and exquisite order of bookish learning in the face of discomforting realities? Perhaps not. Like many of his contemporaries, Parsons thought that the crisis of Western liberalism was more than a social crisis; it was an intellectual crisis – a crisis in social and political thought. If Western societies were tumbling down the road of self-destruction, it was not unreasonable to suppose that this reflected, in part, certain habits of thought. A crisis that so fundamentally challenged Western civilization warranted a study of our most elementary social ideas. Underlying this philosophical or theoretical inquiry was a hope: the possibility that this social theory could contribute to reestablishing secure foundations for Western liberal civilization.

Why focus on the structure of social action? Parsons believed that our assumptions about social action are the most basic or elementary social ideas. Concepts of human motivation, behavior, and goals shape in far-reaching ways the way we think about social institutions, politics, and social change. This is true not only for social theorists but for all of us; each of us holds ideas about the individual and social action, and these shape our broad perception of politics and society. Moreover, everyday social ideas are formed by the broad intellectual perspectives and traditions created by academics and intellectuals. To the extent that social reconstruction requires changes in the way people think about the self and society, theoretical inquiry aimed at changing social ideas would have a deeply moral and political significance.

Parsons was convinced that the principal Western cultural traditions held to contradictory views of society. On the one hand, there were perspectives (e.g., utilitarianism, behaviorism, Marxism, social Darwinism) which conceived of the individual as adapting to physical or social forces beyond her or his immediate control; these forces drove individuals to act in specific ways. For example, instinct theories such as Freudian psychology described individuals as propelled by biological drives; behaviourists explained human conduct by mechanistic stimulus-response patterns; many sociologists explain behavior by appealing to market forces or class position. The key feature of these theories of social action is that the individual is described as merely adapting to objective conditions (biological, psychological, or sociological) which are the chief source of social action. Parsons calls this social perspective, at times, positivism, utilitarianism, or materialism. On the other hand, Parsons notes opposing perspectives (e.g., German idealism, historicism, American pragmatism) that conceive of the individual as the originator and director of his or her own action. Such perspectives involve explanations of behavior that refer to the values or beliefs of the individual. An example is Weber's account of capitalist behavior in terms of the religious vision of the Puritan. Parsons calls social action that is interpreted as expressing subjective motivations and meanings "idealism."

Western culture has been divided between materialist and idealist social ideas. Parsons believed that each perspective has its advantages and drawbacks. For example, idealism asserts the individual as an active agent who can shape her or his own social destiny. However, idealism may be interpreted as blaming individuals for their own misfortunes. Materialism may make society responsible for individual misfortune, but it conceives of the individual as passive or as a product of forces beyond individual control. This may legitimate a culture of manipulation and social engineering. Parsons argued that the division between materialsim and idealism was at the core of social theory and Western culture; it contributed to social and ideological discord and to the present social crisis. In *The Structure of Social Action*, Parsons hoped to fashion a perspective that integrated subjective freedom and objective determinism in order to establish stable intellectual foundations for Western liberalism.

The Structure of Social Action is occupied with detailed textual analyses of the key sociological works of Pareto (Italy), Weber (Germany), Durkheim (France), and Marshall (England). Underlying these interpretive sketches is a far-reaching claim: Despite their different national settings, divergent empirical concerns, and varied ideological and philosophical commitments, each of these European social theorists, almost uncannily, moved toward a common theoretical standpoint that involved the integration of materialism and idealism. Classical European social theory converged towards what Parsons calls a voluntaristic theory of action. "That in the works of the four principal writers here treated there has appeared the outline of what *in all essentials*, is the *same* system of generalized social theory, . . . what has been called the voluntaristic theory of action" [8]. It was Parsons's aim to clarify and fully articulate this new integrated theoretical foundation for sociology and, indeed, Western social thought.

At the core of the so-called voluntarist theory of action is an understanding of human action as involving both freedom and necessity or individual choice and social constraint. Individuals, argued Parsons, do not simply adapt to objective conditions and are not merely driven by them, but direct their own behavior according to subjective interests and values. Approaching human action as a sphere of individual choice requires that the basic social concepts and explanations of sociology make reference to a realm of subjective meanings. Yet a sociology that explains human action only as an expression of individual choice is inadequate since our conduct is always constrained by objective conditions, e.g., our physical and psychological makeup or social class position. Although some of these conditions may be able to be manipulated by the individual, many of them cannot, at least not in the immediate course of action. Accordingly, we need a conceptual vocabulary that speaks to the experience of subjective choice and a language of social structure and power that underscores the constraining features of action. Formally stated, the voluntaristic theory of action assumes an *actor* who exerts *effort* in a *situation* in which some aspects are unalterable (*conditions of action*), while other aspects can be used as *means* to achieve *goals*; both the selection of means and goals are guided by *norms*.

The Structure of Social Action was an exercise in general theory. It was intended to clarify the conceptual premises of a general theory of society. Parsons urges that, in place of either one-sided materialist or idealist premises, our starting point should be an integrated or synthetic "voluntaristic theory of action." Social action is imagined as combining both subjective choice and objective constraint. Although he asserts that this theoretical standpoint is empirically superior to either materialism or idealism, Parsons makes no attempt in this work to specify what empirical concepts, models, or social explanations might derive from his "voluntaristic theory of action." The aim of the *Structure* was only to set out the foundations for a general theory of society.

The stock market crash came in 1929; in 1933, the Nazis seized power; German intellectuals like Adorno and Horkheimer migrated to the United States in the 1930s, bringing with them a sophisticated critical social theory of the West. Parsons spent the decade at work on *The Structure of Social Action*, a book framing social thought as anchored in its image of social action. Yet Parsons was oddly silent when it came to spelling out its moral and political gains. Parsons thought that an investigation into the elementary premises of social thought could speak to the current social crisis; however, he never clarified in what ways this was so.

If Parsons did not feel compelled to give any moral or political account of his theorizing, perhaps it was because he believed that this would force him to acknowledge the moral vision that motivated and informed his work. If Parsons defended the value of the voluntaristic theory of action on strictly conceptual and empirical grounds, perhaps it was because he realized that any other justification would push him into moral and political argumentation. No matter how much Parsons wished to frame his theory of action in a "pure" theoretical language (actor, effort, goals, conditions of action), the plain truth is that he is making a moral statement about human behavior and social ideals. Whether individual behavior is viewed as "free" or "determined" or as involving subjective choice or necessity is a statement of values. Parsons's preference for imagining human action as voluntary yet constrained is a statement of "liberal" social hope, the hope that society values choice and diversity within responsible limits. Parsons refused to concede the moral underpinnings of his theorizing. Perhaps he felt that such a concession would undermine the authority of his argument. Thus, he cloaked his moral vision in a language of value-neutral, objective theory. Indeed, the highly abstract, general character of his theorizing seems related to his wish to remove theory of any moral or political taint. It was as if he believed that the authority of his ideas depended on their being seen as an expression of pure theory, as driven by the abstract, universal dictates of reason.

Functionalist sociology as liberal advocacy

After *The Structure of Social Action*, Parsons's writings went in two directions. On the one hand, he turned to more empirical concerns, as he sought to address current developments [9]. On the other hand, he articulated his ideas about action into a set of premises and concepts that could serve as the basis for a general theory of society. Specifically, Parsons developed a model of society as a functioning system. It is to this general theory that we briefly turn. I focus on his most important theoretical statement, *The Social System* [10].

Whereas the *Structure* clarified the most basic premises about social action, *The Social System* specified the elementary conceptual basis of patterns of interaction or what he calls "the social system." In shifting from analyzing "action" to "social interaction," Parsons wished to retain the dual emphasis on subjective choice and objective conditions. At the heart of *The Social System* is a systems model: Society is composed of three analytically distinct systems (the personality system is composed of individual needs and motivations; the cultural system relates to shared beliefs and values; and the social system consists of a plurality of social roles and norms). It is important to keep in mind that these systems are not actual entities but represent analytical dimensions of social life. Individual needs, social roles, norms, and cultural values are always interrelated. Consider a baseball team. To be a member of the team each player must make the team value of winning (cultural system) his or her own; each player must know what behavior is expected of him or her (social system) in order to promote a goal; finally, each player must identify with the team or have his or her needs met by membership (personality system). A systems approach to a baseball team would, accordingly, propose a multidimensional explanation analyzing the interrelations between the personality, social, and cultural systems. Parsons imagined that his general systems model would form the foundations of a comprehensive science of humanity, while particular sciences would specialize in one "system," e.g., psychology would focus on personality system and anthropology on the cultural system. In this grand scheme, sociology was the study of the social system.

Inspired by this scientific vision, Parsons viewed *The Social System* as laying out the basic concepts that would unify and guide sociologists in analyzing social systems. By social systems, Parsons meant virtually any pattern of interaction that has achieved sufficient continuity to have evolved social roles, statuses, social expectations, and norms, e.g., a baseball team, hospital, university, club, friendship, family, or political party. The key question in analyzing social systems is to explain social integration. Assuming that social systems are composed of a multitude of roles, norms, statuses, obligations, and authority relations and that they are subject to conflict and change, how is social stability and coherence routinely achieved?

Parsons disputed explanations of social order that appealed to notions of a human inclination to civic order or a process of natural selection and survival; individualistic accounts do not explain the coordination of conflicting interests. Similarly, he took issue with perspectives that explained social order as a result of domination, for example, the coercive power of the state or a ruling social class; such accounts leave no room for subjective choice and social consensus. Parsons imagined order as a precarious achievement made possible by a series of complex processes of social coordination and cultural consensus.

Proceeding from the simple to the complex, Parsons argued that well-functioning social systems require a "fit" between the needs and motivations of the individual and the role requirements of the institution or social unit. For example, if professors expect to concentrate on research, but universities value teaching, there would be a great deal of institutional discontent, conflict, and instability. A stable university presupposes that the expectations of professors and university administrators coincide. What Parsons called the "complementarity of expectations" must occur in a multitude of social interactions or role relations in order for social systems to achieve routine order. Thus, not only must there be a fit between professors and administrators but overlap in expectations between professors and students, professors and staff, professors and parents of students, among professors, and so on.

If routine social order presupposes a complementarity of expectations, how does this come about? Parsons's account draws heavily on a notion of cultural consensus. Let me explain. In order for there to be a fit between personal and institutional needs and between individuals and social roles, there must be a minimal level of shared understandings and values. If individuals occupy sharply different worlds of meaning and value, social interaction and institutional functioning would be embroiled in continuous disruptive conflicts. But how does cultural integration translate into social integration? Parsons spoke of "internalization," by which he meant a socialization process where cultural meanings become part of the self; the individual, as it were, takes into him or herself the beliefs, norms, and values of the society. To the extent that there is a shared culture and to the extent that socialization is roughly successful, individuals grow up with similar understandings and motivations. Social order will, accordingly, always exhibit a consensual aspect, i.e., individuals obey social norms and rules because they believe in them, because they express who they are and what they want society to be. To explain routine order, Parsons introduced a second key concept: "institutionalization." Whereas internalization refers to culture becoming a part of the self, institutionalization is a parallel process of culture becoming a part of the institutional order, i.e., defining roles, statuses, norms, and goals. If the same cultural patterns that define the needs and expectations of the individual also define institutional environments, we would expect a fit between individuals and institutions and the achivement of social integration.

Parsons was aware that all of these conditions – the complementarity of expectations, cultural consensus, successful socialization and institutionalization – are never fully present in any society. Social stability is rarely achieved in the absence of a great deal of social conflict. For example, in societies characterized by individualism and social pluralism, cultural consensus and therefore social integration will be precarious. If society permits substantial divergence with respect to ideologies and world views, we would expect conflicting understandings of needs, expectations, social norms, and therefore institutionalized patterns of social conflict and change. Indeed, Parsons expected endemic social disturbances stemming from everyday disruptions in socialization and institutionalization. These strains in the "fit" between the individual, culture, and institutional roles may be "functional" if they encourage social innovation.

There are, however, more threatening sources of social conflict. Parsons spoke of social disturbances stemming from "allocative" conflicts. Social systems are, in essence, concerned with the allocation – and integration – of social resources, personnel, and rewards. If social resources and rewards are scarce, division over who gets what and how much is inevitable. Social systems must evolve mechanisms to allocate resources (e.g., technology and personnel) and rewards (e.g., money and prestige) so that basic social requirements are satisfied. Viewed from the vantage point of allocation, problems of social system integration take on a more "materialist" or structural aspect. Are social systems distributing the social, technical, and human resources of society in a way that ensures individual and social reproduction? For example, is society producing enough food and housing? Is the educational system producing the kinds of skills needed in the economy? Is society producing enough technicians, physicians, or farm workers? Social system integration presupposes not only that the right resources are being produced and distributed at the needed levels, but that the allocation of resources, rewards, and personnel effective keeps individuals satisfied and avoids major social divisions. In other words, social systems evolve mechanisms (i.e., norms of justice, performative standards) that determine how social rewards (e.g., money and prestige) are distributed among personnel. Widespread social perceptions that these allocative mechanisms are unfair will produce the kinds of social conflicts that Marx thought were integral to property-based societies.

Social system strains and conflicts are endemic and inevitable. Disruptions in socialization and institutionalization are unavoidable. Individuals who, for whatever reason, grow up angry toward society will likely rebel against institutional expectations. Cultural diversity inevitably translates into conflicting interpretations of needs, social norms, and roles. Moreover, because social systems must allocate scarce resources, it is inevitable that the enormous problem of coordinating resources, ensuring that social functions receive the right level of inputs and yield the right level of outputs, will result, from time to time, in deficits. Similarly, the allocation of rewards to personnel can hardly avoid strains. If segments of a society perceive that the allocation of resources and rewards is unfair, if people feel that their level of prestige is unjust, further discontent over allocation norms and mechanisms will threaten serious social conflict. Should integration break down because of problems of socialization or allocation, social systems have recourse to the coercive force of the state, e.g., the law, police, military.

The Social System was published in 1951. In his subsequent writing, Parsons elaborated this systems approach in a decidedly more functionalist and formalistic direction [11]. Social systems were now understood as having four functional requirements or needs: adaptation, goal attainment, integration, and pattern maintenance. Considering a whole society (e.g., the United States) as a type of social system, Parsons imagined four subsystems emerging to satisfy the four functional needs. Thus, the economy specializes in securing the material conditions of society (adaptation); political institutions prioritize the goals of society and ensure that they are attained by mobilizing social resources (goal attainment); the legal system plays a key role in maintaining social regulation and solidarity (integration); and the family, religion, and education aim to produce individuals who have the appropriate needs, values, motives, and skills (pattern maintenance). Each subsystem (e.g., economy or the family), moreover, must handle these same four survival problems. For example, the family has problems of adaptation (economic maintenance), goal attainment (making major decisions), integration (coordinating family relationships), and pattern maintenance (transmitting family values to children).

By the early 1960s, Parsons had evolved an enormously abstract, formalistic systems theory whose focus was on functional requirements, cybernetic flows, input/output processes, and interchanges between systems and subsystems. Although Parsons's systems theory moved in a decidedly antihumanistic turn, a language of systems imperatives crowding out a language of individual action and subjectivity, his social vision assumed a much more aggressive defense of Western liberalism. Nowhere is this clearer than in his theory of social evolution.

Liberal America: the end of history

Parsons's *The Structure of Social Action* and *The Social System* were written against the backdrop of social events that threatened Western liberalism, for example, the Russian Revolution, the Great Depression, European fascism, and World War II. In the postwar period, however, American liberal hegemony at home and abroad was consolidated. The renewed economic prosperity of the 1950s and the rise of state bureaucratic welfare systems focused on economic and domestic management raised the hope for many Americans that an era of social peace was beginning. This hope for social harmony was shared by many intellectuals who expressed a strong disillusionment with radical ideologies and movements. Parsons shared this hope. Indeed, he recast this liberal social dream into an evolutionary theory in which an idealized contemporary America marks the virtual endpoint of history [12].

Approaching social change from the standpoint of structural-functionalism, Parsons outlined a vision of humanity evolving from "primitive" to modern societies. The key to change is a process of social differentiation. This refers to 1) the separation and relative autonomy of institutional spheres (e.g., family, economy, law, government, religion); 2) their functional specialization (e.g., family as a socializing agent); and 3) their interdependence (e.g., the family provides the economy with adult workers which, in turn, makes possible the material basis of the family). Social differentiation propels social evolution on a trajectory of social progress. Progress means that, in the course of social evolution, structures emerge that make possible higher levels of social adaptation for all of humankind, i.e., permit greater control over the environment. Parsons calls these structures "evolutionary universals." For example, a money economy, bureaucratic organization, and universalistic norms enhance social adaptation by permitting higher levels of material productivity, more efficient social coordination of resources, and the social inclusion of diverse social groups. In addition, progress means that history reveals a movement towards greater levels of individual freedom, democracy, and social integration. Parsons's perspective on social change as social progress can be clarified by turning briefly to his analysis of modernization [13].

Parsons conceives of modernization as marking an epochal change in history. In premodern periods, "society" was experienced as a natural force determining the fate of individuals; modernity renders society an active, ongoing creation of individuals.

The ruling institutions of early modern Europe, for example, the monarchy, aristocracy, church, the corporate, estate system, meant that individuals experienced society as if it were a fixed, closed, natural force. Individuals were born into a particular status (e.g., serf or noble) that determined their social destiny. There were little mobility and variation in social experience. Society was experienced as constricted and narrow, weighted with burdensome duties, obligations, customs, traditions, and responsibilities. This hierarchical, closed social system was destroyed by three successive revolutions: the industrial, democratic, and educational.

Beginning in the late eighteenth century, the industrial revolution brought about the differentiation of the household and the economy. In Western Europe and the United States, this entailed the emergence of a market economy separate from the activities of the family household. This had two major consequences for social evolution. First, it enhanced the adaptive capacity of Western societies in that material production was enormously more efficient and productive. Second, it greatly expanded individual freedom; individuals had greater choice over occupational decisions which, in turn, meant greater latitude over personal matters, e.g., residence, intimate, and marital arrangements. At a social level, the enhanced levels of freedom and mobility rendered the experience of society as more of a medium for individual choice and action than as a natural force fixing an individual's fate. The experience of society as something created by and for individuals was reinforced by the modern democratic revolutions. Whereas tradition and custom ruled early modern life, the democratic revolutions rendered society, in principle, as the intentional creation of individuals. Insofar as individuals are bearers of political and civil rights, society exists only through their action and consent. Citizenship gives to individuals a feeling of society as their own, as a medium of human wishes and will. Of course, citizenship does not make individuals free if social resources are controlled by an elite or ruling class; society would still be experienced as oppressive, as something to escape from. Thus, the educational revolution is of the highest importance; it breaks down rigid barriers to individual mobility and opens up the social environment to the free play of individual talent and effort. The educational revolution of the twentieth century equalizes social competition; as individual social status reflects personal talent and effort, the experience of society is that of a medium of individual action, a vehicle responsive to the needs and efforts of the self.

Parsons envisions modernization as creating an open, mobile, democratic social order. Central to modernization is the experience of society as an active, ongoing creation of its social members. Individuals feel an identification or a sense of "ownership" with the society as a whole. Nowhere is this social identification more evident than in the development of what Parsons calls a "societal community." Beyond particular attachments to specific class, ethnic, racial, or religious groups, modernity encourages the individual to feel a sense of belonging to a national community, a community of abstract national citizens. The creation of a societal community, of a societal-wide moral community beyond particular moral groupings, makes possible high levels of individualism, pluralism, and social competition without threatening to devolve into social disorder.

Parsons thought that the United States had gone furthest in institutionalizing a modern societal community animated by an activist social ethos. America was settled as a multiethnic, multireligious society while creating an encompassing societal community. For example, religious freedom was established as a private choice; the state was to protect and guarantee freedom of belief by prohibiting the establishment of a state religion. Religious faith was, accordingly, perceived as irrelevant as a factor in national identity and inclusion. Similarly, ethnic group affiliation and identity were encouraged, even celebrated in America, but as a personal choice, not a condition of national inclusion or citizenship. In principle, religious, ethnic, racial, or class affiliation is irrelevant for being an American. This is another way of saying that the United States created a social community apart from, and above, that of particular attachments, a community to which all Americans belong, as national citizens. A point of contrast would be Israel where religious status (being Jewish) defines national citizenship and inclusion. Institutionalizing a coherent societal community renders conflicts over ethnicity or religion less socially divisive as these are not, in principle, conflicts over national identity and inclusion. Moreover, to the extent that particularistic group attachments are not so socially weighted, individuals would be permitted more latitude in such decisions.

Parsons's social imagery is inspiring, even dreamy. For example, contrary to the many critics of modern society – conservative and radical – Parsons highlights the advance of liberties in modernization. "American society – and most modern societies without dictatorial regimes – has institutionalized a far broader range of freedoms than had any previous society." He continues:

> Perhaps they can be said to begin with freedom from some of the exigencies of physical life: ill health, short life, geographical circumscription, and the like. They certainly include reduced exposure to violence for most of the population most of the time. Higher incomes and extensive markets enhance freedom of choice in consumption. Then there is an immense range of free access to various services like education, public accommodations, and the like. There is widespread freedom of marital choice, of occupation, of religious adherence, of political allegiance, of thought, of speech and expression [14].

Modern society is experienced as an enabling medium of individual action, as an open, fluid environment that permits individuals to interact in a relatively free, playful, empowering way. Far from society being imagined as oppressive, as burdened with the weight of tradition and custom, it is imagined as an enabling, secure space for individuals.

The autonomy of theory

Parsons's first major publication was *The Structure of Social Action* (1937). In 1978, at the age of 76, he published *Action Theory and the Human Condition*, a majestic vision of human existence [15]. In between, there were many theoretical essays, books, and some empirically oriented works on American education, race, family, social stratification, and social change. It is as a theorist that Parsons has exercised enormous influence. He was, as he frankly confessed, an "uncurable theorist." It was less his general functionalist, systems, or evolutionary theories that has made him a major figure in twentieth century sociological theory than his insistence on the "autonomy" of theory. Commentators may debate whether his systems, cybernetic model departs from his early action perspective or whether his chief approach is functionalist, systems, or cybernetic. Parsons never wavered, however, from a view of theory as grasping the most abstract, fundamental, and universal features of society and weaving them into a general theory that aspired to comprehend all societies – past, present, and future.

Parsons had a truly Olympian image of theory. To aspire to the heights of universal knowledge, theory had to be thoroughly disengaged from current social and political conflicts. The theorist should be disinterested or interested in nothing more than truth. Whether Parsons was theorizing about social action, the social system, social evolution, or the human condition, his aim was to lay bare the most abstract, elementary, and universal aspects of social processes. He aspired to reach for a concept of the social that was purged of all particular, historical social aspects. Parsons offered a vision of theory as an autonomous, intellectual enterprise, unsullied by social interests or moral advocacy, whose sole justification lay in the general truths that it aspired to reveal.

Talcott Parsons viewed theory as a foundational exercise. Its aim was to clarify the most basic premises, concepts, and explanatory models of sociology and, indeed, social science. Theory was to unify and guide empirical science. Much of Parsons's theorizing aimed to provide conceptual foundations, to legislate a set of concepts and explanatory logics for the human sciences. Parsons wished to elaborate this conceptual foundation into a general theory of society and history; he aspired to an encompassing theoretical system that would, in effect, render his heirs little more than disciples whose work would amount to smoothing out the rough edges of Parsons's grand synthesis. Somewhere in this project is a hope that theory and science will benefit humanity. Unfortunately, nowhere is such a moral aim articulated; nowhere does Parsons clarify the moral or political meaning of his theorizing or offer moral rationales for his theorizing. In Parsons, theory is intended to be cut loose from its moral and political moorings; whatever moral vision animated him, it was buried beneath layers of morally purged vocabularies, muted by the dogma of value-neutrality, objectivity, general theory, and social knowledge. It is the notion of theory as "autonomous," as foundational, as universal, as disinterested – a compulsively *scientific vision* – that has come to be orthodoxy in American sociological theory.

Afterword

Parsons is an odd, even if brilliant, figure in American sociology. Why odd? His grand theory and grandiose social vision is dissonant with American empiricism and pragmatism. Yet this system builder in the rationalist tradition of a Hobbes or Hegel, created a school of functionalist sociology that dominated the discipline through the 1950s and 1960s. Long after function-alism all but disappeared as a force in the discipline, the Parsonian ideal of the autonomy of theory and science has conquered his most bitter foes.

It was inevitable that the Parsonian grand synthesis would be attacked. Few, however, anticipated the degree to which he would come to serve as a site for the battle over the soul of sociology. His vision of an integrated social system that evolves in a slow, gradual, and progressive way was at odds with the spirit of the times. The movements for civil rights and social justice, protests against American colonial policy in Vietnam, and the youth struggles against a parochial, patriarchal, career-oriented, commercial social ideal turned many younger sociologists against Parsons, who came to symbolize the very target of their social and generational rebellion. A ruthless assault on Parsons's sociology occurred in the sixties. A younger generation of sociologists and sociologists who immigrated to the United States or Great Britain from Europe looked to fashion a sociology that was attuned to a language of conflict, power, discord, and change. Parsons was scandalized as a conservative or as simply out of touch with a changing world.

Attacked in the 1960s, Parsons's presence in the discipline was virtually erased in the 1970s. This period saw the rise of new sociologies: phenom-enology, ethnomethodology, symbolic interactionism, conflict theory, exchange theory, and neo-Marxism. Despite considerable differences among them, they shared a fierce hostility towards Parsons. They aban-doned the themes and language of Parsonian functionalism. They sought an agent-centered, process-oriented sociology. The fall of Parsonian sociol-ogy was indeed remarkable. Attending undergraduate and graduate school in the seventies, I was never assigned any readings by Parsons. My only introduction to Parsons was the notorious assault on Parsons, the text that announced loud and clear the end of the Parsonian era, Alvin Gouldner's *The Coming Crisis of Western Sociology* [16]. Parsons's grand vision of sociology and society, his aspiration to announce a universal system of sociology, was criticized by Gouldner as a less than noble effort to legit-imate liberal welfare capitalism in mid-century America. As a graduate student in the seventies, I studied Marx and the classical sociologists, not from the perspective of Parsons, but from the standpoint of neo-Marxism or the new interpretive sociologies that spoke to the issues of the day.

Parsons has fared somewhat better in the 1980s and 1990s. As the turbu-lent period of the seventies passed into the complacent Reagan years of the eighties, it was possible to offer a more balanced assessment of Parsons. Indeed, the resistance of social institutions to change, the decline of social protest, the excess of the sixties, and the loss of hope in a socialist alter-native refocused the attention of sociologists, once again, on integrating and stabilizing social dynamics. Parsons's social ideas and his liberal ideal seemed attractive to many sociologists. The 1980s witnessed serious efforts to resurrect and revise Parsonian sociology [17]. Many sociologists, including myself, have come to appreciate the imaginative and grand character of Parsons's work, his effort to produce an overarching system of sociology that would defend scientific knowledge and a social liberal civilization.

Parsons erected a system of sociology based upon a proposed synthesis of the classical tradition. This was a synthesis, however, that excluded as much as it included. Weber and Durkheim were canonized as "classics" while Marx and Herbert Spencer were marginalized as "precursors" or failed efforts at social science, i.e., ideologists. Parsons's own ideological agenda is exposed in his synthesis. Marx and Spencer were chief representatives of socialism and individualistic or utilitarian liberalism, respectively. Weber and Durkheim pointed the way to an alternative social liberal ideal that Parsons believed represented a "third path" between socialism and individualistic liberalism. Parsons envisioned sociology as a vehicle for a reconstructed social liberalism in the face of the failure of individualistic or utilitarian liberalism and the threat of socialism.

Parsons did not, however, make the case for his social liberal ideal in directly moral or political terms. Rather, he masked his ideological agenda in a theoretical critique of Marxism and individualistic liberalism. Specifically, he challenged the utilitarianism or the "materialistic" view of society and modernity of his ideological foes. By materialism, I mean a perspective that emphasizes the pursuit of economic gain, social security, and power as the dominant principle of human life. For both Marxism and individualistic liberalism (e.g., Locke, Bentham, Spencer), individuals are seen as rationally calculating, self-interested, and economically motivated. Society is depicted as a sphere of economic competition and power struggle to control material and symbolic resources. Modernity is imagined as individualistic, secular, commercial, and class divided. This view of social life, even if it is animated by humanitarian values, is, according to Parsons, illiberal because it ends up justifying a polarized view of society and the deployment of state power to maintain social order; it promotes a culture of cynicism and distrust.

Parsons's voluntaristic theory of social action was intended to provide an alternative basis for thinking about society and modernity. It asserted that subjective beliefs and shared meanings are integral to the human condition. Although I am not convinced that Parsons's "theory of action" is comprehensive or "true," I am persuaded of its enormous sociological importance. By claiming that human action involves meanings (norms, values, beliefs, symbols), Parsons found a basis for opposing a narrow economic, materialistic view of society and modernity. If all social behavior is guided by norms, values, and moral ideals, a materialist view of society is one-sided. Contrary to Marxism and utilitarian liberalism, society is not just a struggle for economic gain and power but involves individuals fabricating shared worlds of meanings, engaged in rituals of solidarity and community, and aspiring to realize social ideals and transcendent goals, for example, salvation, justice, self-fulfillment, or autonomy.

Drawing on Weber and Durkheim, Parsons was a pivotal figure in providing an alternative sociological approach to the materialism of Marxism and liberal social thought. He imagined the possibility of a culture-centered sociology, that is, a sociology that took seriously processes of identity formation, the making of social solidarities, the role of ritual and common values in social integration. Parsons was important in challenging the dominant image of modernity as a secular, rational, economic, materialist universe. Although he never surrendered a deeply Enlightenment vision of modern societies as marching down a path of social progress, he imagined modernity as an epoch with its own myths, rituals, solidarities, sacred beliefs, and redemptive hopes. Against the current of much Enlightenment thinking, Parsons, like Freud and Nietzsche, Weber and Durkheim, before him, found a place in his social perspective for the nonrational, for the deeply emotional and volatile aspects of the human condition.

Challenging utilitarian and materialist views of society was not just of theoretical or "scientific" significance; it was of fundamental ideological importance. It permitted Parsons to approach the individual not only as a self-sufficient economic creature but as a social and cultural one; the individual was viewed as motivated by values and moral ideals, as embedded in institutions and in shared cultural worlds. Parsons's sociological approach allowed him to highlight the importance of trust, shared values, and moral community in the making of a good society. Parsons's sociological critique of utilitarianism and materialism functioned as a vehicle to legitimate a reconstructed social liberalism in a context where the only alternatives were utilitarian individualism, whose legitimacy was enfeebled by the Great Depression and fascism, and Marxian socialism which Parsons abhorred.

In Parsons's late writings, his ideological agenda is obvious. I am thinking of his theory of social evolution. He sketches a narrative of the progress of "civilization" from the ancient Mesopotamian empires to the modern West. Parsons relates a story of the simultaneous advance of autonomy and community, of institutional differentiation and cultural pluralism and the making of a societal community or common value system that unifies a diversified, pluralistic society. Postwar America is stationed as the apex of social evolution. In its scope and grandeur, Parsons's story of Western history compares to the grand vision of Condorcet or Comte.

Parsons, however, does not see his theory of social evolution as simply a story – grand, inspiring, imaginative, but, still, just one tale of human drama. Does it preclude other social accounts? No. Can his story claim to be comprehensive or complete? No. Let me be frank. Parsons's perspective on historical development represents a story told from a particular standpoint, i.e., the standpoint of a White, upper class, heterosexual male living in late twentieth century America who holds social liberal values. Stories of history written from a different standpoint, say, by an African, Native American, lesbian feminist, or Italian socialist would be, as you can imagine, very different. Parsons's account excludes a multitude of other possible perspectives. For example, I can imagine a Latin American asking why Parsons's account neglects the role of colonialism and does not make the rise of a world economic system into the key social drama. An Afrocentrist might wonder why the path of "civilization" shifts from Egypt to Europe and the United States, rather than to Africa. A gay American man might ask why Parsons's narrative of social progress fails to mention changes in sexual meanings, identities, roles, and conflicts. My point should be obvious. Accounts of the social world, no matter how much they are animated by a sincere desire for truth, are never more than stories we tell whose themes and meanings express the social positioning (e.g., class, gender, nationality, ideology) of the storyteller.

Parsons presents his social ideas, whether it is his theory of action, the social system, or social evolution, as science. I do not find such a description credible. Can we really take seriously the view that the social location of the social scientist does not deeply and fundamentally shape the content of her or his ideas? As sociologists, we assume that an individual's gender, class, racial, national, and historical status are directly related to that person's interests, values, thinking, and action. How can we exempt the social scientist from the very logic of social explanation that we apply to all other social actions? Through the absences and exclusions in Parsons's stories, as I briefly alluded to earlier, we become aware of its partial, parochial, and value-laden character. I interpret the social perspectives of Parsons or any social scientist as part of a struggle over social norms, policies, values, ideals, and hopes.

Insisting on the moral and ideological significance of Parsons's sociology does not mean that I wish to reduce "theory" or sociology to moral values or politics. Developing maps of the social world, perspectives on the past and present, critical understandings of social institutions or cultural configurations are, in my view, important. These are valuable efforts to understand ourselves, to defend social norms and ideals, to uncover domination and points of resistance, to guide social struggle, or to achieve a certain personal and social coherence. Sociology provides such social mappings and critical perspectives. In this regard, Parsons's social liberal perspective is a powerful framework that citizens can use to make sense of their lives, to criticize a utilitarian individualistic or socialist perspective, and so on. In fact, I am broadly sympathetic with Parsons's social and moral values. I take issue, however, with his refusal to acknowledge the value-laden, broadly ideological and political character of his sociology. By refusing to acknowledge the moral commitments and broadly ideological implications of his own sociology, Parsons avoided having to give reasons for his social liberal values and ideals. Indeed, by framing his arguments as "scientific sociology," he denied the moral and political impulse and meaning of his work. This is a serious failure. It removes the realm of values, social norms, and ideals from the arena of public debate and argumentation, a rather regrettable lapse for this heir to the Enlightenment.

There is an ironic aspect to Parsons's work, as there is, sad to say, with much sociology. Parsons's sociology was responding to what he perceived as a crisis of Western liberal civilization. The Great Depression, the rise of fascism, and the communist threat greatly weakened the legitimacy of a liberal social ideal. Parsons wished to provide a defense of liberalism against apologists for individualism and advocates of socialism. Sociology was to be the vehicle to give public voice to a reconstructed social liberalism. Parsons thought that only a truly scientific sociology could achieve the degree of objectivity and public authority that could give his social vision credibility and moral force. Accordingly, Parsons in effect buried his moral and political values in obscure analytical or theoretical arguments about social action, systems, and evolution. The sublimation of Parsons's moral and political vision into a scientific system of sociology, however, has had the effect of publicly obscuring his social values. By concealing his values and political advocacy in a theoretical brilliance, Parsons not only effectively undermined the social force of his moral vision but contributed to the very relativism and enfeeblement of reason that he deeply feared.

Science meant a lot to Parsons. He was appalled by relativism. In the context of serious challenges to the American liberal ideal, Parsons wished to find in a scientific sociology a defense of a social liberal American ideal. In the face of the Russian Revolution, the Great Depression, the rise of fascism, Parsons looked, understandably, to a standpoint of certainty. He saw in the work of Durkheim and Weber an emerging science of society that simultaneously rejected both Marxism and utilitarian individualism. Parsons canonized Weber and Durkheim as *the* classical tradition of scientific sociology.

He attempted a grand scientific synthesis, one that would provide the foundation for a social liberal ideal. Parsons may have been a great sociologist; I won't dispute this. However, it is telling that Parsons is not considered a great American social thinker, a public intellectual, say, in the class of a Thorstein Veblen, John Dewey, or C.W. Mills. No doubt there are complex reasons for this. My own explanation is that Parsons was simply unable to articulate his social vision in a language that could speak, powerfully and compellingly, to a broad social public. His vision of a scientific sociology forced him to conceal his values, to retreat into an overdetermined theoretical language that speaks only to a narrow expert culture. How sad that perhaps America's greatest sociologist, an unquestionably towering social mind, was pushed into social obscurity by the very discipline that he hoped would contribute to revitalizing a vigorous social liberal future.

References

1. Henry Hughes, *A Treatise on Sociology, Theoretical and Practical* (New York: Greenwood Press, 1968 [1854]); George Fitzhugh, *Sociology for the South* (Richmond, Va.: A. Morris. Reprinted in Wish, ed. 1960 [1854]).

2. William Graham Sumner, *What Social Classes Owe to Each Other* (New York: Harper & Brothers, 1969 [1883]); Albion Small, *General Sociology: An Exploration of the Main Developments in Sociological Theory from Spencer to Ratzenhofer* (Chicago: University of Chicago Press, 1905); Franklin Henry Giddings, *The Principles of Sociology* (New York: Johnson Reprint Corp., 1970 [1896]); Lester Ward, *Dynamic Sociology, or Applied Social Science as Based upon Statistical Sociology and the Less Complex Sciences* (New York: Johnson Reprint Corp., 1968 [1883]).

3. Max Eastman, editor, *Liberator* (New York: The Liberation Publishing Co., 1918–1924); Floyd Dell, *Love in the Machine Age* (New York: Octagon Books, 1930); Emma Goldman, *The Traffic in Women and Other Essays in Feminism* (New York: Times Change, 1970); Margaret Sanger, *Women and the New Race* (New York: Brentano, 1920).

4. W.E.B. Du Bois, *The Philadelphia Negro* (New York: Benjamin Blom, 1967 [1899] and *The Souls of Black Folk* (Chicago: A.C. McClurg, 1903).

5. Charlotte Perkins Gilman, *Women and Economics* (New York: Harper, 1966 [1898]); *The Man-Made World, or Our Androcentric Culture* (New York: Johnson Reprint, 1971 [1911]).

6. Albion Small and George Vincent, *An Introduction to the Study of Society* (New York: American Book Co., 1894).

7. Talcott Parsons, *The Structure of Social Action: A Study in Social Theory with Special Reference to a Group of Recent European Writers* (New York: Free Press, 1968 [1937]).

8. Parsons, *The Structure of Social Action*, pp. 719–720.

9. Many of his early empirical sociology is collected in Talcott Parsons, *Essays in Sociological Theory* (New York: Free Press, 1954).

10. Talcott Parsons, *The Social System* (Glencoe, IL: Free Press, 1951).

11. Talcott Parsons, *Social Systems and the Evolution of Action Theory* (New York: Free Press, 1977).

12. Talcott Parsons, *Societies: Evolutionary and Comparative Perspectives* (Englewood Cliffs, NJ: Prentice-Hall, 1966).

13. Talcott Parsons, *The System of Modern Societies* (Englewood Cliffs, NJ: Prentice-Hall, 1971).

14. Parsons, *The System of Modern Societies*, p. 114.

15. Talcott Parsons, *Action Theory and the Human Condition* (New York: Free Press, 1978).

16. Alvin Gouldner, *The Coming Crisis of Western Sociology* (New York: Basic Books, 1970).

17. Jeffrey Alexander, *Theoretical Logic in Sociology*, Vols. 1–4 (Berkeley, CA.: University of California Press, 1982–1983); Niklas Luhmann, *The Differentiation of Society* (New York: Columbia University Press, 1981); Richard Münch, *Theory of Action* (New York: Routledge, 1987).

4

The Triumph of Scientific Theory: Postwar American Sociological Theory and the Abandonment of Public Enlightenment

P arsons's *Structure of Social Action* had virtually no impact on American sociology in the interwar years. By the postwar period, however, Parsons had achieved an unprecedented level of authority in American sociology. It was the functionalist vision of *The Social System* that won out in American sociology. By the 1950s, Parsons's abstract language of social systems had been translated into an impressive research program that was used to study everything from industrialization to the race problem and family dynamics. Parsonian functionalism had achieved such disciplinary dominance that Kingsley Davis, in a 1959 American Sociological Association Presidential address, could announce, somewhat tongue in cheek, that functionalist analysis and sociology were one and the same.

The immediate postwar American setting provided the context for the ascendance of functionalism. The defeat of fascism unleashed a wave of national pride, reinforcing Americans' belief in their nation's manifest destiny. This nationalism did not, however, evolve into an active internationalist agenda. Americans returned from the war longing for stability and the good life; they turned to personal, domestic, and career concerns for self-fulfillment. The economic prosperity of the 1950s made this culture of self-realization and domesticity possible. Indeed, the defeat of fascism, the economic boom, and a redistributive welfare system that lessened inequalities produced a widespread national feeling that America was entering a new era of peace and democracy. American's social optimism received intellectual expression in the proliferation of theories that asserted that the great divide between capitalism and socialism was giving way to a new convergence on an "industrial society." Radical ideologies and political movements, such as fascism or revolutionary socialism, were expected to pass into problem-solving, reform politics. Parsons's image of society as an integrated system immune to abrupt changes and internal chaos expressed the sentiments of many Americans weary of conflict and change.

Underlying the surface of social complacency in the immediate postwar years were pervasive social discontents. While some intellectuals viewed the cold war as a passing phase prefiguring a new postindustrial society, others saw in it the possibility of another, even more horrific, holocaust. Although class conflicts seemed to subside due, in part, to economic prosperity and redistributive welfare and tax legislation, new sites of conflict around race, gender, and sexuality surfaced in the fifties. The civil rights movement, the youth culture, and the women's and gay movements originated in the discontents of the 1950s. Moreover, if national tensions were muted, international conflicts were not. Nationalist movements in Africa, Cuba, Latin America, and Asia opposing Western colonialism forced their way into national awareness. In these domestic and international events were the seeds of cultural rebellion against Parsonian functionalism.

No sooner had functionalism triumphed in sociology than a multifaceted assault began in the 1950s. Critics attacked the core of the Parsonian social image: the notion of society as a self-regulating, internally harmonious, functionally integrated system. Functionalists' lack of attention to social conflict and power were criticized. Parsons's formal conceptual edifice was dismissed as out of touch with social realities. Although American sociologists such as C. Wright Mills, George Homans, and Herbert Blumer were aggressive critics of Parsons, those who proved most influential in terms of the development of mainstream sociology in the late 1950s and early 1960s were European critics such as Lewis Coser (Germany), Ralf Dahrendorf (Germany), and Peter Berger (Austria) [1]. Curiously, though these critics drew from their European heritage to contest Parsonianism, it was in the United States that their ideals had the greatest impact. Indeed, all of these critics immigrated, at some point, to the United States. Like their American-born counterparts (e.g., C.W. Mills or Homans), these European-based sociologists criticized Parsonianism in the context of developing alternative sociological theories.

The new "realism" in sociology: conflict and change in the sociological theory of Ralf Dahrendorf, Peter Berger, and Thomas Luckmann

The challenge to Parsons focused on criticizing his structural-functionalist conceptual strategy. Critics contested his preoccupation with order, integration, and evolutionary change. They did not dispute the scientific vision that inspired Parsons. Although they wished to redirect theory in a more empirical and problem-oriented direction, they did not question Parsons's commitment to theory as an autonomous, value-neutral activity. Similarly, while they challenged Parsons's particular choice of concepts and explanatory models, they did not dispute the role of theory as foundational or as providing the basic premises and concepts that could unify sociology. They wished to preserve a vision of sociology as scientific and as an instrument of social progress. However, the experience of fascism and communism made many critics of functionalism skeptical of wholistic, excessively rationalistic grand theories. Prominent among these anti-Parsonian efforts in the immediate postwar years were Ralf Dahrendorf's *Class and Class Conflict in Industrial Society* and Peter Berger's and Thomas Luckmann's *The Social Construction of Reality* [2].

Ralf Dahrendorf

Ralf Dahrendorf came of age in the declining years of Nazi Germany. His sociological perspective was formed in response to both his exposure to Nazism and Soviet communism. Despite Germany's commitment to democratic reconstruction in the postwar years, its link to liberal and democratic values was weak and precarious. As someone who experienced firsthand the horrors of Nazi Germany – Dahrendorf was sent to a concentration camp – and who was disillusioned with Marxism after learning of the horrors of Stalinism, Dahrendorf translated his opposition to social and political authoritarianism into a liberal pluralistic scientific vision.

Dahrendorf's formative experience under Nazi Germany and his exposure to Soviet communism made him skeptical towards radical ideologies. Both Nazism and communism promised a new humanity and a new world order. They were examples of what Dahrendorf called utopian thinking. Utopianism was characterized by social visions that assume a level of social harmony and moral consensus that renders conflict and change "abnormal" or "deviant." Utopias promote, often unwittingly, a hostile attitude towards individualism, pluralism, and change. Like many of his contemporaries, sociologists such as Seymour Martin Lipset, Raymond Aron, and Daniel Bell, Dahrendorf looked to sociology to construct and legitimate an anti-utopian, liberal social ideal [3].

Dahrendorf's conflict theory was articulated in the context of a "positive critique" of Marxism and functionalism, both of which were accused of utopianism. A large portion of Dahrendorf's major book, *Class and Class Conflict in Industrial Society*, criticizes Marxism. He disputes the central Marxian claim that social dynamics and conflicts can be explained by grasping the underlying social class structure which, in turn, is anchored in dichotomous property relations. Dahrendorf questions the importance of property relations in today's industrial societies. The Marxian model is less compelling in light of the proliferation of joint stock companies and the separation of ownership and management in the West. The rise of state bureaucratic regimes in East Europe and the Soviet Union in which authority derives from political status (i.e., party position) likewise weakens Marxism. Dahrendorf disputes the Marxian dichotomous class model by referring to the social prominence of white collar workers in industrializing nations who are neither reducible to the "proletariat" nor the business-owning capitalist class. In this regard, Dahrendorf dismisses the Marxian prophecy that capitalist societies will evolve into a state of class polarization and civil war. "None of Marx's hopes . . . has been refuted more dramatically in social development than his prediction that the class situations of bourgeoisie and proletariat would tend toward extremes of wealth and poverty, possession and depravity. . . . The remarkable spread of social equality in the past century has rendered class struggle and revolutionary changes utterly impossible" [4]. Dahrendorf dismisses the Marxist opposition of capitalism and socialism in favor of an image of history as converging towards a liberal industrial society.

Dahrendorf rejected Marxism as a political ideology and social vision. He valued, though, its image of society as organized by power relations between social groups or classes. Drawing on the Marxian conflict image of society, Dahrendorf confronted Parsonian functionalism. Describing functionalism as an approach to society as a stable, functionally integrated social system, he took issue with its preoccupation with order and social utility; he criticized its neglect of social conflict, power struggles, and change. Dahrendorf argued that, to the extent that Parsons places society outside history and minimizes social conflict and coercion, his functionalist sociology promotes a utopian social vision.

In *Class and Class Conflict in Industrial Society*, Dahrendorf attempted to stake out a conceptual space between Marxism and functionalism. He wished to combine the Marxian emphasis on social conflict and change with the Parsonian understanding of processes of social integration. He designated this conceptual space "conflict theory." Although he described the "coercion paradigm" as needing to be complemented by the functionalist "consensus paradigm," Dahrendorf framed conflict theory as an effort to clarify the elementary grounds of social life, to state a vocabulary of the social that mirrors social reality.

The central premises of conflict theory are virtually the opposite of functionalism: the ubiquity of social conflict, coercion, and change. Elaborating these premises as social categories and explanatory principles, Dahrendorf offered a liberal social perspective. Society is conceived as consisting of a plurality of social institutions and social conflicts. No one institution (e.g., economy, state, or family) has the power to shape the entire society, nor is any one type of social conflict (e.g., class or ethnic conflict) primary in determining the dynamics of order and change for the whole society.

The basic social unit is what Dahrendorf called "imperatively coordinated associations." This refers to any organization (religous, economic, political) composed of social roles organized in hierarchal relations of domination and subordination. Simply put, organizations differentiate social roles by function and authority; specific roles (e.g., professor, manager, corporate executive), give to some individuals institutional power over individuals in subordinate roles (e.g., secretary, laborer, salesperson). Dahrendorf argued that individuals who share similar positions of institutional authority (lack or possess power) share common social interests. As individuals become aware of their common interests and struggle to promote them, they function as a "social class." Class conflict ensues in specific organizations as a struggle over maintaining or reorganizing the distribution of authority and social rewards.

Departing from the Marxist idea of a society divided into two hostile, economically based classes, Dahrendorf viewed class conflicts as anchored in dichotomous authority relations in specific organizations. Moreover, Dahrendorf did not assume that dominance in one social organization implies dominance in any other. "There are a large number of imperatively coordinated associations in any given society. Within every one of them we can distinguish the aggregates of those who dominate and those who are subjected. But since domination in industry does not necessarily involve domination in the state, or a church, or other associations, total societies can present the picture of a plurality of competing dominance (and, conversely subjected) aggregates [i.e., groups] [5]. For example, property ownership may confer authority in economic organizations while educational achievement anchors authority in the university. Moreover, property owners may have authority in industrial organizations but be in a subordinate position in the university where cultural credentials confer status. Thus, Dahrendorf rejected the Marxian idea that individuals can be uniquely placed in a dichotomous class system. He disputed the Marxist view of society as class war.

Major portions of *Class and Class Conflict in Industrial Society* examine the conditions under which common interests and social classes emerge, the social characteristics of dominant social classes, the factors affecting the character of class conflict, especially the likelihood of violence, the relations between classes in different institutional sectors, and the social consequences of class conflict. The details of Dahrendorf's conflict theory are less important than the driving impulse: to offer a liberal pluralistic vision of society as an alternative to the utopian social images of Marxism and functionalism.

Conflict theory was intended to be an alternative to Marxism. It incorporates the insights of Marxism – the ubiquity of conflict and change – but aims to avoid its utopianism and political extremism. By proposing a pluralistic model of classes and class conflict, Dahrendorf believed that his sociological perspective was more realistic. However, I do not believe that Dahrendorf's conflict theory avoids utopianism. Instead, he is committed to his own liberal social utopia. Dahrendorf's utopianism lies in the hope that social pluralism can yield civic and moral harmony, that the plurality of power struggles won't wrench society apart or produce a new leviathan. In a word, Dahrendorf's utopianism is revealed in the claim that power is at the core of society yet social harmony can be based on something other than coercion and domination. His utopianism lies in the hope that modern societies have moved beyond polarizing ideological divisions that incite movements of radical change. Darhendorf's utopianism is that of a liberal weary of the unexpected turns of history but who, in the end, surrenders to a utopia of the present.

Dahrendorf imagined conflict theory as a complement and completion of functionalism. The "coercion paradigm" and the "order paradigm" are approached as two sides of social reality. Dahrendorf's theorizing is inspired by the utopian hope that the eventual unification of conflict theory and functionalism will create an integrated conceptual framework for sociology. Unfortunately, he did not say just how these two sets of antithetical premises can be consistently integrated; he did not explain what such a unified sociological theory would look like or why he thought it to be possible or desirable. Despite his critical engagement of Marxism and functionalism, Dahrendorf never questioned their, or his own, scientific vision. "I cannot see why it should not be at least desirable to try to free sociology of the double fetters of an idiographic historical and a meta-empirical philosophical orientation and weld it into an exact social science with precisely – ideally, of course, mathematically – formulated postulates, theoretical models, and testable laws. The attempt must be made; and although the present study [*Class and Class Conflict in Industrial Society*] remains far removed from its satisfactory completion, I want it to be understood in terms of such an attempt" [6]. Dahrendorf did not bring to his own theorizing a reflexivity that might have clarified the moral hope that animated his own scientific vision.

In the early postwar years, conflict theory emerged as an important alternative to the dominance of functionalism in the United States and Marxism in Europe. Conflict theory was a European response to the theoretical and political disillusionment with Marxism and the world ascendance of American sociology. Parsonian functionalism was challenged in the United States by, among others, George Homans, whose ideas he framed under the rubric of "exchange theory," and Herbert Blumer who codified "symbolic interactionism." However, to the extent that American critics of

Parsons did not have to engage Marxism simultaneously – because its presence was so feeble in America – they gravitated towards a microsociological theory. Thus, Homans sought to ground exchange theory in a behavioristic psychology [7]; Blumer focused on the interpretive construction of reality [8]; and Garfinkel was preoccupied with the microinteractive conditions of social order [9]. Because European sociologists engaged Parsons in the context of the presence of Marxism, their theorizing remained centered on grasping institutional dynamics. In this regard, the synthesis of phenomenology and classical sociology by Peter Berger (born in Austria) and Thomas Luckmann (Germany) stands out as one of the few efforts at the time to offer an alternative to both functionalism and Marxism that incorporates the American focus on microsocial dynamics with the European emphasis on institutional dynamics. Even more than the conflict theory of Dahrendorf, Berger and Luckmann's theoretical synthesis was a challenge to Parsons because they proposed an equally grand theory. However, like Dahrendorf and other critics in the mainstream of sociology, Berger and Luckmann never contested the scientific vision; they defended a strong notion of the autonomy of theory.

Peter Berger and Thomas Luckmann

Berger and Luckmann shared with conflict theorists a disillusionment with the excessively rationalistic views of society and history espoused by Marxism and functionalism. They took issue with images of society as an organic or mechanistic system. Society was rendered so orderly and integrated in such theories that individual freedom disappeared. Despite their substantial differences, Marxism and functionalism conceptualized society as if governed by impersonal social forces. The individual was replaced by the mode of production or functional imperatives as the real social forces. Berger and Luckmann criticized this image of history as beyond individual control. Despite their wish for a society that valued individualism and autonomy, the organismic and mechanistic social imagery of Marx and Parsons devalued, if not excluded, individual agents as a social force. The irony of Marxism and functionalism was that, though their social ideas were inspired by the high ideals of the Enlightenment, their social theories sketched a process of social evolution in which individual choice counted for very little. Berger and Luckmann were convinced that something had gone terribly wrong when Enlightenment ideals promote, even if unintentionally, an antihumanistic social philosophy.

Berger and Luckmann wished to bring real living, acting individuals back into the center of sociological theory. They aimed to replace organismic and mechanistic social imagery with a view of society as a precariously negotiated, fluid order that ultimately resides in the interactions of individuals. The very title of their major work, *The Social Construction of Reality*, underscored the power of the individual to shape society and the open-ended character of history [10]. Paralleling the shift to a more individualistic and dynamic view of social realities in symbolic interactionism and conflict theory, Berger and Luckmann approached social life as produced and reproduced in individual interaction. They sought to recover the "voluntaristic" dimension of social life that was integral to the early works of Marx and Parsons but was submerged in their later, more social deterministic, perspectives.

The subtitle of *The Social Construction of Reality, A Treatise in the Sociology of Knowledge*, signals the unique approach of the authors. The sociology of knowledge was at the time defined as an inquiry into the social origin and function of ideas, in particular religion, theoretical ideas, and political ideologies. Instead of describing ideas as pure expressions of reason, they were understood as wedded to social interests and conflicts, for example, as instruments of class domination. Berger and Luckmann aimed to redefine the sociology of knowledge. Instead of a specialized study of the social role of ideologies, they proposed that it become an inquiry into the ways in which everyday ideas about reality are created and maintained. They reasoned that cultural elites are not alone in defining what is real; ordinary individuals have ideas or produce bodies of knowledge that define reality. The sociology of knowledge should be centered on understanding the way that everyday realities are socially constructed. It was Berger and Luckmann's aim to make the sociology of knowledge into a general sociological theory focused on the everyday social construction of reality.

Berger and Luckmann proposed a dramatic departure from Marxism and functionalism. Unlike Marx who described the social world as produced through labor and class struggle or Parsons who imagined society as a system governed by functional prerequisites, Berger and Luckmann perceived society as a cultural, symbolic construction. Society is neither a system, a mechanism, nor an organic form; it is a symbolic construct or a mindful artifice composed of ideas, meanings, and language. Here is one formulation of their outlook: "Human existence is . . . an ongoing externalization. As man externalizes himself, he constructs the world. . . . In the process of externalization, he projects his own meanings into reality. Symbolic universes, which proclaim that *all* reality is humanly meaningful and call upon the *entire* cosmos to signify the validity of human existence, constitute the farthest reaches of this projection" [11]. Their underlying premise is that ideas about society, including ordinary bodies of knowledge (e.g., proverbs, stereotypes, shared expectations, folk wisdom), are the very stuff of the social world. For Berger and Luckmann, society is a fluid, precarious, negotiated field of loosely connected activities. It is held together, ultimately, by the thin threads of shared understandings and a common language.

Berger and Luckmann set themselves two tasks. First, they would specify the main premises and concepts that clarify the nature of everyday life. Drawing from the phenomenological philosophy of Edmund Husserl and Alfred Schutz, they introduced a range of foundational concepts such as intentional consciousness, multiple realities, the practical attitude, intersubjectivity, and so on. I will not review this aspect of their work, except to say that their intent was to frame everyday life as a fluid, multiple, precariously negotiated achievement of individuals in interaction. Their second and chief aim was to offer a general theory of the social origins and maintenence of social institutions. Their principal thesis was that individuals in interaction create social worlds through their linguistic, symbolic activity for the purpose of giving coherence and purpose to an essentially open-ended, unformed human existence.

Berger and Luckmann's sociological theory synthesized the existential philosophy that was popular at the time and the classical sociological tradition. From the former, they argued that people construct social worlds to give order and meaning to their lives in the face of an awareness of the ultimate meaninglessness of existence in a post-Christian world. The threat of metaphysical anguish never entirely disappears since the social worlds we create are fragile and events threaten to reveal the chaos and meaningless that lurk below a surface of order and purpose. Drawing on classical sociological themes, Berger and Luckmann argued that the social worlds we create always threaten to dominate us. These grand themes are worked into a sociological theory of social institutions.

Social institutions have their origin in individual interaction. Berger and Luckmann described the origin of social institutions as a process of externalization. In *The Sacred Canopy: Elements of a Sociological Theory of Religion*, Peter Berger outlined this process as follows:

> The fundamental dialectic process of society consists of three moments, or steps. These are externalization, objectivation, and internalization. . . . Externalization is the ongoing outpouring of human being into the world, both in the physical and the mental activity of men. Objectivation is the attainment by the products of this activity . . . of a reality that confronts its original producers as a facticity external to and other than themselves. Internalization is the reappropriation by men of this same reality, transforming it once again from structures of the objective world into structures of the subjective consciousness. It is through externalization that society is a human product. It is

through objectivation that society becomes a reality sui generis. It is through internalization that man is a product of society [12].

Human neediness propels individuals into social interaction; recurring social exchanges give rise to patterns of expectations and social norms. Social institutions are little more than recurring patterns of interaction anchored in shared understandings and expectations. Curiously, their argument is decidedly functionalist. Social institutions are functional in that they fix needs, provide a predictable, orderly setting for behavior, and give coherence and purpose to human life.

Following Marx, Berger and Luckmann maintained that humans make their own nature through their social practices. The plastic, open-ended character of human nature is given form and purpose by social processes. Institutions are not necessarily forces of domination but are functional. However, we can become alienated from the social worlds that we create. Alienation is not, as in Marx, a condition of humankind dominated by a real world of objects (e.g., commodities); rather, it appears as an almost natural, inevitable property of the social worlds that we create to take on an objectlike character. Berger and Luckmann refer to a process of objectivation. The origin of institutions as an ongoing negotiated achievement between individuals is, so to speak, forgotten as the social world is experienced as an objectively coherent order. Alienation or what Berger and Luckmann called reification occurs when the institutional order is assumed to have taken on a life of its own independently of human intentions and needs; society is perceived as controlling human behavior. In part, reification appears as an inevitable result of generational dynamics. As a new generation is socialized into a preexisting, taken-for-granted social order, it is experienced as natural. Socialization is described as the process by which the objective world of social institutions is made into the paramount subjective reality. In effect, the socially produced institutional world is internalized by the individual as an objective, natural order.

Paralleling the Marxian dialectic, Berger and Luckmann maintained that reification is never completely successful. Humans reclaim their social creations and themselves as active, creative agents. Between generations, there are different experiences, values, and hopes. Generational discord results in challenges by the younger cohort to the legitimacy and necessity of the existing institutional order. Moreover, routine social events (e.g., intersocietal contacts, social conflicts, illness, and death) disrupt the natural, taken-for-granted character of the institutional order. Social order is always precarious; the merely contingent human origin of social worlds threatens to break through the illusion of its naturalness and objectivity. This, in turn, threatens to confront us with the chaotic and meaningless nature of human existence, an awareness that could undermine social authority and incite social disorder.

The susceptibility to disruption of the social worlds we make calls forth fortifying strategies. Although Berger and Luckmann mentioned coercive means to maintain social order, their focus is on what they call legitimations. In the face of events that threaten to render our social experience fragile and purposeless, individuals react, driven by seemingly unconsciously felt social and personal needs for order and meaning, by developing symbolic systems. Their purpose is to reassert the objectivity of social institutions. This is accomplished by viewing the social order as part of a more encompassing suprahuman order of nature or the divine. Social institutions are granted authority not by mere human will but by divine decree, natural law, or historical destiny. Religion, philosophy, myth, and science have been the chief symbolic strategies of social legitimation. Their aim is to reestablish the perception of the social world as an objective order that can ground our subjective experience as orderly, coherent, and purposeful. Of course, legitimations may be questioned. In fact, Berger and Luckmann believe that, in contemporary Western pluralistic societies, legitimations are perpetually contested. It is precisely modern Western experiences of perpetual epistemological uncertainty, experiences that generate relativism and subjectivism, that have made possible insights into the social construction of reality. Where once legitimations were understood as statements of social reality to be accepted at face value, today we view them as interpretations subject to contestation and social conflict. In the modern world, the conflict of interpretations is unavoidable and is interpreted as a conflict over the will to power.

Berger and Luckmann shared Parsons's vision of sociological theory. They sought to uncover the universal features of social life, to offer a set of premises, concepts, and explanatory schemas that could account for social life – anywhere and anytime. Aspiring to such global theoretical ambitions, they described social life as both an objective order and a subjectively meaningful experience. They produced a grand theory of the social origin, structure, and change of institutions.

No less than Parsons or Dahrendorf, a moral impulse and vision lay at the heart of Berger and Luckmann's theoretical effort. Like their sociological colleagues, their work was camouflaged by the language of science, cleansed of explicit moral judgment. Berger and Luckmann fashioned a liberal, fiercely antiutopian, moral vision forged against the dark history of Nazi Germany. Its liberalism is that of a commitment to the value of the individual as an active, creative force and to the value of diverse, multiple social worlds. It is a cautious and guarded liberalism. Institutions must carry sufficient authority to prevent individualism from deteriorating into chaos and anarchy. Berger and Luckmann were all too aware of the dark forces that lie in our hearts. Institutions must serve as a check and control when these passions are incited. Antiutopianism is at the core of their theoretical synthesis: While humans make and remake themselves and their social worlds, the social order needs to have a solidity and forcefulness, however illusory, to constrain the modern temptation to seek social transcendence. Against all utopian impulses, Berger and Luckmann underscored the dangers of viewing institutions as simply domination and the will to a freedom without institutional constraint; this hubris throws open the floodgate of dangerous passions. Like many liberals living in the shadow of fascism, Berger and Luckmann no longer put their faith in a self-regulating human will or reason; in a post-Christian world, only social authorities have the power to control human passions or channel aggressivity in socially beneficial ways. In the absence of the possibility of a religiously based social order, they pinned their hopes on society to maintain the fragile balance between freedom and moral order.

The flight from public life in the 1970s: the natural scientific ideal of Randall Collins and Peter Blau

The struggle over functionalism was more or less over by the late 1960s, even though the polemics continued into the 1970s. So thoroughly repressed was functionalism that I recall little discussion, none positive, of Parsons in my undergraduate and graduate courses through the 1970s. In place of functionalist dominance came the era of the warring schools. Theorists stepped forward, claiming for their particular theoretical synthesis (e.g., conflict theory, exchange theory, symbolic interactionism, ethnomethodology, phenomenological sociology, Marxism) the successor status to functionalism.

The era of warring schools reflected the state of America. The United States was racked by social conflict: young against old, Black against White, gay against straight, women against men, peace advocates and Vietnam war protesters against the political and military establishment. The movements linked to Black, gay, and women's liberation, to student and youth rebellion, challenged America's basic institutions. New voices of social thought and criticism were being heard – feminist, gay and lesbian, Latino, and African-American. Simultaneously, radical perspectives of social criticism drawn from European neo-Marxism (e.g., the Frankfurt school, structural Marxism) were making an impact, particularly among young sociologists who sought a sophisticated language of social criticism.

Mainstream sociology was not immune to these critical voices. For example, neo-Marxism, feminism, radical sociology, and dependency theory became new, even if peripheral, forces in sociology in the 1970s. Moreover, social conflicts of the period made their way into mainstream sociological theory through the incorporation of the themes of conflict, power, diversity, and inequality. However, instead of mainstream sociological theory turning outward to engage public life, it turned inward to focus on the making of scientific knowledge. While some sociological theorists took over the humanistic, critical impulse of the times, many reacted against this politicization and embraced a narrow model of scientific theory. These scientific theorists viewed theory as a body of knowledge that could be put in the service of empirical research. The hope was that a close link between theory and research would result in the "takeoff" of sociology as a truly scientific discipline. Scientific theorists urged abandoning the grand, overarching theories of their predecessors in favor of more narrowly empirical and explanatory theories. Two sociologists whose theories exemplify this flight from the public world while absorbing some of the moral themes of the era are Randall Collins and Peter Blau.

Randall Collins

Taking his doctorate in Berkeley in the late 1960s, Randall Collins translated the spirit of the period into a no-nonsense scientific theory that he has called "conflict theory." In his major work, *Conflict Sociology: Towards an Explanatory Science*, Collins locates his own theoretical efforts in critical relation to the state of the discipline and of theory [13]. The discipline, thought Collins, is doing well; sociological research has accumulated an impressive body of knowledge. However, sociology's achievements have not been widely recognized by the public nor by many sociologists. One reason is that sociological research is dispersed across various specialty fields (e.g., crime, organization, social psychology, medical, family); few sociologists have sought conceptual integration. Collins was especially critical of sociological theorists whose grand humanistic aspirations have left them either indifferent to, or ignorant of, sociological research. The result is an uncoupling of theory from research, to the detriment of both. Collins aimed to reconnect theory and research by bringing sociological theory into the scientific era. His hope was that conflict theory could be the vehicle to fulfill the promise of sociology to become a true science of society.

Conflict sociology aspires to be a genuine science. The essence of science, in Collins's view, is to explain empirical reality. Not all types of explanations count as science; only those that account for variations in

social behavior across space and time and take the form of general principles or social laws are truly scientific.

> The scientific ideal is to explain everything, and to do it by making causal
> statements which are ultimately based upon experience. . . . Science is a way
> of finding the common principles that transcend particular situations, of
> extrapolating from things we know to things we do not, as a way of seeing
> the novel as another arrangement of the familiar.
>   This aim is no different when applied to sociology than to physics [14].

Science must rely on painstaking empirical research, especially comparative research that permits the development of general explanations about
social behavior. Drawing on available empirical work, Collins's *Conflict
Sociology* proposed hundreds of general explanatory principles.

Collins's hopes for conflict theory were not modest. He aimed to convince the sociological community that it is the only basis for a science of
society. His immodesty is not peculiar among theorists. I would be hard
pressed to think of any modern social theorist – from Condorcet, Comte,
Marx, and Durkheim to Parsons, Dahrendorf, and Coleman – who has not
claimed for his or her theory a breakthrough to a true science. Theorists
compete for the privilege of declaring themselves the Newton of the social
sciences.

The claim to the mantle of science for conflict theory rests, however, on
exceedingly fragile foundations. Collins rests his case for conflict theory on
dubious, largely rhetorical, appeals to realism. For example, he proposes
that social structure be conceptualized as recurring patterns of individual
interaction, rather than as a reality sui generis. Collins might have justified
this approach on the grounds that it opens up new possibilities for research
or resolves certain conceptual problems or encourages liberal social values.
Instead he offered an epistemological justification: The individualistic
approach is claimed to be true in the sense of mirroring social reality.
Collins appealed to commonsense knowledge that only individuals exist
and that conflict is the real stuff of social life. "I believe that the only viable
path to a comprehensive explanatory sociology is a conflict perspective. . . . [It] grounds explanations in real people pursuing real interests. . . ."[15]. Conflict theory is recommended because its premises are
said to be truly nonideological or to correspond to reality as we ordinarily
observe and know it. This is hardly credible in light of critiques of epistemological realism. How do we know that only individuals in a state of
conflict exist? Is it not the case that how we know reality depends on the
concepts and broader perspectives that structure perceptions and understandings? Is the "individual" merely the "body," or does this concept imply

thinking, feeling, and behavioral practices? Are not the thoughts and feelings of an "individual" derived from "society"? If, as most sociologists concede, individuals are penetrated by society in the sense of internalizing social beliefs and values, the distinction between the individual and society would seem to be an analytical one, i.e., perhaps useful for certain reasons but not necessarily mirroring reality.

Collins's distaste for the kind of philosophical reasoning that his claims for conflict theory seem to demand does not mean that his proposal does not merit serious consideration. His strongest defense of conflict theory centers on his assertions of its explanatory power and scope. Collins's hope was that conflict theory would organize empirical research into a coherent body of scientifically valid knowledge.

Conflict Sociology begins with the premise that social life consists of individuals who are motivated to satisfy their own needs and wants. Individuals will use whatever material (e.g., wealth or physical strength) and cultural (e.g., education or verbal skills) resources are available to secure their goals. Moreover, individuals always pursue their self-interest in social encounters in which there is an unequal distribution of resources, i.e., individuals have more or less physical strength, attractiveness, wealth, education, or occupational prestige. Insofar as the desired goods (e.g., wealth, deference, and power) are scarce relative to demand, and assuming that individuals will use their available and unequal resources to achieve their goals, all social encounters will involve conflict and be structured by relations of domination and subordination. The institutional and cultural structure of a society will reflect its system of stratification, i.e., who possesses and lacks power.

Social life is viewed as an arena of struggle and conflict.

> For conflict theory, the basic insight is that human beings are sociable but conflict-prone animals. Why is there conflict? Above all else, there is conflict because violent coercion is always a potential resource. . . . What we do know firmly is that being coerced is an intrinsically unpleasant experience, and hence . . . calls forth conflict in the form of antagonism to being dominated. Add to this the fact that coercive power, especially as represented in the state, can be used to bring one economic goods and emotional gratification – and to deny them to others – and we can see that the availability of coercion as a resource ramifies conflicts throughout the entire society [16].

In specific social encounters, individuals maneuver for advantage, manipulate their environment, deploy whatever symbolic and ideological means are available to press their social advantage, and form alliances with other individuals to gain and maintain social dominance. In this regard, Collins followed Dahrendorf's liberal conflict model, not the Marxian one. Instead of viewing the *whole society* as divided into two social classes anchored in the possession or lack of property, Collins conceived of society as exhibiting multiple, heterogeneous conflicts between groups whose individual membership may not involve significant overlap. He described social stratification as occurring along three relatively autonomous dimensions: economic or between occupational classes, cultural or between status groups, and political or between political parties. Although some individuals might be members of the "dominant" group in each of these conflicts, typically, individuals who are members of a cultural elite will not necessarily be members of the economic or political elite. Moreover, there is no necessary coherence between the social interests of elite or subject groups in these three spheres. For example, business elites may very well be at odds with cultural elites over social policy and social resources. Collins offered a Nietzschean vision of individuals struggling for power but reconfigured into an essentially individualistic liberal social image.

Collins translated his vision of social conflict into a sociological research program. He recommended that sociologists focus on the "power" factor. Conceiving power as an empirically useful variable, Collins suggested that, by analyzing the (material and cultural) resources that individuals possess, we can explain a great deal of social behavior in a range of social spheres (e.g., organizational, political, economic, familial). Collins proposed that the level of resources that individuals command – along with other secondary factors (e.g., social contacts) – directly affects the possession or lack of power which, in turn, affects social behavior and organization. The link between the level of resources and social behavior is twofold: First, differential resources confer differential power; and power has its own social effects. Second, the level of resources affects "social density" or access to social networks that have independent social effects as well as influence power positioning. In the course of applying his conflict approach to a range of empirical areas of research (e.g., organizations, social change, science, education), Collins developed a multitude of general, lawlike principles.

One empirical illustration of Collins's conflict theory is in the sphere of sexual stratification. He assumed that sexual drives are natural or biologically based and that individuals will use whatever resources available to achieve sexual gratification. Moreover, men's chief resource is said to be their natural superior physical strength, while women use their capacity to withhold sexual favors as their main bargaining advantage. Sexual relations are viewed as a sphere of power struggle.

The pattern of sexual stratification depends on two major factors: first, the degree to which the use of force in personal relations is socially regulated, and, second, the respective economic status of men and women. To the extent that there are few limits placed on the use of force, men will deploy their superior physical power to dominate women. Thus, in premodern societies where there were few constraints on the use of force in personal relations, men exercised sexual dominance. However, male dominance varied in these societies with women's economic status. As women's economic power increased, their sexual power would be enhanced, even if male physical strength secured their dominance. By the nineteenth century in the West, the use of force in personal relations lost most of its legitimacy. Men's dominance lay in their economic authority. However, women's power increased to the extent that the separation of the household and the economy encouraged an ideology of marriage as an individual choice, rather than a family decision. Women's power rested on their capacity to withhold sexual favors and to choose their own spouses. Marriage became a social exchange in which men offered security and status in exchange for women relinquishing to them exclusive sexual rights to their bodies. The rise of a marriage market encouraged men to emphasize their economic and social status assets. Maneuvering to enhance their social value, women developed the ideology of femininity (female purity and virginity) and romantic love which increased the value of women's chief asset, sexuality. To the extent that women's economic status has improved in the course of this century, the exchange system that underlay the marriage market lost social credibility. Economic equalization between the sexes, in the context of the complete delegitimation of the use of force in personal relations, brings about higher levels of gender equality in intimate matters.

Collins hoped that conflict theory would be the vehicle to transport sociological theory into the scientific age. A scientific sociology would reduce the universe to a series of general explanations and universal social laws. Theory has a pivotal role to play: it gives conceptual coherence to the impressive body of empirical research that sociologists have accumulated. Collins was convinced that conflict theory can best achieve this end.

Collins's justifications for conflict sociology (e.g., epistemological realism or methodological individualism) are, as we have seen, rather feeble. In the end, his plea for conflict theory rests on its explanatory and empirical adequacy. But here, too, Collins is on shaky ground. For example, conflict theory is recommended primarily because it "works" or is useful in explaining empirical events in a variety of specialty areas, e.g., organization, stratification, family, gender, change, and politics. Yet similar claims regarding explanatory scope are advanced by functional analysis, Marxism, exchange theory, and any number of other theoretical approaches. How do we judge the claims of competing conceptual strategies for superiority on the grounds of explanatory breadth or scope?

Collins seems to assume, moreover, that the meaning of the claim that a conceptual approach is useful or "works" in explaining empirical events is obvious. However, conceptual strategies can "work" or be useful in explaining social phenomenon in a variety of potentially conflicting ways. For example, an explanation might be useful because it permits quantification, enhances conceptual economy, maximizes contextual understanding, provides a wholistic account, opens up new avenues of research, accounts for origins or functional adaptation, or makes possible political mobilization. In other words, what we mean by an explanation being useful varies depending on our purposes and values. In order to make a credible case that any one conceptual strategy is superior to its rivals on the grounds of its explanatory superiority, it would be necessary to make a plausible case that explanatory values or goals can be prioritized. Collins would have to make the case that the explanatory values or purposes to which he is committed (e.g., scope, propositional formalism, abstractness, or generality) are superior to other explanatory values or ends (e.g., conceptual economy, quantification, contextual understanding, historical origins, narrative drama) that would make other types of conceptual explanations useful. Unfortunately, Collins does not provide arguments that might make credible his assertion of the superiority of conflict theory.

If Collins's claims for conflict sociology are on shaky epistemological grounds, and if the appeal to its explanatory power is no less flimsy, his empirical case hardly compensates. Indeed, the examples that he uses to make the case for conflict sociology are schematic and are not credible on the "evidence" alone. For example, it is not self-evident that individuals are born with a sexual nature or biologically based sexual drives. As we will see in chapters 6 and 7, many contemporary theorists argue that what is "sexual" is a social and historical product. Similarly, Collins simply assumes a natural gender order composed of "men" and "women" that operates uniformly throughout history. Yet many scholars argue that the meaning of men and women vary considerably within and between societies and that the very notion of a natural female and male is part of the social construction of gender. Again, while force and economic positioning may be important factors in explaining gender patterns, a great deal of recent research highlights the central importance of religious or scientific-medical institutions and discourses, the mass media and popular culture, and the role of the state. Unfortunately, Collins does not entertain the possibility that the premises and concepts of conflict theory may be quite arbitrary and limiting; he seems unaware that these same premises may gain their credibility as much from their cultural or ideological resonance as from their explanatory value.

Collins's effort to distinguish sociology as a science from sociology as a form of literature, philosophy, or political ideology hardly seems convincing. Moreover, we need not deny that conflict theory offers "useful" empirical or conceptual strategies while, simultaneously, asserting that it carries a broadly moral vision of society. Conflict theory articulates what in the United States is a fairly widespread public ideology: liberal utilitarianism. The language of individual self-interest, resources, competition, social networks, alliance building, symbol as instrument, and so on are deeply ingrained in American folk culture. Unfortunately, inspired by the spirit of science, Collins remains largely blinded to the moral import of his work.

Peter Blau

Blau's sociological theory is animated by the spirit of science and yet exhibits an undeniable moral vision. Even more than his predecessors and contemporaries, Blau approached sociology strictly as a science. Where Peter Berger and, more reluctantly, Randall Collins, seem willing to view sociology as part of a liberal humanistic political culture, Blau wished to establish sociology on strictly scientific grounds. Indeed, his so-called structural sociology is deliberately antihumanistic. Blau admits no role for meaning, cultural symbols, values, subjective feelings, and beliefs. He takes the scientific vision to its logical conclusion: sociology as a wholly formal, logical, quantitative approach that, in principle, excludes any humanistic residue from its basic premises, concepts, and explanations. Yet, Blau's scientific sociology reveals, centrally, a commitment to a politics of liberal individualism and pluralism.

Like many of his sociological colleagues in the 1970s, Blau reacted against the politicizing of sociology in the sixties. Perhaps his personal experience of emigrating from Austria to escape Nazism made him feel that the politicization of science and the university would promote social extremism. In any event, Blau embraced a notion of science as a strictly logical and formalistic enterprise. Ideally, science should aspire to become a system of interrelated general propositions hierarchically organized; at the base would be a limited number of "self-evident truths" or axioms, from which are derived theorems that state relationships among abstract concepts which, in turn, can be empirically tested and falsified. In a strictly axiomatic theory, every theorem is logically derived from an axiom, less abstract theorems are derived from more abstract ones, and each theorem is provisionally accepted until empirically falsified. Whether Blau's own theorizing can be called, strictly speaking axiomatic, is doubtful, but it is, unquestionably, formalistic. Blau emphasizes developing general propositions that explain empirical reality with the hope that, eventually, propositions will interrelate to form a system of social laws.

Peter Blau's *Inequality and Heterogeneity* was one of the most influential proposals for a scientific sociological theory in the 1970s [17]. Its aim was signaled in its subtitle, *A Primitive Theory of Social Structure.* Departing from standard approaches to social structure that focused on social institutions, cultural constructions, or patterns of individual interaction, Blau defined social structure as the distribution of a population among social positions. Blau's definition abstracts *entirely* from the psychology of individuals, the cultural context of interaction, and the actions of individuals or groups. He excluded any reference to psychology, culture, or history in order to propose a formalistic or, in his own words, a "primitive" theory of social structure. Underscoring the distribution of populations among social positions and its effect on social association signals Blau's intention: to offer a theory of social structure that lends itself to a highly quantitative analysis. For Peter Blau, it is a Newtonian scientific vision that seems compelling.

Inequality and Heterogeneity aimed to put sociology on the path to science. To make the case for structural sociology, Blau addressed what he considers the basic question of sociology: how to explain social order. Rejecting consensual models (order as a product of moral consensus) and coercive explanations (e.g., order as a product of class domination), Blau introduced an alternative account that emphasizes the centrality of the sheer rate of social association between social positions.

Clarifying the link between social association and social integration requires an outline of Blau's theory of social structure. Social structure is defined as the distribution of people among social positions or what Blau calls "parameters." These refer to those characteristics that a particular society uses to distinguish people from one another. In the United States, gender, age, race, and income, not eye color or feet size, are parameters. Blau distinguished two types of parameters. "Nominal parameters" divide people into subgroups with distinct boundaries, e.g., gender, religion, and age. "Graduated parameters" distinguish people by placing them in a rank order, e.g., income or education. Nominal and graduated parameters are respectively linked to two major axes of social differentiation: heterogeneity and inequality. That is, nominal parameters mark out horizontal differentiation (heterogeneity) among social positions or social groups; graduated parameters mark out a social space of vertical differentiation (inequality) between social statuses.

Blau's central thesis is that social differentiation along these two axes – heterogeneity and inequality – is a key determinant of the rate and type of social association which, in turn, directly condition whether society is integrated or divided. Simplifying his position enormously, Blau proposed that the "intersection of parameters" or high levels of heterogeneity produce high frequencies of intergroup association which promote social integration. In other words, as social positions (e.g., racial, religion, gender, income) exhibit minimal correlation, for example, gender is not highly correlated with income, prestige, or education, this condition of social heterogeneity is likely to be correlated with high rates of intergroup association and social mobility which promote social integration. Blau's reasoning is that maximizing heterogeneity results in people associating with a large number of small, open, and intersecting groups which has an integrating effect. If heterogeneity promotes integration, inequality signals a social danger. In Blau's language, the "consolidation of parameters" produces high correlations between social positions, for example, gender predicts income, education, and prestige. This heightens social inequalities which, in turn, minimize intergroup association and result in social division and conflict. In other words, if parameters cluster together, such that Whites have high income, high education, similar occupation, schooling, and residential patterns, while Blacks have low income, low education, similar occupations, schooling, and residences, there will be significantly reduced intergroup association and social mobility and heightened social inequality and conflict.

The promise of structural sociology was its claim to provide a unifying, scientific research program. In this regard, Blau spends remarkably little space engaging in argumentation with rival positions. There is virtually no effort to gain a warrant for structural sociology by appealing to the sociological classics. Similarly, despite his curious departure in theorizing social structure, he does not pause to justify his exclusion of psychology, individual agency, or culture. Apparently, Blau's primary audience was not sociological theorists but empirical researchers. The value of structural sociology lay solely in its capacity to offer empirical researchers a language and methodology to explain scientifically "the social" – anywhere and anytime. Blau's formalistic scientific sociology, with its axioms, propositions, and equations, coincided with the ascendance of a discipline-centered, specialty-focused, quantitatively oriented sociology in the 1970s.

Collins and Blau were troubled by the state of sociological theory. To the extent that theorists were preoccupied with developing grand humanistic theories or with providing justifications for conceptual strategies through textual exegesis or metatheoretical discourse, they lost touch with what most sociologists do. Blau and Collins wished to connect theory and research. This required that theory give up its humanistic legacy in favor of a natural scientific model. Instead of spinning out elaborate conceptual frameworks that resemble philosophy, political ideology, or literature, scientific theory aims to develop general explanations of empirical reality.

Both Collins's *Conflict Sociology* and Blau's *Inequality and Heterogeneity* offered literally hundreds of general explanatory propositions. It is not at all clear, however, that the mere framing of discourse in the form of general propositions amounts to science or that, if it does, it achieves what they hoped. Most of the propositions advanced by Blau and Collins are little more than empirical generalizations whose credibility rests on a set of tacit social, philosophical, moral, and ideological meanings. However, whereas a discursive theoretical approach would address these broader meanings, the formalistic approach reduces them to matters of mere empirical status. For example, Blau advanced the following proposition: "Positions of authority over many employees are the source of most authority in contemporary societies" [18]. Not only is it seriously doubtful that such a proposition can be tested, given its high level of abstraction and conceptual vagueness, but it gains its coherence only as it is embedded in a broader social discourse. The question of social authority – who has power, its source and maintenance – is inseparable from broader conceptual and ideological disputes about the structure of society, social inequality and justice, oppression, and struggles of resistance. In other words, the force of propositional claims presuppose a conceptual or discursive context in which narrow empirical statements are entangled in broader conceptual, moral, and ideological perspectives. A formalistic theorist such as Blau or Collins is unable to address this broader discursive context; they are confined to reducing conceptual, discursive disputes to narrow empirical ones.

Collins's *Conflict Sociology* was published in 1975. Curiously, his subsequent work has drawn minimally, if at all, on the hundreds of propositions he formulated in that book [19]. He has made no effort to develop his numerous propositions into anything approaching an axiomatic theory. Indeed, while his conflict theory has had impact among theorists and researchers as a conceptual strategy, his formalistic, propositional program has had none. Similarly, while Blau and some of his associates have pursued structural sociology as a conceptual and research agenda, there has been little effort to force his theorems into a systematic theoretical structure. In short, few sociologists have seriously pursued their formalistic, high-science program. In part, this may reflect the pull sociologists feel toward a more discursive approach, for reasons I indicated earlier. In part, it may be that a formalistic, propositional approach too narrowly limits sociology. If the cost of a scientific sociology is that we must give up a concern with individual psychology, culture, and history – as Blau urges – many sociologists will feel that it is too high a price to pay. If, as Blau seems to recommend, a scientific sociology requires that we must focus on those aspects of social structure that permit an exclusively formal, quantitative precision, sociologists will question the significance of a science that must disavow so much. Collins and Blau seem to want a scientific sociology that is driven by what they consider to be the logical and methodological dictates of science, without either seriously engaging critics of a natural scientific model or reflecting on what makes such knowledge valuable or important.

Whatever the scientific merits of Blau's structural sociology, it does not escape projecting moral values and a vision of the good society. *Inequality and Heterogeneity* projects a liberal, pluralistic social ideal. Horizontal differentiation or enhanced levels of heterogeneity are socially beneficial because they promote an open, mobile, individualistic society tolerant of social differences. By contrast, the major social evil is social inequality which promotes a closed, static society in which individuals are tightly controlled by large primary groups whose relation to one another exhibits in-group/out-group animosity. While inequality and heterogeneity might function, at one level, as analytical axes of social differentiation, they also mark the major axes of moral and political conflict. Indeed, read against Blau's immigration to the United States in the shadow of Nazism, it seems plausible to infer that *Inequality and Heterogeneity* is his moral and ideological coming to terms with this experience. Sociologically speaking, Nazi Germany represented an extreme form of a closed society divided by rigid in-group/out-group tensions, that is, a society characterized by the "consolidation of parameters." Blau's coming of age against the backdrop of Nazism might explain his apparent championing of extreme forms of heterogeneity. Blau's ideal seems to be a society composed of so many small intersecting social circles that this edges into a celebration of a pure individualism. Any group coherence and solidity threatens to evolve into in-group/out-group conflict, scapegoating, and political extremism. Like many European-born theorists whose coming of age was marked by Nazism, Blau's thinking reveals an antiutopianism that links science and a liberal, pluralistic social vision.

There is an irony to Blau's scientism. His liberal humanistic values are thoroughly contradicted by his scientific, structural sociology. In its structural explanations, its exclusion of individuals, subjective intentions, and history, structural sociology projects an image of society controlled by impersonal, nonrational forces, a position that, in principle, justifies an illiberal politics. Unfortunately, Blau seems unaware of how the very spirit of his sociology unwittingly promotes the very illiberal values he so detests.

The search for foundations and disciplinary unity: the canon as boundary maintenance

By the late 1970s, the social turmoil that divided America was pushed from the national public center to the social periphery. Student protests and New Left politics virtually ceased with the United States' withdrawal from Vietnam; the counterculture had been either assimilated into a commercial consumerist culture, or its critical spirit had been sublimated into Eastern religion or New Age self-fulfillment, therapeutic movements. The feminist, gay, and Black movements were under siege by a conservative backlash led by the New Right. The decline of liberal and left reform politics on the national scene led many sociologists to turn their attention and critical energies inward to their discipline.

For many sociologists, the state of the discipline left much to be desired. In particular, theorists were troubled by the conceptual and empirical fragmentation and conflict that seemed to be the legacy of the end of Parsonian ascendance. Although some sociological theorists praised sociology's seemingly permanent condition of "paradigm" conflict as a testimony to its pluralism and vitality, many were distressed by its lack of consensus on the most basic premises, concepts, explanations, and aims. A century after sociology had achieved a stable institutional academic status, its subject matter, logical structure, and purpose were still a matter of dispute.

In the depoliticized social environment of the 1980s, at least for the mostly White, middle-class, heterosexual American-born men who dominated theory circles, the turn inward often meant aspiring to end the era of warring schools. The reform spirit of many sociological theorists, which might have engaged the public world a decade before, now engaged the world of disciplinary theory struggles. Of course, many sociologists hoped that their theoretical efforts would somehow have beneficial impact beyond the academe. Appeals to the public importance of theory were not uncommon; yet they were largely rhetorical, a matter of well-intentioned, politically minded intellectuals hoping that their work was not "merely" academic.

There was, needless to say, little consensus among theorists on how to end the era of warring schools. Theorists split into two broad camps. On the one side, disciplinary integration was to be achieved through a unifying natural scientific vision. On the other side, the case for conceptual integration was made by invoking a grand humanistic scientific project.

Jonathan Turner has been a tireless advocate of the natural scientific program. In his 1988 presidential address to the Pacific Sociological

Association entitled, "The Disintegration of American Sociology," Turner lamented the fragmented, incoherent state of the discipline. "American sociology is clearly disintegrating. It has no accumulated body of knowledge that goes unchallenged; it reveals no real consensus over important problems; it can articulate few abstract laws; its practitioners . . . do not share goals, procedures, discursive forms, or standards of adequacy" [20]. Although Turner invoked many reasons for sociology's dismal state, he is particularly critical of theorists. Theorists have promoted disciplinary fragmentation by focusing on developing specialized theories (e.g., theories of deviance, organization, gender), advocating for their favorite theoretical perspective or school (e.g., Marxism or exchange theory), and abandoning empirical theory in favor of metatheory or philosophical discussions about the logic of sociology. At the root of sociology's conceptual incoherence is its abandonment of the original vision of sociology as a natural science. Accordingly, Turner urged the recovery of the Comtean project. It aims to identify the most basic patterns of social organization (e.g., social differentiation, integration, competition, socializiation, stratification) and their causal relations. Sociology should abandon its organization around subfields (e.g., political, family, religion) and its specialized research and theories in favor of the search for social laws that explain the most elementary, generic properties of the social universe. The hope is for sociology to deliver a catalogue of causal principles that could be used to understand social events for the purpose of social engineering.

The proposal to unify sociology through a natural scientific program has received enthusiastic support among many theorists who share Turner's discontent with the state of theory. Peter Blau added to the case for a formalistic structural sociology with the publication of *Crosscutting Social Circles* [21]. Although apparently abandoning a strict propositional formalism, Collins remains no less insistent that conflict theory marks a nonideological science of society. James Coleman, the 1992 president of the American Sociological Association, was given the prestigious Sorokin Award for the *Foundations of Social Theory*, a book defending an economic model of society on the grounds of its empirical and explanatory scientific rigor [22]. Closer to the spirit of Turner, Walter Wallace has proposed unifying sociology by standardizing its premises, concepts, and explanatory logics along the lines of a natural scientific model [23]. Impressive as these proposals might seem, they offer few good reasons for believing that the natural scientific agenda, one that has been present since sociology's origin, will now capture the hearts and minds of sociologists. Behind this reform impulse is the Enlightenment hope that reason and truth themselves carry the power to heal divisions and bring consensus where little now exists. Unfortunately for purveyors of this dream, the

Enlightenment spirit seems somewhat dulled in an increasingly cynical postmodern era.

It is my impression that the majority of sociological theorists remain wedded to a grand humanistic scientific vision. These theorists insist that underlying, and, to some extent, driving, the antagonistic divisions among sociologists are contradictory premises that are unreflected upon. The task of theory is to clarify these premises or presuppositions in order to arrive at a conceptual consensus. Theorizing must go metatheoretical; it must take as its subject matter the core assumptions that inform empirical research and sociological theory. The hope is that theorists can forge a consensus about presuppositions that will make possible disciplinary unity.

Much theory in the 1980s that moved in a metatheoretical direction brings to mind Parsonian grand theory. In some instances, the connection is explicit and deliberate. For example, Jeffrey Alexander's *Theoretical Logic in Sociology* takes Parsons as his point of departure in addressing the fragmented state of sociological theory [24]. He introduced the concept of a "theoretical logic" as a vehicle of disciplinary consensus. A theoretical logic offers general standards and guidelines for the purpose of clarifying and resolving conceptual disputes among sociologists.

The notion of a theoretical logic presupposes a view of science as multidimensional or as composed of empirical statements, methods, models, ideology, and theoretical presuppositions. Alexander argues that each dimension has an independent impact on science. We must avoid reducing issues at one level (e.g., empirical) to issues at another level (e.g., ideological). Scientific reductionism exaggerates the significance of any specific dispute. If empirical disputes are immediately viewed as markers of broad conceptual and ideological differences, there is little likelihood of sorting out the real – and resolvable – empirical issues. In the hopes of keeping disputes circumscribed and within the bounds of reason, Alexander advocates developing norms of conceptual decision making that address the specificity of each autonomous dimension. The focus of *Theoretical Logic* is on presuppositions about action (instrumental versus normative) and order (individualistic versus collective) which, in Alexander's view, shape sociology's core concepts and explanatory strategies. The promise of *Theoretical Logic* is to deliver normative standards to guide presuppositional disputes; its hope is that consensus at this level could translate into disciplinary consensus at other conceptual and empirical levels.

Parsonian modes of grand theorizing have reappeared in unexpected places. Anthony Giddens, a British sociologist who began his career as a harsh critic of Parsons, has, nevertheless, theorized in a decidedly Parsonian way. His first major book, *Capitalism and Modern Social*

Theory, recommended an historical sociology oriented to substantive problems (e.g., secularization, democracy, social stratification) in place of Parsons's more formalistic, scientific theorizing [25]. Despite the anti-Parsonian impulse of this book, Giddens unintentionally reinforced Parsons's dominance in theory by making his case through an argument about the sociological classics and, indeed, by positioning Weber and Durkheim (and Marx) as *the* classics. In the eighties, Giddens's theorizing has become increasingly formalistic and grand. Parsons's *The Structure of Social Action, The Social System* and *Societies: Evolutionary and Comparative Perspectives* have a strong family resemblance to Giddens's *Central Problems in Social Theory, The Constitution of Society*, and *The Consequences of Modernity* [26]. In the spirit of Parsons, even if urging a decidedly anti-Parsonian direction, Giddens has elaborated a formalistic theoretical system as grand, synthetic, and idiosyncratic as Parsons. From somewhat tentative initial proposals for reconceptualizing action and structure in a way that avoids dualism, Giddens has built the concept of the "duality of structure" into a formalistic edifice – complete with his own glossaries and neologisms – that includes a theory of the self, action, institutionalization, everyday life, nation-states, societal types, social change, modernity, and so on. Functionalist dominance may have come to an end in the 1960s, but the spirit of Parsonian grand theory marches on triumphantly.

As we approach the mid-1990s, there are few realistic prospects for theoretical unity. The hope for disciplinary integration that underlies both the natural scientific and grand humanistic projects seems utopian. Each leans on an Enlightenment faith in the power of reason to govern belief and behavior that stretches credibility in light of the demonstrable power of interest and tradition.

If sociological theory has not achieved theoretical consensus, it does not occupy a terrain of disorder or the anarchic play of difference. The divisions in sociological theory are structured and organized by a dominant set of understandings and conventions that define "theory" in terms of certain key figures, texts, schools, narratives of the past and present, rhetorical or discursive strategies, and disciplinary hopes. In short, sociological theorists have created a canon, an understanding of theory in terms of a precise beginning and development, with classic texts and contemporary heirs and defined by key probems and argumentative strategies.

Parsons has been pivotal in the making of a sociological theory canon and, indeed, in positioning himself as a central figure. He shifted the center of sociological theory from Comte and Spencer – and to lesser extent from American pragmatism – to Durkheim and Weber. Breaking away from and discrediting competing notions of theory as the "history of social thought" or social criticism or sociological explanation, he construed "theory" as an autonomous foundational exercise concerned with clarifying the basic premises and concepts of sociology. With the ascendance of Parsons in the fifties, Durkheim and Weber became *the* classic sociologists, with Parsons himself – and functionalism – as the major heir to scientific sociology.

Critics of functionalism in the 1950s and thereafter consolidated the triumph of Parsons. They never challenged the classic status of Durkheim and Weber, though they sought to legitimate the inclusion of Marx; they never contested the Parsonian view of theory as an autonomous, strictly objective, value-neutral, foundational exercise; they never disputed the claim that the central problems of theory are metatheoretical, for example, the nature of social action, the problem of social order, or the link between materialism and idealism. By the mid-1970s, sociological theory was understood as having a definite beginning (the classic texts of Marx, Durkheim, and Weber), a middle phase marked by a plethora of lesser figures and movements (e.g., the Chicago school, Mead, the sociology of knowledge of Mannheim) but dominated by the Parsonian functionalist synthesis, a post-Parsonian period (mid-1960s–1970s) that featured paradigm conflict, and the current phase marked by continued conflict over a few presumably universal metatheoretical issues (e.g., the micro-macro or the agency-structure link) and by movements towards theoretical synthesis. Giving some moral coherence to sociological theory has been the hope – the Parsonian one – that integration through foundational consensus is about to be realized.

Establishing a sociological theory canon is a boundary maintaining strategy. Canons create order by giving authority to certain texts, figures, ideas, problems, discursive strategies, and historical narratives. By definition, a canon cannot be inclusive. Some texts, figures, problems, and movements are excluded or marginalized; they might be silenced or may lack any authority. However, the lack of consensus among sociological theorists has meant that the sociological canon only loosely or sloppily coheres. That is, its boundaries are likely to be contested; there will be persistent arguments over who and what is to be included and why and who is making these decisions. The sociological theory canon is a "loose canon," a contested one. Disputes over, say, who counts as a classic sociologist (what about Simmel, Spencer, or Mead?) and how to interpret the meaning of classic texts (do they authorize a positivist or interpretive sociology, a natural scientific, or historical vision?) are ongoing. Aside from disputes over "canon borders," there are critics who challenge the canon more centrally. In part 3, I turn to efforts to reassert the centrality of a moral vision in the human studies.

Afterword

The seventies were a period of turmoil in American society and sociology. The rise of movements of social change and the resurgence of Marxism, feminism, and a variety of self-styled radical sociologies challenged not only Parsons but at times the whole tradition of sociology. Social critics attacked sociology as conservative, male-dominated, and racist. From within the discipline, pronouncements of the crisis of sociology were not uncommon. Alvin Gouldner's *The Coming Crisis of Western Sociology* was undoubtedly the most influential statement in this genre of criticism [27]. Gouldner surveyed the historical development of sociology, culminating in Parsons and his critics. He announced a crisis of Western sociology that was said to reflect a crisis of Western civilization. European and American societies were at an impasse, stalled between a failed capitalism and a failed socialist alternative. Sociology and Marxism had become tools of state welfare societies, whether it be the United States, France, or the Soviet Union. Sociological critics of sociological functionalism and Marxism, moreover, had dead-ended, Gouldner argued, in a smug celebration of subjectivity and lifestyle choice, as was evident in the new interpretive sociologies. Gouldner urged the renewal of social theory as critical, reflexive, and publicly engaged.

Sociology was under siege in the United States. However, not all intellectuals and surely not all sociologists criticized sociology. European sociologists who immigrated to the United States or Great Britain to escape fascism and who were hostile to Soviet communism found in sociology an alternative to Marxism and to the corporatist statist ideas of fascism.

These European immigrant sociologists played a key role in the formation of post-Parsonian American sociological theory. They embraced sociology as a vehicle of a liberal, pluralistic social theory and ideology. They aimed to avoid reducing society to a collection of individuals or viewing society as a reality sui generis. They emphasized the interaction between the individual and society; the individual is shaped by social institutions which in turn are a product of individual action and communication. This sociological approach gave expression to both their refusal to assign too much power to society over the individual and to give too much power to the individual, a position that carried the threat of social disorder. Their sociology voiced a hope for a society that valued the individual, but in a stable social and political environment. These European sociologists looked to sociology as a way to defend a liberal social order, one that leaned heavier on individual freedom than on equality and democracy. Sociologists such as Dahrendorf, Berger, Lewis Coser, and Peter Blau were important defenders of sociology; they shaped the configuration of American sociological theory through the seventies and eighties.

One reason that these European sociologists proved influential is that they provided an alternative to Marxism and functionalism which resonated with the liberal values of American sociologists. Like their European counterparts, American sociologists were looking for a sociological alternative to functionalism that captured the spirit of conflict and change of the time. Most American sociologists were not, however, sympathetic to the holistic, class-centered approach of Marxism. Moreover, like their European counterparts, the Americans were critical of positions that advocated the unity of theory and practice. In contrast to radical sociologists who were calling for a partisan sociology, mainstream sociologists defended a disinterested, value-neutral scientific sociology. Like their European counterparts, American sociologists feared that the politicization of science and the universities would threaten liberty. In sum, the 1960s and 1970s saw a major division among sociologists between proponents of a partisan sociology and defenders of a scientific sociology.

By the late 1970s, the proponents of partisanship, of the sociologist as a public educator and advocate, were marginalized. The defenders of a scientific sociology had claimed the center of sociology. Sociological theory was viewed as an autonomous practice, a specialty area with its own problems, topics, technical language, and expert skills. "Theory" was seen as addressing a series of universal problems such as the nature of social action, the problem of social order, the dynamics of social change, the logic of knowledge, and the relation of the individual and society. Sociological theorists were divided into various schools or paradigms according to where they stood on these general problems. Of course, sociological theorists disagreed over the key problems and which theorists, schools, or paradigms were important; much effort was expended on making the case for a particular reading of what "theory" is or which problems and figures should be definitive of theory. Additionally, theorists were engaged in efforts at synthesis, attempts to combine various paradigms into one overarching grand theory. In short, the assumption of the autonomy of theory was firmly entrenched in sociology by the mid-1970s.

It would be a mistake to describe sociological theory in the 1970s and 1980s as divided between advocates of partisanship and defenders of scholarship without further qualification. The champions of scientific sociology were neither unified, nor is their work reducible to this narrow focus. Defenders of a scientific sociology are a diverse lot; some (e.g., Peter Blau and Jonathan Turner) have sought to model sociology on an axiomatic natural scientific ideal; others (e.g., Randall Collins) defended a scientific ideal that amounted to the search for general principles and explanations;

some sociologists (e.g., Berger and Giddens) substituted an interpretive or humanistic scientific ideal for a natural scientific model. Sociologists differed on the blurring they allowed between science and ideology. Blau allowed for very little, whereas, for Giddens, the line between science and ideology is often considerably blurred. However, to varying degrees these sociologists have remained committed to a scientific vision of sociology, to the quest for objectivity, general social truths, overarching theories, and a language that mirrors the social universe.

Sociologists who fashioned a scientific vision of sociology often crafted novel interpretive or critical social analyses. They translated their abstract conceptual strategies into innovative social perspectives on contemporary societies. For example, in *The Social Construction of Reality*, Peter Berger attempted to furnish the conceptual foundations of a universal science of society. However, the premises and concepts of his general theory of society guided a series of influential sociological analyses of modernization, religion, and the family [28]. Indeed, Berger has gradually moved away from, though not necessarily abandoned, a project of scientific sociology to assume the role of a public educator and advocate. His *Capitalist Revolution: Fifty Propostions about Prosperity, Equality, and Liberty* is an effort at public sociology [29]. Similarly, Dahrendorf's general conflict theory of society in *Class and Class Conflict in Industrial Society* guided his sketch of a non-Marxian perspective on Western industrialization. I have no reason to believe that Dahrendorf ever abandoned his scientific vision of sociology. However, in subsequent writings, his standpoint is deliberately philosophical, political, and moral. In works such as *Society and Democracy in Germany*, Dahrendorf steps forward as a public intellectual [30]. Not all sociologists who theorized under the sign of science linked these efforts to an interpretive and public sociology. Peter Blau's sociology is organized, almost exclusively, in response to disciplinary disputes and concerns. His sociology is oriented to an expert disciplinary culture. Between Berger and Blau are Collins and Giddens. Collins's *Conflict Sociology* is a brief for a scientific sociology. Nevertheless, in *Weberian Sociolgial Theory and the Credential Society*, Collins seems to abandon his quest for abstract principles in favor of a more historical, interpretive style whose value lies in offering broad, original perspectives on contemporary industrial societies [31]. Similarly, in *The Constitution of Society* and *Central Problems in Social Theory*, Anthony Giddens is engaged in a foundational quest no less inspired by a hope for a "system of sociology" than Parsons's *The Structure of Social Action*. However, in *The Consequences of Modernity* and *Modernity and Self Identity*, he articulates his general social theory as a novel interpretation of modern Western social development [32]. Neither Collins nor Giddens, in my view, manage to move beyond addressing an expert elite culture to engaging a broader public. They remain academic, not public, intellectuals.

American sociological theory in the postwar years reveals diverse currents. As I have suggested, sociologists who embraced a scientific project were deeply divided on the meaning of science and its boundaries vis-à-vis ideology. Moreover, these scientific sociologists were not necessarily narrowly focused on issues of foundations or elaborating grand theories. Many of these sociologists provided interpretive sketches of social development or critical analyses of social institutions; some functioned as public intellectuals. Nevertheless, the project of scientific sociology, the quest for certainty, objectivity, value neutrality, foundations, general principles, and a system of sociology or an overarching theory of society and history, has won out in sociology. Despite persistent dissenters and despite the fact that partisans of scientific sociology at times assumed an interpretive, moral, and political role, it is the project of a scientific sociology, whether it assumes the form of axiomatic theory, the search for general explanatory principles, a theoretical logic, or an analytical ordering of the social, that has triumphed in sociology and sociological theory.

Has the dominance of scientific sociology had only undesirable consequences? No. I believe that the quest for foundations, universal laws, or a general theory has proved valuable in a number of ways. For example, it has promoted a culture of reflexivity, criticism, and suspicion towards religious and metaphysical claims to truth which have often justified unjust social conditions. Moreover, to the extent that general theories and foundational efforts such as Parsons's *Structure of Social Action* or Giddens's *The Constitution of Society* have been articulated as novel views of the self, society, history, and modernization, they are potentially of social importance. Such perspectives can be used by ordinary people (e.g., citizens, activists, public officials, policy makers) to make sense of their lives, criticize current social arrangements, or suggest sites of political activity or strategies of political mobilization.

Nevertheless, I have serious reservations about the value of the scientific project, especially as it now dominates sociological theory. The quest for foundations, certitude, objectivity, grand theories, or systems of sociology has taken on a life of its own. Instead of approaching such efforts pragmatically or with an eye to their payoff as empirical, interpretive, or critical social perspectives, sociological theory is increasingly stuck in metatheoretical disputes. Instead of speaking to issues of broad public concern, sociological theory is consumed with abstruse, largely philosophical debates over the nature of social action, the problem of social order, the foundations of sociology, the relation of agency and structure, micro–macro analysis, and meaning and power. If the history of such disputes are at all relevant, they appear to be irresolvable. Our preoccupation with metatheory – motivated by our wish to realize our scientific aspirations and by the public authority that would accrue to sociology – has had the social effect, ironically, of insulating sociology and diminishing its public status. Moreover, even when sociological theorists attempt to engage public issues and develop their general theories into interpretive or critical social analyses, they are frequently unsuccessful. Why? I believe that the failure of sociological theory to become an important part of the public conversation about society reflects its language which expresses an exclusive expert culture. Additionally, much sociological theory is organized around primarily disciplinary relevances and considerations rather than framed in the language and terms of existing public debate and social conflict.

The tragedy of contemporary sociological theory is that it has so much to offer but that its promise has gone largely unfulfilled. Much sociological theory has abandoned both the narrow individualistic liberalism of Western, especially American, culture and the social realism of conservative, romantic, and religious social perspectives. Sociological theory represents a rich cultural tradition, a powerful and important approach to address changes in societies and the social problems and conflicts that are central to current social realities. By viewing the self as embedded in social institutions and "society" as produced in and through the interaction of individuals, sociology is in a position to speak powerfully to the major social issues of the day and to be a compelling social voice. Indeed, from Comte's social vision of the rise of a scientific-industrial society and Marx's image of class conflict, to Weber's view of social rationalization and Parsons's notion of social differentiation, sociology has provided powerful critical understandings of Western modernity. Unfortunately, the ascendance of a scientific vision of sociology has frustrated and impeded sociology from assuming its role as one important medium of public education and advocacy. The scientization of sociology has turned it inward and promoted its social isolation. Increasingly, sociological theory has been dominated by narrow, parochial disciplinary concerns, in particular, with metatheoretical issues of foundations or justifications of premises and concepts, discovering general laws or erecting systems of concepts and grand theories.

Sociological theory has lost a public voice. We are proving unable to speak to the broad mass of citizens, to policy makers, public officials, activists, and cultural and social leaders. We have not lost our social conscience or our capacity to enlighten and to educate, nor have we lost our will to shape society according to a moral vision. To realize its promise, sociology must recover its public voice; it must renew its role as public educator and advocate without surrendering its rich tradition of human studies. In part 3, I explore efforts, within and outside of sociology, to imagine a social knowledge that is public and partisan and yet inspired by the sociological imagination.

References

1. C.W. Mills, *The Sociological Imagination* (New York: Oxford University Press, 1959); George Homans, "Bringing Men Back In," *American Sociological Review* 29 (1964); Herbert Blumer, "What is Wrong with Social Theory" in *Symbolic Interactionism: Perspective and Method* (Englewood Cliffs, NJ: Prentice-Hall, 1969); Lewis Coser, *The Functions of Social Conflict* (New York: Free Press, 1956); Ralf Dahrendorf, "Out of Utopia," *American Journal of Sociology* 64 (1958).
2. Ralf Dahrendorf, *Class and Class Conflict in Industrial Society* (Stanford: Stanford University Press, 1959); Peter Berger and Thomas Luckmann, *The Social Construction of Reality: A Treatise in the Sociology of Knowledge* (New York: Anchor, 1967).
3. Seymour Martin Lipset, *Political Man* (Garden City, NY: Doubleday, 1960); Raymond Aron, *18 Lectures on Industrial Society* (London: Weidenfeld & Nicolson, 1967); Daniel Bell, *The End of Ideology* (Glencoe, IL: Free Press, 1960).
4. Dahrendorf, *Class and Class Conflict in Industrial Society*, p. 61.
5. Dahrendorf, *Class and Class Conflict in Industrial Society*, p. 171.
6. Dahrendorf, *Class and Class Conflict in Industrial Society*, p. 9.
7. George Homans, *Social Behavior* (New York: Free Press, 1962).
8. Herbert Blumer, *Symbolic Interactionism* (Englewood Cliffs, NJ: Prentice-Hall, 1969).
9. Harold Garfinkel, *Studies in Ethnomethodology* (Englewood Cliffs, NJ: Prentice-Hall, 1967).
10. Berger and Luckmann, *The Social Construction of Reality*.
11. Berger and Luckmann, *The Social Construction of Reality*, p. 104.
12. Peter Berger, *The Sacred Canopy: Elements of a Sociological Theory of Religion* (New York: Anchor, 1967), p. 4.
13. Randall Collins, *Conflict Sociology: Towards an Explanatory Science* (New York: Academic Press, 1975).
14. Collins, *Conflict Sociology*, p. 2.
15. Collins, *Conflict Sociology*, p. 21.
16. Collins, *Conflict Sociology*, p. 59.
17. Peter Blau, *Inequality and Heterogeneity: A Primitive Theory of Social Structure* (New York: Free Press, 1975).
18. Blau, *Inequality and Heterogeneity*, p. 103.
19. Randall Collins, *Weberian Sociological Theory* (Cambridge: Cambridge University Press, 1985) and *Three Sociological Traditions* (New York: Oxford University Press, 1985).

20. Jonathan Turner, "The Disintegration of American Sociology," *Sociological Perspectives* 32 (1989): 420.

21. Peter Blau and Joseph Schwartz, *Cross-cutting Social Circles: Testing a Macro-structural Theory of Intergroup Relations* (Orlando: Academic Press, 1984).

22. James Coleman, *Foundations of Social Theory* (Cambridge, MA: Harvard University Press, 1990).

23. Walter Wallace, "Towards a Disciplinary Matrix in Sociology," in Neil Smelser, ed. *Handbook of Sociology* (Newbury Park, Ca.: Sage, 1988).

24. Jeffrey Alexander, *Theoretical Logic in Sociology*, 4 vols. (Berkeley: University of California Press, 1982–1983).

25. Anthony Giddens, *Capitalism and Modern Social Theory* (Cambridge: Cambridge University Press, 1971).

26. Anthony Giddens, *Central Problems in Social Theory: Action, Structure and Contradiction in Social Analysis* (Berkeley: University of California Press, 1979); *The Constitution of Society: Outline of the Theory of Structuration* (Berkeley: University of California Press, 1984).

27. Alvin Gouldner, *The Coming Crisis of Western Sociology* (New York: Basic Books, 1970).

28. Peter Berger, *The Sacred Canopy*; Peter Berger, Brigitte Berger, and Hanfried Kellner, *The Homeless Mind: Modernization and Consciousness* (New York: Vintage Books, 1974); Peter Berger, *Pyramids of Sacrifice: Political Ethics and Social Change* (New York: Anchor, 1976).

29. Peter Berger, *Capitalist Revolution: Fifty Propositions about Prosperity, Equality, and Liberty* (New York: Basic Books, 1986).

30. Ralph Dahrendorf, *Society and Democracy in Germany* (Garden City, New York: Doubleday, 1967).

31. Randall Collins, *Weberian Social Theory and the Credential Society* (New York: Academic Press, 1979).

32. Anthony Giddens, *The Consequences of Modernity* (Stanford: Stanford University Press, 1990) and *Modernity and Self-Identity* (Stanford: Stanford University Press, 1992).

PART 3

DISLODGING THE CANON: THE REASSERTION OF A MORAL VISION OF THE HUMAN SCIENCES

5

Between Science and Politics: The Critical Theory of C.W. Mills and Jürgen Habermas

T he institutionalization of sociology in Europe and the United States between 1890 and World War I was accomplished through a series of exclusions. Many traditions of social thought did not find a place in the discipline of sociology. For example, Christian social thought, feminism, Black nationalist, and sex radical discourses did not find a home in sociological theory. These social discourses continued outside of academe, often establishing their own institutional base.

This intellectual pluralism did not mean that all forms of social thinking carried equal social value or influence. In the course of the twentieth century, discourses that successfully acquired the status of science also acquired social prestige at the expense of nonscientific discourses, e.g., religion, ethical thought, or folk traditions. To the extent that sociology could place itself under the sign of science, it could claim a public authority for its discourse. Paralleling other disciplines that assumed the authority of science, sociology marked off clear boundaries between its own discourse and nonscientific ones. The latter were labelled mythological, political, ideological, moral, philosophical, or mere opinion. The concepts, concerns, and argumentative strategies of these nonscientific discourses could be discounted and ignored by the scientific community. Moreover, lacking scientific authority, these discourses could not presume the same entitlement to be heard in matters of public importance as science; they did not have equal access to the public. Asserting the status of science justified social privilege and power for sociology and sociologists.

By the time Parsons came of age as a sociologist (in the 1930s), he did not need to engage, even acknowledge, those traditions of social thought that had not achieved expression in the institutionalization of sociology (e.g., socialism, feminism, Black nationalism, or cultural criticism). Sociology had so thoroughly excluded these social discourses in its formative years that sociological theorists did not protest Parsons's exclusion of them. This silencing of social voices was not necessarily achieved through censorshop or repession; rather, it was more unconscious, a matter of the consolidation of distinctive conventions and codes that marked off the intellectual boundaries of sociology. Discourses whose conceptual conventions fell outside these borders were simply ignored, devalued, or marginalized within the discipline.

Institutionalizing sociology as a privileged social language did not mean the disappearance or even necessarily the public marginalization of nondisciplinary discourses. Religious, humanistic, political, cultural critical, and folk discourses survived, sometimes flourished, outside the institutional walls of academe. The church, public media such as radio, magazines, and newspapers, educational associations, social movements, and the culture of everyday life provided a social base for nonscientific discourses. For example, from roughly the 1890s through World War I, a culture of critical dissent flourished in the United States. A cultural apparatus of journals, magazines, newspapers, conferences, theatre groups, political organizations, public lectures, and publishing companies provided a source of livelihood for independent Left intellectuals. This proved harder in the post-World War II years as universities and policy institutes came to provide the principal source of livelihood for intellectuals. In any event, social thought at the turn of the century was divided between disciplinary knowledges (e.g., sociology or economics) and social discourses outside academe. This was more than a matter of social discourses being located in different institutional settings. Disciplinary social science had its own unique intellectual conventions, language, interests, and aims which carried higher levels of social authority than did nondisciplinary cultures of discourse.

There materialized in twentieth centry social thought in the United States and Europe a division between a university-based scientific social discourse and a culture of social discourse whose institutional base was outside of academe. Occasionally, figures appeared who bridged the two cultures of discourse. These "bridge figures" have typically been academics (usually humanities or social scientific professors) who are intimately connected to a public culture of social discourse. Such figures are crucial in challenging the conventions and orthodoxies of the disciplines. Drawing on the practical-moral and ideological concerns that are central in these public cultures of discourse, these figures may dispute the taken-for-granted premises and aims of the disciplines, in particular, the "pure" scientific interest that presumably guides them. In this chapter, I turn to two key bridge figures who have appealed to the moral and political concerns of a public culture of social discourse to contest the project of a scientific sociological theory: C.W. Mills and Jürgen Habermas.

C. Wright Mills

Although some fourteen years younger than Parsons, Mills was in many ways his chief adversary through the 1950s and early 1960s. The contrast of personalities and intellectual identities could hardly be more starkly drawn. The son of a Congregational minister, educated at the finest private schools (Amherst, London School of Economics, and Heidelberg), Parsons represented the ruling White, Anglo-Saxon, Protestant elite. By contrast, Mills came from a conventional middle class Texan household. He was educated at large state universities (Texas and Wisconsin). Mills and Parsons spent most of their respective careers as sociologists in rival departments. Parsons was at Harvard where he eventually founded, chaired, and dominated the Department of Social Relations. Mills spent the better part of his short and tempestuous career at Columbia, where his department was known for its strong commitment to empirical social analysis. Perhaps most importantly, while Parsons was forging his grand vision of a synthetic scientific sociology, Mills was crafting a moral vision of a critically engaged "public sociology."

In one crucial respect, however, Mills surrendered to the influence of Parsons. Mills appealed to the European classics to legitimate his own vision of sociology. By the 1940s, Parsons's *Structure of Social Action* stimulated a growing interest in the European classics, especially Weber. Indeed, Parsons played a key role in making Weber a "classic." He translated Weber's *The Protestant Ethic and the Spirit of Capitalism* as well as large sections from Weber's *Economy and Society*. Of course, Parsons did more than introduce European social thinkers to American sociologists; he interpreted their significance through the lens of his theoretical synthesis. As we have seen, Parsons saw in the European sociologists a convergence towards a general theoretical system that could serve as the unifying basis for the social sciences. Curiously, one of Mills's earliest publications (1946) was *From Max Weber* (coauthored by Hans Gerth), a translation of Weber's essays [1]. In his introduction to the book, Mills described a strikingly different Weber than that presented by Parsons. Rather than the pure theorist interested in a general theory of society, Mills perceived in Weber a sociologist who offered a sociohistorical perspective aimed at clarifying the social, political, and moral meaning of modernity. Weber epitomized an ideal of the sociologist who is politically and morally engaged with the major public issues of the day, *the sociologist as public intellectual.*

While Mills looked to the European tradition to legitimate his vision of sociology, he positioned himself differently than Parsons with regard to indigenous American traditions. In his effort to effect a major reorientation of American sociological theory by centering the discipline in non-Spencerian and non-Comtean European traditions, Parsons ignored American sociological and philosophical developments. Mills, however, deliberately situated himself in the American pragmatic tradition associated with the social philosophy of William James, John Dewey, Charles Pierce, and George Herbert Mead. His dissertation, posthumously published as *Sociology and Pragmatism*, was on the American pragmatic movement [2]. American pragmatism appealed to Mills precisely because it approached ideas with an eye to their social consequences rather than exclusively focusing on their absolute truth. Pragmatism assumed an activist approach to thinking; ideas acquired value only in relation to their social utility. Mills interpreted the European sociologists through the prism of pragmatism, as intellectuals whose discourses engaged current social conflicts. Mills looked to European sociology in order to find a more elaborate social perspective than that developed by the American pragmatists. Whereas Parsons aspired to a cosmopolitan intellectual standpoint from which to advance a grand theory, Mills was very much the scrappy Texan approaching ideas with regard to their social purposes.

Mills and Parsons represent two strikingly different conceptions of sociology. Parsons envisioned a grand synthetic scientific sociology; theory would furnish the basic premises and categories for a unified science of society. Mills imagined sociology as a publicly engaged social discourse; rather than aspiring to conceptual transcendance, sociology would be deeply historical. To the extent that "theory" had an independent existence, it was to provide conceptual sketches that would guide empirical social analysis. At times, Mills described his project as that of creating a "public sociology."

It was Parsons, not Mills, who achieved dominance in sociology during the 1950s and early 1960s. Specifically, it was the transcendant, universal scientific vision of *The Social System* that captured the sociological imagination in the postwar years. Mills was an outsider to the discipline, even if much acclaimed or, in truth, infamous. His vision of a morally and politically engaged critical sociology was at odds with a discipline that seemed intent on settling down into either grand theorizing or problem-solving empiricism. If Mills was marginalized in sociology, he was perhaps the most influential public sociologist of the time. Much like the sociology of his contemporary, David Riesman, Mills spoke to a broadly educated public [3]. He wrote for the major national liberal and Left magazines and newspapers. Moreover, while Parsons was designing his grand system, Mills was publishing his great trilogy on the shape and meaning of postwar modern society: *The New Men of Power, White Collar,* and *The Power*

Elite. Parsons's functional scientific sociology may have captured the disciplinary center of sociology, but Mills's public sociology shaped national debates for a decade and beyond.

Motivating Mills's sociology is a wish to shake a weary postwar America out of its false sense of security and arrogance. Americans returned from the war and the long, hard period of national Depression longing for domestic tranquility and civic harmony. They turned inward, to concerns of self-fulfillment, family, career, and consumerism. Despite a surface appearance of national prosperity and unlimited personal and social opportunities, Mills was convinced that America was drifting into a bureaucratic, alienated, elitist society in which self-realization amounted to little more than economic security, white collar status, and consumer satisfaction. The underlying social trends threatened liberal democracy but neither ordinary citizens, who were increasingly dazed and dulled by consumerist fantasies, nor intellectuals, who had been bought and sold by government grants, plush academic positions, or corporate money, were willing to address these social dangers. Mills's trilogy and subsequently his rather desperate pamphleteering were aimed at awakening Americans to current dangers and to instigating a renewal of New Deal democratic reform.

The first installment of Mills's trilogy on contemporary modernity, *The New Men of Power*, was his least substantial [4]. It was less self-initiated than a project sponsored by Columbia University's Bureau of Applied Social Research, where Mills was, at the time, the director of its Labor Research Division. Nevertheless, while the bureau was charged with collecting data on labor leaders, Mills provided the interpretive perspective. Disputing Marxist expectations of the politicization of labor as a revolutionary class, Mills was more troubled by the depoliticization and passivity of organized labor. The rank and file had delegated their political will to the labor leaders. Contrary to Marxian hopes, union leaders had abandoned any interest in broad social change. They had become major power brokers in a system that delivered prestige and material rewards. Contrary to liberal reformers, moreover, Mills doubted the widespread belief that labor leaders act as a countervailing force to the state and big business, thereby preserving the values of freedom and democracy. Taking issue with a liberal pluralistic social model that was ascendant in the 1940s, as well as European Marxism, Mills argued that the new labor elite acted in concert with state and managerial elites; their aim was to maintain a well-functioning, stable social system that could deliver to the great social mass economic security, social status, and abundant consumer goods.

Despite the absence of any sustained analysis of the rank and file of blue collar workers, Mills had hit upon one of the great themes of his work: the rise of a social mass – blue collar and white collar – who were depoliticized and manipulated by consumerism and social elites. The depoliticization of the public, moreover, was being ignored by cultural and intellectual elites. Whereas Marxists took flight from the present in their millennial dreams of a coming revolution, liberals abandoned their critical impulse by serving up little more than apologies for the West in the era of the Cold War. Mills himself was not immune to utopian flight; he pinned his hopes on the rise of an independent Left and labor coalition which might form the basis of a third political party inspired by social democratic ideals.

Mills's vision of America as drifting into a bureaucratic mass society in which a debased consumerist culture perpetuates the illusion of freedom and happiness is the chief theme of *White Collar: The American Middle Classes* [5]. As we have seen, Mills had concluded that labor had become a politically passive mass whose elite representatives desired little more than better wages and work conditions while preserving the social status quo. The dramatic appearance in mid-twentieth century America of a new middle class raised social hopes for many intellectuals. Marxists viewed the enormous expansion of white collar workers as marking a new proletariat and reinvigorating a waning union movement. Liberals attributed to the new middle classes a socially and morally stabilizing force in America; as the ranks of the white collar swelled, class conflict and ideological extremism would disappear. Moreover, unlike the old property-owning middle class, the professional ethos of the new middle classes would make them a force promoting social responsibility and democracy. Mills agreed that the character of postwar America would be decisively shaped by the new middle classes. However, he disputed the moral and political hopes that liberals and Marxists attached to this social development. *White Collar* sounded a warning to America: The new middle classes are driving this nation down the road of social totalitarianism.

The story of the new middle classes is part of the history of America as a society decisively shaped by a middle class culture. The absence of a feudal-like aristocratic order in a territory of enormous expanse and rich resources made America the land of the entrepreneur. Before the new middle classes burst on the scene in this century, there were the free farmer and independent trader of antebellum years and, more recently, the captains of industry and robber barons of American lore. The small farmer shared with the captain of industry a fiercely guarded independence and a suspicion toward any institutional dependence. This democratic spirit was rooted in property ownership; economic self-sufficiency bred social independence and a democratic political culture.

The world of nineteenth century America, characterized by economic competition, small-town democracy, and Protestant individualism, came to an end with the rise of corporate capitalism, bureaucratization, and the tremendous expansion of the state. Spurred by technological innovation, a worldwide market forged through Western colonialism, and the creation of new modes of communication and transportation, the small and midsize business gave way to the giant corporation run by salaried, nonowning managers and manned by an army of sales, advertising, and public relations persons, receptionists, secretaries, file clerks, accountants, lawyers, and technicians. Although small businesses survived, along with the ideological celebration of economic competition and the self-made individual, real power shifted into the hands of the managerial and big business elite. The middle class, now transformed into an army of white collar workers, were, for the first time in American history, virtually powerless. Except for the highest level of managers and executives, white collar workers were not corporate owners or institutional decision makers. They merely executed the marching orders issued by the top echelon of a bureaucracy. Even the professions such as law, medicine, or academia experienced a similar dependence on bureaucratic institutions and a considerable loss of economic autonomy and power.

The decline of work autonomy and the bureaucratic standardization of work was compensated for by the status the new middle class attached to white collar jobs. Where blue collar work is physical, white collar work is mental. To the extent that white collar work involves conversation and the production and circulation of texts (e.g., memos, documents, reports) in a context of respectful collegiality, white collar workers can claim the symbolic authority of those who really exercise power. Furthermore, as white collar work turned dull, repetitive, and mechanical, as the differences between white collar jobs blur, making it harder to base a status hierarchy on work roles, the new middle classes looked to consumption and leisure activities to flag social status and to feel free and powerful. Instead of realizing self-fulfillment in consumerism, Mills believed that individuals are captured and manipulated by mass culture. Peddling its wares of false dreams and unrealizable fantasies of satisfaction, the new middle classes find only fleeting gratification and the feeling of power, not the real thing.

Instead of the new middle classes serving as carriers of a revitalized social liberalism, Mills imagined that they would become an inert, depoliticized mass controlled by bureaucratic elites and a profit-driven consumer culture. "Among white-collar people, . . . the absence of any order of belief has left them morally defenseless as individuals and politically impotent as a group. . . . This isolated position makes them excellent material for synthetic molding at the hands of popular culture – print, film, radio, and television" [6]. Preoccupied with self-fulfillment in their private lives, white collar individuals mistake the freedom to consume and work with genuine autonomy. Mills is especially critical of intellectuals. They have forfeited their critical role by retreating into either celebrating the making of a postideological society or by awaiting its self-destruction. White collar America may be our worst nightmare: a society of happy robots unaware that they are tumbling into a social hell.

Mills's social vision has a decidedly pessimistic coloring. In *The New Men of Power*, Mills concluded that the labor movement aimed for little more than its share of America's growing prosperity. Although Mills did not fully relinquish the utopian hope that labor leaders might coalesce with an independent Left movement, he conceded that presently they are becoming a new elite intent on social accommodation. In *White Collar*, Mills analyzed the formation of a new middle class culture that abandoned meaningful political action in favor of the quest for self-fulfillment, status, and security. As America drifts into a mass society, political power concentrates at the social top. In his first two major works, Mills had only a vague notion of a tendency towards the consolidation of an authoritarian political culture. However, in *The Power Elite*, he asserts the existence of an elite that exercises power, not always responsibly, and frequently without social accountability, over a politically dead, atomized social mass [7].

Mills crafted a story of political change. In the nineteenth century, the economy consisted of small businesses and farms locked in fierce competition; political power was dispersed among the local, state, and federal levels as well as between various secular and religious institutions; the military establishment lacked a major centralized social presence. The great territorial expanse of America, its rich resources, an underdeveloped system of transportation and communication, a weak federal government, and competition between local religious and secular elites impeded the development of a cohesive power structure. Political decentralization gave way to centralization and consolidation in this century. The growth of big business greatly stimulated the concentration of wealth; technological advances, colonial expansion, World War I, and the Great Depression promoted the enlargement of the federal government. Additionally, two successive wars and the evolution of a military-industrial complex helped to consolidate the military as a principal social force in the United States. By the postwar years, the concentration of economic wealth in corporate hands, of political power in the national government, and of military power in the federal military establishment had evolved to a point where whomever occupied the top positions in these three institutions exercised enormous power.

Mills's chief thesis was that a power elite had been consolidated in postwar America. The elite were mostly men who held power in either the corporate, political, or military sector. "At the top of the economy, among the corporate rich, are the chief executives; at the top of the political order, the members of the political directorate; at the top of the military establishment, the elite of soldier-statesmen clustered in and around the Joint Chiefs of Staff and the upper echelon. . . . The leading men in each of the three domains of power – the warlords, the corporation chieftans, the political directorate – tend to come together, to form the power elite of America" [8]. Although the power elite do not necessarily act in a deliberate, concerted way, they share similar interests and pursue a common social agenda. In part, the interlocking character of the power elite reflects the interconnecting nature of economic, political, and military institutions. Top-level decision makers in any one institutional sphere cannot avoid consulting and cooperating with policy makers in other spheres. Moreover, there are personal ties binding elites and separating them from the social masses. Elites stand apart from the mass of blue collar and white collar Americans foremost by their considerable wealth. Of course, wealth translates into a whole series of markers that divide the elite from the masses, e.g., education, residence, and social opportunities. Moreover, elites develop a common identity as a result of attending the same prestigious schools and belonging to the same clubs, churches, and social cliques. Finally, the elite often circulate among the top instutitional orders; the high-level corporate executive resigns to become a cabinet officer; the retired general sits on the board of directors of a big corporation. The circulation of elites reinforces their consolidation as a politically effective ruling body.

Mills views the power elite as more of a loosely linked network bound by personal and structural ties and interests than a closed, unitary, conflict-free class. Nevertheless, elites share similar social interests, in particular, an interest in maintaining the current unequal distribution of wealth, prestige, and power. Moreover, they can and do act in concert to implement and enforce their social will. Despite declaring that their interests represent the welfare of all Americans, they are guided, as are all strata or classes, by self-interest. What makes the power elite so dangerous, in Mills's view, is that they not only have the power to shape society but they exercise it with minimal accountability. Who keeps the corporate executive or the appointed military chief or cabinet officer accountable? With a blue collar and white collar mass public captivated by the illusory promises of consumer and domestic bliss, the electoral process turns into little more than a process of ratifying elite rule.

Mills imagined America as evolving into a society divided between a nonpolitical social mass sedated by the illusions of consumerism and ruled by a power elite who almost invisibly shape the future. "The top of modern American society is increasingly unified . . . [by] an elite of power.

The middle levels are a drifting set of stalemated, balancing forces. . . . The bottom of this society is politically fragmented and . . . powerless: at the bottom there is emerging a mass society" [9]. Mills was convinced that the preservation of a democratic society required an alert, educated, politically engaged public. Such a democratic political culture thrived on public debate and critical discourses that translated private troubles into public issues. Unfortunately, many intellectuals had abandoned the role of providing critical perspectives that could address current developments and activate a mass public to regain a democratic spirit. In the face of the communist threat, liberals relinquished critical perspectives on the United States in favor of celebrating American democracy. Meanwhile Marxists turned away from current realities as they waited for the imminent crash of capitalism. Mills rejected both liberalism and Marxism as each turned away from current realities to serve narrow ideological interests. What was needed, thought Mills, was a public intellectual discourse that was critical yet addressed complex social realities in terms of the practical possibilities for democratic renewal.

In the early decades of this century, liberal pragmatists (e.g., William James and John Dewey), muckraking journalists, and independent cultural critics stepped forward as guardians of a democratic public culture. Today these figures are disappearing as the university becomes the dominant intellectual center. However, Mills believed that the classical sociological tradition represented a turn of mind that could serve as a successor to liberal pragmatism. In *The Sociological Imagination*, Mills called on sociologists to take up their calling as public intellectuals committed to safeguarding democratic public values [10].

Sociology has a mission: to be a medium for a critical, publically engaged social discourse. Mills imagined sociology as a public voice whose aim was to provide critical perspectives on the present which citizens would draw on to understand and orient their behavior. The classical European sociology of Marx, Durkheim, and Weber were models of a public sociology. They provided historical perspectives that aimed to clarify the implications of current developments for human freedom and democracy. While the European classics may have embraced the rhetoric of objectivity, Mills interpreted this as little more than a respect for empirical realities. Social analysis can never cleanse itself of political and moral values and commitments. Mills envisioned a sociology that would be simultaneously respectful of empirical realities and passionate in its critical role. His own works were meant to exemplify the ideal of a public sociology.

Inspired by a moral vision of sociology, Mills characterized the current state of sociology as a betrayal of its mission. Sociologists had renounced a public critical role in favor of a scientific vision which, at times, was little more than a thinly disguised veneer for social opportunism, status monger-ing, and social apologetics.

Mills described postwar American sociology as divided between two equally undesirable positions: grand theory and abstracted empiricism. The former sought a universal language of the social. Parsons's effort to state the basic premises, problems, and concepts of social science and to outline a comprehensive theory of society was illustrative. Mills thought such conceptual closure and completeness impossible. Moreover, in their preoccupation with identifying the most abstract general level of social analysis, grand theorists ignore historically specific social dynamics, problems, and conflicts. In place of grand theory, Mills advocated devising "working models" or conceptual empirical sketches that can be used to analyze social dynamics in different societies.

If grand theorists retreated from the empirical world into the realm of "pure mind," empiricists imagined that they could discover truth by sub-merging intellect in the realm of "pure facts." Although abstracted empiri-cists appeal to a natural scientific model to legitimate their sociology, their research typically lacks any conceptually integrating impulse. In reality, empiricists engage in highly specialized, narrowly focused research that may have the trappings of science (e.g., methodological rigor, statistics, the language of science) but lacks the unifying theoretical vision of natural science. Mills interpreted empiricism as animated by the American spirit of problem-solving, liberal reform. However, whereas an earlier tradition of sociological problem solving aimed to improve the condition of the socially disadvantaged, postwar empiricism was in the service of the power elite. Sociologists were now routinely hired by administrators – the institutional managers of the power elite – in a variety of bureaucratic settings for the purpose of maximizing social control. Mills pointed to a shift in the social positioning of sociology. Instead of orienting to a democratic public, Mills saw sociology, at least in its empiricist aspects, as responsive to clients, in particular, to lower-level managers of society. Both grand theory and abstracted empiricism have retreated from the project of the classical tradi-tion as a critical public discourse.

Mills imagined America drifting into a quiet totalitariansim in contrast to the noisy, harsher version in the Soviet Union. Its basic feature is the development of a dependent social mass ruled by an elite through imper-sonal bureaucracies and the media. A totalitarian society is marked by the absence or enfeeblement of public debate and social movements and political parties that influence the direction of society. In the Soviet Union, a state dictatorship undermined the possibility of a democratic society; in the United States, the formation of a mass consumer culture coupled with the consolidation of a power elite threatened the demise of democracy. The illusion of freedom perpetuated by consumerism and electoral politics blinded Americans to their social drift. Mills believed that intellectuals had a key role to play in initiating public awareness and political engagement. Mills spoke of the public role of the intellectual in terms of two goals. "What he ought to do for the individual is to turn personal troubles . . . into social issues and problems open to reason – his aim is to help the individual become a self-educating man. . . . What he ought to do for the society is to combat all those forces which are destroying genuine publics and creating a mass society – or put as a positive goal, his aim is to help build and to strengthen self-cultivating publics" [11]. Unfortunately, the two dominant social perspectives – liberalism and Marxism – retreated from current realities into ideological dogma. Mills looked to a moral vision of sociology to take on the role of defending a democratic public culture. As a public discourse, sociology was to be one, only one, critical perspective in the broader conversation of society that would help transform a passive mass public into a politically engaged social force.

Mills saw himself as desperately alone. The cold war pushed many public intellectuals to retreat into a narrow dogmatism. Moreover, sociologists and other social scientists were increasingly alienated from public democratic life as their main audience shifted from social movements and political parties to bureaucratic managers and academic colleagues. As he became isolated from academics, who were put off by his politicizing of scholarship, and from many public intellectuals, whose liberalism and Marxism he rejected, Mills appeared increasingly as a lone, sometimes quixotic figure in the 1950s. His writings took on a sharper polemical character; sociological analysis became drowned out by the grand pronouncements of doom and gloom and political advocacy. His final works – *The Causes of World War III* and *Listen Yankee: The Revolution in Cuba* – were little more than political manifestos, ossilating between an equally unwarranted dark social pessimism and utopianism [12].

Mills's legacy was mixed. In the 1960s, he was embraced as a major ideological hero of the New Left. In academe, younger sociologists coming of age in the 1960s looked to Mills for a critical sociology in opposition to conservative functionalism. He inspired a tradition, to speak loosely, of sociology as public discourse, e.g., Joseph Bensman and Arthur Vidich, Alvin Gouldner, Todd Gitlin, Richard Sennett, William Wilson, Arlie Hochschild, and Judith Stacey [13]. The Millsean critical tradition was not alone in contesting the sociological orthodoxy. Paralleling Mills, indeed influencing him and influenced by him, was a German-based critical tradition, the so-called Frankfurt school. Unlike the Millsean tradition, the Frankfurt school had its primary roots in Marxism. In the course of the

1970s and early 1980s, critical theory issued a sustained and far-reaching challenge to the scientific vision of mainstream sociological theory.

Jürgen Habermas

Shifting from Mills to Habermas, we travel from the United States to Germany. This geographical passage marks an important intellectual change. Mills fashioned a critical sociology by fusing American pragmatism and classical sociology. In a tradition of Left criticism that links Mills to Thorstein Veblen before him and Christopher Lasch subsequently, these American social critics have weak ties to Marxism [14]. In contrast, the theory and politics of Marxism were at the center of Habermas's theorizing. He forged a social theory whose aim was to preserve the critical spirit of Marxism as a social force in late twentieth century Europe. We need to situate Habermas in the context of the history of Marxism in order to grasp his project of reconstructing historical materialism.

Durkheim and Weber left behind social science paradigms that were gradually absorbed into sociology. The spirit of Marx lived on in the form of a worldwide social movement that has shaped the twentieth century. By the early decades of the twentieth century, Marxism had become a permanent feature of European political culture and the official state ideology of Russian communism. Functioning as the theoretical expression of a revolutionary movement, Marxism challenged academic social science. By the postwar years, if not earlier, Marxism stepped forward as *the* major language of social criticism across a substantial part of the world.

Marx left an ambiguous intellectual legacy. His successors inherited a body of work rife with tensions and contradictions. In his reaction to German idealism, Marx sometimes advocated a one-sided materialism, while at other times he pressed for a multidimensional social theory. Consider his view of human action. On the one hand, Marx described the individual as a natural being driven by biological, materialistic needs; consciousness was sometimes viewed as a secondary effect of bodily drives or material needs. On the other hand, Marx was equally insistent that human behavior is always deliberate, goal oriented, and norm governed. If being and consciousness are both present, if human behavior is purposeful and rule governed, it is inconsistent to claim priority for a materialistic perspective.

The tension between materialism and idealism in Marx surfaces in the pivotal concept of his social theory: labor. It is through our productive activity that we make and transform human nature and the social world. However, Marx was not clear as to whether labor referred narrowly to economic activity or to all productive, practical activity. If it was the former, Marx assumed a fairly simplistic economistic worldview; if labor was interpreted broadly as practical activity, Marx surrendered any special warrant for a materialist or economic social analysis. From this ambiguity in Marx's basic understanding of human action, a whole series of conceptual strains surface. Marx ossilated between a mechanistic base/superstructure model and organic social imagery. In the former, the economic base determines in a one-sided way the rest of society; in the latter, the parts of society are causally interrelated. Similarly, Marx shifted between a mechanistic view of history as governed by invariant laws and a humanistic image of history as produced by human actions.

At the root of classical Marxism is a tension between a scientific and a moral vision of human studies. To the extent that Marx embraced mechanistic social imagery and aimed to uncover the laws of history and society, he endorsed a strong scientific vision. Yet Marx framed his work as social critique of society and social science.

These ambiguities in Marx's social ideas were perpetuated by his heirs. The history of Marxism in the twentieth century evolved in two opposite directions. In the first half of this century, a materialist and scientific Marxism achieved dominance in the West and East. Marxism was understood as a science that discovered the laws of society. History was viewed as the linear, progressive unfolding of successive socioeconomic formations propelled by internal contradictions in the prevailing mode of production. Capitalism was conceived as the last contradictory mode of production; its inevitable decline would usher in socialism and a classless communist society. The Russian revolution made scientific Marxism the official ideology of Communist parties in Europe and the United States In the postwar period, less dogmatic versions of scientific Marxism (e.g., structural Marxism, world systems theory, rational choice theory) found a secure place in the Western academe.

Reacting against the authority that scientific Marxism had acquired in European culture and politics was a tradition that framed Marxism as a social and moral critique. If scientific Marxism highlighted the mechanical, materialistic, and economistic aspects of Marxism, "critical Marxism" appealed to the voluntaristic, dialectical, and activist dimensions of classical Marxism. Society was described as a system structured by multiple, interacting causative factors and history as the contingent creation of human actions. Critical Marxists valued the role of critical theory as a force of social change. The original home of critical Marxism was Germany. Critical Marxists combined the Hegelian idealist emphasis on humankind's self-creation through history with the sophisticated political sociology of Weber and Georg Simmel. They sought to broaden Marxism by connecting its political economic approach to an understanding of culture and politics. They aimed to fashion Marxism into a critical social theory that could grasp the movement of Western industrial societies and its potential for revolutionary change.

Critical Marxism has many voices, from the existential Marxism of Jean Paul Sartre to the Praxis school associated with East Europe [15]. The most important movement of critical Marxism in terms of its impact on the human studies has been the critical theory of the Frankfurt school. The Frankfurt school refers to a group of extraordinary academics – philosophers, sociologists, historians – who worked together at the Institute for Social Research at Frankfurt between roughly the late 1920s and 1935. Its chief intellectual leaders were Theodor Adorno, Max Horkheimer, and Herbert Marcuse [16]. Despite migrating to the United States in 1935 to escape Nazism, they reestablished the institute under the auspices of Columbia University.

The Frankfurt school proposed "critical theory" as an alternative to both scientific Marxism and orthodox social science. Critical theory draws from the empirical disciplines to forge synthetic conceptions of society as an historically developing social whole. Critical theory aims to not only understand society but change it. Repudiating the dogma of value neutrality, the Frankfurt school analyzed the major sites of conflict and social crisis for the purpose of advocating political activity. Critical theory was to be a new type of human study: It would unite philosophy's concern with synthetic analysis and the empiricism of the social sciences, animated by the moral intention of making theory into a force for human emancipation.

A history of dramatic, often shocking, changes separates Marx and the Frankfurt school. Marx's ideas were formed against the hopeful background of imminent social revolution, e.g., the working class revolts of 1848, the Paris Commune of 1870, and the formation of unions and socialist parties in late ninteenth century. By the 1930s, Marxists were considerably less optimistic. Despite recurring economic and social crises, there were no revolutions in Western capitalist societies. Contrary to Marxist expectations, revolution occurred in the economically underdeveloped nation of Russia. Whatever social hope the Russian revolution inspired quickly disappeared as communist Russia drifted into a bureaucratic empire. Complete disillusionment swamped the Frankfurt school as Germany embraced fascism, rather than socialism, as a response to the twin threats to capitalism: economic depression and communism.

Social hope passed into social pessimism for the critical theorists. The Marxist dream of the coming of a new age of freedom came crashing down as a nightmare of social barbarism and mass terror. As the prospects for progressive change disappeared, the Frankfurt school gradually abandoned empirical social analysis in favor of philosophical theories that explained the darkness that enveloped the West. The major thrust of critical theory was to trace the current social hell to some elemental defect in the West, for example, its concept of reason or the dominance of scientific-technological rationality. The shift to a philosophical analysis in the face of the crisis of Western civilization parallels the sociology of Talcott Parsons, except that the latter theorized with a hope of imminent social revitalization. In the face of social barbarism, the Frankfurt school's only social hope was to keep alive the already enfeebled philosophical and aesthetic traditions of critical reason.

Despite the reestablishment of the Institute for Social Research in postwar Germany, it never regained its former unity of purpose and intellectual importance. Many of its key members – Marcuse, Leo Lowenthal, Eric Fromm – remained in the United States [17]. Horkheimer retired in 1958, and Adorno died in 1969. Nevertheless, if the institute no longer served as the social center of critical theory, its spirit was preserved in the person of Jürgen Habermas.

Between the Frankfurt school and Habermas was not only a generational space but an historical one. The founding members of the Frankfurt school came of age in the midst of the Great Depression, the rise of Nazism, and the disillusionment with Soviet communism. Habermas reached adulthood during the democratic reconstruction of postwar Germany and in the context of postwar Western economic prosperity. His intellectual development coincided with the renewal of democratic political activism in the student protests and the new social movements of the sixties. Although the public disclosure of the shocking atrocities of Nazi Germany and Stalinist Russia introduced a profound caution into Habermas's social hopes, his perspective on Western development was much more optimistic than that of his predecessors. Faced with what they considered to be the irrationality of the modern world, Adorno and Horkheimer abandoned the Enlightenment dream that reason could help to liberate humanity. Habermas aimed to recover the modern utopian faith in the beneficent power of reason.

Habermas wished to return to the original aim of the Frankfurt school to integrate philosophy and empirical science for the purpose of moral critique and social change. He rejected the flight of critical theory from empirical analysis into philosophical and aesthetic analysis. Habermas believed that the prospects for progressive change in the postwar West make possible a renewed unity of theory and practice. Critical theory needed to recover the original Marxian aim of clarifying the sites of social crisis and conflict; the value of social criticism lies ultimately in becoming a force in a transformative politic. However, Habermas was convinced that this renewal of social critique required the reconstruction of Marxism.

Habermas gave three reasons for reconstructing Marxism. First, Marxism was too easily dismissed as ideology; accordingly, its social criticisms and political intent lacked public authority. Habermas undertook the daunting task of providing an epistemological justification for critical theory. In other words, he wished to make the case that critical theory is an expression of reason, not prejudice and ideology. Second, the conceptual foundations of Marxism were flawed. The failure of Marxism to explain the absence of revolution in the West and its occurrence in the East, the rise of fascism and, in the postwar years, the rise of the new social movements indicates defects in its most basic premises and categories. Third, Habermas argued that the general conceptual defects in Marxism combined with postwar develop-ments rendered the Marxist theory of capitalism inadequate as a basis for clarifying the major dynamics and prospects for change in today's world. During the last 30 years, Habermas has attempted to furnish a sound conceptual foundation and justification for a critical theory of society.

Social critique as reason

Habermas described Marxism as a critical social science. In contrast to the natural scientific ideal of Comte or Durkheim or the ideal of value-neu-trality of Weber, Marx viewed social theory as commited to promoting human freedom. Theory aimed to reveal the sites of conflict and the prospects for social transformation. Theory was to be a force of change by altering the social perspective of agents of change. Societies were to be judged by their own ideals and social promises. For example, in *Capital*, Marx criticized capitalism by claiming that the ideals of liberty, equality, and justice that were invoked to justify this society were contra-dicted by a reality of exploitation and class rule. In arguing that profit is based on the exploitation of labor or that the accumulation of wealth perpetuates class domination, Marx wished to foster a critical attitude on the part of laborers toward capitalism. Indeed, Marx hoped to con-tribute to the transformation of a mass of blue collar laborers into a politicized working class whose personal discontents would be translated into a public struggle against capitalism. Marxism was to provide the theory of change, socialism the political ideology, and the working class was to unite theory and practice.

The Frankfurt school absorbed the Marxian ideal of "immanent critique." The basis of moral criticism was the social ideals that legitimated institutions and political rulership. Immanent critique exposed the contradictions between reality and social ideals for the purpose of stimulating critical consciousness. According to the Frankfurt school, social critique is a force for social change to the extent that it challenges the dominant social

ideologies that present the existing society as a natural and morally beneficent order. Critical theorists aimed to clarify the socially constructed character of society, to reveal the existence of ruling social groups whose social
world views justify an unequal and unfair social arrangement, and to
identify social agents who have an interest in enacting social change.

The Frankfurt school eventually abandoned the ideal of immanent
critique. They perceived that the broadly liberal democratic values of
modern civilization were declining in the face of fascism and that the
power of reason and the modern ideals of liberty, social equality, and
justice were becoming feeble and peripheral to the legitimation of capitalist society. As reason fled the world, as the positive moral values of the
modern West lost their public authority, immanent critique gave way to a
defense of an abstract philosophical critical reason. The Frankfurt school
became protectors of a rationality that is committed to the values of
reason, morality, and emancipation in the face of the flight of these
values from the world.

Habermas shared the Frankfurt school's perception that immanent critique was no longer an adequate basis for a critical social theory. Although
he was not persuaded that Enlightenment values had fled the West, he was
convinced that their social support was precarious. He urged that the values
of critical reason, autonomy, and democracy needed a justification rooted
more centrally in reason than in elite cultural traditions (e.g., art or philosophy). But how was a critical theory of society to be rationally justified? It
was no longer credible, thought Habermas, to appeal to some notion of
reason that was outside of society and history. The modern tradition, from
Marx through Nietzsche and Freud, convinced us that behind reason are
interests and desires. Although conceding that knowledge is structured by
social interests, Habermas was unwilling to surrender to relativism. This
would render humanity unable to defend itself against the evils of a Nazi
Germany, Soviet communism, or state capitalist society.

In *Knowledge and Human Interests*, Habermas conceded that human
interests structure knowledge [18]. However, instead of thinking of interests and knowledge as thoroughly relativistic, Habermas asserted the
existence of three universal human interests that produce three general
forms of knowledge. In other words, Habermas argued that beneath the
near-infinite variety of human desires are three universal interests. These
human interests give rise to general forms of cognition and knowledge.
This renders knowledge, including critical theory, general and necessary,
rather than merely historical or arbitrary.

Habermas referred to three types of knowledge that correspond to
three cognitive interests, each of which is said to be basic to the ongoing
reproduction of human existence. The empirical-analytical sciences, for

example, the natural scientific ideal, focuses on apprehending empirical regularities and making predictibility possible. They are governed by a "technical" human interest in enhancing control over nature and society. The empirical-analytical sciences are rooted in the necessity of human reproduction through work or controlling our inner and outer environment. Humans need empirical knowledge relating to the causal sequencing of events in order to exercise some control over their environment and their behavior. The reproduction of human life through exercising mastery over the self and world is made possible by our capacity to cooperate, communicate, and share a common world. It is only because we share language and a world of meaning that communication and therefore human survival are possible. This "practical" cognitive interest gives rise to the historical, interpretive, or cultural sciences whose aim is to clarify the meaning of texts, actions, and social events in order to promote mutual understanding. Basic to both the technical and practical cognitive interest is a third "emancipatory" interest. The technical cognitive interest reveals a desire to free ourselves from the constraints of nature so that we may be self-directing. Similarly, the practical cognitive interest exhibits a wish to abolish distortions and blockages in interactions in order to render communication open and free, i.e., free to hear the voice of reason over the noise of particular interests. The emancipatory cognitive interest gives rise to the critical sciences – e.g., Marxism and psychoanalysis. These aim to identify unnecessary internal (e.g., psychological) and external (e.g., social or environmental) constraints on human action with the hope that such awareness will promote autonomy.

Habermas wrote *Knowledge and Human Interests* to show that critical theory cannot be dismissed as mere ideology. Just as positivism is rooted in a general human interest in control and interpretive social science expresses an interest in linguistic communication, critical theory is anchored in a universal human interest in autonomy. Habermas wanted to defend a critical moral standpoint as a form of reason, not ideology. His strategy was to identify a will to freedom or to forms of social life free of unnecessary constraint as embedded in the very structures of everyday life, e.g., in work, communication, or power dynamics. Critical theory is characterized as an expression of a universal drive towards human autonomy.

In response to criticisms surrounding the status of cognitive interests, especially the emancipatory interest, Habermas abandoned the position of *Knowledge and Human Interests*. He did not repudiate the search for a rational basis for critical theory. Instead of trying to identify an emancipatory cognitive interest, he turned to the structure of language and communication to uncover a generalized human interest in autonomy.

In *The Theory of Communicative Action*, Habermas argued that all human action involves language use [19]. Moreover, linguistic communication is impossible without raising what he calls "validity claims." In ordinary conversations, people make claims about the nature of the world (e.g., that it is made up of individuals or that unconscious motives explain behavior) and claims about what social rules are right (e.g., people should stop at a red light or reward achievement). Routine, ongoing social interaction is possible insofar as there is some agreement regarding these validity claims. In order for individuals to share a common social world, to cooperate and coordinate actions, there must be some consensus about what we take to be real and what social norms are appropriate in various situations.

Social consensus is fragile and can easily be disturbed. If validity claims are disputed (e.g., if someone challenges beliefs about what is real or individuals disagree about social norms), individuals may respond by trying to coerce or manipulate a "consensus." However, people may also respond by giving reasons for their beliefs about the nature of reality or which norms are appropriate *with the hope of restoring a noncoerced consensus*. The anticipation of arriving at a "reasoned consensus" implies the possibility that the sheer force of the reasons advanced or the possibility of identifying common beliefs, values, social norms, and interests through reasoned discussion are a powerful force in motivating behavior and structuring interaction. In other words, Habermas maintained that insofar as linguistic communication presupposes an orientation to consensus based on appeals to arguments alone, reason is an integral aspect of daily life.

Habermas took this argument for the foundations of critical theory one step further. At the core of the hope for a rational consensus is a social ideal that is implicit and that Habermas explicitly invoked as justifying the moral standpoint of critical theory. The logic of rational consensus or a consensus shaped by the force of the reasons advanced is unthinkable without assuming a social condition in which discourse is open to all individuals who are not constrained by lack of resources or fear of repercussions in contesting validity claims and therefore power hierarchies. If discourses over what is real and right are not open to all and constraint free, we could not avoid the suspicion that consensus making was achieved through force or intimidation. Rational consensus presupposes what Habermas called an "ideal speech situation," a social condition in which the parties to public discourse are in a situation of equality and autonomy.

Habermas's intent should not be obscured in the detail of his theory of communicative action. He wished to provide a defense of critical theory as a form of reason, not ideology. He intended to justify the commitment of critical theory to social justice and democracy as more than a prejudice or culturally specific value. By identifying an orientation to rational consensus as inherent in everyday life, Habermas thought he had found a rational basis for critical theory. The hope for a society free of constraint, founded on a democratic public culture, is not merely a utopian wish of critical theorists but an ideal built into the very structures of daily life. The values of democracy, justice, equality, and autonomy are not arbitrary or irrational but are the very preconditions of communication, the hidden telos toward which everyday life is directed. In short, Habermas hoped to render critical theory as the very manifestation of an immanent reason arriving at a certain awareness of its own power and purpose.

Reconstructing Marxism as general theory and critique

Habermas detected in Marx a certain reluctance to think through the basic concepts and premises of his social theory. Marx never really clarified his moral standpoint. He appealed to the liberal and democratic values of Western capitalist societies to criticize them. But what if the social ideals invoked are morally ambiguous or what if democratic values are declining? Moreover, Marx assumed that the working class represented the general interests of humanity and that the truth of his social ideas was guaranteed by their inevitable triumph. But what if Marx was mistaken? Indeed, by the mid-twentieth century, the identification of the working class with humanity's freedom was in doubt. The first generation of the Frankfurt school wedded social critique to a relativistic standpoint. As we have seen, Habermas attempted to secure foundations for a critical theory of society.

Marx never adequately clarified the basic concepts of his social theory. As his ideas developed in polemics against idealists and political economists, and in response to current social developments, Marx's core concepts were only sketchily outlined and defended. In fact, Habermas thinks that classical Marxism is conceptually flawed.

At the heart of Marxism is the defense of a materialist social theory. Marx often described materialism as little more than an approach emphasizing economic and political dynamics in contrast to idealism's focus on ideas and cultural development. However, Marx at times presses materialism into an economistic, base-superstructure model that neglects cultural and political dynamics. Habermas believed that the tendency of Marxism to favor one-sided "materialist" social explanations accounted for its growing obsolescence in Western societies. Habermas intended to revive Marxism as a vehicle of critical social analysis by broadening and refashioning its conceptual foundations.

The Marxian theoretical edifice is built around the concept of labor. It is through labor that humans make and remake themselves, society, and history. Yet the concept of labor is confused in Marx and often falls prey to a one-sided materialistic understanding. In principle, labor refers to our materialist struggle to control social and natural forces as a means of survival and dominance. Labor also exhibits an "idealist" dimension in that all behavior is guided by norms and involves shared beliefs and values that make possible social cooperation and regulated social conflict. Marx's multidimensional view of labor should have encouraged him to develop concepts, social models, and explanations that emphasized both materialist dynamics such as technological and organizational development and idealist processes that relate to changing social norms and ideals of justice. Yet Marx's social theory repeatedly edges into a one-sided materialism, either ignoring idealist dynamics or reducing them to secondary effects of materialist social processes.

Habermas addressed the materialism of Marxism in *The Reconstruction of Historical Materialism* (many of the essays appear in the English edition, *Communication and the Evolution of Society*) [20]. Drawing on recent anthropological research, Habermas disputed the Marxian definition of the human species in terms of labor. Labor is not a uniquely human trait since it is characteristic of hominoids. What is distinctive to the earliest stages of human evolution is that labor is organized along kinship lines. Kinship, moreover, is an arrangement defined by language and cultural codes. In other words, Habermas suggested that labor and language or work and communicative or symbolic action are basic to humankind. Accordingly, social theory must build into its conceptual strategies a dual concern with materialist processes revolving around work and the struggle for survival and dominance and idealist processes centered on the creation of a symbolic world of meanings, identities, and social solidarities.

Habermas's effort to reconstruct Marxism as a multidimensional social theory led him to challenge the centrality of the concept of mode of production. According to Marx, the mode of production defines the core structure and dynamics of society. Marx conceived of the mode of production as composed of the forces and relations of production. The former includes raw materials, technology, labor power, organizational skills, and knowledge; the latter refers to the social relations of property ownership. Marx held that the class that owns property exercises control over the forces of production (e.g., determines the division of labor) and over laborers. The forces and relations of production form the economic base of society that determines the cultural and political superstructure. History is viewed as the progressive unfolding of the internal contradictions in the mode of production or economic base. The development of the forces of production inevitably come into conflict with the relations of productions or the social framework of the economy. For example, the development of

commerce and manufacturing in late feudal Europe contradicted the dominance of agrarian socioeconomic relations and institutions. Class conflict is
the mechanism by which a new mode of production is ushered in. Thus,
the struggle of the new bourgeois class against the landed nobility in late
feudal Europe ended in the triumph of the former and a developing capitalist system. The coming to power of the working class and the advent of
socialism will mark the end of history as a story of class conflict.

Habermas argued that a reinvigorated critical theory should abandon this
formulation of historical materialism. The latter is unable to grasp the
interdependency of economy, state, and culture in late capitalist society.
Through the concept of relations of production (i.e., the relation between
property owners and laborers), Marx can explain how the actions of individuals – laborers and capitalists – are guided and ordered. He relied
heavily on an appeal to the power of legal norms and to the economic
and political power of capitalists to account for processes of social regulation and integration. What is lacking in Marx are analyses of nonlegal social
norms and ideals regulating action; there is no understanding that identity
formation is central to both social regulation and conflict; nowhere in Marx
is there an analysis of the creation of solidarity communities among workers
or capitalists.

Habermas accused Marxism of reducing the social base to the economic base. Marx defined the economy as the determining factor in
shaping cultural, legal, and political structures. The same reductionism
is apparent in the Marxist identification of the relations of production
with narrowly economic or property relations of ownership. Marx
assumed that, in all societies, legal ownership of the means of production
determined the relations of production, that is, property owners controlled
labor power, the division of labor, the distribution of wealth, and ultimately the institutional shape of society. Hence, all societies can be
described in terms of economically based class relations: institutional
dynamics are merely the elaboration of this economic base. Habermas
disagreed. He suggested that only in liberal capitalist societies (from
roughly the mid-nineteenth to the mid-twentieth centuries) do the relations of production assume a directly economic form or is the economy
the base for institutional formation. In other societies, noneconomic
domains regulate access to the means of production, determine the distribution of wealth, and define the dominant forms of identity and social
integration. For example, in "primitive" societies, kinship structures form
the social base or institutional core; their formation and functioning cannot be reduced to property relations but are anchored in complex symbolic systems of classification and codes that govern familial, social, and
political roles and relations. Habermas did not discount the importance of

economic relations but objects to the collapse of cultural and political dynamics into economic ones.

Similar concerns motivated Habermas's critical revision of the standard Marxian theory of social change. Classical Marxism explained change as driven by the internal contradictions of the mode of production. At certain critical junctures, the relations of production become an impediment to the development of the forces of production. System imbalance produces a social crisis which is resolved by a "readjustment" of the relations of production to a higher level of development of the forces of production. Habermas argued that the pressure exerted by the forces of production on the relations of production might explain the precipitation of a social crisis; it cannot account for the kinds of institutional and cultural changes that must occur in order for a social revolution to ensue. Major alterations in the "relations of production" involve new social norms, ideals of social justice, institutional arrangements, and altered forms of personal and social identity and integration. Faced with a social crisis that requires innovation in social norms, identities, and social integration, individuals will not be able merely to apply scientific-technical knowledge; rather, a broad institutional shift is unthinkable without an alteration in the character of our moral knowledge; i.e., ideas about social norms, justice, identities, and community. In other words, whereas the evolution of scientific-technical-administrative knowledge can explain the development of the forces of production, only the application of moral knowledge can explain the organization of the relations of production or the institutional framework of society. Social revolution occurs through the application of scientific-technical traditions and moral knowledge as it is embedded in cultural traditions, law, social customs, and social world views.

Whether he was addressing the core Marxian concepts of labor, mode of production, or social evolution, Habermas aimed to reconstruct the very foundations of historical materialism. Central to this effort is the claim that, in order to arrive at a comprehensive understanding of society, our core concepts must be able to grasp not only materialist dynamics centered on economic reproduction but idealist processes concerned with the formation of identities and social solidarities. At the heart of Habermas's social theory is a guiding vision of social action, institutions, and evolution. Humanity is imagined as developing along the dual paths of increased self and social control through scientific-technological progress and undergoing moral evolution through the progress of ethical traditions.

Habermas conceived of social evolution as occurring at the levels of both scientific-technical-administrative development and ethical advancement. Development at the former level involves processes of economic, technological, and bureaucratic rationalization. Advancement is marked by maximizing efficient, effective control over social and natural processes. With regard to moral or ethical evolution, Habermas drew from the developmental psychology of Piaget and the theory of moral development of Kohlberg to sketch a progressive view of history that parallels individual cognitive and moral development. Just as the child progresses from a state of fusion between the self and the world (the symbiotic phase) to a stage in which the self is clearly differentiated from the world and is capable of critical reflexivity (the universalistic phase), moral evolution, as evidenced in our law and world views, undergoes a parallel progression from mythical thought to universalistic ethics to the current Western critical reflective attitude. The story of human evolution that Habermas related is deeply ambivalent; whereas modernity signals an historic breakthrough, making possible unprecedented levels of social control and autonomy, it also unleashes the forces of bureaucratization and scientific-technological rationality that threaten to trap us in a social nightmare.

Failed modernization: moral reason in retreat

The Marxist critique of capitalism was losing credibility in the 1960s. The absence of working class radicalism and the authoritarian turn of Soviet communism precipitated a crisis of Marxism. This was reinforced by the rise of radical social movements among the youth, students, and marginal groups (women, gays, ethnic minorities) whose struggles could not be characterized as class conflicts. In the face of these events, many Marxists sought to revise the Marxian theory of capitalism. Neo-Marxists tried to explain recent events and to preserve a focus on economic crisis and class conflict by analyzing the shift from competitive to corporate, state-managed capitalism.

Habermas was convinced, however, that postwar developments pointed to a major reconfiguration of Western capitalist societies. The Marxian theory of capitalism required a fundamental reconstruction. The primary site of social crisis, conflict, and change has dramatically altered. Social crises have shifted from the economy to the state and culture; the key axes of conflict are around issues of rights, quality of life, protection of the environment, preservation of the integrity of communities, and control over local decisions around education and health, cultural legitimation, and social democracy; the battle for change is now occurring among a multitude of grass-roots-based groups and communities. A critical understanding of these events and movements requires an analysis of the dynamic interrelations between the economy, state, and culture. Habermas sought to produce a new *Capital*, a perspective on late capitalist societies that could provide oppositional groups with a critical understanding of the potential for social crisis and political action.

Habermas's first major theory of late capitalism was *Legitimation Crisis* [21]. He claimed that the major site of social crisis and conflict has shifted from the economic to the political and cultural spheres. Although capitalism continues to experience cycles of growth and recession, state economic management policies (e.g., monetary policies, price supports, purchasing surplus goods) have succeeded in averting a major socioeconomic crisis. Capitalism remains a contradictory society, but its chief crises have shifted to the political and cultural spheres.

Habermas spoke of a legitimation crisis when the public withdraws support from the government due to perceptions that its policies are unfair. Legitimation problems arise because the state must fulfill the contradictory demands of ensuring capitalist growth while maintaining mass public support. The former imperative requires that the state favors the particular interests of property owners and their managers; the latter imperative demands that the state act as if it represents the interests of all segments of society. In other words, the class interests of the state that are revealed in its social policies undermine mass public support which is necessary in a formally democratic society. Legitimation crises are manifested in citizen apathy, mass social discontent, and proposals for social reform, all of which threaten the social status quo. The state responds by increasing material compensations for the broader population in the form of state-funded support services or social welfare programs. However, this strategy has limited impact because it absorbs profit and threatens an economic downturn. A more effective response is for the state to promote a technocratic ideology. If politics is redefined as consisting of technical-administrative problems to be handled by experts, citizens are rendered politically inactive. Democratic politics is reduced to periodic voting which has the effect of reducing legitimation problems for the ruling powers while conferring legitimacy on the state.

Legitimation problems may be recurring in late capitalist societies but only when they are joined to a "motivation crisis" can they provoke a full-blown social crisis. Whereas the concept of legitimation crisis brought the state into focus, the notion of a motivation crisis places the cultural sphere at the center of critical theory. Essentially, a motivation crisis indicates a contradiction between the cultural and economic spheres. Let me explain.

Habermas believed that social institutions function effectively only if individuals have the appropriate set of beliefs, motivations, and values. These behavioral orientations are sustained by cultural traditions that are transmitted to individuals through the family, church, education, and mass media. In late capitalist societies, our lives are centered around work and family or career, consumerist and family ideals. These values are rooted in Judeo-Christian and secular liberal traditions which are today being undermined by secularization, statism, bureaucratization, and radical democratic movements. The cultural underpinning of late capitalist society is being eroded by its core social structural dynamics.

Habermas alluded to two possible outcomes of a motivational crisis. First, society could try to reestablish its institutional order on a technocratic basis. Individuals would accept social roles and institutional policies in exchange for material rewards (e.g., security, order, status) without requiring that institutional norms and goals be justified by substantive values such as justice or freedom. A second possibility is that Western societies will evolve towards social democracy. In the demands by the new social movements for social equality and participatory democracy, Habermas discerned the possibility of a truly democratic society. To the extent that these movements demand that reasons be given for social decisions and policies, they evidence a "communicative ethic" which, if actualized, would transform capitalism into a democratic socialist society.

In *The Theory of Communicative Action*, Habermas's crisis theory of late capitalism was reformulated as part of an encompassing grand theory of social evolution. Central to this theory is a dualistic view of society as both "lifeworld" and "system." The former term refers to a realm of behavior in which social coordination or regulation occurs by means of shared beliefs and values; in the lifeworld, individuals draw from custom and cultural traditions to construct identities, negotiate situational definitions, coordinate action, and create social solidarity. The lifeworld makes society possible by maintaining the identities and motivations necessary for institutional stability. Social life requires not only shared meanings but strategies for coordinating resources and controlling natural and social forces. This is the function of the systems level of society. In the course of social development, population pressures, intersocietal contacts, technological innovation, and wars create a need to organize complex activities and resources with the aid of functionally differentiated bureaucratic administrative structures. Whereas, in the lifeworld, action is oriented to mutual understanding, at the systems level, the emphasis is on instrumental control and efficiency.

Social evolution is viewed as a two-sided rationalization process of the social system and lifeworld. The development of social systems or social rationalization can be charted as a process of increasing institutional differentiation, complexity, and growing organizational predictibility. For example, the emergence of functionally differentiated institutions and roles (e.g., economy, state, education, family), each having its own function, maximizes social control. The evolution of the lifeworld or cultural rationalization is analyzed in terms of enhanced reflexivity, the universalization of beliefs, and the differentiation of value or knowledge spheres (science, morality, and art). In general, Habermas viewed societal development as progressive. The differentiation of functional systems enhances institutional mastery and makes possible higher levels of autonomy. The rationalization of the lifeworld makes possible higher levels of reflexivity and the expansion of a democratic public realm.

Unfortunately, Western capitalism has impeded the realization of the full beneficial human potential of social and cultural rationalization. In particular, capitalism has promoted social rationalization at the expense of cultural development. For example, the advance of bureaucracy has far outstripped the progress of political democracy; the development of scientific-technological rationality has overshadowed the advance of moral and aesthetic reasoning. Capitalist development has favored the bureaucratization of society, its rule by an elite of scientific-technical-administrative experts while devaluing moral rationality and a democratic political culture. Indeed, Habermas spoke, darkly and with echoes of the Frankfurt school, of the "colonization of the lifeworld." He imagined a dominant scientific-technical-administrative rationality and elite seizing control of daily life, translating moral issues into cost/benefit decisions, and redefining political disputes as purely administrative or technical problems. As the "system," with its technological-administrative ways of thinking, penetrates the lifeworld, it disrupts identities, traditional forms of life, forms of social solidarity, and cultural traditions. A traumatized lifeworld threatens the very survival of society. The spirit of Marx reappears in the notion of capitalist society as a contradictory, ultimately self-destructive system.

Despite the self-destructive logic of late capitalism, Habermas was not wholly pessimistic. He pinned his hopes on the new social movements. Marx, we recall, saw in the working class the hopes of humanity in the face of a self-destructive capitalist system. Habermas looked to the new social movements as redemptive agents responding to the destructive impact of the colonization of the lifeworld. "In the past decade or two, conflicts have developed in advanced Western societies that deviate in various ways from the welfare-state pattern of institutionalized conflict over distribution. They no longer flare up in domains of material reproduction; they are no longer channeled through parties and associations; and they can no longer be allayed by compensations. Rather, these new conflicts arise in domains of cultural reproduction, social integration, and socialization; they are carried in subinstitutional – or at least extraparliamentary – forms of protest" [22]. Unlike the working class, the concerns of the new social movements are not wages or work conditions, but "have to do with quality of life, equal rights, individual self-realization, participation, and human rights. . . . The new politics finds stronger support in the new middle classes, among the younger generation, and in groups with more formal education" [23]. The new social movements, which are grass roots, democratic, and motivated by substantive values and moral visions, aim at reestablishing an appropriate balance between social and cultural rationalization; they are the carriers of a rational society.

Afterword

Writing in the shadows of fascism and Stalinism, many liberal social theorists retreated from the Enlightenment hopes that modernity would usher in a new era of freedom and progress. Stunned by the ease with which the dreams of human freedom passed into a social nightmare, liberal intellectuals turned against social utopianism in favor of a defense of the social status quo that masqueraded as social realism. While rejecting an uncritical faith in the progress of humanity, Mills and Habermas, despite the horrors of the time, remained true heirs to the radical strains of Enlightenment social utopianism. The possibilities of human emancipation through critical engagement with the present were the moral impulse of their critical theory.

Central to the Enlightenment vision is the notion that science has a key role to play in human liberation. Science can free us from the ignorance, prejudice, error, and myth that tie humanity to the past and perpetuate a lack of freedom. Science tears the veil of illusions from our lives so that the full grandeur and possibilities for freedom are clearly before our eyes. Mills and Habermas shared this moral vision of science. As we have seen, Mills pinned much of his hope for a good society on the capacity of the independent intellectual, animated by a sociological imagination, to penetrate behind the illusions of the day to make the public aware of its drift into social darkness. Mills's utopianism lay in imagining that the sheer power of truth revealed would transform consciousness and ultimately create a democratic public out of an inert mass. Similarly, Habermas looked to reason, ultimately to an enlarged scientific reason, to uncover a human telos toward freedom.

Departing from a liberal Enlightenment vision in which science, almost unintentionally, is thought to promote social progress, Mills and Habermas conceived of the human sciences as value committed and morally and politically engaged. They offered a moral vision of human studies. Infuenced deeply by the American pragmatic tradition, Mills called for a public sociology, a type of social analysis whose problems come from current public conflicts and whose purpose is to clarify the implications for freedom and democracy of various social agendas. Mills's public sociology was to be a participant in current public conflicts with the hope of shaping their outcome. Situated more squarely in the tradition of Western Marxism, Habermas proposed a critical theory of society; its guiding interest was human liberation. Critical theory aimed to identify the conditions that foster or block autonomy and to justify the very idea of human emancipation as something more than a mere prejudice or illusion. Both Mills and Habermas rejected the value-neutral scientific ideal; both wedded science in its guiding premises and purpose to a moral vision.

Yet, theorizing in the aftermath of humankind's easy fall into barbarism, Mills and Habermas refused to surrender a strong notion of science as truth. They insisted that science was not to be confused with opinion, prejudice, or ideology. Relativism eased the slide into mass terror; it rendered reason impotent as a voice of moderation and restraint.

Habermas and Mills aspired to craft a human studies that would preserve the privileged access to truth claimed by science while enlarging its domain to include moral judgment. For Mills, this vision of a critical science suggested devising conceptual strategies that were historically specific, developed in close connection to empirical concerns and, in principle, susceptible of falsification. Exactly how concepts and explanations, which were value laden and intended to effect change, would be subject to empirical testing or fact-based revision was never addressed. Mills did not satisfactorily integrate the scientific vision of the classical tradition with the social activist agenda of a pragmatic tradition. Where Mills gravitated, even if haltingly, toward a pragmatic justification of critical theory, Habermas abandoned pragmatic and historical justifications. From *Knowledge and Human Interests* to *The Theory of Communicative Action*, he aspired to a transcendent or universalistic justification. He wished to prove that critical theory is not arbitrary or a mere convention but is necessary, i.e., gives expression to the human drive toward autonomy. In his recent social theoretical work, Habermas aims to uncover the real, universal foundations of the social sciences and the laws of social evolution. As Habermas's theorizing moves in the direction of grand theory, it is becoming far removed from public conflicts and the concerns of oppositional movements. Ironically, Habermas's moral vision, animated as it is by this quest to ground or justify critical theory as a form of knowledge, threatens to sever the ties between theory and practice.

Mills and Habermas represent two distinct styles of social criticism. Mills gravitates towards a "pragmatic" type of social criticism; Habermas defends a "foundationalist" type of critical theory. The latter aims to identify a universal basis to justify the values and social ideals of the critic. For example, the social critic may appeal to human nature, reason, some ethical imperative, God, or the laws of history to justify civil rights, equality, or democracy. A pragmatic approach favors justifications of social norms or arrangements that appeal to cultural traditions, situational advantages, or local, context-specific reasons.

Although Mills never directly addresses the moral basis of his social ideas, his critical sociology gains its moral force from appeals, mostly implicit, to cultural traditions and social practices that exemplify the values of autonomy, pluralism, and democracy. For example, his assault on the power elite receives its moral authority from its presumption of the value of representative democracy and citizen autonomy. Nowhere does Mills justify these social values by any foundationalist claims about human nature or arguments about ethical reason or the laws of history. Instead, Mills's defense of citizen rights and political democracy involves appeals, sometimes explicitly, to shared cultural traditions and social conventions among Americans or to the advantages of democracy, for example, that it promotes individual choice, autonomy, and equality. These values receive *their* moral force from appeals to national cultural traditions and social ideals. Pragmatic justifications of social norms, values, and ideals are historical, circular, and to some extent ethnocentric.

Whereas Mills was not much bothered by the moral standpoint of his sociology, Habermas has addressed this issue directly and relentlessly. In contrast to Mills, Habermas has pursued a foundationalist type of critical theory. Habermas has been troubled by a pragmatic or historically oriented type of social criticism. The chief problem with such approaches is that they are vulnerable to the charge of relativism. If standards of moral judgment are tied to cultural traditions, and if cultural traditions are conflicting or open to contradictory interpretations, such standards do not provide a basis to resolve normative conflict. Similarly, a pragmatist might appeal to utility to justify a social norm or practice but cannot identify general values or interests from which to advance objective standards to guide judgments of utility. Lacking such standards, the question persists: "useful for whom?" or "advantageous in terms of whose interests or from what perspective?" Pragmatism edges into relativism or the assumption of a plurality of moral standards. Relativism, Habermas thinks, cannot defend against the replacement of reason by power as the final arbiter of moral conflict.

Habermas urged a foundationalist type of social criticism. The aim is to find a rational moral basis or "ground" for the social critic's values and ideals. In order for this moral strategy to avoid relativism, it must *not* be tied to merely local or historical social conditions or linked to particular interests, traditions, or groups. The aim is to uncover an ahistorical or universal standpoint (e.g., human nature, reason, God, ethical reason) that can generate standards of moral judgment to guide social criticism and politics. As we have seen, Habermas has proposed a moral foundation for critical theory in the nature of communicative reason. In the very act of linguistic communication, Habermas perceived a moral logic of autonomy, equality, and democracy.

I have a great deal of admiration for Habermas as a social theorist. I began reading him in the early 1970s. I found in Habermas an impressive synthesis of Marxism and the classical sociological tradition. His critical theory combined Marxism's commitment to the unity of theory and practice with sociology's multicausal models of society. From the essays collected in *Towards a Rational Society* to his *Legitimation Crisis* and *The Theory of Communicative Action*, Habermas furnished critical analyses of Western societies, spotlighting sites of social crisis, conflict, and movements of democratic change [24]. Moreover, at a time when the social crises associated with capitalism, fascism, Nazism, and Stalinism seemed to demand a serious consideration of the moral basis of social ideas, Habermas was virtually alone among social theorists in engaging this issue. I would be hard pressed to identify another twentieth century social theorist who has so tirelessly pursued the ideal, to its logical conclusion, of a moral and epistemological foundation for human studies. Driven by the belief that only a foundationalist approach to questions of value can offer a "rational" engagement of social and political conflict, Habermas has elaborated a grand conceptual edifice, a theoretical system that includes moral foundations, a theory of the self, language, social institutions, and evolution. It is a system inspired by an uncompromising commitment to the values of autonomy, equality, and democracy. Habermas placed social reason into the service of advocating for social justice. This is a social theory that is insistently foundational, that attempts to anchor its basic premises, concepts, and moral commitments in something fundamental or basic to human existence.

I am not convinced that a foundationalist type of social criticism is necessary or desirable, though I admit a certain caution here. I leave aside the specifics of Habermas's efforts in this regard, in particular, his theory of language which anchors his critical theory. I assume, as an initial premise, that foundationalist arguments are important *only* if they carry social authority. I have no doubt that, in many contemporary societies, foundational appeals and arguments function as legitimations and moral rhetorics. Perhaps Germany, the home of Kant and Hegel, is such a society. On the other hand, Habermas may understandably believe that the weakness of Germany's culture of Enlightenment universalism was partially responsible for Nazism. In this regard, we may interpret Habermas as struggling to give cultural coherence and authority to a culture of

Enlightenment in a society particularly susceptible to illiberal currents. His opposition to pragmatic legitimations would make sense in light of a national history in which historicism and pragmatism were enlisted to serve fascistic ends. I am sympathetic to such an argument, but am I mistaken in viewing this reasoning as a pragmatic argument for a culture of Enlightenment? If this is Habermas's motivation, he overlooked an important point: Foundational appeals, whether they involve invoking God, human nature, or reason, can as easily serve authoritarian ends as democratic ones.

My own view is that foundational arguments, especially as they occur in expert academic cultures, have diminished public authority, at least in the United States. I do not wish to deny that public discourses at times appeal to God, reason, moral or natural law, or the laws of history to legitimate social practices or norms. Rarely, though, do such appeals rely on academic discourses or are foundational academic discourses carried into the center of moral and political debate. The isolation of academic culture from public life in the United States raises serious doubts about the social influence of academic foundational discourses. Moreover, I believe that foundationalist appeals are increasingly viewed with suspicion. I don't think that it's too much of an exaggeration to speak of postwar America as a culture of cynicism. Ideas, especially ideas that make fundamental claims about values, belief, or the nature of things, are perceived as expressions of particular experiences; claims to universality are suspected of masking particular interests; and values, norms and ideals are understood as subjective or tied to particular groups, subcultures, or traditions. Foundationalist arguments have lost a good deal of their moral credibility. More and more Americans, I believe, are living in a culture in which only arguments that acknowledge interests, locality, historical contingency, and practicality carry moral authority. In a word, pragmatism resonates with the broad culture of America, especially with a postwar culture that links knowledge, values, and power.

Speaking as an American, as an intellectual who wishes to engage national debates and conflicts, I favor a pragmatic approach. Pragmatism resonates deeply with the American emphasis on utility, social consequences, and diversity. It is in tune with a culture that, in important respects, is cynical towards universalistic ideas. The new social movements have made Americans increasingly aware of social differences (along the axes of gender, race, ethnicity, sexuality, or age). To the extent that these social differences have been politicized (e.g., through affirmative action programs or legislation banning discrimination or multicultural curriculum reforms), appeals to a unitary human nature, reason, or moral law are viewed skeptically or as acts of power concealing a particular social interest and agenda; such arguments lack moral credibility. Finally, I advocate pragmatic approaches because I am convinced that, at least in the United States, they encourage a public democratic culture. As the language of moral legitimacy assumes a vocabulary of utility, consequences, situational advantages, cultural traditions, and social practices rather than a vocabulary of essences, human nature, reason, natural law, divine right, social and political conflict, it encourages citizen participation and the free give and take among all citizens. A pragmatic culture is not a culture of experts in truth and argumentation; it is a democratic public culture. I imagine, hopefully, that a pragmatic culture would compel the social sciences to engage public conflicts much more seriously and centrally than at present. Perhaps somewhat fancifully, I link a pragmatic culture to a public sociology.

It is with some reluctance that I surrender a foundationalist approach to human studies. Habermas is right to observe that a shift to a pragmatic culture of social and political argumentation carries risks, the risk of cynicism passing into a power struggle that cannot agree on limits or terms of conflict. Yet I am not at all convinced that foundational arguments are a protection against this social danger. Formalistic arguments of the kind suggested by Kant or Habermas would seem to lack social effectiveness or force in a developing postmodern culture; they seem, moreover, unable to translate into specific social norms that can guide action or resolve actual social conflicts. In the end, I remain doubtful that a realm of general interests or norms can be situationally identified and agreed upon, which is presumed by Habermas, for his communicative ethic to have any social force. I have suggested that, in the United States at this historical juncture, universalistic or transcendent justifications of values, norms, or social ideals are losing public authority. I observe the making of a pragmatic culture of justification, one that preserves many Enlightenment values but favors loose, somewhat informal, less certain, more local styles of moral legitimation. In the next several chapters, I explore what such a culture might look like, at least in the sphere of social knowledge.

References

1. H.H. Gerth and C.W. Mills, eds., *From Max Weber: Essays in Sociology* (New York: Oxford University Press, 1946).
2. C.W. Mills's dissertation was published posthumously under the title *Sociology and Pragmatism* (New York: Paine-Whitman Publishers, 1964).
3. David Riesman et al., *The Lonely Crowd* (New Haven: Yale University Press, 1950); Thorstein Veblen, *The Theory of the Leisure Class* (New York: MacMillan, 1899).
4. C. Wright Mills with the assistance of Helen Schneider, *The New Men of Power: America's Labor Leaders*, (New York: Harcourt, Brace and Co., 1948).

5. C. Wright Mills, *White Collar: The American Middle Class* (New York: Oxford University Press, 1951).

6. Mills, *White Collar*, p. xvi.

7. C. Wright Mills, *The Power Elite* (New York: Oxford University Press, 1959).

8. Mills, *The Power Elite*, p. 4 or 9.

9. Mills, *The Power Elite*, p. 324.

10. C. Wright Mills, *The Sociological Imagination* (New York: Oxford University Press, 1959).

11. Mills, *The Sociological Imagination*, p. 186.

12. C. Wright Mills, *The Causes of World War III* (New York: Simon & Schuster, 1958) and *Listen Yankee: The Revolution in Cuba* (New York: McGraw-Hill, 1960).

13. Joseph Bensman and Arthur Vidich, *The New American Society* (Chicago: Quadrangle Books, 1971); Alvin Gouldner, *The Future of Intellectuals and the Rise of the New Class* (New York: Oxford University Press, 1979); Todd Gitlin, *The Whole World is Watching* (Berkeley: University of California Press, 1980); Richard Sennett, *The Fall of Public Man* (New York: Vintage, 1978); William Wilson, *The Truly Disadvantaged* (Chicago: University of Chicago Press, 1987); Arlie Hochschild, *Second Shift* (New York: Viking, 1989); Judith Stacey, *Brave New Families* (New York: Basic Books, 1991).

14. Thorstein Veblen, *The Theory of the Leisure Class* (New York: Macmillan, 1899); Christopher Lasch, *The Culture of Narcissism* (New York: W.W. Norton & Co., 1979).

15. Jean Paul Sartre, *The Critique of Dialectical Reason* (New York: Verso, 1991). A useful overview of an independent East European tradition of Marxism can be found in Erich Fromm, ed., *Socialist Humanism* (Garden City, New York: Anchor, 1966).

16. Max Horkheimer and Theodor Adorno, *The Dialectic of Enlightenment* (New York: Herder & Herder, 1972); Max Horkheimer, *Eclipse of Reason* (New York: Seabury, 1947); Herbert Marcuse, *One-Dimensional Man* (Boston: Beacon Press, 1964).

17. Leo Lowenthal, *Literature, Popular Culture and Society* (Palo Alto, CA: Pacific Books, 1967); Eric Fromm, *Escape From Freedom* (New York: Rinehart, 1941).

18. Jürgen Habermas, *Knowledge and Human Interests* (Boston: Beacon Press, 1971).

19. Jürgen Habermas, *The Theory of Communicative Action*, 2 vols. (Boston: Beacon Press, 1984–1987).

20. Jürgen Habermas, *Communication and the Evolution of Society* (Boston: Beacon Press, 1979).

21. Jürgen Habermas, *Legitimation Crisis* (Boston: Beacon Press, 1975).

22. Jürgen Habermas, *The Theory of Communicative Action*, Vol. 2, p. 392.

23. Habermas, *The Theory of Communicative Action*, p. 392.

24. Jürgen Habermas, *Towards a Rational Society: Student Protest, Science, and Politics* (Boston: Beacon Press, 1970).

6

Knowledge and Power: The French Poststructuralists

As our attention shifts from postwar United States to France, we encounter a strikingly different intellectual milieu. French academic life has centered around a few great universities and a small number of major research centers often headed by a "patron-scholar." French universities exhibit less of the discipline-centered emphasis characteristic of American universities. Moreover, in American academic culture, the figure of the specialized researcher or scholar who aspires to achieve stature in a specific discipline is the ideal. In France, this figure is overshadowed by the general intellectual who, regardless of his or her discipline, is expected to contribute to the national public culture. This unique social positioning of the French academic carries great significance for the moral and political meaning of human studies.

The separation between academic intellectuals and public intellectuals that has been characteristic of postwar America is less defining in France. Since at least the 1950s, the spirit of science and professionalism has governed American universities; academic intellectuals are expected to produce scientific or scholarly studies intended to be read primarily by members of their discipline. Although some American academics have assumed the role of public intellectuals, this is neither expected nor does it necessarily confer academic prestige. In France, academics are expected to be general intellectuals; they aspire to produce original perspectives that will address a broad public beyond academia.

The French cultural ideal is that of the general intellectual. Typically, this person has academic affiliations, preferably with the Sorbonne or the College de France. It is not, however, this academic status or any purely scholarly virtuosity that confers prestige on the intellectual. Rather, status accrues to those who fashion a singular style of writing and a distinctive perspective on the human condition that elicits interest across academic disciplines and social publics. The public intellectual draws on scholarly learning in order to engage current social developments in an original, provocative way. To be a socially engaged intellectual is to be political.

Contrary to American conventions, the public intellectual is not expected to separate scholarship and partisanship or to disjoin knowlege, politics, and ethics.

The existence of a tradition that values public intellectuals in France is crucial to grasping postwar French social thought. It explains, for example, why many of its major social thinkers, figures such as Jean-Paul Sartre, Simone de Beauvior, Albert Camus, Louis Althusser, Henri Lefebvre, Roland Barthes, Michel Foucault, Julia Kristeva, and Jean-Francois Lyotard were not sociologists or social scientists. In turn, many major current sociologists, figures such as Jean Baudrillard, Pierre Bourdieu, or Michel Crozier, can hardly be described as sociologists in the American sense since their work is more in the nature of a general social philosophy. As French human studies is produced by public intellectuals whose ties to a specialized scientific culture are weak, it exhibits a directly moral and political character.

In France, we look less to the narrow academic disciplines of the social sciences to locate the major breakthroughs in the human studies than to broader movements of thought that have an interdisciplinary, public character. And while the tradition of French sociology from Durkheim to the present is an admirable one, the defining shape of postwar French social thought was produced, above all, by two powerful theoretical movements: structuralism and poststructuralism.

Structuralism: a vision of a scientific human studies

Modern French intellectual culture reveals a long-standing division between a humanistic and scientific world view. This cultural conflict was pivotal at the juncture of the institutionalization of the human studies disciplines at the turn of the century. For example, the major opponents to Durkheim's sociological vision were scholars for whom society was the sum of individual decisions. Reflecting a humanistic world view, they opposed sociology, at least in its Durkheimian mode, because its emphasis on social forces was believed to deny individual freedom and moral responsibility. Durkheim's sociological works, from *The Division of Labor in Society* and *Suicide* to *The Elementary Forms of Religious Life*, were successive efforts to make credible a vision of the human world as governed by impersonal social laws and forces.

The tradition of a scientific structural sociology, which connects Montesquieu, Comte, and Durkheim, did not fare well in the French academe. By the end of the Second World War, Durkheimian sociology was in decline. These years saw the aging and death of many leading Durkheimians. In addition, the war resistance movement encouraged a more individualistic and heroic ethos that received a powerful expression in an existentialist philosophy. The marginalization of Durkheimian sociology was further encouraged by the growing importance of Marxism. This reflected, in part, the rise of the French Communist Party to a position of political power. Despite the decline of Durkheimian sociology in the postwar years, its sociologistic vision did not disappear from French intellectual culture. Its image of society as an autonomous realm of social relations and functions flourished in the 1950s as a program of structuralist social analysis.

French structuralism was a reaction against the tradition of humanistic philosophy, particularly existentialism [1]. At the core of a humanistic philosophy is a view of the individual as a self-directing, creative force. Humanism celebrates the individual as the primary active force in the making of society and history. In contrast, structuralism looks to forces beyond the impulses, interests, and values of the individual to grasp the basis of knowledge, society, and history. Indeed, the individual is explained as an effect of impersonal forces. Structuralists hold to the view that beneath the surface appearance of an individual-centered world that is contingent and in flux are universal structures that are manifested in the organization of the mind, knowledges, and human behavior. Structuralism was to be the vehicle for a scientific vision of human studies that aimed to uncover the deep structures that give coherence and order to the human universe.

As is typical of French intellectual culture, structuralism was less an innovation in method than a broad philosophical movement. Structuralism viewed the human world as ordered by unconscious, but rule-bound, principles. Although we can trace its intellectual roots to Marxism, Freudian thought, and the sociological approach of Comte and Durkheim, the most profound source of structuralism lay in developments in linguistics.

Ferdinand de Sausurre (1857–1913), a Swiss linguist, is credited with playing a major role in altering the way Europeans think of language [2]. The conventional view at the time approached language as a neutral medium for representing the world. Words or signifiers were said to acquire meaning by the concept they summon up in our mind. A relation of identity was assumed between word and concept and concept and world. For example, the meaning of the word "man" would lie in a relation of identity this word was said to have to the concept of man whose meaning, in turn, would be derived from its correspondence to the existence of real men.

Saussure challenged this view by conceptualizing language as a system of signs whose meanings lie in relations of difference. Signs conjoin a signifier and a signified or the concept brought to mind by the signifier (e.g., the concept of a tree by the word "tree"). Saussure claimed that the relation between a signifier and the signified or between word and concept is arbitrary in the sense that virtually any signifier (word or sound) can refer to any signified. Is there any intrinsic relation between the sound or word "tree" and its concept? Moreover, Saussure argued that there was no necessary or fixed meaning connected to the signified as well. Words may stay the same, but the concepts they refer to change.

If there is no natural, intrinsic link between word and the concept that it evokes in our mind, how do signs get their meaning? Saussure proposed that the meaning of signs is derived from their relations of difference. Words and concepts get their meaning in the particular ways they differ from other words and concepts in a specific language system. Relations of difference between signifier and signified in a particular language fix meaning. Thus, there is no necessary or compelling reason beyond social and linguistic convention to use the word "man" to refer to the concept we intend. Similarly, there is no reason to believe that the particular idea of men elicited by the word "man" has any fixed meaning.

What is it in the relation of difference that generates the sign's meaning? Saussure appeals to the oppositional or binary relation of signs. Thus, the word "man" takes on meaning not because it has any intrinsic properties that summon up the concept. Rather, "man" takes on meaning because, in the language system of which it is a part, it contrasts to the signifier "woman." Pursuing this further, the structural linguist could relate the man/woman opposition to a more general human/nonhuman animal binary which, in turn, could be linked to an opposition between animals and nonanimal living things and so on. The meaning of signs lies in their relations of difference, particularly in their binary oppositions, in a specific language system.

Saussure abandoned the standard view of language as a neutral medium through which the mind mirrors the world. This view held that, between word and concept and between concept and world, there were relations of identity that fixed meanings. In contrast, Saussure argued for a notion of language as a system of signs whose meanings were generated by their relations of difference. Saussure thought of language as an active, dynamic social force that shaped both the mind and the world. As a self-sufficient system, language can be studied as it is organized and functions in the present.

The project of a structural linguistics was translated into a program of structural human studies by Claude Levi-Strauss. Born in Belgium in 1908, Levi-Strauss immigrated to France as a child where he eventually held a chair at the prestigious College de France. He authored a series of pioneering works – *The Elementary Structure of Kinship*, *Structural Anthropology*, *The Savage Mind*, *The Raw and the Cooked* – that initiated what some have called "the structural revolution" [3].

Levi-Strauss aimed to model human studies after structural linguistics. He assumed that language was the prototype of all social phenomena. Accordingly, the assumptions and methods that guide the study of language can be applied to any social fact. Levi-Strauss analyzed kinship, myth, ceremonies, marriage, cooking, and totemic systems as autonomous systems composed of elementary units (akin to words or phonemes) whose meanings derive from their patterns of difference, particularly binary opposition and correlation. Levi-Strauss invoked language not only as a model of particular social institutions (e.g., marriage, kinship, or religion) but as a paradigm for conceiving society as a whole. Considered in its cultural or symbolic aspect, society is a kind of superlanguage.

Structural social inquiry examines the relations of difference and correlation among the elementary units of social phenomena. It aims to discover the universal laws that govern the functioning of social forms. Levi-Strauss imagines that these general laws are, at bottom, unconscious mental structures. In effect, he is proposing that underlying the social surface, with its seeming contingency, randomness, and individual freedom, are universal structures that operate independently of individual will to create order and social coherence. Indeed, the self or individual is, in this perspective, little more than a vehicle for the unconscious structural codes to enact their order.

In the 1950s and 1960s, the "structural revolution" instigated by Levi-Strauss provided an alternative to the humanism of existentialism and the sociologism of Marxism. Many intellectuals who sympathized with Levi-Strauss's structuralism did not, however, follow his rather literal program to model human studies after structural linguistics. For example, Louis Althusser wished to rethink Marxism in light of structuralism without reducing society to language [4]. In his early writings, Michel Foucault employed a broadly structural approach to the study of madness and the birth of the human sciences but avoided a rigid application of the linguistic model [5]. Nevertheless, even for Althusser and the early works of Foucault, we can detect the structuralist preference for synchronic over diachronic relations, internal system dynamics over narrative succession, and structural analysis of a present system over the historical analysis of events. In the structuralist approach, contingent social events and history move into the background as the analysis of elementary forms, general laws, and static structures prevails.

May 1968: poststructuralism and a politics of cultural revolution

The popularity of structuralism coincided with efforts to rebuild France in the aftermath of a devastating war. Unlike in the United States, World War II was fought on French soil. The end of the war left an economy and society in shambles. Furthermore, it was a war that produced a divided nation. Long-standing hostilities between France and Germany were greatly magnified during the German occupation. Many French believed that it was a national duty to resist German occupation. Divisions surfaced between a powerful resistance movement and those who backed, either passively or energetically, German occupation. Under the leadership of General de Gaulle, postwar France sought to heal the national divisions and reassert national pride.

The immediate postwar years saw the rise to prominence of existentialism, a philosophy that expressed the heroic ethos of the war resistance. However, as the memory of the war faded, and a new national and world order began to take shape, structuralism triumphed. Perhaps structuralism gave expression to a particular French take on the world. This was a world where little dramatic change was expected, and, for many war-weary Frenchmen, desired. General de Gaulle promised neither reform nor revolution but a stable, growth-oriented society. In addition, the rise to superpower status of the United States and the Soviet Union left France a second-rate power. To many Frenchmen, the emerging national and world order seemed to offer few possibilities beyond maneuvering within a fixed structural framework.

The 1950s was a sobering decade for the French. In place of visions of change and aspirations of national grandeur, the French were saddled with the humdrum task of rebuilding an economy and national culture in a world order where France was a sideshow. With the heroic spirit of existentialism dimming and with the revelations of the horrors of Stalinism dampening the ideological vigor of the French Communist Party, structuralism took center stage. With its present-centered, high-minded intellectualism, structuralism seemed an attractive alternative to a depoliticized intelligentsia. If France had to cede world political dominance to the United States and the Soviet Union, at least it could still claim an intellectual dominance by the sheer sweep and brilliance of its ideas.

Postwar social calm came to an end dramatically in May 1968. Student revolts ignited a national crisis. Unlike in the United States, French student discontent assumed a radical coloring. The agenda of the students involved more than democratizing a state-controlled, elitist university system. They wished to revolutionize society: Citizen control, self-government, and sweeping cultural change were at the heart of their rebellion. Their battles shifted from the campus to control over the key social institutions of the French Fifth Republic. Clashes with the police involving thousands of students took place on the streets of Paris. For example, on May 10, some twenty thousand students marched to free imprisoned students and comrades; a clash ensued with the police, injuring hundreds of students. Yet, the students did not retreat; barricades were erected in the heart of Paris as students occupied large sections of the Latin Quarter.

In the United States, the student protests gained mass public support only as an antiwar movement. The radical wing of the student movement, for example, Students for a Democratic Society (SDS), remained isolated. In France, the broad ideological agenda of the student movement was shared by substantial segments of blue collar workers, professionals, and the cultural elite. As one after another campus fell to the students or was closed, blue collar workers went on strike and occupied factories. In alliance with the students, trade unions and the teachers' federation called a general strike on May 13. Within a few days, an estimated six to ten million workers were on strike, bringing France to a virtual standstill. Reinforcing a growing sense of national crisis, physicians, lawyers, journalists, actors, and musicians joined the students and workers by taking over the cultural apparatus of television, radio, cinema, and publishing companies. What began as incidents of student unrest escalated into a broad-based revolt against French capitalism, Catholicism, and consumerism.

Through concessions to the students and unions, military and police force, counterdemonstrations, cabinet shifts, and legislative elections, de Gaulle triumphed. By the end of May, the revolt was, as a practical matter, over. Yet France was not the same. In its reluctance to support the students, the Communist Party lost a good deal of its cultural capital among the Left. De Gaulle's cosmetic concessions and attacks on the students and workers did little to shore up widespread public questioning of the authority of the Fifth Republic. Perhaps less perceptible was a growing feeling that the key institutions of France lacked legitimacy. Moreover, the revolts threw into relief the importance of the structures of personal and social life beyond the state and capitalism. Radicals turned their attention to those social institutions that produce knowledge, shape personal desires and identities, and form our ideas and ideals (e.g., universities, research centers, advertising, consumerism, and popular culture). They developed critical perspectives on consumerism, the culture of everyday life, prisons, mental health institutions, sexuality, gender, and the family.

The revolts of May 1968 were not an isolated or incidental occurrence. France was changing in broader institutional and cultural ways. Major population shifts to cities beyond Paris shook up the country; small, family-owned businesses, traditionally the backbone of the French economy and society, were rapidly disappearing, throwing large segments of the population into turmoil. Under the impact of mass consumerism and popular culture, the shape of daily life was dramatically altered. May 1968 was as much the effect, as the cause, of deep divisions and changes that were shaping France as it began to evolve beyond the task of rebuilding a war-torn nation.

France after 1968 was not a very hospitable environment for structuralism. The renewal of social activism and the experience of social life as fluid and changeable made structuralism, with its scientific formalism, seem irrelevant. Nor were French Left intellectuals prepared to renew their romance with existentialism which lacked a compelling social and political theory. Although Althusser's structural Marxism remained attractive to many on the Left, others were disturbed by the disdainful contempt of the Communist Party toward the student revolts. Moreover, despite the flexibility of Althusser's Marxism, he neglected to analyze seriously the structures of everyday life and social revolts that were not class based.

With existentialism, Marxism, and structuralism losing their grip on the Left, a new intellectual movement took form: poststructuralism [6]. It combined the disruptive gesture of existentialism, the high-minded seriousness of structuralism, and the political engagement of Marxism. It is not too much of an exaggeration to describe poststructuralism as a theoretical expression and continuation of the generalized revolt against authority signaled by May 1968. Like the protesters and rebels, poststructuralists emphasized rebellion and deconstruction rather than social reconstruction. Like their activist counterparts on the barricades of the streets of Paris, these Parisian intellectuals offered few proposals for a good society beyond slogans and rhetoric. Nevertheless, it would be a mistake not to take this theoretical flourish seriously. Poststructuralism signaled the development of a post-Marxian, postcommunist Left standpoint.

Poststructuralism shares with structuralism its antihumanism: The autonomous, rational self is replaced by discursive or linguistic structures as the principal logic of social explanation. Poststructuralists underscore the role of language in forming individual subjectivity and social institutions. Language is the place where meanings are produced; linguistic meanings play a major role in organizing the self, social institutions, and the political landscape. Hence, language is a principal site for the production of social realities and political conflict. Poststructuralists approach language as a system whose meanings derive from relations of difference and contrast. However, they do not share the scientific vision of structuralism. Structuralists aimed to uncover uniform linguistic patterns that gave order and coherence to human experience; binary oppositions were thought to structure psychic and social life in a patterned, universal way. To the contrary, poststructuralists highlight the inherently unstable patterns of linguistic and therefore subjective and social order. Whereas structuralism was a "constructive" project intent on identifying linguistic and social order, poststructuralism had a "deconstructive" aim: to demonstrate that all claims to identify an order to society, knowledge, or morality were unwarranted and concealed a will to power.

The chief figure of poststructuralism is Jacques Derrida [7]. He wished to unfold the logic of Saussure's structural linguistics. Derrida agreed that the meaning of the sign lies in its relations of difference. However, structuralists wrongly assume that meanings are fixed once these contrary relations are established. Derrida proposed that the meaning of the sign is unstable, multivocal, and changing. For example, the binary opposition, man/ woman, may seem universal, but it carries variant meanings depending on national context and considerations of class, race, age, and gender. One discourse may construct women as maternal, emotional, passive, and desexualized; another discourse projects women as erotic and powerful. In short, the meaning of signs are never fixed or static; they are, moreover, subject to contestation because assigning meanings has broad social and political significance.

In this regard, Derrida's break from structuralism is more than a matter of amending its view of signs; it is about the politics of language and knowledge. The structuralist intends to uncover general linguistic and social patterns organized around binary oppositions. The political meaning of this linguistic and social order is not examined. Indeed, Levi-Strauss thought of the binary structuring of language and society as marking fixed mental structures, ultimately lodged in the brain. In contrast, Derrida interpreted the meaning of signifiers – words and sounds – as in a state of continuous flux and contestation. He held that, whenever a linguistic and social order is said to be fixed or meanings are assumed to be unambiguous and stable, this should be understood less as a disclosure of truth than as an act of power, the capacity of a social group to impose its will on others by freezing linguistic and cultural meanings. Poststructuralists opposed efforts at linguistic, social, and political closure. Poststructuralism is a kind of permanent rebellion against authority, that of science and philosophy but also the church and the state. Its strategy of linguistic and political subversion is called "deconstruction."

Derrida thought that he had discovered a hidden logic in Western thought. He called it "logocentrism." The logocentrism of Western culture lies in its quest for an authoritative language that can reveal truth, moral rightness, and beauty. From Plato to Bertrand Russell, Western thinkers charged philosophy with the task of establishing a universal language that could disclose what is real, true, right, and beautiful. Social thinkers, from Rousseau to Levi-Strauss, aimed to disclose the order of society – how it is and how it ought to be. Furthermore, Derrida detected a series of binary oppositions in Western thought that have been pivotal in efforts to establish an order of truth. Dualisms such as speech/writing, presence/absence, meaning/form, soul/body, masculine/feminine, man/woman, literal/meta-phorical, nature/culture, positive/negative, transcendental/empirical, and cause/effect reappear time and again and lie at the core of Western cul-ture. Moreover, the two terms in these oppositions do not represent equal values. The first term is considered superior; the second is defined as derivative, undesirable, and subordinate. For example, the assumption that speech is superior to writing is basic to Western philosophy. Whereas speech is thought to be an immediate and clear vehicle for the mind's ideas, writing clouds our vision by entangling the mind in the rhetorical and metaphorical aspects of language. Relying on such hierarchical opposi-tions, Western thinkers have sought to identify an order of truth and reality that could function as an authoritative basis for judging truth/falsity, knowl-edge/ideology, reality/illusion, or right/wrong.

Instead of proposing his own system of truth, Derrida turned against the very idea of trying to uncover an order of truth. Beginning with his break-through book, *Of Grammatology* and elaborating further in *Writing and Difference* and *Positions*, Derrida attempted to show that claims to intellec-tual authority cannot withstand serious scrutiny [8]. He assumed the unstable, multivocal, and changing meaning of signs. If signifiers (words) carry ambiguous, conflicting meanings, if their sense is always in flux and contested, the search to identify a fixed order of meanings is thrown into doubt. In particular, Derrida exerted his considerable critical energies toward undermining the hierarchical dualities that occupy a supreme place in Western culture.

The subversion of the hierarchical discursive oppositions for the purpose of questioning their authority is the core of the deconstructive critical strategy. Its aim is less to oppose the hierarchy or reverse its values than to delegitimate its discursive force and contribute to its displacement or marginalization. A key strategy is to show that the first and superior sign can be explained as a special case of the second and subordinate sign.

Freudian thought is rich in deconstructive moves. Freud interpreted the "normal" in relation to the pathological. He reversed hierarchies such as conscious/unconscious, sane/insane, real/imaginary, and experience/dream. Freud's thought can also be the object of deconstruction. For example, man/woman and masculine/feminine are pivotal oppositions in Freudian psychoanalysis. Feminists have made a persuasive case that masculinity functions in Freud as the superior sign. For example, Freud repeatedly made the penis the norm of sexuality in general. As women's sexuality is assumed to be centered in the vagina, it is defined by its lacking a penis and therefore as incomplete and dependent. In Freud's theory of psychosexual development, the superiority of masculinity is registered by the centrality of the castration complex for the boy and

204 Dislodging the Canon

penis envy for the girl. Whereas the threat of losing his penis signals the loss of the father's power for the boy, the girl's awareness of lacking a penis generates a self-definition as subordinate and a wish to have a penis. The masculine/feminine hierarchy in Freud is unstable. In order to make women's sexuality derivative and subordinate, Freud assumed that women originally combined both the masculine (clitoris) and the feminine (vagina) aspects. Women are said to mature by giving up their masculine aspect in favor of a vaginal-centered sexuality. A healthy feminine self is achieved at the cost of repressing a clitoral-centered sexuality. However, since it is women who are originally bisexual, Freudian texts allow the conclusion that they are the general model of sexuality, while men are merely the particular, derivative expression of her phallic aspect. Reversing the hierarchy shifts women from the derivative to the foundation, from the periphery to the center, and from the subordinate to the superior term.

The point of deconstruction, however, is not to reverse the value of the signs, for example, to celebrate women's sexuality as superior. This is a limited strategy since it leaves the hierarchy intact and open to reasserting its original form. Deconstruction aims to disrupt and displace the hierarchy, to render it less authoritative in the linguistic organization of subjectivity and society. Subverting hierarchical oppositions allows marginal or excluded signifiers and forms of subjective and social life to gain a public voice and presence.

Deconstruction is not conceived only as a philosophical or literary critical strategy; it involves a politics of subversion. It challenges the institutions and public authorities that sustain linguistic, social, and political hierarchies. Linguistic meanings, be they about gender, sexuality, politics, or nationalism, are not innocent of political significance. Constructions of masculinity/femininity or Western/oriental shape Western social and political life. Thus, imagining femininity as signaling the natural, nonrational, and maternal positions women as socially subordinate or as naturally positioned to assume the wife, mother, and caretaker roles. Linguistic meanings and discourses, however, do not in themselves produce subjectivity and the social world. They are embedded in institutional frameworks and political hierarchies. It is important to trace how signifying and discursive practices empower and give privilege to certain individuals, groups, and forms of social life. Derrida envisioned the deconstructive subversion of signifying hierarchical oppositions as part of a broad critical social and political project.

Unfortunately, Derrida never clarified the social and moral vision that guides the deconstructive project. As in the days of rage in May 1968, the deconstructive opposition is poised as a relentless revolt against authority, *any authority.* Derrida seems to have been reluctant to go beyond a vague hope that deconstructive criticism can somehow open social space to a wider expression of human life. Derrida's poststructuralism is animated by a vision of a society that celebrates the sheer proliferation of different individual and social forms of life. It is as if poststructuralism wishes to be a kind of general voice for all the oppressed differences (e.g., women, ethnic minorities, gays). Although Derrida did not elaborate the social implications of poststructuralism, his colleagues did. In the writings of Jean-Francois Lyotard and Jean Baudrillard, the critical spirit of poststructuralism is taken in a social direction.

From textual to social poststructuralism: Lyotard and Baudrillard

Poststructural social theory exhibits the subversive spirit of deconstructionism. However, it connects textual or discursive practices to institutional and political regimes. Nevertheless, whether poststructuralism pursues a deconstructive textual analysis or a social critique, its goal is to disrupt intellectual and social hierarchies. The critical spirit of poststructuralism is not joined to a positive liberationist program. Poststructuralists may allude to a vaguely democratic pluralistic ideal; the moral force of their social critique seems to be largely drawn from an anarchistic social vision.

Like many French intellectuals, Jean-Francois Lyotard (born in 1924) has been deeply involved in Left politics. Unlike many of his colleagues, Lyotard's activism preceded his intellectual coming of age. He was active in trade unionism, the radical Marxist group Socialisme ou Barbarie, and the May 1968 events. He took his doctorate in philosophy in 1971. In a quick succession of books – *Discours, Figure, Dérive a partir de Marx et Freud, Economie libidinale* – he developed sketches for a post-Marxian critical social theory [9]. Lyotard rejected not only Marx but the core of the modern Enlightenment. Its quest for truth was said to be allied with the establishment of social hierarchy and oppression. Lyotard appeals to a critical "postmodern" knowledge that dismantles foundations, disrupts hierarchy, and speaks on behalf of oppressed peoples.

The distinction between modern and postmodern knowledge is central to the book for which Lyotard is most famous, *The Postmodern Condition* [10]. Lyotard sketched a series of broad historical changes in the character of knowledge. In premodern societies, narrative types of knowledge prevailed. Narratives tell a story; they are organized around a plot, a linear, sequencing of events, a marked beginning and end, and a tale of good and evil intended to shape social behavior. Lyotard reasoned that, in premodern societies, narratives were considered knowledge not because they corresponded to facts but because they conformed to social rules that fixed who has the right to speak, to whom, and when. As long as these social conventions were followed, the stories told, as well as the storyteller, carried authority. Moreover, to the extent that narratives both presuppose and reinforce social conventions, they are said directly to promote social unity.

Modernity is characterized by an assault on narrative knowledge. Narratives (e.g., religion and myth) are dismissed as ignorance, superstition, and as signs of an inferior civilization. In place of storytelling and myth making, which is poetic and evocative, moderns substitute science which is said to yield objective truths. However, whereas premodern narrative is self-legitimating so long as the story and storyteller conform to social custom, science requires an external source of legitimation. This is so because there is no direct link between science and social cohesion. Thus, the question arises: What is the social and moral meaning of science?

Lyotard has suggested that modern science appeals to narratives for legitimation. This is paradoxical because science claims superiority precisely in abandoning narrative. However, science relies on a different type of narrative than premodern ones. Lyotard called them "master or metanarratives" because they are overarching, synthesizing stories that give coherence and meaning to smaller or "local" stories and practices. For example, the Enlightenment story of human progress driven by the advancement of scientific knowledge justifies the practices of the natural and social sciences. Social scientists appeal to the idea that science promotes human freedom by eliminating ignorance and prejudice in order to justify their research. Lyotard viewed the Marxist story of the coming of socialism through class conflict and proletarian revolution as a metanarrative. Local accounts of economic recessions or trade union activity can be interpreted in light of the grand Marxian narrative. Master narratives legitimate social and political practices as well. For example, sex education policies may appeal to an Enlightenment narrative (knowledge liberates); a union strike may gain coherence within a Marxian narrative (class conflict). Grand narratives have been an essential feature or modernity.

Lyotard defined the postmodern condition by the decline of the legitimating power of grand narratives. "I define postmodern as incredulity towards metanarratives" [11]. By metanarrative, Lyotard referred to "making an appeal to some grand narrative, such as the . . . emancipation of the rational or working subject, or the creation of wealth" [12] Faced with the paradoxical condition of relying on narratives for its legitimacy, science gradually abandons the master narrative. Lacking an integrating story or foundation, science is fragmented into a multiplicity of heterogeneous disciplines, area specialties, and paradigms.

What value does science have in the face of the decline of the legit- imating power of metanarratives? Lyotard sketched two possible meanings of science in a postmodern condition. First, science is justified by its social utility. Lyotard spoke of the possible formation of a technocratic society that deploys science to enhance bureaucratic, capitalist state control over natural and social forces. At odds with this technocratic vision is an evolving postmodern science. As evidenced in Einsteinian relativity the- ory, quantum mechanics, Godel's incompleteness theorem, and Heisen- berg's uncertainty principle, postmodern science envisions the universe as unstable and unpredictable; knowledge is always tentative, incomplete, and perspectival.

Postmodern science abandons absolute standards, universal categories, and grand theories in favor of local, contextualized, and pragmatic concep- tual strategies. Thus, instead of pursuing a moral theory that appeals to universal standards or axioms (e.g., the utilitarian pleasure/pain calculus or the Kantian categorical imperative which enjoins us to treat humans as ends in themselves), Lyotard favors a local pragmatic ethical approach. This underscores the specificity of the situation and the ability of the parties involved to develop agreed-upon, tentative, nongeneralizable social norms. Or, instead of aiming to unify knowledge, postmodern science is oriented towards conceptual innovation, disrupting unifying conceptual schemes, and proliferating paradigms, research programs, and conceptual strategies. Its value lies in neither producing liberating truths nor socially useful knowledge. The value of postmodern science consists in making people more aware and tolerant of differences, ambiguity, uncertainty, and conflict. "Postmodern knowledge . . . refines our sensitivity to differ- ences and reinforces our ability to tolerate the incommensurable" [13]. Postmodern science is deliberately antisystematic and irreverent toward conceptual authority; it is, in short, a vision of knowledge as permanent revolution.

Lyotard linked postmodern science to a democratic pluralistic social ideal. Let me explain. Modern science held to the belief that scientific foundations were necessary for human progress. In Lyotard's view, this was a well-intentioned but misguided hope. He argued that the quest for a general theory that would permit us to legislate truth, moral rightness, and beauty is not only impossible but undesirable. It is impossible because no one standard, common language or set of concepts can speak to the irreducible heterogeneity in the ways that people think and speak about reality. The quest for systematic order is undesirable insofar as general theories create hierarchies that marginalize and repress social differences.

For example, despite Marx's good intentions to think of the working class as the hope of humanity, his privileging of class conflict as the key site of social change devalues gender, sexual, racial, religious, ethnic, or national conflicts.

Lyotard drew a parallel between the fracturing of knowledge into heterogeneous discourses resistant to unification and the decentering of society. No longer unified by a common culture or institutional core (e.g., economy, religion, the state, kinship), the postmodern society resembles an incredibly complex labyrinth of cross-cutting discourses. Deploying linguistic imagery, Lyotard views social life in terms of "language games." This refers to a set of linguistic practices, each marked by their unique rules, conventions, and aims. For example, science is a language game whose aim is truth; its rules enjoin conformity to specific methodological and conceptual conventions; its standards of justification are centered on issues of evidence and logic. In contrast, aesthetics entails different aims (judgments of beauty, not truth) and different standards of justification (considerations of spatial form, color, and dimension, not evidence or logic). Society is conceived of as a multiplicity of language games; individuals function as conduits or junctures in these diverse, conflicting circuits of discursive practice.

Lacking a unifying center, social conflicts in a postmodern society are dispersed and local. Lyotard is not denying the continuing importance of the state and the economy as sites of political conflict. He is contesting the idea that these institutions are today the primary sites of conflict and that the diversity of social conflicts in current Western societies can be reduced to a unifying logic, for example, class struggle or the struggle against patriarchy. Educational institutions, hospitals, psychiatric clinics, prisons, and the mass media are major sites of conflict. Moreover, the struggles that take place in these institutional spheres are heterogeneous. Thus, the struggles around sexuality, gender, ethnicity, class, nationality, and cultural status are irreducible to each other; they cannot be subsumed under some unifying conflict. Lyotard imagines postmodern society as manifesting a kind of generalized revolt against centralizing authorities by marginalized and excluded groups. Though reluctant to spell out a social ideal, Lyotard affirms the awakening of differences and renewed opposition that he attributes to the postmodern condition.

The deconstructive assault on textual authority is applied by Lyotard to the sphere of knowledge and society. The quest for intellectual foundations, objectivity, certainty, and universal truths is abandoned. In place of grand theories, Lyotard described and advocated a postmodern condition featuring the proliferation of multiple, conflicting discourses. Whereas Lyotard detected a shift from modern to postmodern forms of knowledge, Baudrillard describes a similar development, but in more global social and historical terms. In often breathtaking and chilling terms, Baudrillard outlines the social contours of a postmodern world.

Reaching intellectual maturity in the 1960s, Baudrillard absorbed the critical spirit of May 1968. Indeed, the University of Nanterre, where he held a chair of sociology through 1987, was a key site in the student revolts. Like Lyotard, Baudrillard's writings in the sixties and early seventies aimed to think through the intellectual and political implications of May 1968. He fashioned a post-Marxian critical theory that drew heavily from the post-structural turn. However, unlike Lyotard, who was strong in philosophical critique and weak in sociological analysis, Baudrillard elaborated poststruc-tural ideas in a more social theoretical direction.

In a series of masterful books, *The System of Objects, Consumer Society,* and *The Mirror of Production,* Baudrillard intended to revise Marxism but ultimately turned against it [14]. He argued that, desite Marx's revolutionary aims, the premises and concepts that guide his social ideas mirror and reinforce Western liberal capitalist society. At the center of Marxism was a utilitarian, productivist ideology that reduced society to labor as an instru-ment of productivity and economic growth. Unwittingly taking over the utilitarian spirit of capitalism, Marxism failed to grasp the cultural or sym-bolic structuring of society. For example, whereas Marx viewed commod-ities as part of the economic division of labor, Baudrillard analyzed commodities as a system of signs that organize the social universe by assigning to people and things a social identity and location (e.g., a gender, class, regional identity). In effect, Baudrillard inverted Marxism. Instead of conceiving of history as driven by natural human need and labor, Baudrillard insisted on the structuring of society by symbolic or linguistic meanings.

Baudrillard sketched a post-Marxian perspective on history. Whereas Marxism outlines stages of successive socioeconomic formations, Baudrillard proposed a history of the "political economy of the sign." He offered an explanation of the changing structure and social role of the sign. In premodern societies, the sign had a clear referent and context-specific meaning. Such societies were organized around what Baudrillard called "symbolic exchange." In these exchanges, communication is immediate, direct, and reciprocal; lacking mediating structures such as the market or mass media, symbolic exchanges are not defined by their instrumental purpose. In acts such as gift giving, religious rituals, and festivities, exchange directly affirms social status and social order.

From the early modern to the recent postmodern period, the structure and role of the sign changes in two key ways. First, the relation between sign and referent or reality is disturbed. Second, the sign forms a "code" that standardizes meanings and social responses. From roughly the sixteenth through the mid-twentieth century, a modern culture was formed; signs (words, sounds, images) were considered to have a more or less clear relation to an object or reality. Modern culture was organized around a series of distinctions between word and world, concept and precept, mind and reality, truth and falsity, essence and appearance, reality and illusion, and so on. By the second world war, these binary oppositions began to collapse. In particular, the line was blurred between sign and reality or word and world. In a "postmodern" culture, signs, words, and codes create their own universe of meaning without any clear relation to a real world of objects and events.

The somewhat nostalgic, obscure notion of symbolic exchange served as a critical ideal for Baudrillard. In the revolts of 1968, he imagined a renewal of symbolic exchange with its directedness, spontaneity, and reciprocity of communication. May 1968 signaled a break from the alienating codes of high-tech capitalism. The appearance of symbolic exchange among disenfranchised groups held out the possibility of political resistance and change. As the hopes of 1968 were dashed, Baudrillard's thinking became decidedly more pessimistic and obscure. History seemed to come to an end as current realities were overwhelmed by a sign system that virtually destroyed any semblance of order, truth, reality, and, for all practical purposes, political resistance.

In a series of books written in the 1980s, most importantly, *Simulations, In the Shadow of the Silent Majorities*, and *The Fatal Strategies*, Baudrillard conceives of contemporary Western societies as inundated by an excess of meanings and cultural representations [15]. Driven by high-tech information and communication systems, linguistic signs and meanings proliferate, multiplying relentlessly to the point where it is no longer possible to fix the meaning of signs, to relate word and object, and to differentiate truth and error, reality and illusion. The social world comes to resemble a flattened, monotone mass leveled by the spiraling weight of signs, meanings, and information.

We have entered, says Baudrillard, the age of the "simulacrum." Simulacra are signs that function as copies or models of real objects or events. In the postmodern era, simulacra no longer present a copy of the world nor do they produce replicas of reality. Today, simulations no longer refer to any reality; they create the idea of a reality which they simultaneously claim to represent. Simulations have no referent or ground in any reality outside themselves. Postmodernity is organized around such simulations. From model homes to models of urban planning, good sex, masculinity, fashion, and personal identity, social reality is structured by codes and models that produce the reality they claim to merely represent.

In the age of simulacrum, we enter a "hyperreal" space. The simulated representations of the real are taken as more real than the reality they are supposed to refer to. Is not the actor who plays the lawyer, doctor, or the homosexual taken as really a lawyer, doctor, or homosexual? Television viewers take the persona of the actor as their true identity. We assume, moreover, that the model (e.g., the representation of the lawyer, doctor, or the homosexual) defines a reality. Indeed, actors themselves confuse their personal identity with their theatrical role. The actor who takes over the persona of his or her theatrical role or who can no longer distinguish acting from reality has moved into a hyperreal space. In a postmodern hyperreal condition, the quest for reality, for experiences that unambiguously mark reality is intensified, a marker ironically of our very inability to distinguish the real from the unreal.

According to Baudrillard, modernity has been characterized by the explosion of new divisions (e.g., science is marked off from literature and philosophy), new forms of differentiation (e.g., sociology is differentiated from anthropology and within each discipline area specialties are further differentiated), and by new cultural distinctions (e.g., between popular and high-brow culture). In contrast, postmodernity features a process of "implosion." Boundaries collapse. Does it make sense to distinguish news from entertainment or to differentiate politics and science or politics and business? The proliferation of interdisciplinary studies, for example, gender, urban, gay, and African studies, suggests the implosion of disciplinary boundaries. Institutional borders blur. Is it meaningful to separate mass and high culture? Is the "social" distinguishable from the "cultural" sphere? As media images, advertising representations, and information flows saturate the social space, as a neutralizing stream of signs and meanings engulf experience, the elementary distinctions of the modern era lose credibility.

As a late capitalist technocracy ushers in the age of simulacra, the modern politics of oppression and revolt give way to a postmodern politics of seduction and surrender. In the modern era, power was lodged in a specific class or in the institutions of capitalism and the state. In the postmodern world, power is isomorphic with the circulation of signs and meanings. Hence, power is today diffuse and saturates the social field. Social dominance operates not through coercion or rationalized power but through the seduction of the individual by mass media imagery and meanings. Indeed, Baudrillard contends, perhaps somewhat tongue in cheek, that the social field has been leveled into one great mass. He speaks, unfortunately, without much precision, of the "end of the social." He means that the view of society as composed of social classes, ethnic, gender, or racial identities, and interlocking institutions is today irrelevant. In place of "the social" are "the masses," a manipulated by-product of the age of simulacrum. In place of modern social theory, Baudrillard urges "fatal theory." The modern politics of revolt is feeble in the face of a system of social domination that operates through the seductive, pacifying capacity of the sign, media image, and simulation. Today, says Baudrillard, resistance must take the form of a deliberate passivity, a refusal to be absorbed into the imploded universe of signs and meanings. Baudrillard seems to believe that our surrender to the "object" or our indifference to the steady eruption of signs and meanings emanating from a cybernetic informational society will somehow lead to the collapse of the system under its own dead symbolic discharge.

Lyotard and Baudrillard take poststructuralism in a social theoretical direction. The aim of deconstructing textual order is directed to the social field. Thus, Lyotard offers a sketch of the rise of postmodern cultural legitimations of knowledge and authority. Baudrillard proposes a sweeping outline of the passing of an era of Western modernity. Nevertheless, neither Lyotard nor Baudrillard anchor their social ideas in an institutional analysis; neither do they frame their ideas in a detailed historical or sociological way. There is a sketchy, sweeping, closed, and authoritative quality to their work that is somewhat inconsistent with their repudiation of the modern will to grand, generalizing theories. The most impressive effort to frame poststructuralism as a form of human studies has been Foucault's genealogical antiscience.

The making of the modern subject: Michel Foucault's genealogy as human studies

If Jean-Paul Sartre was the dominant intellectual force in the 1940s and early 1950s, succeeded by the short reign of Claude Levi-Strauss, Michel Foucault assumed this lofty status in the early 1970s. Foucault was an unlikely successor to the throne of philosopher king of France. Although he flirted with Left politics in the 1950s, Foucault was largely nonpolitical through the sixties. The son of a surgeon who graduated from the elite École Normale Superieure, Foucault's early interests were psychological and philosophical. In the sixties, Foucault began to make his intellectual mark through a series of books, *Madness and Civilization*, *The Birth of the Clinic*, and *The Order of Things* [16]. These books did not significantly depart from the structuralist program of sketching the internal rules and systematic order – especially a binary linguistic order – governing social phenomenon. Through the sixties, Foucault was speaking the language of structuralism, even as he stretched it in a more historical and political direction.

Foucault was born (1926) into the French social elite. Although he was only minimally engaged in the revolts of 1968, Foucault thought of May 1968 as a turning point in French political and intellectual culture. His own work and life seem to have been dramatically altered by the social upheavals of the time. Subsequently, Foucault's writings took a decidedly political turn; the question of power moved to the center of his ideas. Moreover, from the early 1970s until his death in 1984, Foucault became a truly political man, joining mass demonstrations and protests, writing petitions and lobby reports, making political statements, and traveling across the country and the world to lend his name to various causes for social justice.

The revolts of 1968 did not succeed in bringing about lasting institutional change. Foucault believed, though, that May 1968 marked an important shift in the French Left. Prior to 1968, the Communist Party was a principal political player in French national life. The revolts of 1968 and immediately thereafter challenged the dominance of Marxism, and the Communist-Party-controlled French Left. The movements of political opposition were not organized around class politics. Revolts surfaced around prisons, psychiatry, sexuality, gender, and education, in universities, families, cultural institutions, and prisons, and was initiated by prisoners, students, gays, women, professionals, and laborers.

Foucault interpreted these disparate struggles as marking the emergence of a post-Marxian, Left culture. Left politics could no longer be reduced to economic and class conflict; the working class could no longer be assumed to play a privileged historical role as *the* agent of social change; the Communist Party could no longer claim to be the sole legitimate vehicle for political opposition; Marxism could no longer claim to be *the* ideology of the Left providing *the* understanding of history and modernity.

The character of social revolt was shifting. Intellectuals were pressed to rethink their role. If political opposition was dispersed throughout the body politic, what form should social criticism assume? If social conflict was pluralistic, what would be the appropriate role of the social critic? In a word, how, if at all, would this new political culture alter the role of critical knowledge?

Central to the Western Enlightenment tradition has been the idea that scientific reason can contribute to human freedom. By revealing the essential structure and dynamics of society, social theory could prescribe a political agenda of social change. This critical spirit has guided liberal and Left culture. In this regard, Marxism remains heir to the Enlightenment tradition. Marxism has aspired to reveal the laws of history and society, to disclose the chief site of change (economy), the principle drama of social conflict (class conflict), the agent of change (working class), and the future of humanity (communism).

Foucault urged us to abandon this Enlightenment vision: the quest to liberate humanity through uncovering the laws of social order and change and the appeal to theory as providing a standpoint from which to prescribe a program of social reconstruction. Departing from theorists such as Habermas who attempted to reconstruct Marxism in light of postwar social developments, Foucault questioned the Enlightenment premises of Marxism. He objected to a social theory that aims to grasp the essential structure and meaning of a society or an historical epoch. He was suspicious of a view of theory as synthetic and prescriptive. Foucault did not discount the utility of general theories such as Marxism as interpretive or critical perspectives. He denied the necessity and value of defending these conceptual strategies as encompassing, unifying theories. His objections are both intellectual and practical: Totalizing theories are reductionistic and exclusionary. Such theories arbitrarily privilege particular social dynamics and political agendas while excluding or marginalizing others. For example, Marxism renders gender, sexual, racial, or nationalistic conflicts secondary, if not entirely marginal, by insisting that political economy and class is the organizing principle of all societies. In the aspiration to uncover order and purpose in social existence and to base a politics and ethics on this basis, general theories create a false and repressive sense of closure and order. Foucault's critique of general theory calls to mind Derrida's critique of logocentrism and Lyotard's critique of grand narratives: The longing for intellectual foundations and conceptual closure is purchased at the cost of social repression; the will to truth is entangled with the will to power.

In the revolts of May 1968, Foucault saw the surfacing of a multitude of oppositional social groups. Whether it was movements for prison reform, opposition to the psychiatric control of the self, women's and gay liberation, these revolts exhibited a varied social and political character. They can not be subsumed under a unifying concept, such as anticapitalist or antistatist or antiliberal. They can not be described as originating from the same social source, for example, the crisis of capitalism, patriarchy, or imperialism. The dynamics of domination and resistance in these revolts do not evidence an identical social and political pattern. Foucault did not deny that it might be desirable to analyze the interrelations between these social movements. However, he objected to efforts to deduce these varied social revolts from a general theory such as Marxism. These social conflicts need to be understood in terms of their unique social logic and history. Foucault concluded that, if human studies wishes to play a critical role in post-sixties Left politics, it must abandon its synthesizing, unifying, and totalizing strategies in favor of local, pluralistic, and provisional discourses whose value is proven by their political engagement. "The role for theory today seems to me to be just this: not to formulate the global systematic theory which holds everything in place, but to analyze the specificity of mechanisms of power, to locate the connections and extensions, to build little by little a strategic knowledge" [17]. Foucault called his alternative to a scientific vision of human studies "genealogy."

Foucault once referred to genealogy as "anti-science" [18]. Genealogy relinquishes the search for objective knowledge, secure intellectual foundations, essences, deep unifying patterns of meaning, and grand theories that comprehend the origin and endpoint of history. Genealogy does not claim to promote the progress of science or humanity. Indeed, in opposition to the Enlightenment scientific culture, genealogy does not offer a positive agenda of social reconstruction; it lacks a social utopian vision. In the spirit of poststructuralism, genealogy is deconstructive; it aims to disrupt social conventions and norms. Its value lies in imagining the human world as thoroughly social and historical and susceptible to immense social variety and change.

Compared to the Enlightenment scientific vision, the social hopes of genealogy are modest. It intends to show that the dominant discourses defining the social universe as natural conceal particular social interests and power relations. Although genealogy assumes an intimate tie between institutions and discourses, it takes its aim primarily at disturbing the "normalizing" role of dominant discourses. It reveals how the dominant knowledges and ideas of a society shape human life by naturalizing and normalizing the construction of personal and social identities. Discourses that carry public authority shape identities and regulate bodies, desires, selves, and whole populations. Additionally, genealogy aims to show that these knowledges are entangled in a history of social conflict and domination. Central to this history is the exclusion or marginalization of discourses that represent oppressed groups or communities. Foucault intended genealogy to recover the knowledges and the lives of those who gave voice to them that have been excluded for the purpose of deploying them in current social struggles.

Foucault's studies focused on one particular type of discourse, the human sciences. Even in his pre-1970s writings, which he designated by the term "archaeology," Foucault's concern was with psychiatry and the human sciences. For example, in *The Order of Things: An Archaeology of the Human Sciences*, he challenged the Enlightenment idea that the social sciences had discovered the unity of humanity and detailed its unfolding as social progress. On the contrary, Foucault proposed that the human sciences constructed the concept of humanity as an essentially unitary, common essence. The idea of "Man" as the basis and active force producing knowledge, society, and history is the creation of the human sciences.

As the theoretical object of the human sciences, "Man" has been made into the very subject (original source and active force) of science. Reflecting a poststructural standpoint, Foucault maintained that it is language and discourse that are the agents of knowledge and history. Foucault's early archaeological investigations were important because they advanced a social and historical understanding of knowledge. They did not, however, go much beyond a structuralist analysis of linguistic or discursive order. Absent was any attention to the institutional contexts or social effects of discourse – in a word, to the interconnection of knowledge and power.

As Foucault turned his attention to the intersection of institution and discourse in genealogical analysis, his focus remained riveted on the human sciences. Foucault's major studies, *Madness and Civilization, The Archaeology of Knowledge, Discipline and Punish,* and *The History of Sexuality,* examined the human sciences, for example, psychiatry, criminology, penology, demography, sexology, economics, and sociology [19]. However, his purpose was not to determine whether these disciplines are true or to chart a path of scientific progress. Rather, Foucault investigated the *social effects* of these knowledges. He asserted that discourses that aim to reveal the truth of the abnormal personality or human sexuality or the criminal help to create and control the very objects they claim to know. Scientific knowledge functions as a major social power; through the state, the family, hospital, and therapeutic institutions, the scientific disciplines shape our dominant cultural ideas about who we are, what is permissible and unacceptable, what can be said, by whom, when, and in what form. It is this power/knowledge configuration, hitherto submerged or hidden by the Enlightenment scientific vision, that is the critical object of genealogy.

The genius of Foucault is that he did what he proposed. Aside from his rather osbcure book *The Archaeology of Knowledge* and some occasional essays, Foucault refrained from the kind of systematic theorizing that characterizes scientific social theory. The great body of his work consists of critical historical studies. Without doubt, his master work, left unfinished with his untimely death, was his multivolume history of sexuality. I illustrate Foucault's idea of genealogical social analysis by outlining the social context, purpose, logic, and political implications of this project.

Rethinking sexual liberation: Foucault's genealogy of sexuality

It is perhaps not accidental that Foucault came to devote his greatest efforts to the study of the modern culture of sexuality. As a young man, Foucault was deeply troubled by his homosexuality. French society tolerated homosexuality provided that it was kept private. Even enlightened French culture was antagonistic to making homosexuality the basis of personal identity. Homosexuality never became the basis of a community and politics in postwar France. As Foucault traveled to American universities in the 1970s, he encountered a very different sexual culture. Homosexuality was made into an identity; a lesbian and gay community flourished, based upon the presumption of a common sexual identity; and a liberation movement developed that was inspired by an affirmative homosexual identity ("gay is good" became its battle hymn) and demanding the normalization of homosexuality.

Foucault was ambivalent towards this American culture of sexuality. It is reported that he valued the sexual freedom and social inventiveness of gay life in America. He particularly admired the creation of new ways of experiencing the body as a medium of pleasure and the creation of new forms of group life. Foucault was troubled, though, by the anchoring of this culture in what he took to be a restrictive, unitary notion of sexual and social identity. Didn't the affirmation of a lesbian or gay identity reinforce a culture that assigned individuals mutually exclusive sexual identities? Didn't such identities function to control our behavior? Foucault was suspicious of a sexual liberation movement that was wedded to a rhetoric of authenticity, naturalness, normality, and self-realization. Does normalizing gay identities amount to sexual liberation or the consolidation of a society that defines and regulates individuals by assigning them a unitary sexual identity? He was uneasy with a gay movement that seemed bent on becoming a quasi ethnic community. Foucault imagined that such a community would institutionalize a regime of sexual control in the name of a bland assimilationist social idea.

Foucault's concerns about the direction of the gay movement motivated him to investigate what he took to be the root assumptions of a modern Western culture of sexuality. How did it come about that modern societies developed the notion of a human sexual nature? How is it that sexuality is said to reveal the truth of humanity? What social forces rendered sexual desire into a marker of self-identity? What gives the sexualization of self its force and power in our lives? If, as Foucault believed, a culture of sexualization, sexual identity, and liberation carries it own social constraints, what alternative ways of thinking about the body, desire, pleasures, and intimacies could avoid such limitations?

Despite the harmony of voices – sexual liberationists, sexologists, psychiatrists, social scientists – declaring the naturalness of human sexuality and its organization into an order of normal and pathological desires, acts, and identities, Foucault registered a dissent. He relies on two strategies of argumentation. First, he hoped to make us aware of the historically unique, rather than universally natural, character of the modern sexual culture by exposing us to societies that are different. Second, Foucault offered an alternative perspective on the history of sexuality. He proposed a radical rethinking of the origins and meaning of the modern culture of sexuality for the purpose, ultimately, of imagining a postmodern order of pleasures and relations.

Foucault argued that not all societies assume that humans have a sexual nature, that sexual desires can be isolated and assigned a status as normal or abnormal, and that heterosexual and homosexual desires mark off two, mutually exclusive sexual and self identities. In volumes 2 and 3 of his *History of Sexuality*, Foucault intended to undermine the presumed universality of the modern system of sexuality.

Perhaps because the Greek city-states are often invoked as the cradle of Western civilization, and perhaps because Foucault wished to disrupt a story of the linear evolution of Western humanity, this is the starting point for his historical sketch. He argued that ancient Greek intimate culture was *not* organized around a regime of separate sexual desires and acts, some of which, being dangerous or unnatural, were to be prohibited and subject to surveillance and regulation. There was no system of sexual identities. Gender preference did not mark off a dichotomous heterosexual or homosexual identity. The Greek city-states represented a different universe of sexual meaning from modernity.

Instead of a culture organized around "sexuality" (i.e., discrete desires, acts, and identities), Greek culture was centered around "pleasures" and an ethic of self-mastery. Pleasures included not only or primarily sex but eating, exercise, and marriage. Moreover, moral judgment was not attached to specific sexual acts but to the overall shape of a life, in particular, to an individual's capacity to exercise self-mastery. This did not entail self-denial but enjoying pleasures with moderation and assuming an "active" or "passive" role as was appropriate to an individual's social status. For example, adult free men were expected to be active in sexual exchanges, while the subordinate social status of women, slaves, and boys required them to be sexually passive. Disapproval was not attached to particular sex acts or to a particular gender preference but to individuals who were immoderate in their pleasures or abandoned their appropriate role. "For a [free adult] man, excess and passivity were the two main forms of immorality in the practice of the aphrodisia [pleasures]" [20].

Nowhere is the difference between the Greek and the modern culture more evident than in the meaning of homosexuality. Some scholars, gay activists, and sexual liberationists have interpreted the Greek practice of love between adult males and boys as a moral lesson of tolerance and liberated sexuality. Foucault insisted, however, that man/boy love in Greek culture has little, if any, resemblance to modern homosexuality. In contrast to the moderns, the Greeks did not view sexual desires as naturally divided between the same and opposite sexes. Adult free men were expected to have boy lovers and to be married. Man/boy love was not a lifelong alternative to marriage; there was no separate, deviant culture of exclusively homosexuals and there was no stigma attached to man/boy love. This was not because the Greeks were enlightened, but because gender preference was not a chief category of sexual or social classification. Far more central to the Greeks was whether individuals were appropriately active or passive and whether they were moderate in their actions. Love between adult free men and boys was simply one domain of pleasure, not different in its moral aspect from that of eating, exercise, or marriage. It was no less regulated; only free adult males could take boys, not other free adult males, as their lovers. These relations were limited in time as boys became free adults for whom it would be inappropriate to assume a passive sexual role. The relations between male lovers had to exhibit the appropriate forms of moderation, role playing (i..e., active/passive), and self-mastery in order to retain its legitimacy.

An important shift in sexual meanings occurred in the passing of the Greek city-states into the imperial Roman era. Heterosexual intimacy and love assumed a central place in Western culture. In ancient Greece, marriage was organized around a series of social obligations, for example, the maintenance of an orderly and prosperous household. Ideal love was restricted to the love of boys by free adult men. In Hellenistic Rome, marriage took the place of man/boy love as the sphere of true love and intimacy. Foucault spoke of the emergence of a new ideal of an equal, intimate, and sexualized conjugal bond. This narrowing of intimate culture was part of a broader change to a culture preoccupied with "the care of the self" or with the shaping of subjectivity [21]. Foucault related the centering on personal life and the conjugal bond in the first two centuries A.D. to the bureaucratization of imperial Rome.

Foucault interpreted the shift to a self- and marriage-centered culture as a turning point in the evolution of Western society. Sex was emerging as a domain around which prohibitions and formal rules were being formed; in particular, nonmarital sex was becoming the target of suspicion, if not explicit prohibitions.

Christianity marked a break in Western civilization. In the Christian epoch, we can observe the beginnings of a modern sexual culture, with its centering on sexual desires and acts, its exaltation of virginity and marriage, its prohibitions against nonmarital sex and eroticism, and its fashioning of a formal, universalistic code to regulate sexual desires and behavior. Perhaps the most far-reaching change initiated by Christianity was the coupling of truth and sex. In the Christian practice of confession, which enjoined the individual to reveal his or her sexual thoughts and acts as a condition of purification, Foucault found the origins of the modern compulsion to imagine sex as the hidden truth of the self. In the confessional practice, sex is framed as a domain of discrete desires and acts whose power to sin demands vigilant monitoring. Foucault believed that there was a direct connection between the Christian confessional and modern discourses – e.g., sexology, psychiatry, and psychoanalysis – that approach sex an an autonomous psychic and social force. Foucault's death prevented him from writing the volumes linking Christianity and modernity. In the introductory volume to *The History of Sexuality*, he did, however, outline a story of the modern construction of "sexuality" [22].

The practice of confession was confined to the Catholic monastery through the Middle Ages. By the seventeenth century, confessional practices included all Christians. Moreover, the Christian was enjoined to speak frankly and in detail about the far-reaching effects of transgressive sexual desires and acts. The secularization of European societies in the eighteenth and nineteenth centuries did not put an end to the process of making sex a site of knowledge about the self. Confession was replaced by the practice of the "examination" by physicians, psychiatrists, sexologists, and scientists; the religious language of sin and salvation gave way to a secular medical-scientific language and a vocabulary of normal and pathological.

It was in the Victorian period that the making of sex into a sphere of truth was mainstreamed. In contrast to the stereotype of the nineteenth century as the age of sexual repression, Foucault underscores the proliferation of public talk about sex in this period. A spate of sex advice manuals, psychiatric, medical, scientific, demographic, and legal texts on sex exploded into the public realm. Did this profusion of Victorian discourses have as their aim or effect the drawing of a curtain of silence and shame around sex? On the contrary, Foucault suggests that Victorian discourses created the very idea of a natural sexuality, of an order of desires and acts built into the body and obeying its own logic of natural and normal development. Foucault reverses conventional wisdom. Instead of speaking of sex as a natural entity that gave rise to the idea of sexuality, medical-scientific discourses produced a construction of sexuality as if it were an autonomous entity with its own laws of development and natural morality. The idea of sexuality, in turn, has contributed to producing "sex," i.e., a range of thoughts, desires, acts, and relations.

Sexuality is not a natural fact; it is not built into the genetic, chemical-physiological structure of our body. It is, so to speak, an idea, a conception of who we are that has powerfully shaped the experience of our bodies, desires, actions, and social relations. The power of sexuality does not lie solely in the sheer power of a discourse of truth authorized by science. Foucault insisted that the psychic and social force of medical-scientific discourses lie in their integration in social institutions (e.g., hospitals, clinics, schools, the state) and in their being tied to social practices, from therapeutic regimes to the enforcement of legal statutes.

Inspired by an Enlightenment vision of unveiling the truth of humanity, an army of sexologists, physicians, psychiatrists, psychoanalysts, and demographers sought to reveal a hidden, often camouflaged, order of sexuality. In search of humankind's sexual nature, the sciences unwittingly helped to create a population of new sexual selves. Under the modern regime of sexuality, all individuals acquire a sexual identity; bodily and genital desires stamp us as a type of person. For example, prior to the mid-nineteenth century, "homosexual" behavior may have been subject to disapproval, but it was the act, not the person, that was punished. Lacking a notion that homosexual behavior revealed a distinct sexual identity, such behavior was treated in the same way that any criminal offense was handled. By interpreting same-sex desire as indicative of personal identity, the medical-scientific discourses gave birth to a new human type, "the homosexual." Henceforth, homosexual behavior was not merely a transgression of social norms or laws but marked a deviant human type. Social control was aimed not only at punishing the behavior but at marginalizing and abolishing homosexual desire. The regime of sexuality creates a new world of deviant and normal sexual and social identities – homosexuals, heterosexuals, fetishists, pedophiles, masochists, and sadists. The modern self is a sexual self.

Sexual liberationists might celebrate the making of sexual identities as a vehicle of liberating desire and of creating a sexually free and open society. Foucault was more ambivalent. The modern regime of sexuality simultaneously creates sexual subjects and positions them as objects of social control. Foucault proposed, however, that social control operates less effectively by a legal-administrative-social system of prohibitions and censorship. He emphasized a mode of social control that was built into the very regime of sexuality – its system of normal/abnormal identities and its norm of a healthy, fulfilled sexual life.

To the extent that individuals are defined as sexual subjects, people are inserted into a symbolic and social order that fixes how we relate to our bodies and desires and regulates our behavior. For example, if we think of our sexual preference for members of the same sex as making us into a homosexual, regardless of whether we celebrate or lament our homosexuality, this self-identity will regulate our desires, behaviors, and social relations. Placing ourselves under the regime of sexuality should not be imagined as an individual choice. The system of sexuality is built into the fabric of our institutions (e.g., state, law, medical clinics, hospitals, and family), cultural apparatus (e.g., mass media, advertising, and educational system, church), and into the very texture of everyday life (e.g., customs, norms, language, and lifestyle ideals). Thus, individuals whose sexual preference is for members of the same sex do not choose whether they wish to identify as homosexuals. If desire is socially framed in terms of a mutually exclusive identity system of gender preference, if the regime of sexuality is enforced by the dominant practices and culture of a society, individuals are positioned as heterosexual or homosexual persons regardless of their wishes.

Foucault described a system of social control that operates less by coercion and repression than by the very cultural meanings and self-identities that it produces. The regime of sexuality exerts a kind of pervasive, invisible power over us to the extent that we are inserted within it and absorb its cultural definitions, social norms, and self-images. Every time that we look to define ourselves by our sexuality, consult an expert to discover our true sexuality, aspire to liberate our sexuality from guilt and inhibitions, seek self-realization through orgasmic fulfillment, heterosexual intimacy, or·true gay love, we are placing ourselves under the control of "sexuality." We are not liberating our sexuality but putting ourselves under the control of a regime of sexuality. We are reinforcing this regime; the apparatus of cultural definitions, experts, and institutional practices. Thus, the affirmation of gay identity, its celebration and elaboration in the form of a gay culture, does not, in Foucault's view, signal the liberation of sexuality; rather it reinforces a regime that has produced the very idea that we have a sexuality, that sexuality is our essence and that gender preferences defines our sexual identity.

Did Foucault view modern sexual culture as simply social domination masquerading as freedom? Are sexual liberation movements unwittingly reinforcing a system of domination? At times, Foucault seems to have believed this to be the case. However, he never fully surrendered social hope. He was attentive to the ironies of modern sexual culture and its possibilities for individualism and social innovation. For example, Foucault observed that the construction of the homosexual as an abnormal, dangerous individual ironically gave birth to an affirmative lesbian and gay identity demanding legitimation on precisely the grounds for which it was initially scandalized, namely its claims to being natural and normal. Similarly, despite the apparent aim of the medical-scientific discourse to inhibit or dissuade homosexual desire, its consequence has been to intensify and multiply homoeroticism. The homosexual has had no other choice but to attend to those desires and wants which are self-defining. If the homosexual was compelled to focus on same-sex desires, the lesbian and gay man deliberately fashions a life around those desires, producing an immensely prolific and dense culture of homoeroticism. In the development of new forms of eroticism and in the elaboration of sexual desires into new social relations, Foucault saw much to value in modern sexual culture.

Foucault remained, however, a critic of the regime of sexuality. Although he did not trivialize the significance of reversing social stigma or the creation of movements of sexual affirmation, these developments were said to reinforce the regime of sexuality. Foucault's case against the regime was that it reduced sexuality to narrow sexual pleasures, rigidly forced individuals into restrictive, mutually exclusive identities, created stigmatized, deviant populations, and facilitated an efficient system of social control. Unfortunately, Foucault never spelled out his vision of an alternative intimate culture. It seems clear, though, that Foucault favored replacing the regime of sexual acts and identities with a language of pleasures and social relations. No doubt his attraction to ancient Greece lies in its repudiation of a regime of sexuality in favor of a regime of pleasures and an ethics of everyday life that gave the individual wide latitude for self-regulation. Always siding with the anarchistic strain of French culture, Foucault, like his poststructuralist brethen, favored a society that permitted the widest possible latitude to self-expression and cultural innovation without, unfortunately, addressing issues of normative regulation and institutional pressures. To press further into Foucault's social and political ideas, I turn briefly to his broader perspective on modernity.

Imagining modernity: Foucault's disciplinary order

Some questions remain unaddressed in the preceding sketch: what social forces produced the regime of sexuality? And what social ends are served by a construction of a natural sexuality? What kind of society is it that makes individuals into sexual subjects and objects of social control? What was Foucault's image of modernity?

Foucault's perspective on modern societies can be highlighted by contrasting it to a liberal and Marxist view. Central to liberalism has been the belief in the progress of humanity driven by the advance of human reason which replaces error and superstition with objective, universally true knowledge. Was it not enlightened reason that substituted imprisonment with an eye to rehabilitation for the brutal torture of criminal offenders? Did not the science of psychiatry put an end to the confinement of mad persons by substituting humane treatment? Although Marxists qualify a liberal ideology by making capitalist society an intermediary, rather than final, stage in human progress, Marxism falls squarely within the Enlightenment tradition. In addition, liberalism and Marxism share a basic sociological understanding. They imagine modern society as a triple-layered order: the state, civil society (economic, educational, religious institutions), and the family. They agree, moreover, that the main driving force of society lies in the dynamics of civil society, in particular, the economic realm. Disagreement between liberals and Marxists centers on their respective moral and political values. Liberals defend modern capitalism as the height of social evolution; the chief danger to social progress lies in excessive state intervention into civil society and the family. Marxists criticize the class-based character of capitalism as inhibiting the full progressive potential of modernity; they anticipate a new and better society as social classes dissolve into a truly individualistic, postcapitalist order.

Writing in the aftermath of two world wars, a worldwide Depression followed by Nazism, fascism, Stalinism, and Hiroshima, the Enlightenment story of social progress lacked credibility for Foucault. In his investigations into sexuality, prisons, madness, and psychiatry, Foucault stepped forward as a critic of the Enlightenment. For example, contrary to the Enlightenment story of the liberation of sexuality from the tight grip of repression, Foucault related a tale of the making of a sexual subject who is simultaneously an object of social control; the very medical-scientific discourses that were supposed to free our natural sexuality actually create and regulate individuals as sexual objects. Similarly, Foucault disagreed with the Enlightenment account of criminal justice reform. This view described the march of the humanitarian spirit sweeping away barbaric practices of torture in favor of a humanistic program of reform and rehabilitation. In *Discipline and Punish*, Foucault interpreted the prison reform movement as establishing a new, more efficient, system of control [23]. Contrary to its ideology of prisoner rehabilitation, its chief aim is to depoliticize social discontent by incarcerating alienated individuals and regulating them by an apparatus of surveillance and psychological management. Foucault was no less critical of the view that psychiatry marks the beginnings of the humane treatment of the insane and the mad. Substituting treatment and therapy for banishment or imprisonment, the new sciences of the mind are said to epitomize the humanitarian spirit of the Enlightenment. On the contrary, Foucault underscored the growing authority of mental health experts whose therapeutic discourses and practices create new psychological subjects – e.g., the neurotic, the narcissist, hysteric, schizophrenic, the anal-compulsive, the frigid personality – who are objects of psychiatric and state social control.

Foucault departed from liberal and Marxist images of modern society as an organic whole or social system that has a center or unifying dynamic, such as capitalism or the idea of progress. He imagined modern societies as fractured, lacking a social center that gives to them a unity and telos. Neither the state nor the economy is the social center; no one drama of social conflict, not class conflict nor gender, sexual, ethnic, or religious conflict, carries any obvious social or political primacy. No social group or ideology rules society, nor is society organized around the logic of capitalism, patriarchy, bureaucracy, secularization, postindustrialization, or democratization. In short, contemporary societies cannot be described with the imagery of organicism, totality, and system that has dominated both the liberal and Marxist traditions. Foucault viewed the social field as consisting of heterogeneous forces, institutional orders, processes, and conflicts.

Liberal and Marxist social thinkers have focused on the economy and the state and have aimed to delineate global unifying processes such as capitalism (Marx), bureaucratization (Weber), social differentiation (Durkheim and Parsons), or democratization (Tocqueville). Foucault highlighted the importance of smaller, discrete social units such as hospitals, mental asylums, schools, the military, prisons, and universities. His intent was less to subsume these social units under some unifying global process (e.g., capitalism or bureaucratization) than to analyze their specific social logic and local effects. Focault did not abandon all efforts at describing general social processes. He did, however, abandon efforts to infer local social processes (e.g., the making of sexual subjects or prison dynamics) from global processes (e.g., capitalism, bureaucratization, or social differentiation). He shifted our attention to heterogeneous local social dynamics precisely because they are important sites of social conflict today; our totalizing theories (e.g., liberalism and Marxism) have failed to understand their specificity because they have reduced them to a global process or social logic.

Foucault approached contemporary societies as being composed of heterogeneous social dynamics that cannot be said to have a central logic or organizing principle. He did not assume the lack of social coherence nor does he abstain from general descriptions of modern societies. Although Foucault nowhere proposed a general theory of modernity in the mode of Parsons or Habermas, in his various social sketches of sexuality, prisons, madness, and the human sciences, there emerges the outlines of what we might call a disciplinary social order.

Disciplinary-based societies are contrasted to early modern societies which were organized around the centralization of authority in a sovereign ruler. In these societies, social order is maintained by the power of a sovereign to take or give life or to demand obedience; power is organized around repression – the capacity to silence, censor, or deny. For example, in early modern Europe, the law was viewed as an expression of sovereign rule. Its violation was a challenge and offense to the sovereign. The offender was punished by torture to demonstrate that the sovereign is omnipotent. Torturing the body of the offender was a way to manifest publicly the repressive, absolute power of the sovereign.

In a disciplinary society, order is maintained through technologies of control such as spatial separation, time management, confinement, surveillance, and a system of examinations that classify and rank individuals for the purpose of normalizing social behavior. If the exemplary institution of sovereign-based societies is the king, it is the military, factory, hospital, and prison in the disiciplinary society. Order is maintained less through a hierarchy of ruler and ruled than through an apparatus of disciplinary techniques and discourses. Power in a disciplinary order is manifested less in the form of repression than in the production of subjects or social selves who are positioned as objects of normalizing control. For example, in modern criminological practice, the aim is not to punish the body through torture. Instead the body is observed and managed by a sprawling apparatus of surveillance (e.g., guards, television monitors, prison time-tables, and regimented activities). Moreover, it is the psyche of the offender that is the real object of social control. Foucault spoke of criminological discourses and practices as producing a "criminal subject," a personal identity whose essential psychological and social nature is driven to commit crimes. The construction of a criminal subject justifies the creation of a series of technologies of control (e.g., incarceration, surveillance, and strategies of rehabilitation) and experts (judges, wardens, social workers, parole officers, psychiatrists) whose aim is to normalize the behavior of the offender.

Foucault did not deny the importance of the repressive power of the state or ruling social strata (e.g., an economic elite or the power of men). He insisted, however, that the disciplinary-based production of social order in prisons, hospitals, factories, the military, and schools is central to contemporary Western societies. It is not the power to enforce obedience that make possible these social structures; rather, social order is produced by a series of disciplining strategies – from confinement to systems of examinations – whose aim is to regulate behavior by imposing norms of normality, health, intelligence, and fitness.

Foucault offered the most elaborate social historical articulation of post-structuralism. Whereas Lyotard and Baudrillard rarely go beyond schematic statements about social knowledge and society, Foucault offered historically rich, empirically dense social analyses. His studies of sexuality, prisons, madness, psychiatry, and the human sciences offer a serious alternative to the dominant liberal and Marxist approaches to human studies.

In contrast to Enlightenment traditions, Foucault abandoned images of society as a totality, system, or organic whole in favor of a decentered, radically pluralistic concept of social process. In place of the grand evolutionary theories of the Enlightenment that purport to trace humankind's continuous progressive development, Foucault analyzed the making of a plurality of human subjects, underscores historical continuities and discontinuities, processes of order and conflict, without reducing these to a tale of progress or regress. Liberalism and Marxism aim to uncover a global social logic such as capitalism, bureaucratization, social differentiation, democratization, or individualism. Foucault gave up the search for a unifying social logic in favor of investigating heterogeneous social dynamics. Yet, in the rise of a regime of sexuality, a prison system, the human sciences, asylums, and psychiatric regimes of personal reformation, Foucault sensed the contours of a new disciplinary-based social order. Social control operates less through a system of legal, state, or economic repression than through the application of technologies of discipline that spread from the military to prisons, factories, schools, hospitals, asylums, and virtually all organizations. These technologies of control are interlaced with medical-scientific discourses; the latter control the movement of bodies, desires, identities, and behaviors by contributing to their very formation and by imposing on them normalizing rules or norms.

If power pervades the social field, if it is woven into the very texture of everyday life, social conflict and resistance cannot be centralized. Movements of political opposition cannot be subsumed under the banner of antistatism, anticapitalism, or antipatriarchy. Social resistance must be heterogeneous; oppositional practices must be local, diverse, and specific to the social logic of their particular social field (e.g., prisons, schools, sexuality). In further contrast to the politics of liberation that characterize liberalism and Marxism, the politics of resistance in disciplinary-based societies abandons the illusory dreams of a society free of domination and control. Personal and social existence can never be free of constraint and regulation; every society produces its own configuration of bodies, pleasures, identities, and social norms. Oppositional politics struggles against the disciplines (both the human sciences and the technologies of control) for the purpose of expanding possibilities for individualism, social relations, and producing just, democratic forms of life. Unfortunately, Foucault had little to say with respect to the social hopes of political resistance beyond making clear his opposition to the reign of a disciplinary order. He was clear, though, that the role of the intellectual in the politics of a disciplinary order shifts from confronting reality with universal truths to producing detailed analyses of the social formation of specific social fields, e.g., sexuality, prisons, and psychiatry. Foucault considered genealogy as one

possible form that human studies could assume as part of an antidisciplin-
ary politics.

Afterword

Poststructuralism is an important critique of and alternative to the dominant
currents of Western thought. Its concept of a postdisciplinary human studies
that combines a broad idea of social reason with a political will poses a
challenge to the disciplines. I am especially sympathetic to the effort to
offer an alternative perspective on contemporary history to that of liberalism and Marxism. In particular, I think that the French poststructuralists
break new ground in bringing issues of the body, desire, and identity
into the center of social analysis. I am critical, however, of the failure of
poststructuralism to articulate a positive program of social reconstruction. I
think that this reflects a disposition, one which runs deep in French culture,
to look upon all social regulation as domination and therefore to retain an
implicit anarchistic social ideal, which I find sociologically naive.

Poststructuralists challenge key premises of Enlightenment social
thought. In particular, they view assumptions regarding the objectivity
of science, the coupling of scientific progress to social progress, the
unity of humanity, the evolution of humanity from East to West, and
from a state of oppression to freedom, as not merely the innocent
ideas of intellectuals, but values and beliefs woven into the political
and cultural history of the modern West. Enlightenment ideas have
played a social role in the formation of Western industrial societies.
Disputing apologists of the modern West, poststructuralists argue that
the lofty ideas of the Enlightenment obscure and rationalize a history
of domination – of the West over the East, of the middle classes over
peasants and laborers, of European culture over non-White cultures, of a
regime of disciplinary experts over the subjects it creates (e.g., clients,
patients, and consumers). Liberals and Marxists have revised Enlightenment ideas but have not seriously challenged its ideological role in
Western and world history. From Marx to Durkheim, Parsons, and Habermas, the core ideas, values, and institutions of modern Western Enlightenment culture are assumed to be true to human nature or the "fit"
survivals of historical evolution and superior to other civilizations. Poststructuralists have made the politics of the Enlightenment into a core
theme of their social studies.

Enlightenment social thought has gained much of its social power
because its ideas are woven into the culture of everyday life in the West.
A faith in science, social progress, the unity of humanity, and the superiority

of the West is not confined to intellectuals but permeates the culture of daily life. For many of us in the West, however, this culture of Enlightenment is losing its credibility. For example, the postwar generation has come of age at a time when science seems to have lost a great deal of its aura of truth and progress. As science is integrated into commerce and the military, as it is used to sell toothpaste and build bombs, Enlightenment justifications of science as pure knowledge or as a force of social good seem naive. The postwar generation is aware of the dark side of science: Nazism, Stalinism, Hiroshima, scientific torture, genocide, mental asylums, medical dehumanization, and the role of science in pathologizing homosexuals, Blacks, and women. Science and the broader culture of the Enlightenment have lost their innocence. French poststructuralists have grasped this growing public disenchantment with the culture of Enlightenment.

Poststructuralism would not warrant our serious attention if it were simply a movement against the Enlightenment. On the contrary, poststructuralists aim to preserve some of the social hopes and values of the Enlightenment (e.g., choice, pluralism, and democracy), but in a "postmodern" social vision. For example, Lyotard and Foucault reject the grand theoretical and liberatory hopes of modern social science, but not because they are against empirical knowledge or hostile to the hope that human studies can contribute to making a better world. Rather, they insist that the privileging of science as truth and its synthesizing aims limit choice, diversity, and democracy. For example, if science alone yields truth, nonscientific ideas (e.g., religion, literature, art, and folk knowledges) are socially devalued and marginalized as mere ideology, subjective opinion, or myth. Science erects an intellectual and social hierarchy, with the institution of science, and scientists, at the apex. Lyotard and Foucault propose successor projects to scientific social theory, e.g., local narratives and genealogy. Poststructural human studies would continue to develop empirical and explanatory accounts of social realities. However, poststructuralist approaches would replace "modern" Enlightenment justifications of social knowledge (e.g., truth, scientific and social progress) with a "postmodern" rationale: human studies as a deliberately moral and political practice struggling against the disciplinary ordering and normalization of daily life.

Poststructuralists offer new and challenging perspectives on the history of Western societies. Departing from liberal and Marxist social ideas which draw our attention to the economy, the state, organizational dynamics, and cultural values, they center social analysis on processes relating to the body, sexuality, identity, consumerism, mass media, medical-scientific discourses, the social role of the human sciences, and disciplinary technologies of control. Baudrillard's analysis of the cultural processes of simulation, hyperreality, and implosion; Foucault's outline of the rise of a disciplinary order that creates new identities and institutes normalizing techniques (from surveillance to therapies) compels us to shift our conceptual strategies in ways no less dramatic than the "revolution" in human studies linked to classical sociology. Poststructural human studies is a noteworthy alternative to the sociological theory canon and to the dominant Enlightenment paradigms of social thought.

I perceive the culture of the Enlightenment, with its assumptions regarding the unity of humanity, linear progressive evolution, the objectivity of science, the belief in the liberating role of science, and the superiority of the West, as losing credibility. Our everyday awareness of human difference along the dimension of gender, ethnicity, sexuality, class, and nationality raises doubts about the idea of the identity of humanity; worldwide depressions, wars, and periodic socioeconomic crises (famines, riots, wars) elicit suspicion, if not derision, toward the idea of social progress. The line between science, myth, and ideology have blurred as we are aware of the entanglement of science in social and political realities. Western superiority appears to be little more than an embarrassing prejudice, a thin excuse for colonial plunder and imperial intervention.

The social sciences were born in the period of the Enlightenment and have remained wedded to its culture. They are losing credibility as the broader culture of Enlightenment has lost public authority. Western citizens look less and less to the social sciences to provide powerful understandings of Western and world experience. Indeed, the Enlightenment ideas of scientific objectivity, the unity of humanity, social progress, and Western superiority are under attack in many quarters as perpetuating narrow Eurocentric, male-dominated, and heterosexist values. As the Enlightenment-inspired disciplines (sociology, anthropology, and political science) are perceived as entangled in social domination (e.g., the oppression of women, gays, people of color, non-Western populations), poststructuralists urge that we abandon key assumptions of the Enlightenment without, however, repudiating its social hope for a world with more freedom, equality, tolerance, and democracy.

I interpret poststructuralists, at least Lyotard and Foucault in their most hopeful moments, as saying that, if we wish to realize Enlightenment social hopes, we need to translate them into a different social vocabulary and vision of knowledge, power, and society. The poststructural vision is that of socially produced selves whose identities are multiple and unstable, an awareness of the coupling of power and knowledge, a new moral responsibility attached to the production of knowledge, and an image of society as fragmented, pluralistic, and productive of heterogeneous local struggles. There is a keen sense that power works through repression (e.g., the law, state, class rule) *and* through the production and normalization of bodies, populations, and identities (sexual, gender, ethnic). A permanent struggle for specific, local gains in pleasure, choice, expression, social bonding, and justice replaces the modern dream of bringing to an end all social constraint and repression.

Are there unresolved issues and problems in poststructuralism? Most definitely. Neither Baudrillard, Lyotard, nor Foucault are very clear about the moral and political standpoint from which they criticize Western societies. I am troubled by their refusal to spell out their ideas of a good society. Foucault was critical of the culture of modern sexuality, but he refused to say what an order of "bodies and pleasures" might look like and what would make it better. His steadfast silence on the moral and political implications of his own studies calls to mind the culture of scientism that he criticized so severely.

There is a definite strain of antimodernism in poststructuralism. At times, it appears in the implication that all social regulation and constraint is domination. Foucault's interpretation of the regime of sexuality as a system of social control is indicative of this naive sociological position. Why naive? Social life is unimaginable without social norms, identities, and a system of social control. The compelling moral and political issue revolves around the kinds of choices, social differences, and social relations that different systems of social control make possible and the ways they are implicated in democratization and hierarchy. Baudrillard's sketch of the collapse of the social into a great homogeneous, passive, inert mass that is captured and dominated by the seductive charms of consumerism and media manipulation evidences the same kind of deeply felt hostility towards institutional, normative social order. Baudrillard's social vision virtually eliminates *all* social tension. Everyday struggles for civil and social rights, public inclusion, economic justice, political representation, and cultural legitimation find no place in Baudrillard. The tendency in Foucault to collapse all social control into domination and in Baudrillard to flatten the social universe into an undifferentiated manipulated, dominated mass is both sociologically naive and politically suspect.

Poststructuralism has been unable to turn its challenge to the Enlightenment into an entirely cogent social vision. In Baudrillard and Lyotard, "the social" remains an underdeveloped concept. This failure of poststructuralism perhaps reflects a strain in French culture to see in "the social" the oppressive social weight of the Catholic Church, the state bureaucracy, and the corporate economy. Indeed, there is a current of French radicalism, connecting Rousseau, Proudhon, Sorel, and Sartre, which has, at times, recoiled from the hierarchical, statist French social order to embrace a dreamy naturalism or images of a self free of the deadening weight of social conventions. Perhaps residues of this anarchistic dream are preserved in poststructuralism, manifested, say, in the reduction of "the social" to domination or the fantasy of the "masses" as the only hope for recovering genuine, liberating communication.

References

1. A fine overview of French structuralism that emphasizes its sociological aspects is provided by Edith Kurzweil, *Age of Structuralism* (New York: Columbia University Press, 1980); also, Jean Marie Benoist, *Structural Revolution* (New York: St. Martin's Press, 1978). A useful overview of existential philosophy is provided in William Barrett, *Irrational Man* (Garden City, NY: Doubleday, 1958).

2. Ferdinand de Sausurre, *Course in General Linguistics* (New York: McGraw Hill, 1966).

3. Claude Levi-Strauss, *The Elementary Structure of Kinship* (Boston: Beacon Press, 1969); *Structural Anthropology*, Vol. 1 (Garden City, NY: Anchor, 1967); *The Savage Mind* (Chicago: University of Chicago Press, 1970); *Raw and the Cooked* (New York: Harper and Row, 1969).

4. Louis Althusser, *For Marx* (New York: Pantheon Books, 1969) and (with Etienne Balibar), *Reading Capital* (New York: Pantheon, 1970).

5. Michel Foucault, *Madness and Civilization: A History of Insanity in the Age of Reason* (New York: Vintage, 1965).

6. I have found a useful and imaginative overview of poststructuralism in Jonathan Culler, *On Deconstruction* (Ithaca, NY: Cornell University Press, 1982).

7. Jacques Derrida, *On Gramatology* (Baltimore: John Hopkins University Press, 1976).

8. Jacques Derrida, *Writing and Difference* (Chicago: University of Chicago Press, 1978) and *Positions* (Chicago: University of Chicago Press, 1981).

9. Jean-Francois Lyotard, *Discours, figure* (Paris: Klincksieck, 1971); *The Libidinal Economy* (Bloomington: Indiana University Press, 1993); *Dérive a partir de Marx et Freud* (Paris: Union génerale e éditions, 1973).

10. Jean-Francois Lyotard, *The Postmodern Condition: A Report on Knowledge* (Minneapolis: University of Minnesota Press, 1984).

11. Lyotard, *The Postmodern Condition*, p. xxiv.

12. Lyotard, *The Postmodern Condition*, p. xxiii.

13. Lyotard, *The Postmodern Condition*, p. xxv.

14. Jean Baudrillard, *Le Système des objets* (Paris: Denoel-Gonthier, 1968); *La Societé de consummation* (Paris: Gallimard, 1970); *For a Critique of the Political Economy of the Sign* (St. Louis: Telos Press, 1981); *The Mirror of Production* (St. Louis: Telos Press, 1975).

15. Jean Baudrillard, *Simulations* (New York: Semiotext(e) 1983); *In the Shadow of the Silent Majorities* (New York: Semiotext(e), 1983); *The Fatal Strategies* (New York: Semiotext(e), 1990).
16. Michel Foucault, *Madness and Civilization; The Birth of the Clinic: An Archaeology of Medical Perception* (New York: Vintage, 1975); *The Order of Things: An Archaeology of The Human Sciences* (New York: Vintage, 1966).
17. Michel Foucault, "Two Lectures," *Power/Knowledge: Selected Writings and Other Interviews* (New York: Pantheon, 1980) p. 83.
18. Michel Foucault, "Power and Strategies," in *Power/Knowledge*, p. 145.
19. Michel Foucault, *Madness and Civilization; The Archaeology of Knowledge and the Discourse on Language* (New York: Harper Colophon, 1969); *Discipline and Punish: The Birth of the Prison* (New York: Vintage, 1979); *The History of Sexuality*, Vol. 1: *An Introduction* (New York: Vintage, 1980).
20. Foucault, *The History of Sexuality*, Vol. 2: *The Use of Pleasure* (New York: Vintage, 1985), p. 47.
21. Foucault, *The History of Sexuality*, Vol. 3: *The Care of the Self* (New York: Vintage, 1986).
22. Foucault, *The History of Sexuality*, Vol. 1: *Introduction*.
23. Foucault, *Discipline and Punish*.

7

The New Social Movements and the Making of New Social Knowledges

May 1968 ignited a national crisis in France. Students, laborers, professionals, and cultural workers (e.g., editors, actors, writers) united to change France. They opposed the state, the bureaucratization of society, corporate capitalism, the Catholic Church, mass consumerism, and the commercialization of the national culture. The revolts of 1968 aimed at social revolution.

There was no May 1968 in the United States. There were, of course, student revolts in America. However, a coalition between students, blue collar workers and professionals never materialized. Moreover, student protests received broad public support only as they addressed university reform or were aligned with the protests against United States involvement in Vietnam. As students pursued a radical political agenda, they lost much of their mainstream support. Indeed, the withdrawal of the United States from Vietnam sounded the death knell to the student movement.

Social conflict in postwar America surfaced, as well, around issues of race, gender, and sexuality. These conflicts generated two types of social movements: civil rights and liberation movements. The civil rights movements were sparked by the Black campaign against Southern segregation. The sit-ins, boycotts, nonviolent protests, and political lobbying for equal racial rights became a model for struggles by women and homosexuals. These civil rights movements were a source of serious discord in the United States; they disturbed established racial, gender, and sexual hierarchies. Nevertheless, their aim was less to challenge the legitimacy of liberal institutions than to demand that America live up to its ideals of equal rights and opportunity for all individuals.

Paralleling the civil rights campaigns were liberationist social movements. In the North, a Black power movement cohered around an ideology of Black nationalism. Liberal feminists were challenged by radical feminists for whom changing the law was a small part of a broader agenda of dismantling male domination. The struggle for civil rights by lesbians and gay men was overshadowed in the early 1970s by militants who demanded an end to sexual and gender roles. Inspired by ideas of participatory democracy, sexual and gender freedom, and ethnic nationalism, the liberationist movements challenged the legitimacy of liberal America. American radicals attacked a materialistic, commercial, and imperialist culture that was said to benefit a White, middle class, straight male elite. Although the heyday of the liberation movements had passed by the mid-1970s, they continue to influence the contours of American political and intellectual culture.

Despite some parallels between French and American social rebellions in the sixties, there is a striking difference in their political culture. Whereas French rebels were more or less united in their opposition to the social status quo, American radicals lacked a unity of opposition and purpose. The American rebellions were fragmented into a multiplicity of movements, each organized around an imagined common identity. These identity-based movements had their own cultures, organizations, political strategies, and social visions. For example, the Black liberation movement was unified by the assumption of a common Black identity based on the shared experience of racism and resistance; Black liberation spoke for all, and only, Black people.

The postwar United States saw the rise of a new type of politics: identity politics. Appealing to the idea that all members of the same oppressed group share a common identity, individuals assuming identities as Blacks, women, and gays organized into ethnic type political communities.

These new social movements created new subjects of knowledge (African-Americans, women, lesbians and gay men) and new knowledges. Socially positioned as oppressed, Blacks, gays, women, lesbians, and Chicanos developed new perspectives on knowledge, society, and politics. The dominant knowledges in American public culture were criticized as reflecting the standpoint and interests of White Europeans, men, and heterosexuals. Black nationalists, feminists, gay liberationists, and lesbian feminists produced social perspectives that were said to express their personal reality: Afrocentrism, feminism, lesbian and gay or Queer theory. These new knowledges exhibited an ambivalent relation to the Enlightenment paradigm of knowledge. For example, as feminists analyzed the role of science in creating and perpetuating oppressive cultural stereotypes and myths, they criticized the ideology of the separation of scientific knowledge and values as concealing science's entanglement in politics. In these new social knowledges, I perceive an effort to reconsider knowledge, society, and politics in a way that underscores a moral vision of the human studies.

These new social movements have given birth to social knowledges that contest the Enlightenment framework of the social scientific disciplines. This chapter examines these critical knowledges with an eye to their alternative concepts of the human studies. The centerpiece of this chapter is the women's movement and feminism as a critical social knowledge. This discussion is followed by an outline of parallel developments to contest dominant knowledges in the African-American and lesbian and gay movements.

Feminism: from gynocentrism to postmodernism

The contemporary women's movement developed in response to the contradictions of postwar America. On the one hand, women were pursuing college degrees and careers and generally absorbing the American ideology of individualism. On the other hand, women were expected to be wives and mothers, assume most of the childbearing and household duties, and subordinate their personal and career interests to their husbands; they were also still valued as objects of men's sexual desire which made women targets of harrassment and abuse. Inspired by the Black civil rights and liberationist movements, and encouraged by a social atmosphere of liberalization and idealism associated with the Kennedy and Johnson administrations, a late twentieth century women's movement was born.

If the women's movement was the political vehicle for women's social assertiveness, feminism was its ideology. Feminism offered perspectives on American society from the standpoint of women's lives. It interpreted women's personal troubles as social and political in origin. If women were unhappy in marriage, perhaps this reflected socially imposed roles as wife and mother or a norm of heterosexuality that was at odds with their true selves. If women felt displeased with their appearance, what needed to change were male-imposed ideals of feminine beauty, not themselves. Women's discontents were social facts requiring political action, not individual facts requiring therapy, marriage, or regimes of beautification. Feminists offered views of women that positioned them as social and political agents.

Feminism refers to the ideas produced primarily by women for the purpose of changing their self-awareness and behavior. Feminists offered perspectives on the social role of women from the standpoint of viewing women as an oppressed social group. They assumed that men and women are *socially formed* and that *social explanations* can be given for why men are dominant. Feminists asserted that the relations between men and women in the spheres of work, politics, family, and sex reflect patterns of gender inequality.

Feminism holds that men and women are not born, they are socially created. Most feminists maintain that humans may be born male and female but that society makes them into men and women. The social world is a gendered world: feelings, desires, behaviors, social roles, occupations, and whole institutions are considered masculine or feminine or appropriate for men or women. For example, I would guess that most Americans define nurturing, caring, and empathetic feelings as feminine and view nursing, secretarial, or childcare work as women's work. Would I be far off the mark in assuming that most Americans consider the military and public office as masculine? If women are expected to show nurturant feelings and to assume caretaking roles (e.g., wife, mother, nurse, secretary), while men are expected to be aggressive and to assume leadership roles (e.g., military officer, mayor, business executive), it is not, say feminists, a fact of nature but a social fact.

Gender differences between men and women are socially produced for a reason: to maintain male dominance. The gender order is a hierarchical one. Men are consistently placed in positions of dominance over women. If women are expected to be wives and mothers, will they have the time to develop the skills to be corporate executives and military and political leaders? If women are socialized to be nurturing and responsive to the needs of others, will they have the psychological capacities (e.g., aggressivity) to assume leadership roles? If women are expected to seek the approval of men, will they be able to demand equal satisfaction in their intimate lives? The differences between men and women are not politically innocent. Gender difference sustains male dominance.

In most, if not all, societies, men have power over women. Sometimes male dominance is obvious. For example, in the United States, men occupy the highest positions of power in the economic, political, military, educational, and cultural (e.g., newspapers and television) institutions. Men are corporate executives; men are governors and senators; men control the media empires, the military, and the police force. Male dominance is revealed, more subtly, in our personal intimate lives. For example, women are expected to initiate and sustain heterosexual intimacy. Men make the key decisions around sex and money. Men's dominance is evidenced in the multibillion dollar cosmetic industry directed to women, in the ideal of slim, adolescent-like sexualized beauty that women aspire to in order to feel attractive, in women's exclusion from the highest levels of institutional power across society, in the obscene rates of rape and wife-beating; in the proliferation of households headed by single women who raise children with little or no financial or social support from the biological father.

Like any group that benefits from being in power, men have an interest in maintaining their dominance. As the realities of rape and women-beating indicate, men will use violence if necessary to keep power. They will resist the movement of women into positions of institutional power. A more subtle, and perhaps more effective, strategy of male dominance is to control the public images of gender. If the dominant cultural images define the "normal woman" as destined by nature to be a caretaker, wife, and mother, men will not need to use coercion to keep women subordinate. Men have deployed science, medicine, and popular culture to perpetuate the illusion that nature dictates gender difference and hierarchy; defining women's self-realization as wives and mothers reinforces men's social dominance. At the core of feminism is a reversal of conventional wisdom. Feminists view the idea of natural gender difference as an ideology intended to conceal the social and political formation of an unequal, male-dominated order.

Feminism is the theory of the women's movement. It describes the world of men and women as a social and political universe. Individuals learn to become men and women. Moreover, women are socialized into a subordinate role to men. Women have rebelled against male control throughout history. However, the ideology of natural difference, social norms pressuring women to conform to caretaking, servicing roles, and the deployment of men's superior political, economic, and cultural resources have succeeded in perpetuating male dominance. Although feminists agree that gender is a social and political sphere, they are divided about the source and dynamics of male dominance and the aim of the women's movement. I will outline the varieties of feminism in the women's movement from the mid-1960s through the 1970s. Despite differences among second-wave feminists, they agreed that women are essentially identical in their interests and values. This assumption has been challenged in various strains of feminism in the 1980s and 1990s.

The varieties of feminism and the identity of women

In 1963, Betty Friedan published *The Feminine Mystique* [1]. She argued that science and popular culture perpetuate a myth of women as finding true happiness as wives and mothers. In her interviews with suburban housewives across America, however, she found a pervasive discontent. Many women believed that, if they applied themselves energetically and skillfully to their romantic and domestic tasks, they would find happiness; some pursued therapy and regimes of beautification as a remedy. Friedan was convinced that these women were victimized by the idea that their femaleness destined them to a life organized around men and the household. She criticized the myth of gender difference that underpinned the feminine mystique. To the extent that women were defined as destined by nature to lives revolving around men and domesticity, society was relegating them to second-class critizenship. The ideology of gender difference left a legal system intact that denied women equal rights and opportunities. Women had the franchise, but they did not have equal rights at work or control over their reproductive capacity. Friedan advocated the abolition of all legal barriers to women's equality; she advocated women's equal right to pursue a career.

Friedan's ideas represent the dominant ideology of the women's movement: *liberal feminism.* Liberal feminists perceive a link between social norms of gender difference and male dominance. They emphasize the importance of public attitudes, laws, and legislation in maintaining gender inequalities. Liberal feminists aim to integrate women on an equal basis into the mainstream of the United States. Their chief strategy is public education and legislation. Liberal feminists have campaigned to abolish legal and legislative barriers to equal opportunity for women. The chief organizational vehicle of liberal feminism is the National Organization for Women (NOW), founded in 1966 by Betty Friedan. Its stated purpose is "to take action to bring women into full participation in the mainstream of American society now, exercising all the privileges and responsibilities thereof in truly equal partnership with men." The agenda of NOW has centered on the campaign for the equal rights constitutional amendment and reproductive rights.

Liberal feminists do not entirely reject the notion of natural differences between men and women. They deny that nature requires rigidly separate and unequal social roles. They do not diminish the value of women's role as wives and mothers. However, they object to the social forces pressuring women to a life centered exclusively in the family and household. Liberal feminists advocate choice for women with respect to marriage, family, career, politics, and the military.

Liberal feminism has dominated the politics of the women's movement. *Radical feminism* has captured its soul. Radical feminists contest the reform politics of liberal feminism. If radical feminism could be assigned a birth date it would be October 17, 1967. Disillusioned with the liberal reformism of NOW, a group of women left the October 17th meeting of NOW to form a new radical feminist organization which they initially called "The October 17th Movement," subsequently changing its name to "The Feminists."

Radical feminism describes a variety of social perspectives and politics. However, radical feminists share a commitment to broad institutional and cultural changes beyond altering attitudes and laws. In particular, they emphasize the importance of the norm of heterosexuality, the family, and a sex role system in sustaining male dominance.

The dominant emphasis in the early years of radical feminism (between the late 1960s and the early 1970s) underscored the physical, psychological, and social similarities between the two genders. Society, not nature, produced differences. Radical feminists explained gender inequality as a result of a socially learned gender role system that assigned to men and women different social roles. This gender system positioned men as socially superior to women. The family was viewed as a major institution enforcing gender inequality. Children were taught to reproduce a male-dominated heterosexual order. This unequal gender order was "normalized" and legitimated by scientific, medical, and popular ideas that reflected the standpoint of men. Radical feminists assailed this public culture; they criticized male-dominated family arrangements and socialization patterns. They advocated nontraditional families based on choice and equality; they imagined an androgynous ideal that would free people from restrictive gender norms.

Radical feminism captured the heart of the women's movement. Feminists such as Ti-Grace Atkinson, Shulamith Firestone, Robin Morgan, and Jill Johnston spoke boldly and eloquently against women's oppression [2]. They envisioned a beautiful life for women free of male dominance; they moved the hearts and minds of millions of American women. With images of women struggling against male victimization, radical feminism carries a redemptive power lacking in liberal feminism. It is radical feminism that has provided the passion for the energetic community-building efforts of women across the country.

Many feminists, however, were uncomfortable with the imagery of a gender war, female victimization, and an agenda of separatism espoused by radical feminists. *Socialist feminism* offered an equally critical alternative to liberal feminism. Marginalized in mainstream women's politics, the pioneers of socialist feminism, such as Juliet Mitchell, Gayle Rubin, and Nancy Chodorow, have had their greatest impact in academe [3].

Socialist feminists share with radical feminists a commitment to a large-scale critique and transformation of society. However, they depart from radical feminists who isolate gender from political-economic and class dynamics. Socialist feminists aim to combine the feminist focus on gender inequalities with the Marxist analysis of economic-based class divisions.

Socialist feminists assert the interlocking relations of economy and family and of class and gender. For example, the economic positioning of women in the paid work force influences their autonomy in the family. High-paid career women have more control over their intimate lives than do lower-paid working women. The latter feel pressure to shape their sexuality to please men in order to enhance their prospects of marriage and economic security. Patterns of male dominance are said to structure economic dynamics. Thus, job segregation by gender or gender typing certain occupations as feminine functions to maintain gender division and inequality. Socialist feminists link the spheres of sexuality and family with political-economic and class dynamics.

Despite the variations in feminism from the late 1960s through the 1970s, *gynocentrism unified feminism.* Gynocentrism assumes the identity of women by virtue of a shared biological, psychological, or social experience. Women were said to be unified by the universality of male dominance; they shared similar experiences, dispositions, values, and interests by virtue of male oppression and female resistance. Male dominance, ironically, created a unified, resisting female subject. Whatever disagreements surfaced among women with regard to social visions and political agendas, their common oppression and resistance was said to unify them. Feminists appealed to the reality of women's common identity and bonds of sisterhood to justify their ideas and politics.

Gynocentric feminism came under attack in the 1980s. Feminists of color and self-styled sex radicals provided the initial criticisms. A postmodern feminism has emerged as the successor to gynocentric feminism, although some fear that it is a betrayal of the women's movement.

Postmodern feminism: rethinking gender identity

From the vantage point of the mid-1970s, feminists had good reason to be confident. Between 1972 and 1974, Congress passed the equal rights amendment as well as women's rights legislation covering employment, education, property, and marriage rights. The 1973 Roe v. Wade Supreme Court decision guaranteed women their reproductive rights. As mainstream feminism absorbed radical feminist concerns with issues of sexuality, health care, and violence towards women, the women's movement assumed an ideological unity that has since eluded it.

An antifeminist backlash swung into full gear by the late 1970s. The New Right mounted a campaign against abortion rights which was translated into legislative successes. For example, the Hyde amendment, which cut off Medicaid funds for abortion, passed in 1977. The equal rights amendment failed to attain the 38 state ratifications needed for its passage. Key parts of the feminist agenda, for example, national childcare, health care reform, and equal pay, were stalled by the conservative gender politics of the New Right and the Reagan administration.

To make matters worse, in the face of a well-organized antifeminist campaign, the bonds of sisterhood were strained from within. Internal divisions over issues of lesbianism and race, dissensus around questions of alliances with the gay movement or the New Left, and conflict over broad ideological disputes around political strategy and goals threatened to unravel the fragile bonds of feminist solidarity.

As the women's movement was threatened by internal discord and a rising tide of social backlash, there was a shift in feminist thinking in the late seventies. Feminists rallied around a theory and politics of gender difference. Women's unique ways of being and thinking were celebrated while men were viewed as dangerous. Feminist perspectives highlighted the victimization of women by means of pornography, sex, rape, and physical violence. Men, rather than gender roles, were taken as the source of women's oppression. In Susan Griffin's *Rape*, Andrea Dworkin's *Our Blood*, and Susan Brownmiller's *Against Our Will*, women are viewed as victimized by a violent, uncontrollable male desire to dominate women [4]. In certain radical feminist versions of the ideology of gender difference, a political separatist agenda was defended. Women were encouraged to build a women's community to protect and nourish female culture against male values and violence.

Themes of gender difference that celebrate women while devaluing men surfaced in academic feminist theory. Two of the most important feminist statements of the late seventies and early eighties were Nancy Chodorow's *The Reproduction of Mothering* and Carol Gilligan's *In a Different Voice* [5]. They underscored the psychological, social, and moral differences between men and women. Moreover, Chodorow and Gilligan propose that women's empathetic, nurturing, and caring ways of relating are indicative of a superior moral and spiritual state.

By the close of the decade of the seventies, feminism retreated into a rigid gynocentrism. Departing from earlier currents of feminism that emphasized gender similarity, and institutional sources of women's oppression, the new gynocentrism underscored gender difference and women's victimization by men and affirmed a separatist agenda. The appeal to the identity of women no longer meant simply a state of shared oppression and resistance. Womanhood now referred to common psychological dispositions, values, and ways of thinking and being that unified women across history.

Gynocentric feminism engendered a critical response. The differences among women that had always been present, and, from time to time, noted and forgotten, found a more insistent voice as the claims to a unitary female identity grew sharper. By the early 1980s, these dissenting voices mounted into a crescendo of feminist discontent by working class women, Jewish women, postcolonial women, and differently abled women. Perhaps the most compelling criticisms of gynocentrism came from radical women of color and feminist sex radicals.

The leadership of the women's movement had been in the hands of White, middle class, often university-educated women since the late 1960s. Questions of race and class had bothered feminists through the seventies. Yet it was not until the early eighties that women of color coalesced into an organized force to speak with a public voice that could no longer be silenced. A new "radical women of color" perspective made its way into feminist public culture.

In a series of important public statements, radical women of color criticized the women's movement for reflecting the experiences, values, and interests of White, middle class women [6]. Gynocentrism feminism was attacked for not speaking to the lives of women of color. For example, gender oppression for Black women was said to be inseparable from racial and class oppression. These interlocking systems of identity and oppression could not be separated. As the Combahee River Collective states in its Black feminist manifesto: "We . . . find it difficult to separate race from class from sex oppression because in our lives they are most often experienced simultaneously" [7].

Radical women of color insisted that gender cannot be isolated from racial or class identity. Women are always of a particular race and class. The social positioning of women of color is therefore different than for White, middle class women. For example, only feminists who enjoy the privileges of (White) race and (middle) class status could afford, economically and politically, to pursue a separatist agenda. Women of color experience not only gender, but racial and often class oppression; they need to forge bonds of solidarity with men to fight racism and classism, in part, against White, middle class, even feminist women.

Gynocentric feminism excluded or marginalized the lives of women who were not White or middle class. Women of color could not find their experience reflected in the images of women and in the vision of women's liberation that were dominant in the women's movement. Women of color found themselves oppressed by the very movement that claimed to represent their emancipation! As Audre Lorde, a leading spirit of Black feminism, observed: "As white women ignore their built-in privilege of whiteness and redefine women in terms of their own experience alone, then Women of Color become 'other,' the outsider whose experience and tradition is too 'alien' to comprehend" [8]. Feminists of color aimed to expand the category of woman to include them by viewing gender, race, and class as interconnected.

Gynocentric feminism received its second major challenge from sex radicals. The 1980s witnessed what some feminists have called the "sex wars." Lesbianism had long been an issue of feminist contention. The women's movement was frequently attacked for its presumed hidden lesbian agenda. Many feminists were uncomfortable with lesbianism and an agenda of sexual rebellion. Although the redefinition by lesbian feminists of lesbianism as a political act of women bonding with women against male dominance went a long way to accommodating straight feminists, the broader issue of a feminist sexual ethic and politics did not go away.

Feminists were divided over whether the women's movement was a sexual liberation movement and what that meant.

The gynocentric feminism of the late 1970s invoked the unity of women's gender identity to justify a particular concept of female sexuality. Gynocentric feminists asserted the dichotomous nature of female and male sexual values. Appealing variously to nature, socialization, women's culture or oppression, gynocentric feminists portrayed female sexuality as person-centered, diffusely erotic, nurturing, loving, and monogamous. Male sexuality was described as body- and genital-centered, driven by pleasure, power, and promiscuity. Gynocentric feminists may have proposed this sexual theory to account for what they perceived as an epidemic of violence against women and as a way to energize the women's movement in the face of internal divisions and external backlash. Yet, this sexual theory assumed the force of a feminist sexual norm. Women for whom sex was body- and pleasure-centered or involved role playing or pornography or included multiple partners, were stigmatized as deviant or as male-identified, i.e., alienated from their true female gender identity.

A gynocentric feminist sexual ethic and politics met with stiff opposition. For many feminists, the women's movement stood for sexual choice, diversity, and the affirmation of the body as a site of pleasure. Gynocentric feminists were accused of legislating an unnecessarily restrictive, prudish sexual ethic. The appeal to a unitary female sexual identity and ethic functioned to oppress women whose sexual desires, values, and behaviors were different. By the early eighties, gynocentric feminism was on the defensive. Books such as *Powers of Desire, Pleasure and Danger,* and *Women Against Censorship,* which defended a libertarian sex ethic, challenged the notion of a common female sexual nature [9]. The intent of these feminist critics was to bring sexual choice and diversity squarely under the umbrella of feminism.

Radical women of color did not intend to subvert the foundational status of the category of women. They wished to expand it to include their experiences. They continued to appeal to the idea of "women" to comprehend the racial and ethnic gender identities that they proposed, for example, Black women or Latina women or Asian women. They wished to expand the range of legitimate identities that women could claim. They insisted that a common female identity varied along the axes of race and class. Thus, there would emerge a diversity of feminist standpoints (e.g., Black feminism or Latina feminism), each reflecting a distinctive racial and class positioning of women. While the intent of radical women of color was to multiply the possible articulations of women's identities and politics, this strategy raised doubts about the very idea of a unitary female identity. If women differ by class or race, in what sense, if any, can we speak of the unity of women? Similarly, sex radicals intended to expand the range of legitimate sexual expression for women. However, they placed in doubt the idea of the unity of women. If women's sexual experiences and values vary widely, does it make sense to posit a unitary female identity? Women of color and sex radicals raised doubts about the very idea of the unity of women.

By the mid-1980s, gynocentric feminism had lost cultural and political credibility. A multitude of voices announcing women's social differences circulated. New feminist identities surfaced: women of color, working class women, sadomasochistic lesbians, and postcolonial women. They defended the women's movement against backlash critics; simulta- ✗
neously, they attacked gynocentric feminists for repressing women's diverse experiences and for imposing new controls on women's bodies and behaviors. Mainstream feminism was criticized for functioning as a disciplining, normalizing force that reinforced dominant Eurocentric, middle class, White social norms. Drawing on the poststructuralist critique of essentialism and foundationalism, a new social and cultural force in feminist cultural politics was born: postmodern feminism.

Women of color and sex radicals challenged the exclusionary and disciplining effects of gynocentric feminism with the aim of making feminism more inclusive. Postmodern feminists suggested a broad challenge to the core premise of the women's movement: the idea that "women" refers to a shared essence or common identity that forms the necessary basis of feminist knowledge and politics. They contest the legitimacy, necessity, and desirability of appealing to "women" as the foundation of the women's movement on the grounds that such a concept is incoherent, exclusionary, and has normalizing or disciplining effects.

Postmodern feminists assert that the category of "women" is normative and political. Gender identity is not fixed, either by nature or society. There is no core gender identity based on common psychological dispositions, cultural values, or social positioning that neatly marks off women from men. Gender always bears multiple, conflicting, and shifting meanings; it is a site of ongoing social conflict. In place of appealing to a pure idea of women or female gender identity to organize knowledge and politics, postmodern feminists favor using categories involving multiple, composite selves (e.g., White, middle class, heterosexual, twentieth century women) and acknowledging the permanent multiplicity and instability of feminist knowledges and politics.

Postmodern feminism often draws on the poststructural approach to language as a system of signs whose coherence rests upon internal relations of difference. From this perspective, "women" acquires meaning only in its contrasting relation to "men" in a particular language system. The meaning of signs, including the significations, women and men, are always unstable, multivocal, and subject to contestation. Since individuals are positioned differently with respect to the multiple axes (gender, class, race, sexuality) of social hierarchy, the meaning of gender will vary and exhibit a surplus of meanings. Moreover, the signs, women and men, will serve as a site of social conflict to the extent that gender is an axis of social stratification. We cannot avoid a politics of language. Defining women as intuitive, nurturing, and maternal in contrast to men who are described as rational, ego- and goal-oriented positions the former in socially subordinate roles, e.g., caretaker, support and service social functions. From a post-structural standpoint, gender identity is an unstable, multivocal, and shifting site of meaning and contestation. Efforts by feminists or their critics to fix gender meanings or to assert a unitary gender identity are described as strategies to consolidate a social hierarchy.

The force of postmodern feminism does not lie in the claim that gender is an illusion. Instead, paralleling Foucault's reversal of the relation between sexuality and sex, postmodern feminists assert that gender is an effect of a discourse of bipolar gender identities. Discourses (e.g., science and popular culture) and social practices (e.g., law, violence, and the institution of heterosexuality) that figure humans as bipolar, unitary gendered selves – women or men – do not mirror an objective reality, nor do they engender mutually exclusive masculine and feminine selves. They do, however, produce cultural codes and social norms that carry public authority. Through their absorption into the family, religion, mass media, and the languages of science and mass culture, these bipolar gender meanings shape our lives. We imagine ourselves in their images; if they do not serve as mirrors of ourselves, they function as templates in relation to which we fashion ourselves. Although social forces conspire to shape our lives in the image of these models, and although we often describe ourselves by these gender simulations, our psychic and social lives lack the coherence of the model.

Sketches of postmodern feminism

Central to the postmodern challenge of mainstream feminism has been its "decentering of women" as the origin and agent of knowledge and history. Postmodern feminists propose replacing unitary images of woman with a concept of fractured, multiple identities. For example, in a densely imaginative essay, "A Manifesto for Cyborgs: Science, Technology, and Socialist Feminism in the 1980s," Donna Haraway offers the "cyborg," a boundary-confusing, protean hybrid creature, part fact, part fiction, part animal, part machine as a metaphor for postmodern composite identities [10]. She recommends abandoning the appeal to women's common identity as the basis of feminist politics in favor of a coalitional politic organized around affinities of interest and values. "Identities seem contradictory, partial, and strategic. . . *"* There is nothing about 'being' female that naturally binds women.". . . . Painful fragmentation among feminists along every possible fault line [e.g., race, class, sexuality] has made the concept of women elusive. . . . The recent history of much of . . . U.S. feminism has been a response to this kind of crisis by . . . searches for a new essential unity. But there has also been a growing recognition of another response through coalition – affinity, not identity" [11]. Haraway imagines "women of color" as a cyborg identity, a fusion of outsider identities whose unity is based more on affinities of (gender, race, and class) interests than on a common identity.

Haraway does not abandon the deployment of identity categories. "Women of color" functions as a new identity label. I imagine that Haraway would argue that the composite character of this category or its fusion of gender and race aspects make it inherently fluid, indeterminate, and resistant to a politics of ethnic separatism and normalization.

Postmodern feminists do not aim to give up all appeals to gender identity but to abandon ahistorical or universalistic ideas of womanhood as necessary for authorizing feminist theory and practice. Many postmodernists continue to invoke the category of women but only as an historically situated, socially composite, multiple identity. Nor do all postmodern feminists feel compelled to surrender a generalizing, theoretical vantage point; some wish only to give up strong foundational moves in favor of pragmatic justifications of social knowledge.

In their important programmatic statement "Social Criticism without Philosophy: An Encounter between Feminism and Postmodernism," Nancy Fraser and Linda Nicholson counsel against appeals to the unity of women to justify feminist knowledge and politics [12]. Abandoning references to a common gender identity means, as well, giving up the search for transhistorical theories of gender and gender inequality. However, in contrast to many postmodernists, Fraser and Nicholson do not surrender a commitment to generalizing theories of gender, critical theoretical knowledge, and synthesizing stories of male dominance. In order to advocate general social knowledge without having recourse to a notion of the unity of women or some claim to philosophical foundations, they propose an historicist, politically oriented conceptual approach. They outline their position as follows:

Postmodern critique need forswear neither large historical narratives nor analyses of societal macrostructures. This point is important for feminists, since sexism has a long history and is deeply and pervasively embedded in contemporary societies.

However, if postmodern-feminist critique must remain theoretical, not just any kind of theory will do. Rather, theory would be explicitly historical, attuned to the cultural specificity of different societies . . . and to that of different groups within societies. Thus, the categories of postmodern-feminist theory would be inflected by temporality, with historically specific institutional categories like the modern, restricted, male-headed, nuclear family taking precedence over ahistorical, functionalist categories [13].

Fraser and Nicholson envision a nonuniversalistic but still theoretical version of postmodern feminism. Feminism cannot abandon generalizing theories or big narratives because sexism is a large, organizing social dynamic. However, feminists are urged to give up the search for foundations and for one overarching true set of categories and theory. Postmodern feminism would accommodate a plurality of theories and stories of gender; its analyses would be driven less by demands for truth or theoretical knowledge than by situational political considerations.

The postmodern angling of Fraser and Nicholson is evident in their strategic endorsement of a multiple, composite self in place of the unitary gender identity of gynocentric feminism. "Postmodern-feminist theory would dispense with the idea of a subject of history. It would replace unitary notions of women and feminine gender identity with plural and complexly constructed concepts of social identity, treating gender as one relevant strand among others, attending also to class, race, ethnicity, age, and sexual orientation" [14]. Like Haraway, Fraser and Nicholson recommend a postmodern turn in feminism on the presumption of its usefulness for feminist politics. Gynocentric feminism may indeed promote internal solidarity but at the cost of silencing differences and impeding coalition building. With its imagery of multiple, composite identities and strategic political mobilization, postmodern feminists hope to encourage alliances among women and between feminists and other movements. They aim to break down the insularity of identity-based communities, thereby facilitating the building of broad-based, politically effective coalitions.

Haraway, Fraser and Nicholson imagine postmodern feminism as offering alternative conceptual strategies to gynocentric and standpoint feminisms whose value lies in promoting coalitional politics. A parallel effort but one that draws heavily on French poststructuralism is Judith Butler's proposal for a critical feminist genealogy of gender.

Judith Butler and the performative production of gender

Gender Trouble: Feminism and the Subversion of Identity is a series of studies of mostly French feminists influenced by Lacanian psychoanalysis and Derridean poststructuralism [15]. Butler intends to undermine the credibility of the appeal to women as a secure basis or foundation of feminist theory and politics. She maintains that asserting identity may be enabling for feminism but also constrains the possibilities of sexual and gender politics. Indeed, Butler calls attention to the ways in which feminism has unintentionally reinforced the binary gender order that it criticizes. In place of the feminist project of forging a general theory of women's oppression and liberation, Butler imagines a "critical genealogy of gender." Its aim is to analyze the performative production of gender and its entanglement in a system of male dominance and heterosexuality. She wishes to disrupt the illusion of a unitary gender identity for the purpose of opening up new possibilities for sexual and gender choice and politics.

Despite the variations in women's lives, feminists have assumed that a coherent gender identity exists. Invoking women as the subject of history and knowledge has seemed necessary, moreover, to promote the political visibility and empowerment of women. Butler does not deny the political value of deploying the category of women in light of a history of women's invisibility and disempowerment. Feminism seems to be caught in a dilemma. On the one hand, there is the apparent necessity to invoke the category of women to resist women's exclusion in a male-dominated society. On the other hand, every appeal to "women" and attempt to specify female gender identity has the effect of excluding and disempowering some women.

Feminists have reacted to this dilemma by urging a variety of strategies, for example, multiplying gender identities but assuming an overarching commonality, or acknowledging the fiction of the category of women but deploying it for political reasons. Butler urges that feminism abandon a strong claim of gender identity as a basis for feminist theory and politics. Many feminists already perceive the category of women as incoherent and undesirable. Critiques of Eurocentric, middle class feminism by women of color and postcolonial women have made feminists aware of the normative and political status of their discourse. Many feminists have concluded that there is no way to state what a woman is without excluding and stigmatizing some women. Butler asks: What political possibilities are foreclosed in the appeal to women as the foundation for feminism? What would feminism look like if it surrendered the foundational status of women without necessarily giving up the category of women?

The idea of gender identity is basic to modern Western societies. It has been assumed not only by feminists but by men and women who defend the notion of a binary feminine and masculine identity. The view of men and women as two distinct, opposite human types is so vigorously enforced by custom and law that this social compulsivity suggests an unconscious political force at work. Is there not some social power operating, seemingly behind our backs, that compels us to think of our bodies and behaviors in terms of a grid of fixed, antithetical gender identities? Drawing from Freud and poststructural French theorists, Butler interprets the unconscious compulsion enforcing the production of a binary gender order to be a system of compulsive, normative heterosexuality. Making humans into two opposite gender types, each with their own unique physical, psychic, and social nature and each imagined as incomplete without the other, ensures a system of reproductive heterosexuality. The claim that gender identity is driven by the taboo against homosexuality is suggested by the pressure felt by individuals to exhibit heterosexual desire as proof of a natural and normal gender identity. For example, men who exhibit feminine gestures or behavior are suspected of homosexuality. Linking a binary gender order to a regime of male-dominated heterosexuality provides Butler with a critical standpoint towards discourses and practices that appeal to a model of unitary, bipolar gender identity. To the extent that feminism assumes such a model, even if it reverses the dominant cultural values of femininity and masculinity, it reinforces a system of heterosexuality.

A system of heterosexuality may underpin the making of binary gender identities, but it does not explain the microdynamics of gender. In this regard, Butler proposes a performative theory of gender. I will review this theory in the broader context of feminist discussions of gender.

Butler advances a general claim about gender as a social category. Of course, virtually all feminists believe that gender is a social, not a natural, fact. However, most feminists, in fact, propose a fairly limited social explanation of gender. They assume that humans are, by nature, differentiated as female and male, an assumption shared by many nonfeminists. Through a social process, females and males become women and men. Feminists depart from nonfeminists, first, in the claim that society, not nature, explains the shape of women's and men's lives. Second, feminists claim that gender identities are formed in a manner that illegitimately gives men power over women. However, at least some feminists have not questioned the assumption, commonplace in Western cultures, that there exist two, antithetical sexed (female and male) and gendered selves (women and men). These feminists have not challenged the idea that gender identity is an essential defining core of the self that can explain behavior, including male dominance and women's resistance or lack thereof.

Feminists and nonfeminists may dispute the relative importance of social and natural forces in producing gender and disagree over the extent and legitimacy of gender hierarchy, but there has been little dispute over the assumption that humanity divides into two opposing human types: women and men. Feminists have sought to explain the passage of females and males to women and men in a way that perpetuates men's dominance. Despite its critical politics, feminism is entangled in the maintenance of the very binary gender order that it wishes to alter or abolish.

To recover its critical impulse, Butler believes that feminism must give up the notion of a core gender identity. Appeals to women's unitary identity are not only incoherent but unintentionally contribute to reproducing the binary gender order and a system of compulsive heterosexuality. Instead of charting the social production of "women" and "men" as unitary gendered selves, Butler proposes that we imagine gender as a performance that is susceptible of subversion and disruption. Let me explain.

Feminists have viewed gender as a social accomplishment. Individuals are born female and male but become women and men. Becoming a woman means adopting a core feminine identity which, in turn, forms the basis for women's actions. For example, feminists might refer to women's unique psychology or sociology to explain their specific approach to sex and love. An influential feminist account of behavior that appeals to gender identity is Nancy Chodorow's *The Reproduction of Mothering*. Chodorow wishes to explain how mothering is reproduced over generations. She assumes that the decision to become a mother cannot be entirely explained by social learning or coercion. Her explanation is that females acquire a feminine gender identity that functions as a kind of psychological force driving them to become mothers. Chodorow uses a psychoanalytical model. Girls identify with their mothers; they internalize their mothers as ideals of who they want to be. Girls become mothers because, in a sense, their mothers are lodged within their psyche. To be a mother is part of who they are as feminine selves. In other words, mothering behavior is viewed as an expression of a socially acquired feminine gender identity.

A critique of Chodorow from the standpoint of Butler's performative theory would be instructive. Butler would challenge Chodorow's story of gender identity. The meaning of identification and internalization would be interrogated. In this regard, Butler argues that children do not identify with actual persons but with fantasies or idealizations of them. Children's identifications, moreover, are multiple, often conflicting. Girls might identify with their mothers but also with their older sisters or an aunt or best friend. Children identify with both men and women and absorb these idealized gendered figures in contradictory ways. Boys may absorb feminine images; girls take in combinations of masculine and feminine traits. Further-more, Butler has doubts about the idea of internalization. Do we really internalize our idealized images of others, as if these significant others get lodged in some deep psychic space within us? Butler argues that, if our idealized gender images are "absorbed," it is the surface of our bodies, not some imagined inner psychic terrain, that is the arena of gender enact-ment. Rather than characterize gender as an inner core of the self that underlies the surface of behavior, Butler reverses this imagery: Gender is a learned, situational performance whose dramatic effect is the illusion of an inner gendered self.

Butler proposes a performative theory of gender. Neither nature nor society produces core gendered selves, if by that we mean an organizing psychic center of women's and men's lives. The idea of women and men as unitary contrasting selves is an illusion created by our repeated gender performances. Just as we learn to use language situationally, we learn how to "act" as if we are women or men. Through imitation, a system of rewards and sanctions, and our command of cultural and linguistic conventions, we learn to stylize our bodies and gestures, dress, walk, and talk, and use grooming and grammar to project ourselves as women or men. If we exhibit on the surface of our bodies the stereo-typed figures of masculinity and femininity, this may be interpreted as expressing our authentic gendered selves. There is, though, no true self that guides our behavior. Our gender performances are modelled after idealizations or fantasies of what it means to be a woman or man that are embodied in dominant cultural representations and social practices. In other words, gender is the realm of symbol and power. Representations of gender identity may be fictitious but they are not socially and politically innocent. The illusion of a core feminine and masculine gender identity conceals the social and political forces that fashion humans into sexed, gendered, and sexualized selves; it conceals the role of gender identity in the regulation of our sexuality, in particular, in the perpetuation of the institution of reproductive heterosexuality.

Approaching gender as a performance has far-reaching implications for feminist theory and politics. Butler marks off her own project of "critical genealogy" from the gynocentric project. The latter aims to develop the-ories of the formation of gender identity, sexism, and male dominance. Critical genealogy aspires to reveal the illusion of gender as an inner truth of the self and to identify the social forces that produce this illusion. Deconstructive analyses of discourses and social practices aim to show how they produce naturalistic images of the body, sex, gender identity, and sexuality that conceal the link of gender to a male-dominated regime of reproductive heterosexuality. Subverting constructions of gender identity becomes the task of a critical feminist genealogy. Butler envisions parody as a key strategy of gender subversion. She refers to "drag" as exemplary of its subversive potential since cross-dressing spotlights disjunctions between anatomical sex and gender identity and, Butler believes, reveals the social, imitative character of gender. Gender subversion aims to denaturalize the body, sex, gender, and sexuality for the purpose of exposing their social and political construction. Echoing the poststructural celebration of play and resistance as subversion, Butler imagines gender subversion as creating alternative ways of being embodied, sexed, gendered, and sexualized.

Butler is not proposing to replace a feminist politics of social equality for a politics of identity subversion. Her performative theory of gender aims to displace "women" as the foundation of feminist politics. If the self is produced in the very act of doing, if there is no "doer behind the deed," feminism cannot assert a unitary identity, "women," in whose name it speaks and acts. Deconstructing women as a category of identity does not mean doing away with "women," but making this category permanently open to contestation and to new social and political deployments.

> I would argue that . . . "identity" as a point of departure can never hold as the solidifying ground of a feminist political movement. Identity categories are . . . always normative, and as such, exclusionary. This is not to say that the term "women" ought not to be used. . . . On the contrary, if feminism presupposes that "women" designates an undesignatable field of differences, one that cannot be . . . summarized by a descriptive identity category, then the very term becomes a site of permanent openness. . . . To deconstruct the subject of feminism is not then to censure its usage, but, on the contrary, to release the term into a future of multiple significations, . . . to give it play as a site where unanticipated meanings might come to bear [16].

Making women the site of conflicting meanings creates new possibilities for politics. For example, Butler's own provocative bridging of sexuality and gender and disjoining of sex and gender creates new bases for social alliances, say, between feminists, lesbians and gay men, between feminists and sex radicals or minorities struggling around issues of body norms.

The postmodern subversion of gender identity has been troubling to many feminists. If feminists abandon women as foundational, what will replace it? Doesn't feminism need a unitary image of women to create solidarity? Don't women need affirmative, even celebratory, images of themselves to offset their devaluation in the male-dominated cultural mainstream? What social vision of liberation will mobilize women to make social changes? Granted, postmodernists may speak of affinities of interest or coalitional subjects, but this talk is maddeningly vague and abstract, say critics of the postmodern turn. Moreover, is it not suspicious that, at the moment when women find a public and empowering voice, they are, once again, being denied their identity? Is it not suspicious that so-called post-modern feminism is, to date, dominated by mostly White, upper middle class, academic women? Is not the idea of women as a fiction, a normative political category, precisely the claim made by critics of feminism?

Many feminists are reluctant to surrender identity-based politics. The appeal to "women" has functioned as the cornerstone for fashioning an affirmative identity, community, and politics for nearly three decades. Many feminists have built their lives around women's communities and the symbolism of sisterhood and patriarchy. Feminists are not alone in resisting the postmodern turn. African-American intellectuals have been resistant to relinquishing racial identity as the basis of knowledge and politcs. It is noteworthy, in this regard, that African-American feminists have been decidedly cool toward postmodernism or at least toward the abandonment of identity categories as the foundation of their theorizing and politics. African-American intellectuals have, in the main, turned away from the postmodern subversion of identity in favor of a variety of Afrocentric social perspectives. However, the instability of the category of "African-Ameri-can" has given rise to African-American theory that moves on a postmo-dern terrain.

African-American social thought: between Afrocentrism and postmodernism

Postwar Black politics, like its feminist counterpart, was a response to the failed promise for autonomy and equality in postwar America. Rising expectations for the good life and social justice were dampened by the reality of racism and sexism. Between the two movements, however, there were major differences. The women's movement was primarily dri-ven by White, middle class women who were responding to the contra-dictions between their growing social, educational, and economic opportunities and their sustained political subordination and cultural posi-tioning as inferior. The Black movement was a movement by the poor, the working class, and an aspiring, but still marginal, strata of educated Blacks who had only promises and hope, with little reality of social progress.

The Black movement was divided. In the South, the movement took the form of a struggle to tear down a legally enforced, racially based caste system. Fighting laws and customs that enforced a system of racial segrega-tion that denied them equal rights and opportunities, Blacks struggled for civil rights and social equality. There was no caste system in the North.

However, Blacks encountered a system of segregation enforced by racism and political economic powerlessness. They faced the devastation of indigenous Black institutions and traditions that followed their northern migration and their "ghettoization" in America's cities. Northern Blacks generated a distinctive movement: Black power or Black liberation. Where the civil rights movement emphasized equal rights, opportunities, and integration, the Black power movement was nationalistic and radical. Leaders such as Huey Newton, Eldridge Cleaver, Imamu Amiri Baraka, Angela Davis, and Stokey Carmichael emphasized racial pride and unity; they held that racism was institutionalized and not merely a matter of attitudes or laws, and they appealed to a history of racism and to shared African-American traditions to assert their racial unity. The assertion of an affirmative African-American identity would form the foundation for an ethnic nationalist community and politics.

Feminism and Black liberationism are identity-based political movements. They invoke a unitary personal identity as the basis of community and politcs. However, the fate of identity politics has varied. Gynocentric feminism came under severe criticism for its exclusionary politics; postmodern feminism has emerged as a possible successor project. There has been decidedly less dissatisfaction over a racialist foundation in the African-American movement. Indeed, by the mid-1980s, the ethnic nationalism of Black liberationism had passed into an Afrocentric philosophy that celebrates a unitary African-American identity. Yet, Afrocentrism exhibits multiple strains; if the politics of difference in feminism got played out ultimately in postmodernism, there are efforts to bring postmodern themes into an Afrocentric paradigm. I take Molefi Asante as representing a standpoint of Afrocentrism that is critical of the Eurocentrism of the Enlightenment tradition while in other respects remaining within it. I interpret Patricia Hill Collins as intending an Afrocentrism that absorbs the politics of difference without surrendering identity as the foundation. In the recent work of Bell Hooks, Cornell West and, most importantly, Kwame Anthony Appiah, I see a movement towards a postmodern African-Americanism [17].

Identity and difference in Afrocentrism: Molefi Kete Asante and Patricia Hill Collins

By the late 1970s, the African-American struggles for social justice were stymied. Indeed, from affirmative action programs to Head Start and minority scholarships, the gains of the preceding two decades were under attack. Many Blacks perceived a resurgence of public racism in cities and campuses across the country. With the growing public authority of the New

Right and neoconservatism, Blacks were, once again, being blamed for their own oppression as family instability, drug use, and welfare dependency were said to be the chief sources of their plight. As the White and Black middle classes fled the inner city, along with government and private aid, many Black communities were left devastated. The election of Ronald Reagan, whose administration was frankly hostile to civil rights legislation, reinforced the perception of the period as one of retreat for Black Americans.

In this social context of anti-Black backlash, some African-Americans called for an ethic of self-reliance and individualism; others redoubled their political efforts to publicize Black victimization through racism; still others sought to emphasize the creation of a culture of ethnic nationalist pride and community building. The latter response was advocated by a Black middle class that had achieved a level of socioeconomic security without the commensurate cultural status. Middle class Black Americans continued to be culturally devalued and inferior despite their class position. The message of Black ethnic pride was well received in poor Black communities that were devastated by drugs, unemployment, violence, and a sense of hopelessness. Paralleling the popular movement to redefine Blacks as African-Americans, a people with their own history and culture, academics were advancing an African-centered philosophy that they called Afrocentrism. I interpret Afrocentrism as part of a broader movement to counter the racist cultural inferiorization and political disempowerment of African-Americans by creating and instilling affirmative identities, ethnic national pride, and a standpoint of political agency.

Molefi Kete Asante, a professor of African-American studies, has been a key figure in the fashioning of an Afrocentric social theory. In *Afrocentricity*, he sketched Afrocentrism as a broad philosophy and program of community building and activism [18]. In *The Afrocentric Idea*, he explores Afrocentrism as a critique of the social sciences and as an alternative paradigm of social knowledge [19].

Afrocentrism is an approach to knowledge from the standpoint of African experiences and traditions. Social perspectives that express African values have been excluded or marginalized in the popular and academic culture of the West. In the scientific disciplines in American and European societies, "Eurocentric" paradigms of knowledge are dominant and imposed as universal. Eurocentrism pervades the popular culture of the West, thus reinforcing the public invisibility and devaluation of African-centered ideas and experiences. Asante describes the Eurocentrism of American culture as a kind of cultural colonization of African-Americans. Indeed, "symbolic imperialism, rather than institutional racism, is the major social problem facing multicultural societies" [20].

Symbolic imperialism alienates African-Americans from their own community; it aims to minimize their social discontent by absorbing African-Americans into White, European culture. Afrocentrism provides Africans with perspectives and traditions that are self-empowering because they reflect their lives.

Asante contrasts Eurocentrism and Afrocentrism as distinct, equally valid cultural traditions. Eurocentrism is said to express an Anglo-European civilization. Eurocentrism underlies Western knowledge from ancient Greece to the era of the modern sciences. Eurocentrism is characterized as dualistic (e.g., mind/body, reason/emotion, culture/nature), linear (e.g., evolutionism), and materialistic (e.g., Marxism). By contrast, Afrocentrism is anchored in early African civilizations. Afrocentrism places African experience at the center of its view of the world. Asante assumes that, despite the diversity of African cultures, there is a core African identity. It is apparent in Africa and in the African diaspora. Afrocentrism emphasizes wholistic approaches to knowledge and society; it values harmony, unity, and spiritualism.

Asante does not deny, at least in principle, the value of Eurocentrism in its particular Western context. He objects to its claims to be valid in all societies and to the imposition of European-based values and perspectives on non-Western peoples. At times, Western cultural ethnocentrism is obvious, as in the case of European societies transplanting their culture, along with their economic or military might, in foreign lands. More typically, Eurocentric cultural colonization is more subtle. For example, to the extent that the dominant paradigms of knowledge in the West (e.g., social sciences, philosophy, or literary theory) assume that Western culture and institutions are superior or register a movement of social progress, non-Western experiences and paradigms of knowledge will be ignored or interpreted as indicating a state of social backwardness or "primitiveness." Eurocentric arrogance obliterates African traditions or renders them inferior. As Eurocentrism pervades the social sciences, they unwittingly perpetuate the oppression of non-Western peoples. The assertion of an Afrocentric perspective opposes symbolic imperialism with the intention of giving a critical voice to African people.

Asante's Afrocentrism appeals to a unitary African identity as its foundation. Although he states that African traditions are diverse, he believes that a core set of values and traditions underlies an African identity. Repudiating biological notions of race as the basis of African identity, Asante emphasizes a cultural and historical concept of African identity. He asserts a unique African view of reality. "African society is essentially a society of harmonies, inasmuch as the coherence or compatibility of persons, things, and modalities is at the root of traditional African philosophy" [21]. For example, whereas Western law seeks to establish guilt in order to punish, in African law, the aim is to restore "communal balance, therefore, peace." Or, instead of the separation between speaker and the public characteristic of Western oratory, in African culture, public speaking is seen as a collective experience in which speaker and audience are expected to participate, as is indicated in the prominence of improvisation and the use of call and response between the speaker and public.

Asante connects the African cultural centering on harmony and spiritual unity with the special role of "the word" as a dynamic expressive force generating reality and community. In a series of provocative, sometimes brilliant, observations on the unique culture of communication and public discourse among African-Americans, Asante makes a compelling case for Afrocentrism. For example, he refers to the importance of "rhythm" and "styling" in African-American communication. This involves regulating the flow of words by using pauses, altering cadences and pronunciation, shifting verbal tone and accent, and visible gesturing. "In an education meeting at a university, where a young [Black] speaker gave his view of education, he began by saying "Education is for C-O-M-M-U-N-I-T-Y. I mean com-mu-ni-ty." He was styling, and every person familiar with the "tradition" knew that the speaker had seized upon this stylistic device to have an impact. Between the speaker and the audience was an authentic bond, created by the spoken word" [22]. In rhythm and styling, as in the emphasis on improvisation, lyricism, and call and response, Asante detects the traditional African reverance for the generative, transcending power of the word.

Through a series of deft analyses highlighting the differences in communication and public speaking between Afrocentric and Eurocentric cultures, Asante tries to make credible his assertion of a unitary African identity. Afrocentric cultures are said to be oriented to harmony and spiritual unity through the generative power of the word. Asante intends to challenge the imperialism of Eurocentrism; he aims to legitimate the idea that African cultures and peoples require their own African-based paradigms of knowledge. Yet in making what I consider a plausible case against the Eurocentric bias of Western paradigms of knowledge, Asante upholds a somewhat forced and overdrawn duality between Europe and Africa or Eurocentrism and Afrocentrism. The problem is not just that such a duality unavoidably perpetuates antagonistic stereotypes, but that it obliterates internal differences within the "European" or the "African" experience. Does not class or gender shape the European and African experience and identity? Indeed, does not gender serve as a site of identity and politics that may involve African women aligning with European women against both African and European men? Feminists have made a plausible case in this regard, but it finds no place in Asante's Afrocentrism. Patricia Hill Collins proposes one strategy to accommodate Afrocentrism to feminism.

In *Black Feminist Thought*, Collins responds to the blindness to gender in Afrocentrism and the marginalization of race in feminism [23]. She proposes an "Afrocentric feminist" social theory whose roots are in a unique intellectual tradition forged by Black women (e.g., Bell Hooks, Barbara Smith, Audre Lorde, Alice Walker) and which is to be anchored in the unique experiences and struggles of ordinary African-American women [24].

Black feminism exhibits contradictory strains reflecting the different social positioning of Black women along the axis of class, sexuality, nationality, and so on. Collins likens Black thought to a "shifting mosaic of competing ideas and interests" [25]. Yet African-American women share a history of racism and sexism that is often interconnected with class oppression to mark out a distinctive social standpoint. If this common history is not expressed in a uniformly coherent world view, Black women's thought does exhibit a unity around core themes. For example, Collins underscores the emphasis in Black feminism on the interlocking of gender, race, class, and sexuality as sites of identity, social formation, and politics. A key theme of Black feminism has been the suppression of Black critical thinking in the social mainstream, including the university, as one strategy for maintaining White, male, middle class social rulership. Black women's voices have been excluded or marginalized in public life. Accordingly, Black feminism has found its chief social location outside the dominant institutions of knowledge and cultural production, e.g., in churches, families, political networks, or among poets, writers, and musicians.

Collins maintains that Black thought in America has its roots in African culture. As Africans were enslaved, their Afrocentric values and world view found nourishment in American soil. Drawing on Afrocentric theorists, Collins conceives of Afrocentrism as a unique paradigm of knowledge. However, Black women are not only positioned by their history as Africans, but share with White women a history of sexism and certain core experiences relating to female biology, sexuality, motherhood, and roles in the household and workplace. Rather than emphasize the potential differences and conflicts between Afrocentrism and feminism that stem from their divergent social standpoints, Collins highlights their similarities.

Collins describes a unique Afrocentric feminist type of social knowledge. In contrast to the Enlightenment paradigm of knowledge that is dominant in the social sciences and mainstream feminism, Afrocentric feminism asserts that knowledge is socially anchored in the experiences of particular groups; the multiple social standpoints of agents of knowledge (e.g., Black women, Latino men, White middle class lesbians, working class women) produce a plurality of knowledges, each viewed as partial; knowledge involves the feelings, personal values, and interests of its producers and therefore carries broad social and political implications. For example, Collins highlights the role of concrete personal experience and feelings as a standard to assess knowledge claims. Being subjected to the reality of multiple oppressions and distrusting the dominant paradigms of knowledge, Black women rely on their own experience to survive and to determine what is real and true. In short, Afrocentric feminism conceives of knowledge as an effort to give expression to particular social experiences and as entangled in the making of society.

Deconstructing African identity: Kwame Anthony Appiah

Despite the diversity of Black women's experiences in the United States, Collins asserts a common experience and identity. She rejects, however, efforts to provide a biological basis for Afrocentric feminism. She conceives of Afrocentricity as a social and historical reality. It reflects a history of resistance to racism and shared African values and beliefs. This foundational assumption of a socially produced core African identity, which is at the root of both Collins's and Asante's, work is questioned by Kwame Anthony Appiah.

Raised in British Ghana, educated at Cambridge University, and recently a professor of African-American studies at Harvard University, Appiah contests the coherence of asserting a unitary African or Black identity on a biological, social, or historical basis [26]. His comments on the great African-American social theorist and leader W.E.B. Du Bois are instructive. Du Bois embraced the concept of race and assigned to the Negro race a unique social and moral role to play in history. Yet he wished to avoid a biological concept of race. Race referred to a people who shared a common history. Appiah raises doubts about this view. He observes that Du Bois himself, though a Negro, was the descendant of Dutch ancestors. Is it coherent to say that he shared a common history with Africans, with whom he had no known descendants, but not with the Dutch? If Du Bois is united with Africans, it is not because they share a common history, but because he assumes that they are all members of the same race by virtue of their skin color. The idea of defining race by a common history is credible only if the various peoples who are said to share this history (e.g., Africans, American Blacks, Caribbean Blacks) are already assumed to be an identifiable group by virtue of their skin color. Du Bois's social account of race, in the end, relies on a biological concept.

Is there any compelling evidence for biological accounts of race? Appiah sums up conventional wisdom among contemporary biologists.

Every reputable biologist will agree that human genetic variability between the populations of Africa or Europe or Asia is not much greater than that within those populations. . . . Apart from the visible morphological characteristics of skin, hair, and bone, by which we are now inclined to assign people to the broadest racial categories – black, white, yellow – there are few genetic characteristics to be found in the population of England that are not found in similar proportions in Zaire or in China. . . .

A more familiar part of the consensus is that the differences between peoples in language, moral affections, aesthetic attitudes, or political ideology . . . are not to any significant degree biologically determined [27].

If biology or common history cannot justify the assertion of an African identity, what about shared culture? Asante and Collins assert a common African cultural sensibility, e.g., the power of the word and the orientation towards harmony and holistic thinking. Appiah's work is troubling in this regard. Appealing to the diversity of precolonial, colonial, and postcolonial experiences across the African continent, Appiah finds little credibility in the presumption of African cultural identity. Compare, he says, the

Asante monarchy, a confederation in which the king is [guided by] . . . his elders and paramount chiefs, with the more absolute power of Mutesa the First in nineteenth-century Buganda; or the enclosed horizons of a traditional Hausa wife, forever barred from contact with men other than her husband, with the open spaces of the women traders of southern Nigeria; or the art of Benin – its massive bronzes – with the tiny elegant goldweight figures of the Akan. Face the warrior horsemen of the Fulani jihads with Shaka's Zulu impis. . . . Surely differences in religious ontology and ritual, in the organization of politics and the family, in relations between the sexes and in art, in styles of warfare and cuisine, in language – surely all these are fundamental kinds of difference? [28].

Do not Blacks share a history of racial oppression that unites all Africans and Black Americans? Appiah places this social logic in doubt. If Black Americans share an experience of racial oppression with Africans, do they not share this same oppression with Asians? Moreover, Appiah observes that racially based oppression is not a seamless, uniform experience. The system of racial slavery in the American South was very different from the racism of Northeastern urban centers in postwar America; these are hardly comparable to the experience of colonial subjection in British Ghana or to the system of apartheid in South Africa. Racism can be experienced, for example, as more or less personal or systematic and as susceptible to diverse forms of resistance. Finally, the struggle against racism is not exclusive to racially oppressed peoples. To the extent that Whites put themselves in the place of a Black as an imagined victim, they can, and do, both identify with the racially oppressed and with antiracist struggles.

Appiah sums up the preceding points: "Whatever Africans share, we do not have a common traditional culture, common languages, a common religious or conceptual vocabulary [and] . . . we do not even belong to a common race" [29]. Despite the conceptual incoherence of the varied attempts to authorize Black solidarity based on the concept of a unitary African identity, Appiah does not wish to completely relinquish the idea. African unity remains a compelling cultural and political aim, in part due to commonalities in African history and social struggles. Invoking African identity, moreover, is useful in order to bring about political mobilization, to negotiate civic peace within and between African tribes and nations, to build national alliances across Africa and the globe, and to focus international attention on Africa and the African diaspora. Appiah wishes to defend the appeal to African identity without the strong, and misleading, claims to unity. Although he is aware that the term "African" is already circulating and "fixed" by virtue of history and present realities (e.g., African Development Bank, the Olympics, political parties and agencies, anticolonial struggles), he urges that African identity be viewed as chosen, changeable, permanently contestable, and partial. While the practical needs of politics and social organization compel the assertion of an African identity, we – intellectuals and citizens – should not forget that identities are multiple: familial, tribal, national, gender-based, or religious. In the end, Appiah opts to combine a strategy of disrupting hardened, unitary images of the African while defending a pragmatic, case-by-case appeal to African identity.

The conceptual and political dilemmas involved in organizing selves, communities, and politics around an identity has plagued feminism and Afrocentrism. How can social and political gains of asserting a common identity be preserved while avoiding its contradictions and exclusionary, normalizing effects? Questions of identity and politics have been central to the lesbian and gay movement. Indeed, perhaps more than the feminist and African-American movements, the lesbian and gay movement was organized around the task of the making of a new identity and community.

Lesbian and gay theory: sexuality, identity, and politics

Sex and race were categories of identity as early as the founding years of the American republic. Americans defined themselves as men or women, as White or Black (or colored or negro). The same was not true for sexuality. Historians report that heterosexuality and homosexuality were not a basis for personal identity until the early twentieth century in the United States [30]. Previously, homosexuality was viewed as a behavior. In fact, historians have documented a middle class culture accepting of romantic involvements between women, at least as complements to heterosexual marriage [31]. This came to an end in the first decades of this century. A medical-scientific discourse announced to the public the existence of a new human identity: the homosexual. Characterized as a gender-confused, sexually perverse deviant, the homosexual was a disreputable figure.

A public culture organized around homosexuality as an identity did not develop until the postwar period. The 1950s saw the rise of homosexual organizations, cultures, and politics. Mainstream homophile groups viewed homosexuality as a minor psychological deviation that did not justify discrimination against homosexuals. Some imagined the homosexual as a new social minority. Homosexual politics aimed at eliminating the legal and attitudinal barriers to social assimilation through public education.

The cautious politics of homosexual assimilation was abandoned by a new generation inspired by the spirit of pride and rebellion visible in the Black and women's movements. Central to the gay liberation movements of the 1960s and 1970s was an affirmative politics of identity. If it was hard for women and people of color to find affirmative images of themselves and a forceful public voice, it was even harder for homosexuals. At least women and Blacks were a visible part of American culture. Blacks had fought in America's wars; there was a Black public culture that could offset mainstream racist images of personal inferiority. Women have been valued in their roles as wives, mothers, and social caretakers; twentieth century women could draw on women's rich cultural and political history. Homosexuals were invisible. They fought in wars, but no one knew; they were everywhere, but no one saw them. They were "closeted" or hid their identity for fear of losing their jobs and their families. Homosexuals lived through most of the twentieth century with a submerged, hidden identity that imbued their lives with shame and fear. Is it any surprise that the gay movement made the personal and public assertion of an affirmative lesbian and gay identity the cornerstone of a movement?

Gay politics of the 1970s was organized around the affirmation of a lesbian and gay self. Gay knowledges reversed the cultural logic of the social mainstream: Homosexuality may have indicated a unique human type, but the homosexual, now transfigured into the "lesbian" and "gay man," was the psychological, moral, and social equal to the heterosexual. Although there were disagreements over the degree of commonality between gays and straights, gay perspectives maintained that the lesbian or gay man indicated a distinctive social identity. The experience of heterosexism, the shared reality of being closeted and coming out, the multiple forms of oppression (e.g., by law, discrimination, violence, and cultural stereotyping) and resistance produced a common gay identity. As much as the lesbian and gay movement has rallied behind an affirmative personal identity, divisions were never far from the surface. In particular, gender conflicts gave rise to a persisting division. The gay movement split in the early 1970s into a lesbian-feminist and a gay, predominantly gay male, culture. Each organized their social discourses around the assumption of a unitary identity. They generated powerful social perspectives on sexuality and society. However, by the early 1980s, the success of the lesbian and gay movement and its consolidation of a liberal social center came under attack from without and from within. Whereas the antigay attack led many gays to embrace a strong naturalistic defense of homosexuality, the internal divisions, initiated by voices of difference and AIDS activists, spawned discourses and politics disruptive of identity politics.

Lesbian-feminism and gay theory as identity and community building projects: Adrienne Rich and Jeffrey Weeks

A public lesbian and gay culture materialized in the 1950s. It centered around bars, informal networks, and political organizing. The development of a postwar gay culture was seriously limited by an atmosphere of homosexual persecution; lesbians and gay men were dismissed from jobs and the military and harrassed on the streets; bars were raided and their patrons' names were made public. The power of the state was mobilized to keep homosexuals socially invisible and publicly scandalized.

The broad social liberalization of the 1960s and the appearance of student protests, feminism, Black liberation, and the counterculture favored the development of a lesbian and gay movement. In the course of the 1970s, lesbians and gays built their own subcultures anchored in an affirmative self-identity. In major urban centers such as New York, San Francisco, Chicago, Los Angeles, and Houston, lesbians and gay men created their own institutions, cultural apparatus (e.g., newspapers, book publishers, theatre, art), and political organizations. By the early 1980s, virtually every mid-sized city in the United States had its own public lesbian and gay community. A central part of this community-building effort was the knowledges produced by lesbians and gay men. In particular, lesbian feminism and gay social constructionism were new knowledges that proved pivotal in shaping the identity, community, and politics of these developing movements.

Lesbian feminism was a response to the perceived sexism of the gay movement and to the heterosexism of feminism. Lesbian feminists wished to separate lesbianism from male homosexuality and align with the women's movement. Their strategy involved redefining lesbianism. Rejecting views of lesbianism as a sexual preference or lifestyle, lesbian feminists asserted that a lesbian is a woman who rebels against patriarchy by centering her life around other women. Lesbian feminists argued that heterosexuality underpins male dominance. Heterosexuality refers to a constellation of social practices, including norms of sexual and gender behavior, the ideology of heterosexual romance, and the institution of marriage and the family. The system of heterosexuality perpetuates male dominance by centering women's lives around the interests, values, and needs of men. The culture of romance and the institutions of marriage and the family osbcure male dominance while positioning women in socially subordinate roles, i.e., wife and mother. To become a lesbian was a political act of rebellion against male dominance; it contested the exclusive legitimacy of heterosexuality and male dominance. It positioned women as independent, as living for themselves and highlighted the bonds of solidarity between women. The lesbian stepped forward as the exemplary feminist: independent and women centered.

Lesbian feminism developed in the early 1970s. Theorists such as Ti-Grace Atkinson, Jill Johnston, Rita Mae Brown, and Charlotte Bunch offered novel social perspectives analyzing the linkages between sexuality, gender, and capitalism [32]. These were pivotal statements not only in that they aligned feminism and lesbianism but in their conceptual reach and imagination. However, lesbian feminism created new tensions within the women's movement. It suggested that only lesbians could be true feminists, which alienated heterosexual feminists. A key statement of lesbian feminism, but one intended to soften that message, was Adrienne Rich's "Compulsive Heterosexuality and Lesbian Existence" [33]. Rich asserts the basic lesbian feminist thesis: Normative heterosexuality underpins male dominance. She argues that women are not born heterosexual; heterosexuality is neither natural nor normal. Moreover, heterosexuality is not chosen. Women are coerced, sometimes mildly, other times violently, to become heterosexual. Societies marshall an impressive range of resources to shape women's sexuality so that their heterosexuality is felt as natural and normal. Compulsive heterosexuality is enforced by a system of laws, economics, public policy, a culture of heterosexual romance, pornography, female sexual slavery, and the recourse to violence against women who deviate. Central to the making of heterosexual women is the deployment of a vast cultural apparatus, including the mass media and science, aimed at rendering lesbianism invisible and deviant. The lives of lesbians have been hidden from history, submerged in academic culture, and excluded in public life. Much of feminism has contributed to this public devaluation and silencing of lesbian lives by its presumption of the norm of heterosexuality.

As a political institution implicated in male dominance and the creation of deviant sexual populations, heterosexuality has been resisted throughout history. Despite the powerful machinery that society enlists to enforce heterosexuality, "a central fact of women's history [is] that women have always resisted male tyranny." For example, Rich refers to "the refusal of some women to produce children" or women's assertion of an "antiphallic sexuality" or a commitment to abstinence or the networks of women supporting each other that are part of women's lives [34]. Rich says that women who resist male dominance or who live their lives in important ways around women are part of the "lesbian continuum." All feminists can be located on this continuum. But not all feminists live what Rich calls a "lesbian existence." This refers to women whose primary sexual and intimate lives are organized around women. A key point is that lesbian existence is distinguished from male homosexuality. Whereas men, either straight or gay, retain gender power, women, whether straight or lesbian, are positioned as subordinate to men. Gay men may simply make their homosexuality into a lifestyle; women who choose to become lesbians are making a political statement as it positions them in revolt against male dominance.

Rich assumes that heterosexuality is socially imposed. For example, women marry because they have no choice. They marry for economic survival, to have children, to avoid social ridicule, or to fulfill male-imposed ideals of feminine self-fulfillment. "Within the institution [of heterosexuality] exist, of course, qualitative differences of experience; but the absence of choice remains the great unacknowledged reality" [35]. Women are forced to become heterosexual and surrender their sexual, social, and political autonomy. Choosing lesbian existence is to choose freedom. Rich assumes that the vast social machinery enlisted to maintain the heterosexual norm suggests the natural force of lesbianism. This does not, however, follow. Documenting the social forces conspiring to maintain a heterosexual norm does not imply anything about the relative natural force of homosexual or heterosexual impulses. Women may feel a forceful impulse to bond with women, but this need not preclude the existence of an equally impressive force to bond with men. The assumption that the heterosexual norm will be experienced by all women as necessarily coercive does not follow.

Rich assumed the universality of lesbian existence. She held that there have always been lesbians and that the meaning of lesbian existence is uniform across history. Just as heterosexuality is imagined to be a seamless, uniform order of domination, lesbian existence is assumed to have an essential meaning. This assumption of a universal lesbian continuum and identity that unites women across different histories has been the target of a great deal of criticism. From the mid-1970s through the following decade, independent scholars and academics fashioned a new gay scholarship that emphasized the socially constructed character of sexuality and variations in the meaning and social roles of homosexuality.

The British historian and social theorist Jeffrey Weeks is a pioneer of social constructionism [36]. Weeks reacted against two major currents of social thought. First, the formation of a lesbian and gay community was accompanied by an insistent claim that "the homosexual" is a distinct person with a specific identity. Gay historians produced lists of famous men and women in the past whose true homosexual identity was revealed. Although claiming a noble ancestry may have been useful to legitimate a homosexual identity, it failed, according to the constructionist view, to capture what was unique about the social formation of homosexuality in the present. Second, although Weeks absorbed a Marxist critique of an ahistorical approach to homosexuality, he criticized Marxism and feminism to the extent that they explained sexuality as an effect of class or gender dynamics. Such arguments delegitimated gay and lesbian theory and politics and reinforced the invisibility and devaluation of gay lives. Issues of sexuality and homosexuality were connected to dynamics of class and gender, Weeks argued, but they were not reducible to them. Sexuality had its own history and social patterns, requiring its own theories and politics. Weeks imagined homosexuality, like all forms of sexuality, as a social and historical phenomenon whose meanings vary and whose social and political patterns demand an independent gay or sexual theory.

Declaring the social character of sexuality was hardly news. Freud made sexuality into the driving force in human behavior and social dynamics; Freudo-Marxists such as Wilhelm Reich and Herbert Marcuse had linked sexuality to capitalism. Anthropologists such as Bronislaw Malinowski and Margaret Mead described the social organization of the sexual lives of "primitives." These diverse approaches exhibit, however, a common set of assumptions about sexuality that Weeks calls "essentialism." This approach views sex as a natural instinct built into the biological structure of the individual. Moreover, the essentialist concept of sex assumes it to be a powerful force driving the thoughts and behavior of individuals. Although essentialist approaches to sexuality disagree over its natural or normal development and therefore over the appropriate role of society in regulating sex, there is little disagreement that sexuality and society stand in a relation of antagonism. Sex is a natural force pushing from deep within the self for public release; as the guardian of order and morality, society represses and regulates sex.

Instead of assuming the opposition of sex and society, Weeks proposes a social constructionalist perspective.

First, . . . we can no longer set "sex" against "society" as if they were separate domains. Secondly, there is a widespread recognition of the social variability of sexual forms, beliefs, ideologies and behavior. Sexuality has . . . many histories. . . . Thirdly, . . . we must learn to see that sexuality is something which society produces in complex ways. It is a result of diverse social practices that give meaning to human activities, of social definition and self-definition, of struggles between those who have power to define and regulate, and those who resist. Sexuality is not given, it is a product of negotiation, struggle and human agency. [37]

Rather than approach sex as a matter of personal desire and behavior, Weeks views sexuality as social, as involving bodies, behaviors, meanings, social norms, institutions, and conflicts. Sex is not an instinct whose nature is fixed; it is a site where the personal and the political, the body and society, become a focus of social meanings and struggles.

Weeks's social constructionist approach can be nicely illustrated by outlining his perspective on homosexuality. Conventional wisdom assumes that the human population is divided between individuals who are, by nature, either heterosexual or homosexual. Same-sex sexual desire and behavior are thought to indicate a distinctive homosexual human type or identity. Dominant knowledges have emphasized the processes by which homosexuals arrive at self-knowledge and the impact of social conditions on the homosexual. The politics of homosexuality has revolved around the question of whether society should tolerate homosexuals. Gay politics has absorbed this culture of homosexuality; self-defined homosexuals appeal to the naturalness of the homosexual identity and recommend its normalization by, for example, demanding civil rights.

In *Coming Out: Homosexual Politics in Britain from the Nineteenth Century to the Present*, Weeks proposes that the idea that homosexual behavior reveals a human identity did not emerge in Western societies until the late nineteenth century [38]. In previous centuries, homosexuality was often subsumed under the broad category of sodomy which included a range of illegal homosexual and heterosexual acts. The notion that acts of sodomy indicated a type of person and that sexual desires mark off a distinct homosexual identity from heterosexuals was alien to Western societies prior to the late nineteenth century. The sodomite was punished by law and custom for his or her particular behavior, not as a deviant person. The homosexual stepped forward recently, and only in the West, as a unique physical, psychological, and social identity marked in all these ways by his or her sexuality.

Weeks places a great deal of importance on the rise of a science of sexuality in the making of the modern homosexual. Paralleling the rise of economics, sociology, anthropology, and political science, a new science of sexuality – sexology – materialized in Germany and Britain and subsequently in the United States. Sexologists aimed at discovering the sexual nature of humankind. They sought to chart the development of the sexual instinct and document its manifold forms and its normal and pathological evolution. From the twelve volumes on homosexuality published by the German sexologist Karl Heinreich Ulrichs to the thousands of interviews of the sex lives of Americans by Alfred Kinsey, sexology has sought to uncover the hidden truth of the self that was thought to be buried in the lower regions of human sexuality [39].

Between 1898 and 1908, over 1,000 publications appeared on homosexuality. Sexologists seemed obsessed with charting the development, types, and psychological and behavioral manifestations of homosexuality. Sexologists did not create the homosexual; there were already individuals engaged in homosexual behavior and networks of such individuals. Sexology did, however, contribute to creating the idea that humans have a specific sexual nature and identity, that humans divide naturally into "heterosexuals" and "homosexuals", and that all sexual desires, behaviors, and identities can be classified as either normal or abnormal.

The ideas of the sexologists had great social impact. They were taken up by the state, lawyers and judges, psychiatrists and psychoanalysts, popular culture and the mass media. Weeks highlights the role of sensational public events in giving social impetus to the circulation of sexologists' ideas. In public events such as the 1890s British trial of Oscar Wilde for his alleged homosexuality, the idea of a homosexual identity gets absorbed into popular, everyday culture through massive, sustained publicity. The language of sexuality and sexual types, the opposition of heterosexual and homosexual, and an ethic of sexual normality and abnormality become part of the language of daily life through such public dramas. By the early decades of this century, self-defined homosexuals had become a part of the public sphere. Although the language of homosexual identity stigmatizes the individual, Weeks observes that it also stimulates a heightened homosexual awareness. This, in turn, facilitates the creation of networks that have eventuated in movements of homosexual liberation. This did not happen immediately, but, by the postwar period, a plurality of movements of lesbian and gay affirmation, which often drew on science and sexology for legitimation, had reversed the cultural meanings of homosexuality. Movements affirming lesbian and gay identities appealed to the very ideas of normality and naturalness that originally scandalized them.

Deconstructing gay identity: Diana Fuss and Eve Kosofsky Sedgwick

Despite his critique of the theory of the homosexual as a natural, universal type, Weeks's social constructionist theory of homosexuality was very much influenced by the identity-based gay community-building efforts of the period. Weeks may have historicized gay identity, but he did not doubt its positive role. In effect, he endorsed, for political reasons, an ethnic model of gay identity while recognizing its historical and social origins. Weeks was attentive to the tendency of an ethnic model of identity to be exclusionary and to defuse its critical political potential by evolving in a separatist or liberal assimilationist direction. In this regard, he advocated that lesbian and gay identities be articulated in relation to differences of class, race, and gender, as well as other patterns of sexuality. He did not question the identity framework of gay life but saw it as a necessary historical fiction in shaping a positive sense of self and community. Nor is this surprising given that his own coming of age as a gay man was inseparable from the flowering of a movement of gay affirmation in the seventies. Moreover, the efforts at community building through identity politics paid off. Lesbians and gay men made many important social gains through the 1970s.

By the early 1980s, the social positioning of gays had changed significantly. On the one hand, a powerful antigay backlash campaigned to roll back the gains of the preceding decade. On the other hand, the consolidation of what we might call a gay mainstream came under attack by lesbians and gays of color and a renewed spirit of political radicalism fueled by AIDS activists. Two responses to this crisis of gay life are apparent. First, in response to antigay attacks and growing internal divisions around the meaning of homosexuality, some gays retreated into a biological essentialism, asserting a common genetic basis for homosexuals. Others took the crisis as reason to rethink gay identity and politics, in particular, to go beyond lesbian feminism and social constructionsim and the opposition of identity and difference. Paralleling the renewal of radical politics among AIDS activists and Queer Nation groups, we can observe a theoretical politics that took as its target both the straight and the gay mainstream. Just as Queer Nation groups were criticizing the normalizing effects of the gay mainstream, some theorists were challenging the key premises of gay theory and politics. In contrast to an earlier generation of gay theorists who were either independent scholars, historians, or social theorists, the new theorists were mostly professors of English who were deeply influenced by poststructuralism.

Much gay theory in the postwar period has assumed that homosexuality is a condition or identity of a segment of the human population. Although all humans might have homosexual feelings, only a minority of humanity are truly homosexuals. Gay theory has sought to explain the making of a homosexual minority. Despite disagreements between essentialists and constructionists or separatists and assimilationists, virtually all gay and lesbian theory has theorized homosexuality as a minority experience based upon a unitary homosexual identity.

Poststructuralists contest the perspective that theorizes homosexuality as a social minority. In place of analyzing the natural or social production of a gay minority, with its focus on the acquisition of a gay identity and the building of a community against social oppression, they substitute the analysis of the situational, social production of the very categories of homo-sexuality and heterosexuality. Shifting attention from the making of homo-sexuals to the making of a society in which homosexuality is pervasive and structured into the basic cultural categories and language of society, post-structuralists aim to render gay theory into a general social analysis.

The disruption of the assumption of a unitary coherent homosexual identity is the occasion to inaugurate this broad shift from theorizing homo-sexuality as a minority experience to viewing it as a major organizing principle of Western societies. The case against a unitary gay identity should, by now, be familiar. Asserting a unitary gay identity entails the exclusion and devaluation of a range of experiences and values. Every attempt to define what it means to be a lesbian or gay man inevitably presupposes a particular social (i.e., class, race, gender) standpoint. More-over, as there are an infinite possible combinations of these "subject posi-tions" or social variables, any assertion of identity will be partial and privileging. Multiplying identities such as Black lesbian or White working class gay man simply reproduces this exclusionary effect. For example, White working class gay men may vary considerably by age, religion, race or ethnicity. In addition, multiplying identities has the potential effect of weakening efforts at unifying political mobilization.

Diana Fuss advances a distinctively poststructuralist critique of gay iden-tity standpoint theory. She argues that it reproduces the opposition between homosexual and heterosexual, thereby reinforcing a social logic of exclu-sion and the production of deviant others. "Deconstruction . . . view[s] . . . identity as difference. To the extent that identity always contains the specter of non-identity within it, the subject is always purchased at the price of the exclusion of the Other, the repression or repudiation of non-identity" [40]. Fuss contends that the identity of a person or object is implicated in its opposite. Heterosexuality has meaning only in relation to its opposite, homosexuality; the coherence that the former is built on depends on the exclusion and repression of the latter. The hetero/homosexual symbolic coupling forms a mutually interdependent, hierarchical relation of meaning. The logic of identity is, according to Fuss, a logic of boundary defining that produces excluded, subordinate others. The social gains of coherence in asserting identity are purchased at the price of a social logic of hierarchy and the production of deviant identities. In other words, Fuss maintains that the hetero/homosexual opposition creates a kind of normative social and political logic that is, unwittingly, reproduced by the assertion of affirmative lesbian and gay identities. Fuss urges a shift from theorizing homosexuality as a minority experience to contesting the hetero/homosexual hierarchy as it pervades the dominant cultural images and social conventions of American society.

The shift from theorizing homosexuality as a minority experience to theorizing the hetero/homosexual opposition as a social logic is central to Eve Sedgwick's *The Epistemology of the Closet* [41]. Instead of approaching homosexuality in terms of questions of identity and the politics of oppression and resistance, Sedgwick analyzes how the hetero/homosexual opposition structures the core modes of thought, culture, and identity in the twentieth century. The "*The Epistemology of the Closet* proposes that many of the major modes of thought and knowledge in twentieth century Western culture as a whole are structured – indeed, fractured – by a chronic, now endemic crisis of homo/heterosexual definition. . . . The book will argue that an understanding of virtually any aspect of modern Western culture must be, not merely incomplete, but damaged in its central substance to the degree that it does not incorporate a critical analysis of modern homo/heterosexual definition" [42]. The hetero/homosexual definition not only assigns identities to individuals but shapes broad categories of Western thought and culture. For example, the hetero/homosexual definition frames peoples experiences, regardless of sexual orientation, in terms of self-disclosure. In other words, "coming out" and the "closet" spread from the homosexual to his or her friends, family, and co-workers. The relative of a gay person must reiterate the latter's experience of the closet and coming out. Moreover, heterosexuals' experiences entailing secrecy and disclosure are framed as coming out experiences. As the title of Sedgwick's book suggests, the closet and coming out become general categories of knowledge and cultural organization in societies featuring the hetero/homosexual definition.

Sedgwick imagines the hetero/homosexual symbolic figure as a kind of master social logic, akin to the masculine/feminine gender code. It structures identities, the basic categories of knowledge and culture, and the normative organization of society. In other words, the issue of homosexuality is no longer simply an issue for a social minority, nor is it an issue exclusively of rights, integrity, institutional respect, and equality, but one that touches on the whole of the society by affecting the cultural order. Gay theory is no longer a minority theory; it becomes a general critical cultural analysis of the social productivity of the hetero/homosexual definition in the service of a heterosexual norm. At one level, the aim of poststructural deconstructive gay theory is to show the pervasive, structuring presence and power of homosexuality. At another level, it attempts to feature the instability of this binary opposition for the purpose of diminishing its force and releasing new possibilities for desire, identity, thought, and social organization.

In Fuss and Sedgwick, we can observe an important effort to shift gay theory and politics away from a minority theory to a broadly critical cultural theory. It is the hetero/homosexual opposition that structures the basic categories and orders of cultural life and that needs to be revealed and disrupted. This implies a version of a poststructural politics of subversion: if not subverting identity, then subverting the hetero/homosexual opposition itself. A poststructural gay theory seems to envision a broad cultural politics, struggling against the situational social production of hetero/homosexual cultural texts and meanings. Like their French originals, however, the American counterparts are maddeningly value when it comes to spelling out what such a politics of subversion would look like and towards what goal it would strive.

Afterword

The social knowledges generated by the new social movements challenge the Enlightenment human studies tradition. Feminist, Afrocentric, and gay theorists contest the separation of knowledge, values, and politics; they bring into the center of social analysis issues relating to the body, sexuality, gender, race, and identity; they enlarge the sphere of politics to include the politics of the self, culture, and knowledge. Paralleling French poststructuralism, there is an emphasis on cultural politics, for example, the role of discourses and representations in producing identities and configurations of power. In short, the constellation of beliefs associated with the Enlightenment (e.g., progress, the unity of the subject, the superiority of the West, science as truth) are criticized. The social knowledges produced by the new social movements represent important efforts to rethink how modern values of choice, freedom, pluralism, democracy, solidarity, and justice can be defended from a post-Enlightenment perspective.

From Condorcet through Durkheim, Parsons, and Levi-Strauss, science has been distinguished from religion, ideology, or personal opinion by the presumed irrelevance of the (racial, class, gender, national, or sexual) identity of the scientist to the validity of knowledge. Science was said to represent a disinterested, objective, and universal standpoint. This made possible the production of scientific knowledge as a mirror of the external world. The erasure of the scientist's subjectivity was accomplished through the institution of science, for example, its norms of empirical falsification, criticalness, universality, and rules of evidence. If the scientist could be transfigured into a universal mind aspiring to truth, scientific knowledge could be free of particular social prejudices and interests. Moreover, if only science yields objective truths, then only scientists could be trusted to guide social policy and public education. Science would be a haven from ideological conflict where reliable, valid knowledge would be produced for the purpose of ensuring social progress. The Enlightenment tradition imbued science with enormous significance: as producing objective, nonideological knowledge, educating humanity, and directing social progress. The culture of the Enlightenment has been central to the organization and legitimation of the social scientific disciplines.

Feminist, Afrocentric, and gay theorists have contested the Enlightenment paradigm. For example, feminists described Western science as androcentric or reflecting the interests and values of men. The masculine coloring of science was said to be exhibited in its chief problems and topics (e.g., the economy and government rather than gender, sexuality, or families), basic categories and explanations (e.g., wage labor rather than domestic labor or class explanations rather than gender-role accounts), and methodology (e.g., quantitative rather than ethnographic). The very criteria of knowledge was said to be gender biased. Thus, the identification of knowledge with formal-rational, objective, value-neutral standards is said to reflect men's abstract, formalistic culture. By contrast, women are thought to prefer a personal, experiential, dialogic, and contextual approach to knowledge. If scientific knowledge was identified with men's values, women's ways of knowing were devalued as inferior or prescientific. Feminists accused the social sciences of contributing to the reproduction of an unequal gender order.

Some feminists have wished to defend the Enlightenment paradigm of knowledge. They argued that women's experience can not only provide a corrective to male-biased science but can be the basis for true knowledge. I am skeptical. Why should women's experience supply an objective basis of knowledge rather than simply a different standpoint reflecting their particular interests and values? Moreover, if there is no identical or common experience among women but only a multiplicity of gendered experiences, reflecting the virtually infinite ways gender intersects with class, race, nationality, sexuality and so on, there will be as many women's knowledges as there are possible women's standpoints. Feminist stand-point theory is suspect from an additional perspective. The critique of science as value and interest driven can be turned against feminists. Feminist knowledges can be contested as Eurocentric or heterosexist. Criticizing science as androcentric, Eurocentric, or heterosexist implicates the values and interests of the scientist in the production and content of social knowledge. This critique raises doubts about the value-neutral, objective, universal, and socially beneficent character of knowledge.

Feminists, African-Americans, lesbians, and gay men have contested the Enlightenment view of the social sciences from their own social position-ing in postwar America. In their struggles for social justice, the new social movements often found themselves in a practical and political relation to the social sciences. For example, psychology and sociology have been central in producing "scientific" perspectives defining women as maternal, emotional, and nurturing. These gender definitions pressure women to assume the roles of wife, mother, and social caretaker (e.g., nurse, secre-tary, or social worker). Similarly, psychology has been a formative social force in shaping a culture that views heterosexuality as natural and nor-mal while stigmatizing homosexuality as abnormal and deviant. In its discourses of deviance and "the family," sociology has often normalized heterosexuality and nuclear organized families. The social sciences have constructed non-Western societies as backward, primitive, static, and authoritarian. From Marx to Habermas, social science has been a major source in constructing "Orientalism" or the contrast between the pre-sumed superior West and the inferior, subordinate East. In the discourses of the new social movements, science is often viewed as a major social and political force. It is entangled in social practices of exclusion, margin-alization, and devaluation, from justifying the denial of civil rights to gays to promoting colonialism as a benevolent gesture of social progress. Science is not, however, intrinsically evil; it is not simply, and only, a force of oppression. It has also been used to combat heterosexism, sex-ism, and Eurocentrism. My point is that feminists, African-Americans, and gays are in a practical and political relation to science.

I feel a close kinship with these movements and their criticisms of the Enlightenment tradition of knowledge. I reached adulthood in the late 1960s. Between 1967 when I graduated high school and 1970 when I enrolled in college, I was part of the counterculture and the antiwar movement. I was rebelling against the conceit of middle class, Enlight-enment culture. I protested its arrogance in assuming that the modern West had discovered a natural order of things that included building a life around a career, the normality of heterosexuality, marriage, and a nuclear family and the assumed superiority of Western science and

Christianity. I recall dabbling in non-Western religion and culture because modern Western culture seemed too rationalistic, formalistic, and emptied of a sense of unity between the individual, nature, and society.

Social experimentation was everything in the sixties. We tried drugs and music to experience new ways of recovering our feelings and connecting to nature and creating community. We played with gender roles: Men grew their hair long and wore bright flowery clothes, while women wore jeans and discarded makeup and beauty regimes to achieve an androgynous look. We rebelled against the normalization of sexuality. Guilt-free sex and sex that was no longer confined to heterosexuality, the bedroom, and love was proudly tried. Whether it was protesting United States involvement in the Vietnam War or needlessly restrictive sexual and gender roles, I was part of a generation that registered large doubts about the modern Western view of the "natural order of things."

Like many of my friends, I perceived a decline in the movements of social rebellion by the early 1970s. Drugs, money, in-fighting, burnout, or simply the lack of a viable social direction for our personal hopes led many of us to replace our bell-bottoms with business suits. My years of psychological and physical travels came to an end. I returned to college and found myself pursuing a doctorate. Why? I imagined that the university would provide a tolerant place where I could be relatively free of many routine institutional demands. I thought that its intellectualism would preserve some of the creativity and authenticity of the counterculture. Much to my surprise, I took great pleasure in intellectual pursuits. I became a sociologist. Somewhat ironically, my first book traced the Enlightenment origins of sociology and Marxism [43]. I defended the Enlightenment tradition against attacks by romantic or religious critics. The problems of our society were due, I thought, to the failure of the Enlightenment ideals to be fully realized.

My romance with the Enlightenment changed rather dramatically in the early 1980s. Among the key events in this sea change was the integration of my homosexuality into my life. I redefined myself as gay. As a gay man, I found myself in a changed *social* relation to Western social institutions. I realized that my prior heterosexual identity had positioned me as normal and conferred a range of privileges, from familial and peer approval to legal and state support of my sexuality. As a homosexual, I was now positioned as a criminal in the eyes of the law and a deviant vulnerable to ridicule, violence, and the loss of job, housing, and even my son. As a gay man, I was in an immediate practical, moral relation to science. For example, I discovered that science had played a major role in constructing the homosexual as an abnormal, deviant, immoral human type. The marginal, deviant status of homosexuality was reinforced by the social sciences through their exclusion of homosexuality as a topic of investigation or through their normalization of heterosexuality. As a gay activist, I found myself in a directly political relation to science. Antigay forces deployed science to justify denying me civil rights and child custody and excluding me from the military and the church. Progay forces appealed to science to claim the normality and naturalness of homosexuality. In assuming a gay identity, I could no longer view science through the prism of the Enlightenment. It was not that I rejected the Enlightenment or science, but that both were viewed as social and political forces involved in the making of selves, identities, social norms, and social institutions. I gravitated towards post-Enlightenment social knowledges.

Advocating a post-Enlightenment approach to social knowledge raises serious questions: If there is no objective, universal standpoint from which to generate categories and explanations, if all standpoints are partial and perspectival, how are knowledge and social criticism possible? If all foundations reflect a shifting, unstable assortment of specific social interests and values, are not all claims to truth relative and lacking in credibility? If feminists cannot appeal to women or gays to homosexuality to authorize their claims to knowledge and politics, don't these movements lose their moral legitimacy? Abandoning the possibility of an Archimedian standpoint from which to generate valid knowledge and values would seem to endorse an anarchistic, nihilistic vision of society in a permanent civil war. And, yet, for many of us, Enlightenment traditions lack credibility; the appeal to the objectivity of knowledge, the universality of values, a unitary identity, and the progress of science and society obfuscates the Enlightenment's role in the making of a multiplicity of social and political hierarchies along the axes of class, race, nationality, sexuality, gender, and body-abledness.

The alternative to the Enlightenment is not chaos and nihilism but living with uncertainty and a tolerance of ambiguity. For example, abandoning the appeal to secure foundations of knowledge does not mean surrendering all claims to knowledge. Asserting the value- and interest-based condition of knowledge excludes objective, universal knowledge, but it makes partial and perspectival knowledges possible. Securing foundations for social knowledge may be impossible, but that does not exclude all justifications for knowledge. Instead of justifying knowledge by appeals to empirical truth, a post-Enlightenment epistemology deploys pragmatic rationales, for example, appealing to the moral and political effects or goals of knowledge. A post-Enlightenment culture is suspicious of all claims to knowledge, truth, values, and political legitimacy; it assumes that all discourses are involved in the making of selves and societies. It therefore urges that we approach discourses, including its own, as permanently contestable, as containing values, social interests, and a will to shape human history.

Many people will no doubt find this critique of the Enlightenment objectionable. It is hard to surrender old certainties, especially for a culture that can only promise permanent uncertainty, ambiguity, endemic conflict, shifting, fractured identities, and the loss of a moral and social center. Personally, I find that the lack of a fixed center and certainties permits new possibilities for knowledge and social practice. I believe that a pragmatic approach to knowledge that assumes that there is no neutral agency to resolve differences and that we must struggle, case by case, to negotiate identities, norms, and common understandings promotes a beneficent pluralism and democracy.

References

1. Betty Friedan, *The Feminine Mystique* (New York: W.W. Norton, 1963).
2. Ti-Grace Atkinson, *Amazon Odyssey* (New York: Links, 1974); Jill Johnston, *Lesbian Nation* (New York: Simon & Schuster, 1973); Robin Morgan, *Going Too Far* (New York: Random House, 1977); Shulamith Firestone, *Dialectic of Sex* (New York: Morrow, 1970).
3. Juliet Mitchell, *Women's Estate* (New York: Panetheon, 1971); Gayle Rubin, "The Traffic in Women: Notes on the 'Political Economy' of Sex," in Rayna Reiter, ed., *Toward an Anthropology of Women* (New York: Monthly Review Press, 1975); Nancy Chodorow, *The Reproduction of Mothering* (Berkeley, CA: University of California Press, 1978).
4. Susan Brownmiller, *Against Our Will* (New York: Bantam, 1976); Andrea Dworkin, *Our Blood* (New York: Harper & Row, 1976); Susan Griffin, *Rape* (New York: Harper & Row, 1979).
5. Nancy Chodorow, *The Reproduction of Mothering*; Carol Gilligan, *In a Different Voice* (Cambridge, MA: Harvard University Press, 1982).
6. See Audre Lorde, *Sister Outsider* (Freedom, CA: The Crossing Press, 1984); Angela Davis, *Women, Race, and Class* (New York: Random House, 1981); Cherrie Moraga, *Loving in the War Years* (Boston: South End Press, 1983); Gloria Anzuldua and Cherrie Moraga, eds., *This Bridge Called My Back* (New York: Kitchen Table Press, 1981).
7. Combahee River Collective, "A Black Feminist Statement," in Zillah Einstein, ed., *Capitalist Patriarchy and the Case for Socialist Feminism* (New York: Monthly Review Press, 1978).
8. Lorde, *Sister Outsider*.
9. Ann Snitow et al., eds. *Power of Desire* (New York: Monthly Review Press, 1983); Carole Vance, ed., *Pleasure and Danger* (Boston: Routledge & Kegan Paul, 1984); Varda Burstyn, ed., *Women Against Censorship* (Toronto: Douglas

& McIntyre, 1985); Feminist Anti-Censorship Task Force, *Caught Looking* (Seattle, WA: The Real Comet Press, 1986).

10. Donna Haraway, "A Manifesto for Cyborgs: Science, Technology, and Socialist Feminism in the 1980s," *Socialist Review* 15 (1980).

11. Haraway, "A Manifest for Cyborgs," p. 73.

12. Nancy Fraser and Linda Nicholson, "Social Criticism without Philosophy: An Encounter between Feminism and Postmodernism," in Linda Nicholson, ed., *Feminism/Postmodernism* (New York: Routledge, 1990).

13. Fraser and Nicholson, "Social Criticism without Philosophy," p. 34.

14. Fraser and Nicholson, "Social Criticism without Philosophy," p. 35.

15. Judith Butler, *Gender Trouble: Feminism and the Subversion of Identity* (New York: Routledge, 1989).

16. Judith Butler, "Contingent Foundations: Feminism and the Question of Postmodernism," in *Feminists Theorize the Political*, Judith Butler and Joan Scott, eds. (New York: Routledge, 1992), pp. 15–16.

17. Bell Hooks, *Ain't I a Woman* (Boston: South End Press, 1982); Cornell West, *Prophetic Fragments* (Trenton, NJ: Africa World Press, 1988); Kwame Anthony Appiah, *In My Father's House: Africa in the Philosophy of Culture* (New York: Oxford University Press, 1992).

18. Molefi Kete Asante, *Afrocentricity: The Theory of Social Change* (Buffalo: Amulefi, 1980).

19. Molefi Kete Asante, *The Afrocentric Idea* (Philadelphia, PA: Temple University Press, 1987).

20. Asante, *The Afrocentric Idea*, p. 56.

21. Asante, *The Afrocentric Idea*, p. 79.

22. Asante, *The Afrocentric Idea*, p. 40.

23. Patricia Hill Collins, *Black Feminist Thought: Knowledge, Consciousness, and the Politics of Empowerment* (London: Harper Collins, 1990).

24. Bell Hooks, *Talking Back* (Boston: South End Press, 1989); Barbara Smith, ed., *Home Girls* (New York: Kitchen Table Press, 1983); Audre Lorde, *Zami, A New Spelling of My Name* (Trumansberg, NY: The Crossing Press, 1982); Alice Walker, *The Color Purple* (New York: Washington Square Press, 1982).

25. Collins, *Black Feminist Thought*.

26. Kwame Anthony Appiah, *In My Father's House*.

27. Appiah, *In My Father's House* p. 35.

28. Appiah, *In My Father's House* p. 25.

29. Appiah, *In My Father's House* p. 26.

30. Jonathan Katz, *Gay/Lesbian Almanac* (New York: Harper & Row, 1983); Steven Seidman, *Romantic Longings* (New York: Routledge, 1991); Lillian Faderman, *Odd Girls and Twilight Lovers* (New York: Columbia University Press, 1991).

31. Carroll Smith-Rosenberg, "The Female World of Love and Ritual: Relations Between Women in Nineteenth-Century America," in *Disorderly Conduct* (New York: Alfred A. Knopf, 1985); Lillian Faderman, *Surpassing the Love of*

Men (New York: William Morrow and Co., 1981); Anthony Rotundo, *American Manhood* (New York: Basic Books, 1993).

32. Ti-Grace Atkinson, "The Institution of Sexual Intercourse," in *Women's Liberation: Notes From the Second Year* (New York, 1970) and "Lesbianism and Feminism," in Phyllis Birkby, et al., eds., *Amazon Expedition* (Washington, NJ: Times Change Press, 1973); Charlotte Bunch, "Lesbians in Revolt," in Nancy Myron and Charlotte Bunch, eds., *Lesbianism and the Women's Movement* (Baltimore: Diana Press, 1975); Jill Johnston, *Lesbian Nation* (New York: Simon & Schuster, 1973); Rita Mae Brown, "The Shape of Things to Come," in Myron and Bunch, eds., *Lesbianism and the Women's Movement.*

33. Adrienne Rich, "Compulsory Heterosexuality and Lesbian Existence," in Anne Snitow et al., eds., *Powers of Desire* (New York: Monthly Review Press).

34. Rich, *"Compulsory Hetrosexuality,"* p.195

35. Rich, *"Compulsory Hetrosexuality,"* p.202

36. Jeffrey Weeks, *Sexuality and Its Discontents* (London: Routledge, 1985).

37. Jeffrey Weeks, *Sexuality* (New York: Tavistock Publications, 1986), p. 26.

38. Jeffrey Weeks, *Coming Out: Homosexual Politics in Britain from the Nineteenth Century to the Present* (London: Quartet Books Limited, 1977).

39. Karl Heinrich Ulrichs, *Forschungen über das Ratsel der Mann Mannlichen Liebe*, 12 vols. (Leipzig, 1898); Alfred Kinsey et al., *Sexual Behavior in the Human Male* (Philadelphia: W.B. Saunders, 1948) and *Sexual Behavior in the Human Female* (Philadelphia: W.B. Saunders, 1953).

40. Diana Fuss, *Essentially Speaking: Feminism, Nature and Difference* (New York: Routledge, 1989), p. 103; also see "Inside/Out," in Diana Fuss, ed., *Inside/Out: Lesbian Theories, Gay Theories* (New York: Routledge, 1991).

41. Eve Kosofsky Sedgwick, *The Epistemology of the Closet* (Berkeley, University of California Press, 1990).

42. Sedgwick, *Epistemology of the Closet*, p. 1.

43. Steven Seidman, *Liberalism and the Origins of European Social Theory* (Berkeley: University of California Press, 1983).

8

Post-Enlightenment Paradigms of Disciplinary Knowledge: Refashioning Sociology

T he social sciences experienced dramatic growth in the period following World War II. An era of peace, middle class prosperity, and state subsidies of higher education encouraged the belief that a college education was a social right and economic necessity. Sociology benefited greatly from the postwar educational boom in the United States. For example, between 1960 and 1974, there was a fivefold growth in sociology majors, from 7,147 to 35,915. This was paralleled in the growth in the numbers of graduate students, doctoral degrees, and faculty during this period. In the postwar period, sociology became an important institutional base for producing social knowledge.

Successful institutionalization encouraged the professionalization of sociology. This included the standardization of study areas (e.g. formal organizations, crime, demography, urban, political), the consolidation of a technical language, specialization, the canonizing of a theory tradition, the mathematization of research, and the belief that only science yields social knowledge. While many sociologists continued to view their role as that of public educator and critic, the dominant impulse of the discipline was towards the scientization of sociology. Professionalizing sociology entailed the creation of a culture in which sociologists were rewarded for addressing specialized problems and contributing to the "solution" of isolated conceptual, methodological, or empirical issues, deploying the technical jargon of the discipline, and for promoting sociology as an objective, value-neutral, scientific discipline. Even sociologists who addressed public issues were often isolated from the public because their ideas were framed in a language and rhetorical style that reflected an insulated expert culture.

The movements of the 1960s and 1970s were, at one level, a blessing for sociology. The social protests allowed sociologists to claim public relevance. Public officials, managers of schools, prisons, state institutions, and the military desired information and perspectives on these rebellions. However, these movements challenged sociology. Many activists viewed sociology as either irrelevant or as part of the social status quo. Some movement intellectuals, many of whom had one foot in academe, argued that mainstream sociology did not speak to their issues, for example, gender, race, or sexual inequalities or considerations of cultural and media politics. Such concerns were neither central to the classical tradition nor to contemporary paradigms such as functionalism, conflict theory, Marxism, exchange theory, or symbolic interactionism. Moreover, sociology was seen as tied to Enlightenment ideas such as the objectivity of knowledge, social progress, and the superiority of the West that were discredited in these movements.

The social protests of the period challenged the core premises and aims of disciplinary knowledges. Two currents of social thought have proved pivotal in refashioning our image of society and social knowledge: poststructuralism and the liberationist discourses of the new social movements.

In France, poststructuralism challenged the dominant disciplinary view of society and knowledge. In Derrida, Lyotard, Baudrillard, and Foucault, we can observe a shift to post-Enlightenment models of human studies. They rejected an approach to knowledge as objective, comprehensive, and scientific. They conceived of scientific knowledge as integrated in power relations and in the very making of society. They explored alternatives to disciplinary knowledge, such as genealogies, deconstruction and local social narratives. Departing from classical and contemporary models of society, French poststructuralists proposed alternative images of society that urged a shift in focus, from issues of class, economy, and state and from a language of individualism and materialism, to a focus on discourses, the body, sexualities, identities, mass media, cultural codes, and "intermediary" institutions such as hospitals, prisons, and schools.

In the United States, poststructuralism had little impact on the social sciences through the 1980s. The major challenge to these disciplinary knowledges came from the new social movements. As we have seen, these movements generated new subjects of knowledge (feminists, African-Americans, lesbians, and gay men) and social knowledges (feminism, African-American thought, lesbian and gay studies). Although some activists employed social science for their own political ends, many viewed the disciplines as part of the dynamics of social domination. In their struggles against social inequality and injustice, feminists, gays, and African-Americans often criticized sociology and the social sciences for constructing gender, sexual, and racial hierarchies. The new movements edged toward post-Enlightenment views of knowledge, underlining its moral and political character, and the role of dialogue, critique, and political engagement. Moreover, paralleling the poststructuralists, the discourses of the new movements shifted attention to the social organization of bodies, desires, identities, to the mass media, cultural politics, and to the formative power of families, schools, prisons, and psychiatric institutions.

In the course of the postwar period, the disciplines assumed a central place in the social organization of knowledge. Simultaneously, there emerged social movements contesting the human studies disciplines. Although many of the producers of critical knowledges were academics, the practical politics of social protest shaped their social perspectives. In other words, a series of new social perspectives on the self, society, and knowledge emerged outside the disciplines. These new social ideas edged toward post-Enlightenment paradigms of knowledge and society. They challenged the social and cultural privileges of the disciplines and aimed to refashion social knowledges favoring publicly engaged knowledges.

Through the 1970s and the early 1980s, these post-Enlightenment paradigms were ignored by the disciplines. For example, sociology was minimally, if at all affected, by poststructuralism. Even today, its presence is only weakly felt. The critical knowledges produced by the new social movements left the barest traces on sociology through the early 1980s. Feminism, African-American thought, and lesbian and gay studies were largely isolated or ignored. This began to change in the eighties. Post-Enlightenment social perspectives are now being incorporated into the disciplines.

We can observe this refashioning of the disciplines in sociology. I will review three important efforts to reconfigure sociology in light of a post-Enlightenment paradigm of knowledge: the project of sociology as public philosophy by Robert Bellah, the idea of a postmodern sociology by Zygmunt Bauman, and the materialist feminist sociology of Dorothy Smith. These sociologists are symptomatic of a contemporary struggle over the intellectual and social form of disciplinary knowledge. The outcome of this conflict will have much to do with the shape of social knowledge in the next century.

Robert Bellah

By his own account, Robert Bellah (born 1927) is a religious man. This describes less a denominational affiliation or set of beliefs than the importance to him of transcendent religious values in assessing and guiding personal behavior and social affairs. The interconnection between sociology and religion runs through his work and life. For example, as a student at Harvard in the early 1950s, he was deeply influenced by both the liberal, humanitarian sociological vision of Talcott Parsons and the anguished, existential religious world view of the great theologian Paul Tillich.

Bellah initially sought to accommodate his religious values to sociology by approaching religion as a primary social fact. Influenced by the Weberian analysis of religion as a key factor of social change, Bellah's writings up until the late 1960s focused on religion as a force of modernization, cultural system, and an aspect of the human condition. He published important studies of religion in Japan, the Far East, and Asia. Inspired by Parsons, Bellah issued general theoretical statements on religion and society. In general, Bellah drew on his religious sensibility to craft a culture-centered sociology.

By the end of the sixties, Bellah's concerns and themes had noticeably altered. His attention passed from the non-West to the United States. Moreover, although he continued to produce broad statements on the sociology of religion, his sociology took on a more directly prophetic quality. For example, in "Civil Religion in America," Bellah asserts the existence of a cluster of sacred symbols (e.g., July Fourth and the Lincoln Memorial) and beliefs (e.g., America as a chosen people) that give coherence and purpose to America [1]. Events in postwar America, in particular, the social protests of the sixties, are said to signal a crisis in the American civil religion. Bellah goes beyond examining the social impact of religion to offering a vision of America in the 1960s as undergoing a great moral ordeal. As his sociology assumed a more critical cast, the liberal optimism of Bellah's earlier Parsonian-inspired sociology receded. The Vietnam war and the protests of the sixties reinforced Bellah's positioning as a social critic, though one who remained deeply committed to the promise of America. The optimistic liberal version of Parsons gave way to a more pessimistic, Left social vision akin to that of Jürgen Habermas and C.W. Mills. The change is clearly marked in *The Broken Covenant*, a book that dramatically announces America's lost innocence and spiritual malaise [2]. Henceforth, Bellah sounds a prophetic critical voice alerting Americans to their drift into a spiritless, directionless civilization. In *Habits of the Heart* and *The Good Society*, Bellah took his message of social crisis to the broad American public. He called upon Americans to recover and enact the great promise of America, to realize the moral vision of a nation whose greatness should be measured in terms of its commitment to democracy, social compassion, moral virtue, and tolerance, not by its military might or social affluence [3].

Bellah's religious and moral sensibility and concern with issues of moral coherence, public virtue, and community favor a cultural view of society. Although he is not blind to issues of power and institutional constraint, Bellah imagines society as a realm of shared meanings, symbols, and social norms. Society is envisioned as an order that weds the individual to higher social goals and moral ends beyond self-interest, material gain, and power.

It is one of the oldest of sociological generalizations that any coherent and viable society rests on a common set of moral understandings about good and bad, right and wrong. . . . It is almost as widely held that these common moral understandings must also in turn rest upon a common set of religious understandings that provide a picture of the universe in terms of which the moral understandings make sense. Such moral and religious understandings produce both a basic cultural legitimation for a society . . . and a standard of judgement for the criticism of a society. . . . [4].

Lacking a culture of common values, belief, and symbols or a culture that shapes individuals to aspire to social goals and a shared life, society deteriorates into a war of all against all – a profane, debased human condition.

From at least the early 1970s, Bellah sounded a view of America in crisis. At the heart of this society is a lack of moral coherence and direction. In *The Broken Covenant*, he underscores a deepening cultural crisis. "In the eighteenth century, . . . there was a common set of religious and moral understandings rooted in a conception of a divine order under a Christian, or at least a deist, God. The basic moral norms that were seen as deriving from that divine order were liberty, justice, and charity [and] a concept of personal virtue as the essential basis of a good society" [5]. In contemporary America, "the erosion of common moral and religious understandings [has resulted in] a decline of belief in all forms of obligation: to one's occupation, one's family, and one's country. A tendency to rank personal gratification above obligation to others correlates with a deepening cynicism about the established social, economic, and political institutions of society" [6]. America has evolved from a nation inspired by the high ideals of community, justice, civic virtue, and democracy to a society celebrating greed, commerce, and self-interest. The signs of cultural crisis are everywhere: in the materialism of daily life, the colonization of public life by commerce, the celebration of lifestyle in place of commitments to community, and the drift of individuals through jobs, residences, fashions, and therapies. America suffers from a failure of its religious-moral traditions to forge a people into a unified social body.

In many ways, Bellah began his career as a fairly conventional sociologist. His early comparative work on religion and society was framed within a broadly Enlightenment scientific approach. Moreover, as Arthur Vidich and Stanford Lyman have shown, there is a long tradition in America of religiously inspired sociologists [7]. Many American sociologists in the early decades of this century were deeply influenced by the Protestant social reform movement. However, Bellah did more than draw on his religious convictions to guide his sociology; spurred perhaps by the movements for social justice in the postwar period, Bellah gradually blurred the boundaries between religion and sociology. His sociology became a vehicle to express a deeply religious and moral vision, a perspective on the crisis of America and its prospects for redemption. By the mid-1970s, Bellah had turned away from the narrow expert circles of social scientists and academics to speak directly to Americans. In this regard, he has sought to refashion sociology into a public philosophy.

In the course of his evolution from a sociologist of religion to a "religious sociologist," Bellah not only became a critic of society, but a critic of sociology. If the moral unity of America was unravelling, one sign of this erosion of a civic moral order was the dominance of scientific technological values in sociology. Sociology in the United States reflects the broader utilitarian, individualistic culture of America. It has become a specialized, discipline-centered discourse oriented to experts and in the service of a bureaucratic welfare state. Just as it had been difficult to turn into a public critic at the society that he admired, even if ambivalently, it was with some anguish that Bellah became a critic of the discipline that introduced him to a fresh vision of the world. Nevertheless, Bellah has abandoned a narrow scientific vision of sociology, which the sociologist retreats from an ethical responsibility to address fellow citizens on matters of common concern in order to chase the false idol of objectivity and scientific progress. For the past two decades, Bellah has stepped forward as an advocate of a moral vision of sociology, asserting that it is part of the responsibility of the sociologist to acknowledge the moral commitments of one's sociology and to give reasons for such value or normative preferences. Bellah envisions a sociology which is continuous with a long tradition of ethically driven social analysis linking Plato, Aristotle, Machiavelli, Durkheim, and John Dewey.

Sociology as public philosophy

Bellah has proposed the idea of sociology serving as a public philosophy as an alternative to the standard view of scientific sociology [8]. In response to America's social crisis, sociology's mission is to awaken Americans to this reality. He urges his colleagues to surrender a narrow scientific vision in favor of a moral vision of sociology that can address the current crisis. Sociology as public philosophy is an effort to refashion sociology into a more public-centered, interdisciplinary inquiry combining empirical social analysis and moral advocacy.

Bellah conceives of sociology as a type of ethical reflection whose aim is to provide a synthetic, critical view of society. In Bellah's mind, contemporary sociology has unfortunately largely abandoned integrated or holistic views of society. Departing from the classical tradition, sociology has pursued a scientific model that emphasizes discipline-centered problems, specialization, narrow social research, and the vigorous exclusion of values and politics from its concepts and research. Scientific sociology has contributed to a fragmented view of society; the interconnections, long-term trends, and broad moral and political implications of social events are ignored. Sociology as public philosophy intends to recover the holistic view of society that was integral to the Greeks, the classical sociological tradition, and its Parsonian and Marxian elaborations. Bellah recommends approaches to human studies that delineate the relations between the self, society, and history; he values broad narratives of societies that trace their origin, evolution, and possible futures. Of course, such a synthetic, integrative social analysis would be interdisciplinary and combine empirical analysis, philosophical speculation, and ethical reflection.

A central feature of sociology as a public philosophy is that its primary audience shifts from academics to the educated public. Bellah observes that Marx and, to a lesser extent, Weber and Durkheim, wrote for a public of educated citizens, activists, and public officials. This tradition of a public-centered social discourse links Plato and Aristotle to Marx and the sociological classics. Unfortunately, sociology, and the social sciences in general, have turned inward as they have produced discourses that speak almost exclusively to experts. The language of human studies has become technical, its research specialized and needlessly quantitative, its papers published almost exclusively in professional journals. Sociology has evolved into an insulated academic expert culture that has its own rewards, career strategies, jargon, and relevances. This has had the undesirable effect, in Bellah's view, of weakening the realm of democratic public life. When social scientists claim expert status on social problems, public discussion of social issues by ordinary citizens is devalued as mere opinion. Bellah advocates a sociology that effectively engages the educated public. As we will shortly see, he imagines sociologists to be part of an ongoing conversation about society on matters of common interest, e.g., freedom, justice, poverty, war, and community.

At the heart of Bellah's view of sociology as a public philosophy is its explicitly moral meaning. Sociologists have aspired to avoid moral values and commitments in order to defend their claim to producing objective knowledge. This purging of values from sociology has not, and cannot, succeed, in Bellah's view. Despite the armor of value neutrality, objectivity, and the rhetoric of knowledge for the sake of knowledge, sociological research and theory have not been able to shield themselves from accusations that they make value judgments and form ideas that carry definite social, moral, and political consequences. The effect of sociology's claim to objectivity and value neutrality is not the avoidance of moral and ideological values, but a corrosive cynicism toward all moral beliefs.

Contrary to conventional disciplinary wisdom, Bellah maintains that sociology is inherently value committed. Sociology is part of society; its basic premises, categories, and explanatory models express the values and ideas of the society of which the sociologist is a member. Is it not the case that sociology rests upon the premise that ideas are socially situated and shaped by the social location (e.g., by the class, gender, and nationality) of their producers? How can sociologists claim that this is true for everyone but sociologists?! Instead of trying to neutralize the value-laden character of our ideas, we should admit the moral aspect of sociology and address questions of ends, social goals, norms, and ideals. Sociology can and should aspire to be one medium of social understanding, criticism, and hope.

Bellah's vision of sociology as a synthetic, public-centered, ethical reflection is anchored in a concept of sociology as part of a public social conversation. However, sociologists and citizens speak less as individuals than as members of a tradition. The conversation about society is thought of as a dialogue between traditions that makes claims about the origin, development, present meaning, and future possibilities of society. Let me explain.

In Bellah's view, social ideas are based on encompassing conceptual frameworks or what he calls "traditions." This is true for sociologists as it is for activists, ordinary citizens, or politicians. Our ideas are not isolated fragments freely put together by individuals in unique ways. Rather, social ideas are part of configurations of beliefs, values, and social norms. When we speak about social realities, it is always from the standpoint of a tradition or a mix of traditions. Bellah is suggesting that social knowledge is not rooted in individual experience or the creation of the isolated self but is social, perspectival, and moral. We never speak from an Archimedean or "God's-eye" point of view, but from a tradition. The aim of sociology is to enter into dialogues with fellow members of a society about things that matter to all participants, for example, the meaning of freedom, justice, moral order, community, or the role of the state. These dialogues may be seen as conversations between traditions or between various ways of interpreting and judging social realities. As sociologists and as citizens, our aim is to clarify the social and moral vision in each tradition and state their implications for our lives, i.e., how specific ideas of self, freedom, and justice, if realized, would construct our lives. For what purpose? To reflect upon our world, to clarify the core beliefs and hopes underlying our institutions and guide our behavior, and to assess these social norms and ideals with the intent of possibly advocating social changes.

America's cultural crisis and the tasks of a moral sociology

The concept of sociology as public conversation is central to *The Broken Covenant, Habits of the Heart,* and *The Good Society.* In these books, Bellah engages in an ongoing conversation about America. He imagines his fellow interlocutors – interviewees, commentators, imaginary readers – as representing diverse traditions in speaking of the self, society, freedom, justice, and community. He listens to what his interlocutors have to say and tries to hear in their words their broad social, moral, and political vision of America. He does not simply listen to understand; his aim is not only to provide a map of social interpretations of America, e.g. religious, Marxist, individualistic, Christian, liberal, and conservative. He engages his interlocutors for the purpose of assessing their ideas. He tries to persuade us of the limits, flaws, disadvantages, or advantages of their social stories by showing how their images of self and society undermine or promote the grand hopes of America to realize a just society. He wants to convert us to the power of his moral vision and social ideals for America. He appeals to the very core values, beliefs, and aspirations of the American experiment to justify his critical standpoint.

In *Habits of the Heart,* Bellah and his colleagues engage the public in a discussion about the way Americans think of the individual, community, private and public life, freedom, success, and justice. They wish to explore the way that Americans imagine the self as giving purpose and coherence to personal and collective life. Questions of the self, society, and moral life are, in their view, matters of urgent social importance, as evidenced in public debate over abortion, homosexuality, prayer in schools, health care, the role of welfare, the moral role of the state, and the ends of American Foreign policy. Bellah wishes to engage Americans in a dialogue about these important social and moral matters. In part, the dialogue is carried on with intellectuals (e.g., professors, writers, social commentators, policy makers) who have made public statements on these issues. In addition, Bellah wishes to let ordinary Americans contribute to this dialogue. Drawing on in-depth interviews, *Habits* is filled with the voices of everyday folk. This book is intended to be a public conversation about matters that go to the heart of the meaning of America. His purpose is to persuade Americans to adopt a particular view of America's current malaise and its social remedy. It is an exercise in sociology as public philosophy.

The intent of *Habits* is to have a public conversation about America among equal participants, but the reality, make no mistake, is that the terms of the dialogue are fixed by the authors. Bellah has set up the terms of the conversation. Interlocutors (e.g., interviewees, writers, readers) are viewed as representing distinct traditions of constructing self and society. The authors outline four such traditions: biblical, republican, utilitarian, and expressive individualism. Each of these traditions are said to have shaped in powerful ways the culture and institutional life of the United States. These traditions are integral to the way that Americans imagine themselves, past, present, and future. They comprise a kind of cultural infrastructure of America, providing the underlying, core images of self and world, freedom and authority.

These traditions need to be introduced, even if our characterization is admittedly quite sketchy. The *biblical tradition* is anchored in our Protestant and more broadly Christian heritage. It figures the self as a part of a social community; self-realization is tied to living an ethical and spiritual life or a life fused with social goals. The Puritan John Winthrop exemplifies this tradtion. For Winthrop, success means "the creation of a certain kind of ethical community," while freedom suggests doing what is "good, just and honest" [9].

The *republican tradition* is rooted in classical and early modern social thought. The self is viewed as a participating member of a political society. Self-realization is accomplished through democratic participation in the shaping of the present and future of society. Thomas Jefferson stands out as an adherent to this tradition. "The ideal of a self-governing society of relative equals in which all participate is what guided Jefferson all his life" [10]. In the republican tradition, freedom combines an emphasis on individual rights with the pursuit of an ethical and good society inspired by a vision of transcendent justice.

Utilitarian individualism stands as a counterpart to the biblical and republican traditions. Whereas the latter underscores the unity of self and society and asserts self-realization through social goals, the former views the self as a separate, self-sufficient agent. In this tradition, the individual creates social institutions for instrumental purposes, for example, in order to amass wealth or to secure protection, competitive advantage, and power. Institutions are a means or a barrier to self-realization. Freedom is associated with diminished social control and obligations; success means personal gain; justice refers to the distribution of resources and rewards according to individual merit. With his regime of self-improvement aimed at advancing personal gain and success, Benjamin Franklin embodies the spirit of the utilitarian tradition.

Expressive individualism is a self-centered, individualistic world view. If utilitarian individualism views the individual as a maximizer of self-interest, as a risk taker in pursuit of material gain and power, expressive individualism imagines the self as oriented to developing his or her distinct human potential. The poet Walt Whitman is exemplary of this tradition. "For Whitman, success had little to do with material acquisition. A life rich in experience, open to all kinds of people, luxuriating in the sensual as well as the intellectual, above all a life of strong feeling, was what he perceived as a successful life" [11]. Human freedom is conceived of as a personal struggle to express the self by overcoming internal and external obstacles.

The conversation that Bellah engages in and, indeed, orchestrates, is one where the interlocutors stand in for these four traditions. These traditions are assumed to be basic to American society. They continue to shape the character of the self, social values, and the institutions of this society. American life reflects, in no small way, the configuration of these traditions.

What is the present configuration of these traditions in the United States, with what social and moral implications? The chief theme of the story of America, according to Bellah and his colleagues, is clear enough. America was founded assuming the centrality of the biblical and republican traditions. These traditions provided a unifying cultural framework that linked individuals and institutions, personal and social ends, individual self-interest and the general good of the society. The individualism promoted by the utilitarian and expressive traditions was not disruptive of moral order, institutional legitimacy, or individual and social coherence because of the restraining, socially integrating role of the biblical and republican traditions. De Tocqueville's *Democracy in America* depicted this American social ideal – a nation of small communities organized around a culture of entreprenurial risk-taking, participatory democracy and unified by the solidarities of family, voluntary associations, and the church [12].

From the mid-nineteenth century through this century, the major social, economic, and cultural developments have greatly weakened the social force of the biblical and republican traditions. The rise of corporate capitalism, bureaucratization, the growth of a warfare/welfare state, secularization, and the consumer and therapeutic ethos of American culture have favored the advance of the utilitarian and expressive traditions at the expense of socially and morally unifying traditions. The erosion of the biblical and republican traditions has released the culture of individualism from its religious and moral framework.

The American culture of individualism is to be valued for its great social and economic accomplishments and its defense of personal and political liberties. However, Bellah maintains that it is also responsible for a good deal of the incoherence and malaise in our lives. Our individualistic beliefs and values frame social institutions as a barrier or, at best, a mere means for the self; social obligations and the pursuit of social ends are considered burdensome or secondary to the principal source of personal value, namely, the improvement or achievements of the discrete self. This individualistic culture has contributed to the weakening of the authority of our key institutions, from the family to the government. It has separated individuals from the very communities (families, neighbors, church, or colleagues) that nurture them; it pits individuals against one another in a fight for survival and dominance. The crisis of meaning and legitimacy prompted by the American culture of individualism is evidenced in high rates of illegitimacy, divorce, illiteracy, high school dropouts, a church torn between fundamentalism and secular accommodation, and a passive electorate.

Bellah is not arguing that America has become a mere collection of individuals. Americans continue to be members of groups and institutions and to pursue social goals such as volunteer work or public service. However, as much as their lives are involved in group life and tied to social ends, Americans cannot coherently express these social commitments and values within the language of individualism. This world view does not allow us to recognize our shared goals, moral commitments, and social interdependence. Americans cannot make sense of their social involvements and obligations, give reasons for pursuing social goals, grasp institutional life as a world of social norms, solidarity, and moral order, or articulate their ties to a public life of shared meanings, values, symbols, and goals. The language of individualism does not permit Americans to understand and articulate their ties to generations past, present, and future. Of course, the absence of such a language of social connectedness doesn't mean the absence of social bonds. However, it suggests that Americans cannot make sense of this aspect of their lives; they cannot adequately assess their collective lives. A weak language of social connection weakens such bonds.

This enfeebled culture of communal ties is particularly dangerous today. In *The Good Society*, Bellah and his colleagues argue that we live in a world of corporations, big business, huge government bureaucracies, a global economy, and sprawling media empires [13]. To preserve the democratic individualism that Americans cherish, they need to think in terms of social relations, interdependencies, institutional responsibilities, and public participation in decision making. Social processes such as bureaucratization and economic globalization require that Americans understand their lives as interconnected with social institutions and assume responsibility for their shape in the present and future.

The fate of American individualism is tied to Americans adopting a more social understanding and communitarian ethic. A cultural shift is urged in which the self is viewed as a social creature, institutions are perceived as the chief site of our lives, and personal goals are perceived as fused with social goals. Advancing democracy will require the reestablishment of a common religious-moral framework. In this regard, Bellah urges the critical renewal of the biblical and republican traditions that have been and continue to be so central to America. Bellah invokes a past that is still alive in the present as the basis for his critique of the present and his vision of the promise of America's future.

There is a texture of high drama in Bellah's sociology. Perhaps it is the sense of social urgency that he evokes. Modern America is in a cultural crisis. The culture of individualism has incapacitated Americans to a language of social obligation, virtue, community, and social interdependence. The cultural crisis of American society is echoed in sociology which is dominated by a problem-solving, individualistic, utilitarian spirit. Bellah counsels a reorganization of sociology and society in which a language of moral solidarity is integrated into a dominant individual-centered vocabulary. To play a role in social renewal, sociology must reorient its conceptual center around public life rather than narrow, specialty area disciplinary problems. Bellah envisions a sociology that acknowledges its moral and political role. Sociology as public philosophy is Bellah's proposal for a postscientific sociology. Its aim to engage the public in a dialogue about its core beliefs and values for the purpose of revitalizing a democratic society.

Zygmunt Bauman

As our attention turns from Bellah to Bauman, we find ourselves in a very different national, social, and intellectual terrain. We pass from the United States to Great Britain via Poland. Moreover, despite the influence of European thought on Bellah, he is fundamentally a product of American soil; his vision of an ethically engaged public sociology bears strong traces of Paine, Emerson, Du Bois, Dewey, Walter Lippman, and C.W. Mills. By contrast, Zygmunt Bauman's (born 1925) formative experience was in Europe, specifically in Poland, a nation that lost its independence first to Nazism and then to communism. Bauman migrated to Great Britain in 1955 and is currently a professor of sociology at the University of Leeds. Thoroughly European in his social thinking, Bauman draws on French poststructuralism and the Frankfurt school of critical theory to refashion a sociology for the postmodern era.

Bauman's Jewish birthright and his coming of age as an intellectual in Poland under communist rule were crucial in shaping his social ideas. Poland lost its independence in 1939 as a result of the German invasion. Subsequently, Poland was freed from German dominion only to surrender to Soviet communist rule. Though subject to a Soviet military threat, Poland was not a Stalinist state, in the way, say, of Hungary or Rumania. For example, an independent Marxist tradition flourished among academic intellectuals. The experience, however, of Nazism, antisemitism, and communism disposed Bauman to distrust claims of reason to fashion a social order or remake humanity in its image. Indeed, as we will see, Bauman came to reject the conventional view of Nazism and communism as accidents or aberrations of modern history. These two social formations, with their mission to design a perfect, controlled order, revealed the true spirit of modernity. The defeat of Nazism and the subsequent collapse of communism signaled the failure of modernity and its grandiose aspirations to fashion an ideal world order.

Unlike many European intellectuals who immigrated to Great Britain or the United States to escape Nazism or communism (e.g., Peter Berger, Lewis Coser, or Peter Blau), Bauman did not substitute a liberal social standpoint for a Left critical theory. Perhaps the maintenance of a tradition of independent Marxism in communist Poland allowed Bauman to preserve a socialist-inspired critical theory. Marxism was, however, abandoned on the grounds that its rationalist utopian impulse was emblematic of the increasingly tattered dreams of modernity. In place of Marxism, Bauman, drawing heavily on poststructuralism and critical theory, has attempted to refashion sociology into a critical tool that can respond to the movements of global transformation in a postmodern world.

From modernity to postmodernity

Like Lyotard and Foucault, both of whom offer a grand story of Western development while asserting that postmodernity will be organized around local discourses, Bauman sketches a sweeping narrative of Western history. Departing from the Enlightenment stories of the progress of reason and freedom, Bauman relates a tale of social control and the advance of reason as domination. Moreover, whereas classical and contemporary sociological theorists assert that the division between capitalism and socialism is the principal site of social conflict and hope, Bauman substitutes the division between modernity and postmodernity. From this perspective, capitalism and socialism represent social variations in the dynamics of modernity. Despite his conceptual rebellion against "modern" sociology, Bauman's social narrative has a decidedly Enlightenment cast: It is a story of humankind's struggle for freedom and the still-lingering hope that reason can make a difference.

Bauman outlines a typology of premodern, modern, and postmodern societies. His story begins with premodernity. Furnishing only the barest sketch, Bauman characterizes premodernity as a decentralized, fragmented type of society. Premodern societies were composed of a plurality of self-sufficient communities, each with their own tradition and way of life. These societies were highly stratified and were stabilized by a dominant religious culture and a well-established social hierarchy of power relations. Notwithstanding their social inequalities, Bauman admiringly underscores the respect for social differences, local traditions, and the coexistence of social diversity that obtained in premodern societies.

Between the collapse of premodernity and the consolidation of modernity in the seventeenth century, there was a brief period of social freedom. European societies experienced an openness to social differences and an acceptance of the uncertainty and contingency of existence. A social life evolved without the authority of God or a secular sovereign to impose order, certainty, and purpose. "It was in that brief interlude . . . that diversity was . . . lovingly embraced and hailed as the sign and condition of true humanity. Openness, readiness to refrain from condemnation of the other and . . . settling for the credible instead of chasing the absolute – were all conspicuous marks of the humanist culture" [14]. Unfortunately, the humanist celebration of difference and ambivalence did not last.

Faced with a growing population of vagrants, the poor, the mad, and the discontented, Western societies responded with new forms of social control. Premodern local communities were unable to respond effectively to the heightened social chaos and the escalating administrative requirements of the time. Vast resources, human and nonhuman, had to be administered: detailed, specialized information on labor, health, fertility and national and international developments was needed for national growth and survival in an emerging era of industrial colonialism, and a system of transportation and communication that spanned huge stretches of territory was a pressing need as commerce spread. In short, a new modern social order arose in response to the failure of premodern social controls.

Modernity is characterized by a multi-leveled system of control which includes law, disciplinary strategies, and ideological control. At the center of modernity is the state. Bauman states that the modern centralized bureaucratic state, with its concentration of resources, monpoly over the use of violence, and its army of civil service workers, police and military might, is the foundation of modernity. With its mission to control, regulate, and order the social and natural environment, the state expresses the essential spirit of modernity.

The modern state did not simply evolve in response to a functional need for new forms of social control. It consolidated power at the expense of local authorities, traditions, and ways of life. The modernization of governmental authority entailed the transfer of power from local agencies and communities to the state. In effect, the centralization of state authority involved a war on local communities, an effort to wrestle power away from them. This was paralleled by a cultural war. In order for the state to administer society in an orderly and efficient manner, it tried to impose a standardization of social norms, values, and beliefs. The state waged a cultural war against local, diverse cultural traditions. In the name of progress, secularism, science, democracy, freedom, individualism, and health, the modern state uprooted local cultures and destroyed particular traditions and unique regional, ethnic, and cultural communities. The birth of modernity was purchased by means of a relentless assault against local traditions, social pluralism, disorder, ambiguity, and uncertainty. It is this will to order, classify, design, or control everything that is at the heart of modernity.

The modern state represents a new concept of governing. It is not simply that powers that were previously dispersed are now centralized; the very character of the modern state is historically unique. It was born of the wish to create, impose, and maintain order; its mission is to shape society and to mould its people, institutions, and cultures to reflect a rational social design. The modern state is not merely intent on maintaining order; it aims to fashion humanity to mirror an ideal. Bauman describes the modern state as a "gardening state." It aspires not merely to rule, keep order, protect its citizens, or ensure prosperity, but to tame and domesticate the disorder of human impulse and desire.

The modern state is inconceivable without intellectuals. To run the bureaucratic apparatus of modernity requires information about human behavior, the dynamics of populations, institutions, and whole societies. Expert knowledges are required for the management of schools, factories, welfare institutions, prisons, hospitals, and local and national governments. Additionally, the modern state requires legitimation; its war against local, diverse traditions, authorities, and communities, its interest in concentrating power and resources, and its social goals must be justified. The modern state and Enlightenment social science emerged simultaneously and exhibit an affinity of interest and spirit.

Bauman disputes the conventional view of the Enlightenment. This perspective assumes that modernization marks a giant step towards freedom, tolerance, and social progress. The social sciences, born in the age of Enlightenment, are described as a humanitarian force struggling against bigotry, fanaticism, and the evils of the excessive power of the church and the state. In contrast, Bauman argues that the true spirit of the Enlightenment revolves around the quest for control and certitude. The triumph of the Enlightenment has meant the victory of what he calls "legislative reason." This type of reason is hostile to genuine forms of individuality and pluralism and intolerant of ambiguity and uncertainty. Legislative reason strives to fashion the world in accordance with general principles, laws, rules, or norms. The Enlightenment may, in principle, celebrate individualism and diversity; in practice, it is repressive. For example, the ideology of social progress has been used to justify the destruction of local traditions and communities or to colonize non-Western peoples who are defined as backward or primitive. The claim of science to objective truth has discredited and silenced nonscientific knowledges and the social experiences that they express. In short, the chief ideas of the Enlightenment, the malleability of humans, the doctrine of social progress, the unity of humanity, and the truth of science, are viewed as part of a project of legislating order, controlling the unruly, labeling deviant those who differ or who do not conform to conventional norms of health, fitness, beauty, normality, and virtue.

Bauman has no love for modernity. Reversing conventional wisdom that sees modernity as redemptive or as marking the breakthrough for all of humanity towards a freer, more rational society, Bauman figures modernity as a ruthless, relentless drive to wipe out all chaos, ambiguity, ambivalence, difference, and uncertainty. "The typically modern practice, the substance of modern politics, of modern intellect, of modern life, is the effort to exterminate ambivalence: an effort to define precisely – and to suppress or eliminate everything that could not or would not be precisely defined" [15]. This spirit of control and intolerance characterizes the modern state, Enlightenment thinking, the social sciences, and disciplinary structures (e.g., prisons, factories, hospitals, schools). Western history is framed as a history of the progressive advancement of social controls in the service of order and inspired by the illusion of a life free of ambiguity and ambivalence.

The modern era has not abruptly come to an end. Nevertheless, Bauman believes that its failure is evident in the recent history of Nazism, the collapse of communism, and the growing crisis of Enlightenment culture in the West. The end of modernity is signaled, moreover, in the changing social role of intellectuals. Indeed, the theory of postmodernity is the product of the changing social position of intellectuals. Let me comment further on the link between postmodernity and intellectuals.

Bauman maintains that the state no longer needs intellectuals for legitimation. Why? Social control in postmodernity is less dependent on state repressive measures or on shared cultural values than on "seduction." In the modern era, individual loyalty to social and governmental institutions was tied to strategies of punishment and deterrence, disciplinary strategies of normalization, and appeals to common beliefs, values, and norms, e.g., the ideology of individualism, progress, or political democracy. In a postmodern era, citizens are socially integrated and their institutional loyalty secured through the agency of the market. Individual needs, desires, identities, and social lifestyles are wedded to consumption. Post-modern selves fashion identities and social lives through patterns of con-sumption. They are seduced into social conformity by the fantasies, dreams, and hopes that commodities are designed to evoke. Disciplinary strategies of social control, from surveillance to the medicalization of social behavior, have shifted their focus from mainstream populations to those marginalized groups outside the reach of the market, e.g., the poor and the deviant.

Intellectuals in postmodernity are politically dispossessed. The state has reduced needs for expert knowledges and for discursive legitimation. Moreover, their role as arbiters of culture is also significantly dimin-ished. As the cultural domain has been fashioned into a sphere of enter-tainment and popular consumption, a new cultural elite of gallery owners, managers of the mass media, publishers, and mass cultural entrepreneurs have squeezed out intellectuals. Lacking political or cultural authority, intellectuals rethink knowledge and power. No longer called upon to legislate standards of truth, goodness, and beauty or to arbitrate knowl-edge and culture, intellectuals now emphasize the plurality of knowledges and cultural standards and their rootedness in particular traditions or communities. As intellectuals lose social authority in their legislative role, they adopt an "interpretive" role. Their aim is less to dictate stan-dards or laws than to affirm social diversity and facilitate communication between diverse traditions. This interpretive role gives to intellecatuals a new social value; their advocacy of postmodernity is tied to their own aspirations for social power.

Postmodernity does not mark a complete break from modernity. Bauman conceives of the former as the development of submerged or marginal aspects of modernity. The values of choice, diversity, criticalness, reflexiv-ity, and agency are modern ones and are preserved in postmodernity. Yet, there is a profound antagonism between modernity and postmodernity. The guiding spirit of modernity revolves around creating order, bound-aries, classifications, aspiring to certitude and transparency; it is an epoch of formal reason, laws, typologies, classifications, boundary maintenance, uniformity, and universality. Postmodernity is said to embrace plurality, ambiguity, ambivalence, uncertainty, the contingent, and transitory; it is disruptive, irreverent, relentlessly critical, and oppositional.

The postmodern, above all, stands in opposition to the modern ideal of a uniform, standardized culture composed of individuals who are, ulti-mately, seen as similar or identical instances of a common humanity. It is the assumption of shared humanity that makes the idea of deducing a universal human interest, truth, or standard of value plausible. In contrast, postmodernity assumes and celebrates the irreducibly pluralistic character of humanity and culture. Humankind proliferates a multiplicity of traditions, communities, and cultures. In place of the modern notion of the identity of humanity, the postmodern era substitutes the idea of irreducible human differences, of individuals whose interests, values, and beliefs vary within and between societies. Humanity is always instantiated in multiple forms, while the idea of the unity and identity of humanity is seen as a rhetorical, normative claim, an expression of ethnocentric arrogance. Instead of invoking humanity or the self or the individual, in the postmodern world, we would speak of individuals only as they are stamped by their particular, local social location and character.

Central to postmodernity is the abandonment of any basis for claiming certainty or for appealing to universal standards of truth, goodness, and beauty.

> The main feature ascribed to "postmodernity" is thus the permanent and irreducible pluralism of cultures, communal traditions, ideologies. . . . Things which are plural in the postmodern world cannot be arranged in an evolutionary sequence, or seen as each other's inferior or superior stages; neither can they be classified as "right" or "wrong" solutions to common problems. No knowledge can be assessed outside the context of the culture, tradition, language game, etc. which makes it possible and endows it with meaning. Hence no criteria of validation are available which could be themselves justified "out of context." Without universal standards, the problem of the postmodern world is not how to globalize superior culture, but how to secure communication and mutual understanding between cultures [16].

As Bauman suggests, in a postmodern world, there is no authoritative standpoint from which to know the world. Human knowledge is always situated; we know from a particular standpoint, tradition, or cultural community. Knowledge is always pluralistic, as are values, social norms, and aesthetic styles. Claims to truth have value or credibility in relation to a specific tradition or perspective. As the realm of knowledge, values, norms, and aesthetics, culture is a major site of social conflict and contestation. In the face of endemic conflict, the postmodern individual doubts the credibility of appealing to any neutral, Archimedean standpoint from which to resolve cultural clashes. Instead, a postmodern standpoint proposes a case-by-case, local strategy of negotiation that does not aim to abolish ambiguity, ambivalence, and uncertainty. Postmodernity affirms a decentered, fragmented social order that, ideally, creates the institutional spaces for continuous discourse, contestation, and negotiation in the face of endemic sociopolitical conflicts.

Postmodernity and sociology

Bauman assumes that the structure of sociology is closely tied to the social role of the intellectual. In the modern era, there is an alliance between the state and intellectuals. Reflecting the broad culture of intellectuals, sociology was shaped to assume a "legislative role," i.e., its aim was to discover the principles of social organization and evolution. Although modern sociology claimed legitimacy on the basis of its assertion of truth and general social utility, it was integrated in the grand goals of the modern state to create and administer a rational society. The preoccupation of modern sociology with principles of social organization and integration, and problems and disorder such as deviance, crime, and mental illness reflects the governing "legislative" spirit of modernity.

The social transition to postmodernity has altered the relation between the state and intellectuals. As we have seen, the state has less need for intellectuals; their legitimating role diminishes as the market replaces the state as an integrating social mechanism. The disempowerment of intellectuals renders their legislative role obsolete. If sociologists, as one sector of the intelligentsia, are no longer called upon to legislate social order and cultural norms, what social role and conceptual task will define sociology? Bauman suggests several possibilities.

Unfortunately, some sociologists will simply ignore the shift to postmodernity. This is a grave mistake. As sociology is needed less by the state and its role as a cultural arbiter diminishes, it will become obsolete if it does not refashion its premises and aims. The appeal to knowledge for knowledge's sake to justify a scientific sociology sounds increasingly hollow and implausible in a postmodern culture. Sociology ignores postmodernity at the risk of its own social relevance, if not survival.

Some sociologists acknowledge the arrival of postmodernity, but they deny that the changes described by that term indicate a noteworthy development. In particular, Bauman notes that many sociologists read postmodernity as signaling a crisis of modernity. The preoccupation by postmodern thinkers with identity, instability, fragmentation, and change is interpreted as an indicator of a cultural crisis of modernity. The championing of radical pluralism, decentered identities, and relentless criticism is criticized as reinforcing the disintegrative, anomic, and pathological conditions of Western modernity. Bauman is sharply critical of this perspective: "I suggest . . . that the phenomena described collectively as 'postmodernity' are not symptoms of systematic deficiency or disease; neither are they a temporary aberration with a life-span limited by the time required to rebuild the structure of cultural authority. I suggest instead that postmodernity . . .

is an aspect of a fully-fledged, viable social system which has come to replace the 'classical' modern, capitalist society and thus needs to be theorized according to its own logic" [17].

Bauman's perspective on postmodernity suggests a major reorientation of sociology from a legislative to an interpretive role. Surrendering the search for foundations or an overarching language of the social, sociology takes up the task of facilitating the mutual understanding of diverse communities. Valuing the plurality of cultural traditions, subcultures, and communities, the sociologist defines his or her goal as making coherent and intelligible these social differences. "A postmodern sociologist is one who, securely embedded in his own, 'native' tradition, penetrates deeply into successive layers of meanings upheld by the relatively alien tradition to be investigated. . . . In the person of the sociologist, two or more traditions are brought into communicative contact. . . . The postmodern sociologist aims at 'giving voice' to cultures which without his help would remain numb or stay inaudible to the partner in communication" [18]. The value of a postmodern sociology is in rendering social differences less threatening, fostering tolerance for diversity, making the unfamiliar familiar, and giving voice to submerged or marginal experiences and communities. In a postmodern world of public cultural clashes, the interpretive sociologist has a role to play in facilitating mutual understanding and suggesting local, case-by-case, negotiated strategies of conflict resolution. A postmodern sociology suggests a shift in sociological practice to being more qualitative, ethnographic, interpretive, and textualist.

Bauman imagines as an additional possibility the refashioning of a critical sociology in a postmodern direction. Sociology as social criticism has been a key part of the sociological tradition. However, social critique, from Marx to Habermas, has typically appealed to universal standpoints, foundations, historical or social laws, and science to wrap it in an aura of legitimacy. A postmodern social critique would preserve the emancipatory hopes of the modern but without the anchor of certitude. The postmodern critic would acknowledge the situated and contingent – merely historical – basis of the interests and values that ground social criticism. The rationalist language of modern criticism, for example, that of foundations, grounds, and laws, would give way to a local, historical language of values, interests, purposes, and hopes. Postmodern social critics abandon, moreover, the dangerously redemptive vision of social change that has proven so seductive to moderns. "The faith in a historical agent waiting in the wings to take over and to complete the promise of modernity using the levers of the political state . . . has all but vanished" [19]. Postmodern critics imagine change as less millennial; they look less to the state as an agency of change. Bauman gestures toward a postmodern criticism whose aim is to enlighten citizens, if not to their redemptive role in history, then to the social forces (e.g., the market and consumerism) that threaten to diminish freedom and political democracy.

There is one final possibility that in one sense involves the least possible shift change for sociology, while suggesting a fairly dramatic overhaul of its conceptual apparatus. Bauman proposes a sociology of postmodernity. This would not entail a departure in the goals of sociology. Sociologists would strive to understand the origin and social organization of post-modernity in a way similar to classical and contemporary efforts to fashion a sociology of modernization. However, just as a sociology of modernity required sociologists to adopt assumptions and categories that reflected modern Western societies, a sociology of postmodernity would pressure sociologists to replace modern premises, concepts, models, and explanatory schemes with postmodern ones.

What would a postmodern conceptual reorientation of sociology look like? Sociology would abandon its chief modernist assumptions and ideas (for example, the view of society as a system, organism, or mechanism), the parallel view of the individual as a natural agent of action, a centering on the categories of labor, production, the division of labor, values, and ideologies, the emphasis on social class as the agency of change, a focus on the nation-state as the unit of analysis, and assumptions of continuous, linear development and progress. In place of these modern premises, a post-modern sociology would emphasize the fluid, multiple character of social realities, the local or situationally produced character of social institutions, the role of the interpretive efforts of individuals in making social realities, and the individual as a socially produced identity. There would be a shift in the axial categories of sociology to center on consumerism, the market, disciplinary technologies, body, self and identity formation; a deliberately international horizon in sociology; and approaches to social change that address discontinuous, unpredictable, and contradictory social trends.

Sociologists have been slow and resistant to acknowledge the great transformation from a modern to a postmodern era that has transpired in postwar Europe and America. To the extent that they remain wedded to modern premises and approaches, sociologists will continue their current drift into social insularity. As its social utility lies solely in producing narrow technical information for institutional administration, sociology is destined to intellectual parochialism. Bauman offers possibilities for renewal. Sociology must shift to a postmodern axis. It should abandon its legislative role (e.g., providing foundations, general principles, laws, overarching theories, systems of sociology) in favor of a more modest interpretive role. Sociologists would aim to enhance mutual understanding among different communities or to clarify and criticize the emerging postmodern epoch. The world has changed, and sociology, Bauman insists, must change fundamentally to preserve its social value and role. We must give up an Enlightenment paradigm of knowledge and society; only a shift in the culture of sociology to a post-Enlightenment paradigm of knowledge and society can save it from its growing obsolescence.

Dorothy Smith

Entering the textual universe of Dorothy Smith is a challenge to both the mainstream of sociological theory and its chief critics. Even critics of sociology such as Mills and Habermas or Bellah and Bauman fall squarely in the mainstream by occupying a conceptual universe that is frankly a man's world. Smith pressures sociological theory to approach theory and society from the vantage point of women's experience. She imagines a feminist sociology.

Feminism did not originate in the 1960s. Feminist ideas have been integral to western Europe and the United States from at least the eighteenth century. There was a flourish of feminist thought and politics in the 1780s and 1790s, the period from the 1840s to the 1860s, and between 1880 and World War I. From Mary Wollstonecraft's *A Vindication of the Rights of Women*, Sarah Grimke's *Letters on the Equality of the Sexes*, and Condorcet's *On the Admission to Women of Citizens' Rights* in the eighteenth century, to John Stuart Mill's (with Harriet Taylor) *The Subjection of Women*, Friedrich Engels's *The Origins of the Family, Private Property and the State*, and Charlotte Perkins Gilman's *Women and Economics* in the nineteenth century, to Simone de Beauvoir's *The Second Sex* in this century, feminism has been a noteworthy feature of Western culture and politics.

Sociological theory has not incorporated or even responded to feminism. Classical sociology, from Comte to Weber, Durkheim to Albion Small, has largely ignored, devalued, and marginalized feminist concerns and perspectives. Classical sociological theory is a male-centered universe. Indeed, feminists have made the case that much of classical theory is decidedly antifeminist in that it legitimates the notion of women as naturally different and inferior. For example, Durkheim positions women in the domestic sphere as a matter of nature and social necessity, while stationing men in the world of institutional power.

The relation between feminism and sociology changed somewhat in the postwar period. The sixties and seventies witnessed a dramatic resurgence of feminism in Western societies. Some feminists were sociologists, and many women sociologists were deeply influenced by the women's movement. They brought feminist ideas into sociology. However, as Judith Stacey and Barrie Thorne have observed, feminism has had minimal influence on sociological theory and has not significantly shaped the basic premises and concepts of sociology [20]. Sociologists have incorporated feminism by either isolating and marginalizing feminist sociology or making gender one sociological variable among many. In the main, feminism has been integrated into sociology without contesting the Enlightenment paradigm of scientific sociology. If sociologists, including many feminist sociologists, have sought to accommodate feminism to sociology, postwar (male) sociological theorists, almost without exception, have simply ignored feminism. I would be hard pressed to find even the faintest traces of feminism in the canonical works of mainstream sociological theory, from Talcott Parsons to Ralf Dahrendorf, Peter Berger, Peter Blau, James Coleman, Jeffrey Alexander, and Anthony Giddens.

The flowering of feminist social and political theory in the 1970s and 1980s occurred largely outside of sociology [21]. There have been exceptions. Nancy Chodorow's *The Reproduction of Mothering* was enormously infuential among feminists in the early 1980s [22]. However, Chodorow's book is a psychoanalytically oriented theory of gender identity which, for all its brilliance, lacks an institutional and cultural theory. A notable exception to the absence of feminist theory in sociology is Dorothy Smith. As early as the beginnings of the 1970s, Smith addressed the state of sociology in order to produce a feminist sociological theory. Born in 1926, Smith took her doctorate in sociology at the University of California at Berkeley in 1963. She is currently a professor of sociology at the Ontario Institute for Studies in Education in Toronto, Canada. Virtually ignored through the 1970s and 1980s, Smith is now recognized, and deservedly so, as a leading feminist sociological theorist in the postwar period.

Smith situates her work centrally in relation to the women's movement. Feminism criticized society as male dominated, which included a critique of the controlling ideologies of society. Feminists charged that disciplinary knowledges (e.g., sociology, anthropology, economics, and philosophy) exhibit a male perspective and function as social forces perpetuating women's oppression. Feminists have sought to develop alternative, women-centered knowledges.

Smith has applied a feminist perspective to sociology. She views the sociological tradition as male centered. Her aim has been to craft a sociology by and for women that looks to women's experiences, interests, and values as the basis of social knowledge and politics.

At the core of Smith's feminist sociology is the claim that women are socially positioned differently than men. Their unique social location provides women with a distinctive basis for developing their own sociology. A feminist sociology would be critical of an androcentric sociology and society. Its aim would be to enhance women's understanding of the social forces that shape their lives, that both oppress them and make possible their resistance. Smith's feminist sociological theory is morally and politically committed to abolishing male dominance. Although Smith places her own work squarely in the tradition of feminism, I perceive strong parallels to poststructuralism, in particular, the linking of power and knowledge, the critical, deconstructive impulse of her work, and, as we will see, the focus on knowledges and discourses as a new, central axis of social formation and domination. Smith offers a powerful, imaginative moral vision of a sociology and a society in which knowledge is both the dominating power and our social hope.

Sociology from the standpoint of women

As a feminist, Smith assumes that gender is a master category of social analysis. Like class, gender structures subjectivity, institutions, culture, and the politics of a society. In contemporary Western societies, human feelings, desires, identities, conduct, occupations, institutions, and ideas are gendered as masculine or feminine. Gender is a master framework that functions to shape and regulate the lives of individuals and whole populations for the benefit of men. The gendered character of the self and society is true for human sexuality, social roles, and knowledges, including the sciences. Asserting the gendered imprint of knowledge means that there is no universal, Archimedean standpoint from which to know the social world. "There can be no theory, no method, and no knowledge . . . that is not made by men and women and made from a definite standpoint in the society and in the interests of those who make it" [23].

Smith asserts that, in contemporary Western societies, men and women are socially positioned differently and unequally. Smith does not wish to claim that all men and all women share identical experiences, interests, values, or social positioning. She is aware that women differ by class and race and in many other ways, as do men. These differences suggest variations in women's knowledges. Yet, Smith holds that, despite such social variation among women, it is still valid to claim, however tentatively, a common gender experience. Specifically, in relation to men, women continue to be primarily responsible for household duties, for the care of the physical, material conditions of society, e.g., cooking, cleaning, caring for the bodies of children and men, and the routine material care of the self – child and adult, male and female, in sickness and in health. Women center their lives around domestic, household, caretaking tasks. This terrain of activity is formative and defining for women in ways that are not true for men.

As women's lives are centered in domestic, nurturing, service-oriented roles, their experiences are organized around a range of specific, detailed, daily activities. These behaviors are anchored in particular localities, times, and social relations. Women's lives are centered around their homes, neighborhoods, and relations to children and other women. Smith suggests, moreover, that women's values and view of the world reflect their unique social experiences. Accordingly, women's conceptual values or knowledges tend to emphasize locality, the particularity of behavior, time, and place, specific social relations, and the dense, complex interrelation of individuals.

Smith argues that women's experiences, values, and conceptual orientations are conspicuously absent from the dominant cultural discourses, including the scientific disciplines. For example, sociology may aspire to be the science of the social, but it has not been the science of *all* that is social. "Its method, conceptual schemes and theories [have] been based on and built up within the male social universe" [24]. Sociology has crafted a sociology of men; they are its chief actors and script writers. Women have been excluded from its key perspectives; the activities of women that make possible men's public roles are ignored, as are women's active roles in making sociology and society. The chief topics and subject matter of sociology reflect men's values and experiences, namely, the world of paid labor, politics, and formal organizations. Women's world of the household, children, sexual reproduction, affective ties, and voluntary work is either neglected or marginalized. By making men's experiences, values, and knowledges into the very nature of social experience and knowledge, sociology contributes to erasing and devaluing women's distinctive experiences and values. By making men's sociology into general sociology, the discipline of sociology has served, perhaps unwittingly, as a vehicle for alienating women from their own lives.

Sociology reflects men's experience. Despite men's more recent involvement in household tasks, the core organizing center of their lives in contemporary Western societies is the public world. Smith leaves no doubt that, whatever changes have occurred in the post-World War II period, the formative experience for men continues to be in the public world of big business, government, sports, and the military.

Men hold the positions of power and privilege in the key institutions of society or what Smith calls the "relations of ruling." A central feature of rulership in Western societies is the role of "objectified knowledges" or textually mediated discourses, e.g., scientific-medical, and psychiatric, demographic texts, and hospital, prison, and educational records. In contrast to everyday understandings of human behavior that speak of actual individuals in specific situations, objectified knowledges, from psychiatry to census and coroners' reports, abstract from the particular actualities of real living individuals to construct general identities and classifications of individuals and groups (e.g., by age, income, race, and gender). To the extent that the lives of men are centered in the public world, they consider an abstract, impersonal way of mapping the world as natural. Furthermore, since men have dominated sociology, their conceptual values – abstraction, generality, anonymity – have become dominant. Sociology has been a form of knowledge produced by and for men. Despite the fact that many sociologists see themselves as reformers, sociology is part of the relations of ruling that benefit men, the propertied class, and White Europeans. Like all ruling ideologies, sociology does not see its own ideological role. It fancies that its own ideas are universal. It takes its topics, problems, and conceptual strategies as universal. Sociology masks its gendered character by speaking abstractly of humanity, the individual, society, and moral agency, rather than of gendered selves, behaviors, and experiences. Sociology resists admitting a gendered order because it would threaten to reveal its patriarchal character.

Smith advocates a sociology for women. This challenges the claim to universality of a male-centered sociology. It exposes sociology as a political enterprise. A feminist sociology aims to liberate women from the patriarchal system of social rulership.

What would a sociology for women look like? In contrast to a male-centered sociology that aspires to map abstract entities and processes, a feminist sociology would take women as they find themselves in their particular local settings, social relations, and daily activities as the starting point for social knowledge. Smith conceives of a feminist sociology modeled after the presumed social realism of Karl Marx. In contrast to much sociology, past and present, Marx's historical materialism begins with real individuals with actual needs, located in specific times and places, and engaged in a myriad of specific social relations. Social consciousness or culture is approached as expressive of actual social relations. For Smith, as for Marx, ideology describes a way of thinking in which ideas are separated from their social origins in the actions of real individuals. An ideological method renders abstractions such as freedom, values, reason, mind, and attitudes into the active forces of society and history, while real individuals disappear. A human drama is acted out in which the movement of these abstract fictitious entities (e.g., reason, freedom, values) replace the daily, local, specific struggles of real living individuals.

Smith's feminist sociology is inspired by Marx's "nonideological" method of social inquiry. Her starting point is women's actual lives.

> Inquiry starts with the knower who is actually located; she is active; she is at work; she is connected with particular other people in various ways; she thinks, laughs, desires, sorrows, sings, curses, loves just here; she reads here; she watches television. Activities, feelings, experiences, hook her into extended social relations linking her activities to those of other people and in ways beyond her knowing. . . . The standpoint of women never leaves the actual. The knowing subject is always located in a particular spatial and temporal site, a particular configuration of the everyday/every-night world. Inquiry is directed towards exploring and explicating what she does not know – the social relations and organization pervading her world but invisible in it [25].

A feminist sociology aims to recover the integrity of women's lives, give a public critical voice to women, and push women into the center of society and knowledge.

Smith rejects a narrow Enlightenment legitimation of knowledge that appeals to scientific progress to justify sociology. However, a sociology for women is not mere opinion or political partisanship. The fact that all knowledge, including feminist sociology, is socially situated and interested, does not mean that valid knowledge is impossible.

Smith wishes to steer a middle course between objectivism and relativism. She refuses the aspiration to arrive at one true, comprehensive language of social reality. She is equally critical of relativism or the position that assumes that we can proliferate a near-infinite number of possible theories, knowledges, and standards of truth. Smith asserts that knowledge is both situational and objective. We can know society because we have created it. Sociology is always an "insider" sociology. Our categories of knowledge are expressive of the actual social organization of our lives. If sociology cannot produce a comprehensive, totalizing theory, it can at least yield reliable knowledge of "how things work" which may prove useful for women in understanding the social conditions that shape and constrain their lives.

Smith is convinced that only by defending a representational concept of truth can social criticism be credible. Feminists must be able to claim truth for their statements about gender inequality. I think that Smith is mistaken in this regard. Knowledge can be reliable and useful without being true. The fact that knowledge helps us to do something or achieve some goal does not mean that it is true, i.e., that there is a correspondence between idea and reality. Moreover, Smith does not need to claim a strong truth value for her sociology in order for it to be useful for women. To the extent that social ideas contribute to women understanding their lives and to changing those social conditions that are needlessly constraining, they may be said to be useful but not necessarily true. The real issue is whether a feminist sociology can produce knowledge that women can use to change their social conditions. Do we really need a justification of knowledge beyond its social utility? Questions might, of course, be raised about the social goals or values of feminist sociology or practice. However, Smith does not provide anything approaching a justification of the values and social ideals that guide her feminist criticism. My own opinion is that she does not need a serious philosophical justification. The values that she invokes to criticize sociology and society, such as equality, freedom, autonomy, and democracy, are hardly contestable in most Western societies. An appeal to cultural traditions and social ideals strikes me as sufficient. I doubt, in any event, that any grounding that cannot appeal to such traditions will have much moral force.

Smith's project is clear: a women-centered, feminist sociology. Its aim is to analyze how configurations of power shape and constrain women for the purpose of promoting a critical, political awareness and practice. Smith imagines a feminist sociology that contributes to transforming women into social agents who purposefully make their own lives.

Relations of ruling: patriarchy, discourse, and domination

A feminist sociology underscores the centrality of gender inequality and women's oppression in society. Smith departs from other feminist theorists, for whom the source of women's oppression is a sex role system, the family, the norm of heterosexuality, or a patriarchal state. Smith underscores a neglected but central mechanism of social domination: objectified knowledges and discourses.

Smith does not neatly separate the structures or processes that disempower women from those that are oppressive because of one's sexual orientation, race, or class. She speaks very broadly of relations of ruling as including the government, big business, the professions, scientific, medical, and mass media discourses, and the personnel involved in administering these institutions. The relations of ruling exhibit the intersection of male dominance, racism, and capitalism. It is not Smith's purpose, however, to provide an institutional analysis of the interlocking dynamics of racism, sexism, and capitalism. Rather, she focuses on an underlying, common, and central feature of the relations of ruling in contemporary Western capitalist societies: the role of knowledge as a social force of domination. Smith's distinctive contribution to a feminist sociological analysis of domination lies in her analysis of the centrality of objectified knowledges and discourses in relations of ruling.

In modern Western societies, social domination operates through texts, e.g., medical records, census reports, hospital records, psychiatric case studies, marriage records, and employment files. These texts facilitate social control. They create a world of individual and social types and impersonal processes that can be manipulated and controlled. Individuals appear as instances of a group or social type (e.g., the sick, mentally ill, unemployed, married, White, criminal, or disabled); social realities are framed as governed by impersonal processes (e.g., as an expression of "values," "attitudes," "illness," or "poverty"). The texts of rulership are characterized by their abstraction from real acting individuals in their particular local social settings. Objectified knowledges translate real-life experiences into a language that is anonymous, impersonal, general, and objectifying. Objectified knowledges transfigure real-life experience into individual and social types classified by age, class, race, sex, sexuality, gender, normality, health, employment, and so on. Institutions that function by objectifying the social world aim to control society in ways that benefit men, propertied classes, and White Europeans.

By way of illustrating the substitution of "virtual realities" for actual realities and the link of objectified knowledges and domination, Smith refers to the psychiatric discourse on "mental illness." Psychiatric discourses deploy a medical model of mental illness. This model asserts that, for reasons of nature or environment, some individuals become mentally ill. Illness is manifested in psychological or behavioral symptoms (e.g., depression, sadness, phobias) that impede "normal" social functioning. The "mentally ill" find their way to a psychiatrist or mental health practitioner and are diagnosed. This means inferring from symptoms (e.g., nervousness, anxiety, impotence, failures at work or love) an underlying mental disorder or illness (e.g., neurosis, character disorder, narcissism) and prescribing a treatment. In the medical model, mental illness is discovered by the mental health practitioner and appropriately labeled and treated. Smith notes that many sociologists who analyze variations in mental illness by gender, race, or class rely on this model. Sociologists who depend upon the data provided by mental health practitioners routinely assume a correspondence between psychiatric categories of mental illness and reality.

Smith registers grave doubts about this model and its social effects. For example, she observes a bias towards associating mental illness with women. Many categories of "emotional distress" that are predominant among men are excluded from the category of mental illness in most mental health practices (e.g., alcoholism or drug abuse). This has the social and political effect of viewing women as more unstable and vulnerable to mental illness than men, as more in need of medical and social supervision than men, as less able to fulfill social roles involving power, stress, and social responsibilities than men. In a word, psychiatric discourses position women as socially subordinate to men.

Smith raises doubts about the scientific status of the medical model. Drawing on the work of critics such as Thomas Szazs, Smith holds to a social constructionist view of mental illness. Psychiatric interventions do more than discover and treat a preexisting mental illness; they create it as a social identity and place the individual under its institutional control. Smith doesn't deny that there are individuals who suffer from emotional distress; she takes issue with the warrant and social consequences of medicalizing such distress. With respect to the validity of this knowledge claim, Smith favors a constructionist interpretation of psychiatric discourse. With respect to the social effect of such discourses, Smith underscores its stigmatizing, dehumanizing, and disempowering effects. Psychiatric knowledges take away moral agency and responsibility from the individual and transform the psychiatric self into an object of control. Let me explain.

An individual who is troubled experiences distress in personal, specific, and local ways. Personal distress may be linked to particular situations, perhaps particular people, and experienced in the context of an individual's actual history and complex, specific social relations. Personal distress does not necessarily define that individual's primary self experience or relation to the world. However, defining an individual as mentally ill transforms that individual's experience of self and world. The individual's actual context of actions, social relations, history, and complex relationships with the world is set aside or rendered irrelevant in the psychiatric discourse. Only the individual's symptomatic behavior is considered important and interpreted in light of a general, impersonal system of categories or meanings – a schema of normalty and abnormality, of symptomology and treatment strategies. The individual's actions are seen as expressive of a psychological abnormality or illness; the person loses his or her sense of being an agent, of being a responsible, knowledgeable, self-monitoring social actor.

The psychiatric universe of meaning and social relations replaces the individual's actual history, social relations, and experiences as the reference point for interpreting behavior; he or she becomes a case history, psychological type, disease, syndrome, and treatment possibility. In other words, the individual is lifted out of the actual practices of his or her life, erasing agency, locality, specificity, and history. The person is placed in a different set of social relations – a world of patients, case histories, diagnoses, nurses, psychiatrists, insurance companies, and the state. Smith interprets psychiatry as an agency of social control aimed at defining and managing socially inappropriate local behavior that cannot be defined or managed by other agencies of control, e.g., prisons, hospitals, schools, and families. Psychiatric discourses and practices are integral to defining and regulating bodies, selves, and populations in accordance with the interests and relevances of the ruling institutions and groups.

To the exent that sociology relies on the texts of the relations of ruling (e.g., psychiatric discourses, census records, and crime statistics) for its social knowledge, it is part of the relations of ruling. Its subject matter and topics are those of the ruling powers. "Mental illness, crimes, riots, violence, work satisfaction, neighbors and neighborhoods, motivation, and so on – these are the constructs of the practice of government" [26]. Sociology speaks the language of rulership. Its concepts and schemas are extralocal, general, and impersonal; its guiding concepts substitute abstract entities and processes (e.g., mind, values, attitudes, roles, and interests) for the actualities of lived experience. Sociological knowledge receives its shape less from the concerns and dilemmas of real individuals in their actual social relations than from the interests in control, regulation, and normalization by the welfare state, professional associations, and public bureaucracies.

Dorothy Smith envisions an alternative sociology whose purpose is to challenge the relations of ruling. In particular, she imagines a feminist sociology that can transform society in a nonpatriarchal way. This is a vision of sociology as a moral science, a critical inquiry into the everyday conditions of domination for the purpose of altering them.

Afterword

Sociology has never been without its critics. Liberal humanistic critics have assailed sociology for minimizing individual choice and moral responsibility. On the other hand, Marxists have attacked sociology for legitimating capitalism by celebrating the individualism and social progress of the industrial West. Despite the differences between liberal and Marxist critics, they share a basic commitment to "modern" Enlightenment social values and visions.

In the postwar period, a series of critical discourses challenged the Enlightenment foundations of sociology and Western culture. French post-structuralists contested the core of "modernism," for example, the unity of "man," the identity of humanity, science as truth, Western superiority, and the idea of social progress. In the United States, the new social movements politicized science and Enlightenment culture. These critical perspectives on the human sciences and Enlightenment culture had little impact on the human sciences through the seventies. Efforts to incorporate feminism, Afrocentricity, or lesbian and gay theory into the disciplines were either marginalized or achieved by accommodating to the dominant Enlightenment paradigm. The significance of Bellah, Bauman, and Smith is that they have drawn from post-Enlightenment paradigms to rethink sociology and society. Indeed, these sociologists wish to challenge the core culture of sociology. Despite their being situated differently socially and intellectually, Bellah, Bauman, and Smith advocate the unity of theory and practice, knowledge and power, view human studies as a practical and moral enterprise, emphasize the social role of knowledges and discourses, and shift the discussion of social realities away from a narrow focus on class-based stratification and organizational dynamics, which have been the central axis for sociology. Yet, these three sociologists offer very different approaches to sociology and society.

Bellah's vision of society remains deeply rooted in the classical tradition of sociology. He draws heavily on the cultural views of society found in Durkheim and Weber and elaborated in Parsons and functionalist social science. In particular, I see Bellah as absorbing the Durkheimian concept of society as a religious-moral order. Pushing Durkheim and Parsons to the Left, Bellah's social ideal is a society in which individualism and democracy flourish within the framework of a religiously anchored social order. Bellah departs from a Durkheimian tradition in his advocacy of sociology as a publicly engaged ethical reflection. Drawing on an American populist and pragmatic tradition, as well as European critical theory, Bellah aims to shift sociology from a narrowly scientific to an interpretive, moral, and critical type of human studies. Instead of viewing society with an eye to engineering social control, Bellah offers a view of sociology as part of an ongoing, public conversation about the origin, development, meaning, and possible futures of society. For Bellah, the value of sociology lies in fostering and defending a democratic culture.

I share Bellah's dissatisfaction with the retreat of sociology from public engagement. His advocacy of social science as public philosophy has the dual advantage of revitalizing sociology as a social language that speaks to an educated public and contributing to a democratic public culture. I think, moreover, that the idea of sociology as public social discourse has strong roots in the modern tradition of social thought. The idea of human studies as contributing to public enlightenment and practical action links Marx to C.W. Mills, Robert Park and E.A. Ross to Arlie Hochschild and William Wilson.

I would, however, wish to expand the slate of participants in the public dialogue and perhaps alter somewhat the topics of conversations framed by Bellah. The voices in his dialogue are almost all White, heterosexual, and middle class. I believe it is a mistake to assume, as Bellah does, that the culture and institutions of America and Western societies narrowly mirror the interests and values of this group. This is especially troubling in light of the challenging of the social mainstream by oppressed groups and minorities and their successes in "mainstreaming" in the past two decades. Does not the exclusion of other voices (people of color, lesbians or gay men, working class, the disabled) in the conversations orchestrated by Bellah reinforce their marginalization or public silencing?

The issues that inspire Bellah are clear enough: the viability of moral order and social solidarity, the corrosive effects of individualism, and the decline of democratic culture in the absence of a religious-moral cultural framework. I don't doubt their broad social and moral importance. Moreover, Bellah is among the most powerful social critics of the American culture of individualism. I mostly agree with his analysis. Americans do not seem to have available a moral vocabulary that defines the self as social, situates individualism within a context of social obligations, institutional norms, and public goals, and views the individual as wedded to an interdependent social universe. American individualism is too often pitted against social institutions and values, despite the fact that our lives are filled with social roles, responsibilities, and commitments. I interpret Bellah as a social pragmatist. Americans should think of their lives in a language of social connection because it would help us to see individualism, social solidarities, and democracy as depending on social policies, institutional supports, and political behavior. It would make us all the more vigorous in our defense of the social institutions that support democracy and social justice. I agree.

Yet I have some reservations about the dialogue on individualism and society that Bellah orchestrates. My chief concern relates to the abstract level at which the issues of individualism, democracy, and solidarity are posed. I question the social effectiveness of a social critique that is so sweeping and broadly framed that it addresses no group in particular and whose proposed remedies (i.e., reviving a biblical and republican tradition or more democracy) seem removed from present debates over policy and specific struggles over institutional changes. Which groups are expected to initiate the desired changes, and what are the social sources instigating such political engagement? For whom is the issue of the failures of personal and social coherence, as Bellah describes this state, sufficiently compelling to act politically? And what political form might such a cultural politics assume? I have doubts about the value of posing questions of cultural coherence in the absence of any serious effort to connect the themes of individualism and moral order with an analysis of social oppression and movements of resistance. Why is there no effort to address issues of self, justice, success, and community in the specific context of the struggles of women, gays, Latinos, African-Americans, the disabled, and the poor, many of whom are struggling for ways to create new images of self, democracy, and community?

Perhaps my reservations simply underscore a difference in approach and aim. Instead of posing in a general manner the question of individualism and moral order, I would prefer, for reasons of intellectual prejudice and political efficacy, to frame such issues in relation to specific social conflicts. The advantage, as I see it, of framing moral dialogue in relation to specific social struggles is that issues of self, community, and justice are directly tied to issues of power, political strategy, and transformative social visions. Lacking this connection, there is a politically disengaged character to this discourse of moral crisis. Such reservations should not detract from the importance of stimulating public awareness of such issues and introducing into the public a language of self and society that is presently marginalized.

For all of his anguish over modern history and America's future, Bellah never quite relinquishes the Enlightenment promise of science and modernity. Bauman does. Whereas Bellah's ideas fall into a pattern of ambivalence toward modernity that was typical of Marx and classical sociology, Bauman edges, however reluctantly, toward a critique of modernity. In Bauman's mournful tale of modern history, we hear the pessimistic lament of critical theory and poststructuralism.

Bauman has provided the most compelling sociological articulation of postmodernism. His vision of premodernity, modernity, and postmodernity as unique periods in Western history, is a powerful legitimation of the concept of postmodernity. In particular, the contrast between modernity, as an epoch in the grip of a compulsive drive for a rationally designed order, and postmodernity, as an era pivoted upon the proliferation of social differences and the acceptance of a decentered self and society, parallels the classical typologies of traditional and modern societies. Bauman has forced sociologists to take seriously the claim of postmodernity as a stage of social history.

To his credit, Bauman considers the implications for sociology of this second great social transformation. I am in broad sympathy with his proposal for a postmodern interpretive sociology that facilitates communication between communities and gives voice to submerged traditions. A postmodern sociology departs from the Enlightenment paradigm by surrendering an explanatory, truth-seeking knowledge whose justification appeals to the progress of science and society. A postmodern sociology is engaged in the making of social realities. This critical interpretive approach to human studies has deep roots in sociology, for example, in the Chicago school, phenomenological sociology, or symbolic interactionism.

For all of his efforts to reconfigure sociology in a postmodern fashion, Bauman never escapes the seductive charms of modern and grand theory. He offers a totalizing history which, in its scope and moral sweep, easily compares to the grand narratives of Marx and classical sociology. Bauman furnishes a story of humanity's evolution from premodernity to modernity and postmodernity. In a way similar to Marx, Comte, Durkheim, and Weber, Bauman collapses very different national experiences (e.g., United States, Germany, Italy, Spain, Belgium) that occurred over centuries into one, supranational, epochal meaning – premodern, modern, or post-modern. Is it credible to take specific developments that occurred in the course of seventeenth century France as indicative of a whole period of history of virtually any industrializing society? Does not Bauman's typology of societies in terms of premodernity, modernity, and postmodernity reflect the categorizing, ordering, legislative reasoning of the Enlightenment that he detects? Bauman theorizes postmodernity, but his theorizing in many ways expresses the generalizing and normalizing standpoint of modernity.

Indicative of this modernist impulse in Bauman is a tendency simply to reverse the standard Enlightenment story of history. For example, the orthodox Enlightenment paradigm describes modernity as liberating the individual from local, religiously ordered premodern communities. In contrast, Bauman laments the loss of a culture of social pluralism and individuality in the name of social uniformity, cultural standardization, and state control. Reversing the Enlightenment celebration of modernity as the great leap forward to freedom and reason, Bauman describes it as exhibiting the advance of a social logic of control and domination. Bauman's tendency to retreat from ambivalence, a hallmark of modernity, is striking in his view of Soviet-styled communism as revealing the true spirit of modernity. "Communism was modernity in its most determined mood and most decisive posture; modernity streamlined, purified of the last shred of the chaotic, the irrational, the spontaneous, the unpredictable" [27]. Collapsing all industrializing nations into one "modern" type and then identifying the imperial ambitions of the Soviet communist state with the essence of modernity strikes me as exemplary of the repression of ambiguity, ambivalence, and difference characteristic of modern legislative reason. This unidimensional characterization of modernity contradicts Bauman's own view that the postmodern affirmation of pluralism, difference, ambivalence, and spontaneity articulates the preexisting, even if marginal, condition of modernity.

For both Bellah and Bauman, the social position or character of the sociologist is not scrutinized. They theorize as if the sociologist were outside of society and history. Bellah acknowledges the sociologist as an interested, value-committed moral agent. Yet he does not consider how his own social positioning, for example, his particular racial, gender, class, and sexual location, shapes his perspective and politics. Similarly, Bauman seems to imagine himself as a kind of free-floating, marginal intellectual whose outsider or stranger status provides a privileged standpoint to gain knowledge. He does not reflect on the ways in which his particular national location, gender, class, race, sexual, or religious status may decisively shape his ideas. It is as if neither Bellah nor Bauman has yet to engage the discourses produced by the new social movements, discourses that have insisted on the socially situated, political character of social knowledges.

By contrast, Dorothy Smith situates her theorizing squarely in the women's movement and, more particularly, in the experience of being a woman. Knowledge is always situated for Smith, stamped by the gender, class, ethnic, and racial status of the sociologist. In this regard, Smith agrees with Bellah and Bauman, both of whom, in principle, abandon the idea of an overarching, comprehensive, complete system of knowledge. Social knowledge is always partial, from a specific perspective and reflective of the interests and values of its producers. Yet, Smith maintains that the situated, interested, value-committed character of sociology does not mean that it is merely subjective or ideological. Sociologists produce ideas that reflect a particular social standpoint but that are still valid forms of knowledge. She believes that some claim to "realism" or the idea that our social ideas represent or mirror a world "out there" is necessary and defensible in order to judge competing perspectives and values and to justify one's own social vision. It must be said that Smith does not offer any serious arguments on behalf of "realism"; nor does she justify her values and social vision beyond appealing to social conventions and traditions.

I am not convinced that an appeal to realism or truth is necessary or credible today in order to adjudicate social and intellectual conflicts. Consider the argument that Smith herself proposes. Knowledge, she says, is situated. In particular, she asserts that gender structures knowledge. She intends to use this position to justify feminist knowledge. However, I think that this same position undermines her claim to realism or representational truth. Let me explain.

Smith asserts that women's experience is both a basis of objective knowledge and subject to immense variation. If, however, Smith concedes women's diversity, if women's experiences differ by race, class, sexuality, nationality, age, and so on, she must concede that these differences can be multiplied indefinitely. Smith must agree that, in principle, these prolific social differences among women can be articulated in a near-infinite variety of feminist knowledges, some of which will be contradictory. This acknowledgment of difference would seem to render the category of "women" little more than pragmatic or political. Or, to say it otherwise, if women's standpoints can be multiplied ad infinitum, and Smith does not provide any arguments to the contrary, feminist claims to truth would likewise multiply relentlessly, rendering validity claims a feeble basis for conflict resolution. If Smith wishes to maintain that women's experience provides a general basis for social truths, she must assume a substantialist concept of women or a unitary gender experience. However, as we have seen in the previous chapter, this claim seems indefensible both on conceptual and practical-political grounds. Smith hedges her position, gently pushing the idea of a common female experience while making gestures toward the diversity of women's lives.

As sociologists such as Bellah, Bauman, and Smith edge towards a post-Enlightenment paradigm of human studies, there is still some reluctance to abandon the promise of truth. If it is no longer wedded to hopes of scientific and social progress, the will to truth is judged to be indispensable in preserving a critical human studies. They may be right. However, I am less convinced that truth claims, not particular empirical claims, carry much social authority. Perhaps, as Baudrillard suggests, a world of hyperreality and an information-saturated culture where the line between reality and illusion is blurred undermines the social force of truth claims. Perhaps, a culture grown cynical by a relentless critique of ideology has lost a capacity to be persuaded by claims of truth. For many of us in the West, this possibility raises the specter of relativism, nihilism, and anarchy. I am less terrorized by this possibility than are some because I imagine the substitution of a culture of pragmatic justification for our Enlightenment rationalist culture. Pragmatic justifications would not appeal to ultimate grounds or foundations, such as human nature or the nature of reason, or social and historical laws to legitimate social norms, values, and institutions; rather, behavior and norms are justified by appealing to social conventions, traditions, and ideals. I imagine circular arguments that move back and forth between claims about what society is and should be, between social ideals, traditions, and conventions. Admittedly, pragmatic justifications would make our judgments and reasons contingent, ambiguous, always matters of judgment and negotiation, always contestable. But don't these conditions of ambiguity and contestation make possible a world of choice, individuality, tolerance, and democracy? These are the wages of postmodernism.

References

1. Robert Bellah, "Civil Religion in America," in *Beyond Belief: Essays in Religion in a Post-Traditional World* (New York: Harper & Row, 1970).
2. Robert Bellah, *The Broken Convenant: American Civil Religion in Time of Trial* (New York: Seabury Press, 1975).

3. Robert Bellah et al., *Habits of the Heart: Individualism and Commitment in American Life* (Berkeley: University of California Press, 1985) and *The Good Society* (New York: Alfred A. Knopf, 1991).
4. Bellah, *The Broken Covenant*, p. ix.
5. Bellah, *The Broken Covenant*, p. x.
6. Bellah, *The Broken Covenant*, p. x.
7. Arthur Vidich and Stanford Lyman, *American Sociology* (New Haven: Yale University Press, 1985).
8. Bellah et al., "Social Science as Public Philosophy," Appendix to *Habits of the Heart*; Robert Bellah, "The Ethical Aims of Social Inquiry," in Norma Haan et al., eds., *Social Science as Moral Inquiry* (New York: Columbia University Press, 1983); Robert Bellah, "Social Science as Practical Reason," in Daniel Callahan and Bruce Jennings eds., *Ethics, The Social Sciences, and Policy Analysis"* (New York: Plenum Press, 1983).
9. Bellah, *Habits of the Heart*, p. 29.
10. Bellah, *Habits of the Heart*, p. 30.
11. Bellah, *Habits of the Heart*, p. 34.
12. Alexis de Tocqueville, *Democracy in America*, J.P. Mayer, ed. (New York: Doubleday, 1969).
13. Bellah, *The Good Society*.
14. Zygmunt Bauman, *Intimations of Postmodernity* (New York: Routledge, 1992), p. xiii.
15. Zygmunt Bauman, *Modernity and Ambivalence* (Ithaca, NY: Cornell University Press, 1991), pp. 7–8 and *Modernity and the Holocaust* (Ithaca, NY: Cornell University Press, 1989) and *Legislators and Interpreters: On Modernity, Post-Modernity and Intellectuals* (Ithaca, NY: Cornell University Press, 1987).
16. Bauman, *Intimations of Postmodernity*, p. 102.
17. Bauman, *Intimations of Postmodernity*, p. 52.
18. Bauman, *Intimations of Postmodernity*, p. 42.
19. Bauman, *Intimations of Postmodernity*, p. 109.
20. Judith Stacey and Barrie Thorne, "The Missing Feminist Revolution in Sociology," *Social Problems* 32 (April 1985).
21. Important statements of feminist social and political theory outside sociology include: Nancy Harstock, *Money, Sex and Power* (New York: Longman, 1983); Catherine MacKinnon, *Toward a Feminist Theory of the State* (Cambridge, Mass: Harvard University Press, 1989); Zillah Eisenstein, *Feminism and Social Equality* (New York: Monthly Review Press, 1989); Peggy Sanday, *Female Power and Male Dominance* (New York: Cambridge University Press, 1981); Linda Nicholson, *Gender and History* (New York: Columbia University Press, 1986); Nancy Fraser, *Unruly Practices* (Minneapolis: University of Minnesota Press, 1989): Gayatri C. Spivak, *In Other Worlds* (New York: Routledge, 1988); Iris Young, *Justice and the Politics of Difference* (Princeton: Princeton University Press, 1990).

22. Nancy Chodorow, *The Reproduction of Mothering* (Berkeley: University of California Press, 1987).

23. Dorothy Smith, *The Conceptual Practices of Power: A Feminist Sociology of Knowledge* (Boston: Northeastern University Press, 1990), p. 32. Also, Dorothy Smith, *The Everyday World as Problematic: A Feminist Sociology* (Boston: Northeastern University Press, 1987); Dorothy Smith, *Texts, Facts, and Femininity: Exploring the Relations of Ruling* (New York: Routledge, 1990).

24. Smith, *The Conceptual Practices of Power*, p. 23.

25. Dorothy Smith, "Sociology from Women's Experience: A Reaffirmation," *Sociological Theory* 10 (Spring 1992), p. 91.

26. Smith, *The Conceptual Practices of Power*, p. 15.

27. Bauman, *Intimations of Postmodernity*, p. 167.

Epilogue

T he promise of the modern social sciences has been that they would contribute to human freedom and social progress. By eliminating ignorance and prejudice and revealing the laws of society and history, humankind would control its destiny. We would design institutions, laws, and social customs to conform to the truths about human nature and the social order. This would be a world that combined freedom and a rational social order.

The moral role of science as a vehicle of human emancipation is to be made possible by the scientist's renunciation of political partisanship. For science to function as an instrument of human advancement, it has to obey a rather austere regime involving the erasure of the particular values, interests, and ideology of the scientist. As a citizen assumes the role of the scientist, she or he undergoes a self-transformation analogous to the shift from a civilian to a soldier or a nun. The instrument of this alteration is the institution of science which imposes upon individual behavior a set of supposedly universal rules (e.g., empirical verifiability, methodological procedures, and principles of concept formation and explanation). The institution of science guarantees that only those ideas that mirror the objective world are to be accepted as knowledge.

The balance between human studies as science and as moral commitment is viewed as delicate. Straining too far toward the latter, one surrenders to partisanship. On the other hand, a scientific human studies that is too insulated from public life threatens to render the human sciences socially irrelevant.

From its inception, science has been wrapped in contradictory images: science as truth, as universal knowledge, and science as emancipatory, as liberating humanity from the darkness of ignorance and prejudice. This concept of science has guided modern human studies from Montesquieu, Condorcet, Comte, Marx, Durkheim to Parsons, Blau, Collins, Habermas, and Coleman. Between the high hopes of Condorcet and Comte, Marx and Durkheim, and the equally high hopes of Parsons, Collins, Blau, and

Coleman, something happened. It was *not* that the moral role of science was abandoned. Coleman no less than Comte, Blau no less than Marx, Parsons no less than Condorcet imbued science with moral and social value. Classics and contemporaries alike share the promise of sociology to help make a better world. It is the *scientization of human studies* that has rendered social science isolated from public life and less capable of effectively assuming the role of public educator and advocate.

How did this scientization of the human studies happen? Let me suggest one possible social account. Between the eighteenth and twentieth centuries, science became *the authoritative language for speaking the truth about social realities.* Claiming scientific status for social ideas conferred public authority on the scientist and her or his ideas. Accordingly, the task of justifying social knowledge as science became a focus of attention not only as a matter of discerning truth but as a practical, political matter, i.e., as an issue of whose ideas would be heard and would exert social influence.

Social scientists may have varied in their concepts of science but have consistently believed that science means knowledge of the world "as it is" in contrast to subjective or ideological beliefs that reflect a world of personal experiences or particular, ethnocentric social (e.g., class or ethnic or national) interests and values. Social perspectives are discredited by being characterized as nonscientific or ideological, for example, by revealing the particular social interests or values informing their basic concepts or by linking a "scientific" paradigm to a political agenda. As science functions to legitimate knowledge, a unique culture of truth develops in the human studies. Discussion centers around what ideas count as scientific and what standards should guide decisions between rival conceptual and empirical perspectives. The hope is that such general discussions would yield conceptual foundations for social knowledge or a broad-based agreement about basic premises, concepts, models, and explanatory strategies. "Theory" becomes an "autonomous" practice; its charge is to address foundational concerns, for example, to take a position on the problem of objectivity, the relation between the individual and society, materialism and idealism, order and change, solidarity and conflict, power and meaning, and the logic of knowledge. There develops a set of argumentative strategies that carry persuasive power in disputes (e.g., appealing to evidence, methodological procedures, "classic" texts, and philosophical arguments). Central to this culture of theorizing is the exclusion of moral advocacy and political partisanship. As "theory" is preoccupied with "metatheoretical" or foundational concerns and its attention turns to disputes over the nature of social action and order, the logic of objectivity and knowledge, conflict versus order paradigms, the micro–macro or the agency–structure linkage, and as explicit moral advocacy and political partisanship are excluded, theorists have turned away from public life, or they have simply lost touch with a language with which to address social concerns in ways that are meaningful to various nonacademic publics.

The tension in the human studies between science and morality runs through its history. I believe, though, that the consolidation of the social scientific disciplines in this century greatly expedited the process of scientization. We must not forget that Montesquieu, Condorcet, Comte, and Marx did not develop their social ideas in departments of sociology or as university professors. Their ideas coalesced in response to social events and addressed broad publics. Their social perspectives gained public authority only to the extent that they engaged citizens, from the powerful to the disenfranchised. It was only with the generation succeeding Comte and Marx that universities became an important social institution shaping social knowledge. In the course of the twentieth century, especially in the United States, the human science disciplines (e.g., sociology, anthropology, political science, psychology, economics) became *the* principal social site for the production of knowledge. The disciplines have been valuable in furnishing a range of useful empirical information, varied social perspectives, and critical ideas. However, disciplinary knowledges have been shaped in key ways by the institutions that support them, for example, the state, universities and colleges, big business, and funding agencies. Moreover, the disciplines have evolved their own cultures. For example, sociology has its own jargon, specialty areas, topics, themes, and conventions of empirical research and argumentation. To some extent, this "autonomy" permits some slippage between disciplinary knowledge and public life. Perhaps this is justifiable as it allows a vantage point from which to produce and assess social knowledge somewhat removed from public controversies. However, if this slippage is too great, if disciplinary knowledges are too rigidly governed by these expert cultures, they become insulated and lose a vital connection to public life. Unfortunately, this is what happened in the course of the disciplining of social theory; such social insularity is especially prominent in recent sociological theory.

If I am not mistaken, a scientific social theory that aims to establish the foundations for social knowledge and aspires to uncover a vocabulary mirroring the structure of society is collapsing under its own dead weight. The failure to achieve its goal, indeed, even to make credible this aspiration, and the growing perception in and outside of the discipline that sociological theory has lost its moral bearings have precipitated an almost perpetual sense of crisis.

If the project of scientific human studies is in doubt, perhaps this is symptomatic of a broader crisis in the culture of the West. As I have suggested in previous chapters, Enlightenment paradigms of knowledge and society are losing credibility. Central to the culture of the Enlightenment has been the presumption of scientific and philosophical reason laying bare universal truths about humanity, history, and nature; the assumption of the unity of humanity; the idea of Western development as marking a general path of social progess; and the role of scientific knowledge in promoting enlightenment and human freedom. The core Enlightenment ideas have been under suspicion for some time. They seem to ring less true today; at a minimum, they have the status of a belief, not a faith. In part, this is because critics have uncovered in the culture of Enlightenment a paradigm that legitimates sexism, professional social control, Eurocentrism, heterosexism, and colonialism.

The perception of cultural crisis is perhaps not a cause for despair. Admittedly, some critics have responded to this cultural crisis by advancing anti-Enlightenment values and social agendas, for example, calling for a return to religious culture or to a patriarchal family or to a corporatist, statist order. I believe, however, that most critics are looking for ways to preserve the Enlightenment values of autonomy, tolerance, equality, and democracy, but in ways that either greatly modify the Enlightenment heritage or articulate a post-Enlightenment perspective.

The term "postmodern" captures some of these cultural shifts. Critics see in postmodernity the triumph of relativism and nihilism, the collapse of standards and ideals, the loss of a vision of human progress and freedom, or a surrender to the commercialization of Western culture. I disagree. I favor Bauman's humane, progressive vision of postmodernity. At the heart of a postmodern culture is the acceptance of the irreducible pluralistic character of social experiences, identities, and standards of truth, moral rightness, and beauty. In place of the abstract, universal, identical self, a postmodern culture asserts selves that are differentiated and individuated by class, gender, race, sexuality, ethnicity, nationality, physical and psychological ableness, and on and on. In place of a universal, unitary concept of reason and uniform cultural standards, in a postmodern culture, we speak of traditions of reason and a plurality of cultural standards that express different traditions and communities. If modernity is organized around a series of neat divisions (family/economy, science/ideology, politics/morality) and hierarchies (e.g., male/female, high/mass culture, reason/desire) and foundational premises (e.g., reason, science, individualism, the subject, progress, the West, the identity of humanity), postmodernity underscores a process of dedifferentiation or the collapse of boundaries, the disruption of hierarchies, and the questioning of modern foundations and indeed all ultimate beliefs and values. Postmodernity may renounce the dream of one reason and one humanity marching forward along one path towards absolute freedom, but it offers its own ideal of a society that tolerates human differences, accepts ambiguity and uncertainty, and values choice, diversity, and democratization.

The end of the era of the disciplines, as we have known them, will not mean the end of the human studies or even of the hope that knowledge has a role to play in making a better world. As I outlined in part 3, I see new paradigms of human studies developing in the postwar West. They have, to varying degrees, broken away from Enlightenment assumptions without surrendering many of its values and social expectations. These new paradigms originated outside of the disciplines and have only recently begun to be incorporated into them. In the main, they are interdisciplinary and public centered and do not retreat from moral advocacy or partisanship.

How do post-Enlightenment paradigms of human studies contrast with the standard Enlightenment model? Three assumptions are fundamental to the Enlightenment paradigm. First, the social scientist is assumed to be capable of sufficient detachment from society and history to function as a "pure" medium of knowledge. The institution of science purges the scientist of his or her particular social interests, allowing the scientist to assume a universal, impartial interest in truth. Second, it is assumed that the object of knowledge – society or the social – exhibits an underlying universal structure. Whether the identity of the social universe is imagined to lie in universal laws or a core set of general problems (e.g., the problem of social action and order, the micro–macro or agency–structure or individual–social structure relation) that present themselves to any inquirer who has assumed the universal standpoint of the social scientist, the key point is that "society" functions as a fixed, constant, or identical object of knowledge. Human studies is imagined as a dialogue across generations about the nature of "the social." Third, the aim of the human studies is to arrive at a vocabulary that mirrors the structure of the social universe or, at least, illuminates its core processes and organizing principles. Although the accumulation of social knowledge is a value in itself, the ultimate value of science lies in its contribution to public enlightenment and social progress.

Post-Enlightenment paradigms of human studies may be contrasted along the same three dimensions. First, the social scientist is described as inextricably bound to his or her particular social and historical conditions. The social scientist cannot escape his or her social and historical identity. Social knowledge is said to bear the imprint of the gender, race, ethnicity, class, sexuality, nationality, and historical juncture of the social scientist. Social knowledge is, accordingly, always partial and perspectival and exhibits particular moral and ideological meanings. Second, it follows that, whether or not "the social" can be imagined as revealing a constant and universal structure, social scientists *construct* the social through the lens of their particular social standpoint. A post-Enlightenment paradigm favors a view of human studies less as a general, transhistorical reflection on "the social" than as a response to historically specific social conflict. Third, a post-Enlightenment paradigm links knowledge and power. To the extent that social scientists are seen as ordinary social actors whose interests and public concerns are carried into the realm of science, their products – social knowledges – are efforts to shape public life or alter the outcome of social disputes. Social knowledges, including the social sciences, are involved in the making of selves and societies. From sociology to psychology, the social sciences have been important social forces shaping social identities (e.g., deviant, criminal, heterosexual, female) and social norms (e.g., norms of health, normality, and success). The social sciences have been deeply implicated in struggles over sexuality, gender, race, ethnicity, work, politics, and education. Post-Enlightenment paradigms acknowledge the moral and political significance of the human studies; theorists in this tradition assume the role of public educator and advocate.

As Western societies edge into a postmodern era, we can expect to see changes in the social organization of the human studies. Paralleling broader social dynamics of dedifferentiation, I anticipate the blurring or collapse of disciplinary boundaries, a breakdown of the rigid separation of science, morality, and politics, deepening exchanges of expert knowledges and folk or public knowledges, the rise of social knowledges that combine genres (e.g., autobiography, empirical-analytic, fiction, and nonfiction), disciplinary languages, rhetorics, and styles of argumentation from diverse cultural traditions and communities. In the postmodern reorganization of knowledges, I anticipate the consolidation of a morally and politically engaged human studies that is anchored less in expert cultures than in public debates and conflicts, that is interdisciplinary, ecletic, moves between varied publics, and is deliberate in its moral commitments and pragmatic in its justifications.

In a postmodern culture, human studies would not be justified by appeals to knowledge for knowledge's sake or by the vague hope that knowledge yields progress. Today, we perceive knowledge as inextricably in the making of selves and societies. It can be a force of good or evil. The point is that knowledge is not innocent; its moral and political implications need to be considered.

The value of knowledge in a postmodern era would be related to the kinds of lives that it shapes and the ways that it anticipates a good society. Postmodern knowledges would require pragmatic rationales. We would need to ask: What do knowledges do? What ends or purposes do they, in principle, promote and with what consequences to individuals and institutions? Of course, we would expect that questions of social goals and values will be in dispute. Arguments would need to be made about the kinds of societies we want and why. In place of foundational appeals to human nature, God, reason, the laws of history and society, I imagine a postmodern culture in which appeals to cultural traditions, social practices, and conventions or arguments that draw on social and historical comparisons carry rhetorical authority. If the institutions of knowledge lost their legitimacy as sites of truth, in a postmodern culture, they would be defended as spaces where social actors can openly and freely debate the shape of society – what it is and ought to be. The institutions of knowledge would be valued as part of a democratic society that provides safe social space where its citizens can contest the contours of their social existence. In the end, human studies would stand for a commitment to an open, ongoing, inclusive conversation about society – who we are and where we are and should be going – where all views are welcome and where values and social ideals are stated frankly and debated.

Knowledge in the age of postmodernity will be permanently contested, not because truth surfaces only, and rarely, in the heat of battle, but because knowledge has come to be inseparable from power and is no longer assumed to be beneficent. An age of innocence is passing, an age when knowledge promised only hope. Today, knowledge – scientific, Western reason – bears the scars of its many wars. Its dreams are tattered and its confidence irrevocably shaken. In generations past, science and Western reason triumphed grandly by means of a relentless assault on its competitors: religion, myth, narrative, moral philosophy, folk knowledges. Today, it is as if those repressed rivals have returned to take their revenge. The towering grandeur of scientific reason has all but crumbled under a barrage of assault from those who claim to be its victims: people of color, non-Westerners, women, lesbians and gay men, the disabled, and the poor and economically disempowered. Its promise of freedom has a dark side: a ruthless wish to control and order everything and an intolerance toward the unruly and the deviant. Many will lament this loss of innocence and naive hope; I do . . . at times. However, as we enter a new age of permanent contestation and possible disaster, I envision hopeful futures. These are not dreams of an unencumbered, unrestrained self or society; they are hopeful imaginings of a human habitat that is respectful of differences, values expanded choices, offers increased options for social bonding and community formation, and encourages spirited efforts at negotiating just institutions and common social spaces.

Bibliographic Essay

Introduction

The assertion that sociology is in a state of crisis was advanced, in an influential formulation, by Alvin Gouldner in *The Coming Crisis of Western Sociology* (New York: Basic Books, 1970). Gouldner argued that sociology had abandoned the critical spirit of the Enlightenment. Sociology was either being absorbed into a state corporate welfare system as a tool of social control or had dead-ended in a pointless empiricism. Gouldner's critique echoed the ideas of C. Wright Mills's *The Sociological Imagination* whose own critical views reach back to Robert Lynd's *Knowledge for What* (New York: Grove Press, 1939) and Thorstein Veblen's *Higher Learning in America* (Standford: Academic Reprint, 1954 [1918]). My own discontent with social and sociological theory shares much with this current of the American pragmatic tradition. I am troubled by the tendency in sociological theory to abandon its moral and political public role in favor of the idol of scientific knowledge or the quest for a theoretical system. As sociological theory is removed from public debate and the conflicts, it becomes an insulated expert culture.

The idea of a publicly engaged sociology, a type of human studies that combines empirical social analysis with moral advocacy and political engagement, is gaining in appeal as the human sciences drift into either social irrelevance or become a tool of social control. My own ideas of a public sociology have been outlined in "The End of Sociological Theory," *Sociological Theory* 8 (Fall 1991), "Postmodern Anxiety: The Politics of Epistemology," *Sociological Theory* 8 (Fall 1991), and "Postmodern Social Theory as Narrative with a Moral Intent" in Steven Seidman and David Wagner, eds., *Postmodernism and Social Theory* (Oxford: Basil Blackwell, 1991). There is a considerable body of literature that sounds similar critical themes regarding the state of sociology. I recommend Richard Brown, *Society as Text* (Chicago: University of Chicago Press, 1987) and *Social Science as Civic Discourse* (Chicago: University of Chicago Press,

1989); Charles Lemert, "The Uses of French Structuralisms in Sociology," in George Ritzer, ed., *Frontiers of Social Theory* (New York: Columbia University Press, 1990); Ben Agger, *Socio(onto)logy* (Urbana: University of Illinois Press, 1989); Norman Denzin, "Postmodern Social Theory," *Sociological Theory* 4; and Ann Game, *Undoing the Social* (Toronto: University of Toronto Press, 1991). A similar critique of disciplinary science and theory has surfaced powerfully in anthropology. I refer the reader to James Clifford and George Marcus, *Writing Culture* (Berkeley: University of California Press, 1986) and Renato Rosaldo, *Culture and Truth* (Boston: Beacon Press, 1989). Also see Michael Shapiro, *Reading the Postmodern Polity* (Minneapolis: University of Minnesota Press, 1991) and Stephen White, *Political Theory and Postmodernism* (Cambridge: Cambridge University Press, 1991) for a similar argument in the context of political science. These movements challenging disciplinary knowledges draw heavily on the writings that I survey in part 3, in particular, the French poststructuralists and the writings of postmodern feminists. The work of Richard Rorty has been pivotal in the reorientation of the human studies toward a public-centered, pragmatic approach. See his *Philosophy and the Mirror of Nature* (Princeton: Princeton University Press, 1979) and the *Consequences of Pragmatism* (Minneapolis: University of Minnesota Press, 1982).

Chapter 1

Scholars disagree about the origins and meaning of the human sciences. The period between the early eighteenth and the early nineteenth centuries, the so-called Age of Enlightenment, is considered pivotal for the rise of a scientific human studies. The best general overview of the Enlightenment in English, especially as it relates to the rise of the social sciences, is the two-volume work by Peter Gay, *The Enlightenment* (New York: Norton, 1977). Gay disputes views that imagine the Enlightenment social thinkers as naive worshippers of individualism and progress. Nevertheless, he defends the Enlightenment as a major step forward in human progress; he celebrates the Enlightenment science of society as a carrier of liberal, progressive ideas and values. This remains the dominant interpretation by social scientists of the Enlightenment. This perspective is basic to Talcott Parsons's *The Structure of Social Action* (New York: Free Press, 1937), Jonathan Turner's and Leonard Beeghley's *The Emergence of Sociological Theory* (Belmont, CA: Wadsworth, 1989), Randall Collins and Michael Makowsky's *The Discovery of Society* (New York: Random House, 1989), and George Ritzer's *Classical Sociological Theory* (New York: McGraw-Hill, 1992). An alternative critical perspective holds that much of sociology abandoned, if not directly opposed, the critical progressive aims of the Enlightenment science of society. This influential interpretation has been advanced by Herbert Marcuse in *Reason and Revolution* (Boston: Beacon Press, 1968), Irving Zeitlin in *Ideology and the Development of Sociological Theory* (Englewood Cliffs, NJ: Prentice-Hall, 1987), Ernest Becker in *The Structure of Evil* (Glencoe, Il: Free Press, 1968) and *The Lost Science of Man* (New York: G. Braziller, 1971), and Goran Therborn in *Science, Class, and Society* (London: NLB, 1976). Recently, a somewhat new critical perspective on the Enlightenment has challenged the preceding understandings. For example, Michel Foucault's *The Order of Things* (New York: Vintage, 1966) interprets the Enlightenment as elaborating a new system of conceptual order aimed at social control. Foucault argues that the hidden meaning of the social sciences is that they functioned as part of a new disciplinary order defining and regulating bodies and behaviors. This critical perspective has been elaborated by Zygmunt Bauman in *Legislators and Interpreters* (Ithaca: Cornell University Press, 1987), a position that recalls the perspective of the Frankfurt school, for example, Theodor Adorno and Max Horkheimer, *Dialectic of Enlightenment* (New York: Continuum, 1972). Prior to the Frankfurt school and Foucault, there were romantic and conservative critics of the Enlightenment. They described the Enlightenment as destroying organic social bonds, undermining moral order, and setting in motion social forces of chaos and nihilism. This interpretation of the Enlightenment is powerfully developed by Robert Nisbet in *The Sociological Tradition* (New York: Basic Books, 1966) and Arthur Mitzman in *Sociology and Estrangement* (New York: Knopf, 1973).

There are many fine historical interpretations of the European social origins of the human sciences. In addition to those mentioned previously the reader might consult: Wolf Lepenies, *Between Literature and Science* (Cambridge: Cambridge University Press, 1988); Bruce Mazlish, *A New Science* (Oxford: Oxford University Press, 1989); Steven Seidman, *Liberalism and the Origins of European Social Theory* (Berkeley: University of California Press, 1983); Alvin Gouldner, *The Coming Crisis of Western Sociology* (New York: Avon Books, 1971); and Geoffrey Hawthorne, *Enlightenment and Despair* (Cambridge: Cambridge University Press, 1987).

Auguste Comte is recognized as the founding figure of sociology. Comte coined the term "sociology" and was perhaps the first European thinker to write as a sociologist. His main work is *The Positive Philosophy* (1830–1842) and the *System of Positive Polity* (1851–1854). Comte's *A General View of Positivism* (New York: R. Speller, 1957) provides an accessible introduction to his social thought. Unfortunately, there is no standard intellectual biography of Comte in English. There are some useful overviews available. I recommend Raymond Aron, *Main Curents in Sociological Thought*, Vol. 1 (New York: Anchor Books, 1968); Jonathan Turner and Leonard Beeghley, *The Emergence of Sociological Theory* (Belmont, CA: Wadsworth, 1989); Lewis Coser, *Masters of Sociological Thought* (New York: Harcourt Brace Jovanovich, 1971); and Frank Manual, *Prophets of Paris* (Cambridge: Harvard University Press, 1962).

Sociologists and social scientists disagree over whether to count Karl Marx as a social scientist, ideologue, or a moral philosopher. Parsons's *Structure of Social Action* positions Marx as a precursor to the true takeoff of a scientific social theory in Weber and Durkheim. On the other hand, some Marxists define Marx as marking a breakthrough to science in contrast to the bourgeois ideology of sociology and economics. This is the position of Therborn's *Science, Class, and Society*. The trend in the 1980s and 1990s is to view Marx as a distinctive voice in the development of a science of society. Moreover, even the fiercest critics of Marx acknowledge his enormous influence on the human sciences.

Marx's writings have been collected in Karl Marx and Friedrich Engels's *Collected Works*, 50 vols. (New York: International, 1976–1993). His major works include *The Economic and Philosophical Manuscripts of 1844*, *The German Ideology* (1845–1846), and *Capital*, 3 vols. (1867). The works of his chief collaborator Friedrich Engels should not be ignored, in particular, the *Condition of the Working Class in England* (1845) and *The Origin of the Family, Private Property, and the State* (1884).

The life of Marx has been detailed in a fine biography by David McLellan, *Karl Marx* (New York: Harper Colophon, 1973). An excellent personal and intellectual biography has been written by Jerrold Seigel, *Marx's Fate* (Princeton: Princeton University Press, 1978). There are many excellent overviews of Marx's social thought. I recommend Shlomo Avineri, *The Social and Political Thought of Karl Marx* (London: Cambridge University Press, 1968); George Lichtheim, *Marxism* (Columbia University Press, 1964); Louis Dumont, *From Mandeville to Marx* (Chicago: University of Chicago Press, 1977); G.A. Cohen, *Karl Marx's Theory of History* (Princeton: Princeton University Press, 1978); and Bertell Ollman, *Alienation* (Cambridge: Cambridge University Press, 1971). Particularly influential are interpretations of Marx from the perspective of French structuralism, for example, Louis Althusser's *For Marx* (New York: Vintage, 1970) and (with Etienne Balibar) *Reading Capital* (New York: Pantheon, 1977) and from the perspective of German critical theory, for example, Jürgen Habermas, *Knowledge and Human Interests* (Boston: Beacon, 1972), and, more recently, from the perspective of rational choice theory, for example, Jon Elster, *Making Sense of Marx* (Cambridge: Cambridge University Press,

1985) and John Roemer, ed., *Analytical Marxism* (Cambridge: Cambridge University Press, 1986). Marx's social ideas have proven enormously fruitful. His ideas have contributed to the formation of a great many important thinkers and schools of thought, for example, Antonio Gramsci, Georg Lükacs, Karl Korsch, Louis Althusser, Herbert Marcuse, Wilhelm Reich, structural Marxism, the Frankfurt school, existential Marxism, socialist feminism, conflict theory, and world systems theory.

For general overviews of the development of Marxism through the twentieth century, I recommend Leszek Kolakowski, *Main Currents of Marxism*, 3 vols. (New York: Oxford University Press, 1978); Alvin Gouldner, *Two Marxisms* (New York: Seabury Press, 1980); Perry Anderson, *Considerations of Western Marxism* (Chicago: University of Chicago Press, 1976) and *In the Tracks of Historical Materialism* (Chicago: University of Chicago Press, 1984); and Russell Jacoby, *Dialectic of Defeat* (Cambridge: Cambridge University Press, 1981).

For critical assessments of Marxism from a broadly sympathetic perspective, I recommend Stanley Aronowitz, *The Crisis in Historical Materialism* (South Hadley, MA: Praeger, 1981); Isaac Balbus, *Marxism and Domination* (Princeton: Princeton University Press, 1982); Anthony Giddens, *A Contemporary Critique of Historical Materialism* (Berkeley: University of California Press, 1981); Annette Kuhn and AnnMarie Wolpe, eds., *Feminism and Materialism* (London: Routledge, 1978); Lydia Sargent, ed., *Women and Revolution* (Boston: South End Press, 1981).

Chapter 2

The years between 1890 and 1920 have been described as the "classical" period of the human sciences. It was a watershed period in sociology. In Germany and France, sociology announced its arrival as a discipline and valid form of knowledge. Although such figures as Georg Simmel, Ferdinand Tönnies, and Gabriel Tarde were highly regarded in their time as social thinkers, the work of Durkheim and Weber, above all, has shaped the human studies through this century.

Durkheim's major works include *Montesquieu and Rousseau* (1983), *The Division of Labor in Society* (1893), *The Rules of Sociological Method* (1895), *Suicide* (1897), and *The Elementary Forms of Religious Life* (1912). He was the author of important posthumously published books: *Socialism* (1928), *Education and Society* (1922), *Professional Ethics and Civil Morals* (1957), and *Moral Education* (1973). The standard intellectual biography of Durkheim is Steven Lukes, *Emile Durkheim* (New York: Penguin, 1977). Many excellent overviews of Durkheim's social ideas are available in English: Robert Jones, *Emile Durkheim* (Newbury Park, CA: Sage, 1986); Steve Fenton, *Durkheim and Modern Sociology* (Cambridge; Cambridge University Press, 1984); Robert Nisbet, *The Sociology of Emile Durkheim* (New York: Oxford University Press, 1974); Stjepan Gabriel Mestrovic, *Emile Durkheim and the Reformation of Sociology* (Totawa, NJ: Roman and Littlefield, 1988). The more theoretically oriented reader should consult Parsons's *The Structure of Social Action* and, from a similarly Parsonian point of view, the second volume of Jeffrey Alexander's *Theoretical Logic in Sociology* (Berkeley: University of California Press, 1983). The second volume of Jürgen Habermas's *The Theory of Communicative Action* (Boston: Beacon Press, 1987) offers a powerful theoretical interpretation of Durkheim which integrates a Parsonian and broadly Marxian perspective. Anti-Parsonian interpretations of Durkheim include Whitney Pope, Jere Cohen, and Lawrence Hazelrigg, "On the Divergence of Weber and Durkheim: A Critique of Parsons's Convergence Thesis," *American Sociological Review* 48 (1983) and Anthony Giddens, *Emile Durkheim* (Cambridge: Cambridge University Press, 1972). Some recent interpretations have sought to break away from Parsonian-dominated discussions of Durkheim. In this regard, see Jennifer Lehman, *Deconstructing Durkheim* (New York: Routledge, 1993); Frank Pearce, *The Radical Durkheim* (London: Unwin Hyman, 1989); and Mark Cladis, *A Communitarian Defense of Liberalism* (Stanford: Stanford University Press, 1992).

Unlike Marx, Durkheim did not generate a wide range of schools, paradigms, or movements of social thought. He did create a Durkheimian school of sociology which was important in France in the first half of this century. The reader should consult Charles Lemert, ed., *French Sociology* (New York: Columbia University Press, 1981). However, his main influence has been on the rise of American functionalism: see Jonathan Turner and Alexandra Maryanski, *Functionalism* (Menlo Park, CA: Berganen/ Cummings Publishing Company,1979). More recently, Durkheim has been viewed as influencing a tradition of American microsocial analysis: see Randall Collins, *Three Sociological Traditions* (Oxford: Oxford University Press, 1985).

Weber's major works include *The Protestant Ethic and the Spirit of Capitalism* (1904–1905), *The Religion of China* (1916), *The Religion of India* (1916), *Ancient Judaism* (1917–1919), and the volumes collected under the title *Economy and Society* (Totawa, NJ: Bedminster Press, 1968). His *General Economic History* (1927) and *The Agrarian Sociology of Ancient Civilizations* (1896) remain important works. The essays collected under the title *The Methodology of the Social Sciences* (1903–1917) detail his views on science. Readers should not miss his powerful political and existential statements "Science as a Vocation" and "Politics as a

Vocation," both collected in Hans Gerth and C.W. Mills, eds., *From Max Weber* (Oxford: Oxford University Press, 1958). The standard and only detailed biography remains that of his wife, Marianne Weber, *Max Weber* (New York: Wiley, 1975). Reinhard Bendix's *Max Weber* (New York: Doubleday, 1962) remains the most accessible comprehensive overview of Weber's social ideas in English. Weber's political ideas have been detailed in Wolfgang Mommsen's monumental *Max Weber and German Politics* (Chicago: University of Chicago Press, 1984). Other excellent interpretations of Weber's political ideas are to be found in Robert Beetham, *Max Weber and the Theory of Modern Politics* (London: Allen & Unwin, 1974) and Robert Eden, *Political Leadership and Nihilism* (Tampa, FL: University Presses of Florida, 1983). There are quite a few superb overviews of Weber's social thought. I recommend the following for their accessibility and intelligence: Wolfgang Mommsen, *The Age of Bureaucracy* (New York: Basil Blackwell, 1974); Dirk Kasler, *Weber* (Chicago: University of Chicago Press, 1988); Frank Parkin, *Max Weber* (New York: Tavistock Publications, 1982); and Rogers Brubacker, *The Limits of Rationality* (London: Allen & Unwin, 1984). Interpretations that stress Weber as a social theorist have been influenced powerfully by Parsons's *Structure of Social Action*. In this regard, I recommend the outstanding volumes by Jeffrey Alexander, *Theoretical Logic in Sociology*, Vol. 3 (Berkeley: University of California Press, 1983); Jürgen Habermas, *The Theory of Communicative Action*, Vol. 2 (Boston: Beacon Press, 1987); and Wolfgang Schluchter, *The Rise of Western Rationalism* (Berkeley: University of California Press, 1981). From a decidedly non-Parsonian perspective, the reader should consult Anthony Kronman, *Max Weber* (Stanford: Stanford University Press, 1983); Alan Sica, *Irrationality and Social Order* (Berkeley: University of California Press, 1988); Guenther Roth and R. Bendix, *Scholarship and Partisanship* (Berkeley: University of California Press, 1971); Stephen Turner and Regis Factor, *Max Weber and the Dispute Over Reason and Value* (London: Routledge, 1984); and Martin Albrow, *Max Weber's Construction of Social Theory* (London: Macmillan, 1990). Weber's perspective on history and modernity is the focus of Lawrence Scaff, *Fleeing the Iron Cage* (Berkeley: University of California Press, 1989); Arthur Mitzman, *The Iron Cage* (New York: Grosset & Dunlap, 1969); and Scott Lash and Sam Whimster, eds., *Max Weber, Rationality and Modernity* (London: Allen & Unwin, 1987). An interesting feminist perspective on Weber is provided by Roslyn Bologh, *Love or Greatness* (London: Unwin Hyman, 1990).

Weber did not originate a school of sociology. There is no distinctively Weberian tradition of sociology or social thought. Yet he produced a body of work that has proven enormously fruitful in shaping twentieth century social thought. In particular, Weber has been pivotal in shaping social action theory in the tradition of Talcott Parsons; he has influenced the rise in an interpretive sociology, for example, the phenomenological sociology of Alfred Schutz and Peter Berger. Along with Durkheim, Weber has been central in shaping a cultural sociology, for example, the writings of Robert Bellah (see chapter 8) and Robert Wuthnow, *Meaning and Moral Order* (Berkeley: University of California Press, 1988). Weber has been claimed as a pivotal figure in giving shape to a comparative historical sociology, a tradition exemplified by Reinhart Bendix, *Kings or People* (Berkeley: University of California Press, 1978) and S.N. Eisenstadt, *Tradition, Change and Modernity* (New York: Wiley, 1973). Finally, Weber has been claimed as both central to legitimating so-called conflict theory and as promoting the cultural criticism of the Frankfurt school. Weber's writings on religion and modernization, bureaucracy, social stratification, and charisma have generated fruitful research traditions.

There are many fine overviews of the formation of classical sociology. In particular, I recommend Robert Nisbet, *The Sociological Tradition* (New York: Basic Books, 1966); Anthony Giddens, *Capitalism and Modern Social Theory* (Cambridge: Cambridge University Press, 1971); Alvin Gouldner, *The Coming Crisis of Western Sociology* (New York: Avon Books, 1971); Goran Therborn, *Science, Class, and Society* (London: NLB, 1976); Steven Seidman, *Liberalism and the Origins of European Social Theory* (Berkeley: University of California Press, 1983); Jonathan Turner and Leonard Beeghley, *The Emergence of Sociological Theory* (Homewood, Il: Doresey Press, 1981); Wolf Lepenies, *Between Literature and Science* (Cambridge: Cambridge University Press, 1988); Alan Wolfe, *Whose Keeper?* (Berkeley: University of California Press, 1989); and Geoffrey Hawthorne, *Enlightenment and Despair* (Cambridge: Cambridge University Press, 1976). However, these interpretations, while often critical in their impulse, are decidedly Eurocentric and male-centered in their conception. We have, as yet, to see the appearance of multiculturalist histories of social thought. In this regard, the recent publication of Charles Lemert's *Multicultural Social Theory* (Boulder, CO: Westview, 1993), suggests a new wave of histories that will substantially rewrite the story of the rise of the human sciences.

Chapter 3

I have relied upon a great many excellent accounts of the early history of American sociology. The following books have proved most helpful: Roscoe Hinkle, *Founding Years of American Sociology: 1881–1915*

(Boston: Routledge, 1980); Stephen Turner and Jonathan Turner, *The Impossible Science* (Newbury Park, CA: Sage, 1990); Arthur Vidich and Stanford Lyman, *American Sociology* (New Haven: Yale University Press, 1985); Ernest Becker, *The Lost Science of Man* (New York: George Braziller, 1971); Dennis Smith, *The Chicago School* (London: Macmillan, 1988): Robert Bierstedt, *American Sociological Theory* (New York: Academic Press, 1981); Herman Schwendinger and Julia Schwendinger, *The Sociologists of the Chair* (New York: Basic Books, 1974); Thomas Haskell, *The Emergence of Professional Social Science* (Bloomington, IL: Indiana University Press, 1977); David Lewis and Robert Smith, *American Sociology and Pragmatism* (Chicago: University of Chicago Press, 1980); and Dorothy Ross, *The Origins of American Social Science* (Cambridge: Cambridge University Press, 1991). Unfortunately, there has yet to be a history of American sociology written from the point of view of feminism or from an African-American perspective. The standard histories, even the preceding ones which are mostly excellent, continue to relate a story that excludes or marginalizes women, people of color, and various radical movements of social thought.

Moreover, there are no comprehensive histories of American sociology. Most histories focus on the early years. There are no accounts that span the founding years to the post-World War II period. We lack historical overviews that place American sociologists in a broad social and intellectual context, relating them to both European and American developments. It is my contention, of course, that any such history would have to place Talcott Parsons at the center. It would have to account for how a Parsonian reconfiguring of American sociology could occur in light of the dominance of Comtean, Spencerian, and pragmatic traditions of social thinking.

Talcott Parsons was enormously prolific. Unlike Comte, Marx, or Weber, he wrote exclusively as a sociologist. His major works include *The Structure of Social Action* (1937), (with Edward Shils) *Toward a General Theory of Action* (Cambridge: Harvard University Press, 1951), *The Social System* (Glencoe, IL: Free Press, 1951), *Societies* (Englewood Cliffs, NJ: Prentice-Hall, 1966), and *Social Systems and the Evolution of Action Theory* (New York: Free Press, 1977). Many of his most important empirically oriented statements are collected in *Essays in Sociological Theory* (New York: Free Press, 1954), *Structure and Process in Modern Societies* (New York: Free Press, 1960), and (with Gerald Platt), *The American University* (Cambridge: Harvard University Press, 1973). Interpretations of Parsons have been deeply divided between defenders and critics. For example, Alvin Gouldner's *The Coming Crisis of Western Sociology* (New York: Basic Books, 1970) is among the earliest and more sophisticated critical interpretations. Benton Johnson, *Functionalism in Modern*

Sociology (Morristown, NJ: General Learning Press, 1975) defends Parsons. In the last two decades, a more nuanced and appreciative, even if critical, literature on Parsons has appeared. Among the more important and accessible of this literature, I recommend Jeffrey Alexander, *Twenty Lectures* (New York: Columbia University Press, 1987); Leon Mayhew, ed., *Talcott Parsons* (Chicago: University of Chicago Press, 1982); and Robert Holton and Bryan Turner, *Talcott Parsons* (London: Routledge, 1986). For the reader interested in the more theoretically demanding debate over Parsons today, I suggest volume 4 of Jeffrey Alexander's *Theoretical Logic in Sociology* (Berkeley: University of California Press, 1983) and Richard Münch, *Theory of Action* (London: Routledge, 1987).

Chapter 4

In this chapter, I offered a very selective interpretive sketch of the development of sociological theory in post-World War II United States. I focused on particular theorists and texts to make some general points about the shape of American sociological theory. I do try, however, to at least allude to the historical context and social meaning of these intellectual developments. Unfortunately, I was unable to rely on existing historical work since virtually none exists. Most books on contemporary sociological theory provide only the barest, if any, allusion to the social and historical context of theory. Typically, such books classify theory into schools or paradigms that are viewed as responding to a limited set of identical problems or topics, for example, the nature of society, or the explanation of individual behavior, social order, and change. Each theory school is presented with an eye to major figures, texts, and strengths and limits. For example, in *Contemporary Sociological Theory* (Englewood Cliffs, NJ: Prentice-Hall, 1991), Ruth Wallace and Alison Wolf begin with a short chapter defining sociological theory, followed by chapters on functionalism, conflict theory, rational choice theory, symbolic interactionism, phenomenology, and alternative perspectives which include structuralism, structuration theory, and sociobiology. I take issue not only with their particular typological approach to theory but, more to the point, with their ahistorical presentation of theory. Theorists are presented as if theory is a permanent dialogue on a set of universal problems addressing the nature of society. Unfortunately, this textbook is typical of discussions of contemporary sociological theory. I have tried to place theorists and their work in their specific social setting, as enmeshed in the events and conflicts of the time. If my specific observations fail to convince, I hope the reader at least comes away with a view of theory as meaningful only in relation to a specific social and intellectual historical context.

Peter Berger's major works include (with Thomas Luckmann) *The Social Construction of Reality* (New York: Doubleday, 1966), *The Sacred Canopy* (New York: Doubleday, 1969), *A Rumor of Angels* (New York: Doubleday, 1970), (with Brigitte Berger and Hansfried Kellner), *The Homeless Mind* (New York: Doubleday, 1973), and *Capitalist Revolution* (New York: Basic Books, 1986). Assessments of Berger's sociology can be found in James Hunter and Stephen Ainlay, eds., *Making Sense of Modern Times* (London: Routledge, 1986). Berger's work is heavily influenced by classical sociology and by the philosophical movements of existential phenomenology, in particular, the ideas associated with Edmund Husserl, *Ideas* (New York: Macmillan, 1975); Jean-Paul Sartre, *Being and Nothingness* (New York: Washington Square Press, 1971); and Martin Heidegger, *Being and Time* (New York: Harper, 1960). Especially relevant for Peter Berger is the work of Alfred Schutz, *Collected Papers*, 3 vols. (The Hague: Martinus Nijhoff, 1962–1966) and Thomas Luckmann, *The Structure of the Lifeworld* (Evanston, IL: Northwestern University Press, 1973).

Ralf Dahrendorf's key sociological works are *Class and Conflict in Industrial Society* (Stanford: Stanford University Press, 1959), *Essays in the Theory of Society* (Stanford: Stanford University Press, 1968), *The New Liberty* (London: Routledge, 1975), and *Life Chances* (London: Weidenfeld and Nicolson, 1979). Dahrendorf has been interpreted and largely engaged in American sociology as a conflict theorist. See the critical discussions by Peter Weingart, "Beyond Parsons? A Critique of Ralf Dahrendorf's Conflict Theory," *Social Forces* 48 (December 1969), Jonathan Turner, "From Utopia to Where: A Strategy for Reformulating Dahrendorf's Conflict Model," *Social Forces* 52 (December 1973), and Randall Collins, *Three Sociological Traditions* (Oxford: Oxford University Press, 1985).

Randall Collins's main works are *Conflict Sociology* (New York: Academic Press, 1975), (with Michael Makowsky) *The Discovery of Society* (New York: Random House, 1989), *The Credential Society* (New York: Academic Press, 1979), *Sociology since Midcentury* (New York: Academic Press, 1981), *Weberian Sociological Theory* (Cambridge: Cambridge University Press, 1985), and *Three Sociological Traditions* (Oxford: Oxford University Press, 1985). Collins draws from classical European sociology, the micro-interactionist or interpretive tradition associated with ethnomethodology, symbolic interactionism, and the work of Durkheim and Goffman, at least with regard to their emphasis on the ritualistic structuring of daily life. A recent clear statement of Collins's position is "Conflict Theory and the Advance of Macro-Historical Sociology," in George Ritzer, ed., *Frontiers of Social Theory* (New York: Columbia University Press, 1990).

Peter Blau's major theoretical statements include *Exchange and Power in Social Life* (New York: John Wiley, 1964), *Inequality and Heterogeneity* (New York: Free Press, 1977), "Elements of Sociological Theorizing," *Humboldt Journal of Social Relations* 7 (Fall–Winter, 1979–1980) and (with Joseph Schwartz), *Cross-cutting Social Circles* (Orlando, FL: Academic Press, 1984). Blau's work was initially situated in the context of so-called exchange theory. For accounts of this theory and Blau's relation to it, see Karen Cook, ed., *Social Exchange Theory* (Newbury Park, CA: Sage, 1987); Anthony Heath, *Rational Choice and Social Exchange* (Cambridge: Cambridge University Press, 1976); and M.J. Mulkay, *Functionalism, Exchange, Theoretical Strategy* (New York: Schocken Books, 1971). Blau's later work has been described as representing a distinctive paradigm of "structural" sociology. For discussions of American structural sociology and Blau's role in this so-called paradigm, see Jonathan Turner, *The Structure of Sociological Theory* and Craig Calhoun et al., eds., *Structures of Power and Constraint* (Cambridge: Cambridge University Press, 1990).

Sociological theory in the 1980s and 1990s cannot be easily summarized or reduced to a few key movements, figures, or texts. Nevertheless, I have highlighted certain important developments in light of the broad social and historical sketch that I outlined in chapters 3 and 4. I emphasized the resurgence of a strong natural scientific program for sociology in reaction to the politicization of theory in the previous two decades. I referred to the following work as signaling this trend: Jonathan Turner, ed., *Theory Building in Sociology* (Newbury Park, CA: Sage, 1989) and *The Structure of Sociological Theory*, Part 6, and "In Defense of Positivism," *Sociological Theory 3* (1985); Walter Wallace, "Toward a Disciplinary Matrix in Sociology," in Neil Smelser, ed., *Handbook of Sociology* (Newbury Park, CA: Sage, 1988); Thomas Fararo, "The Spirit of Unification in Sociological Theory 7 (1988); James Coleman, *Foundations of Social Theory* (Cambridge: Belknap Press of Harvard University Press, 1990); Randall Collins, *Theoretical Sociology* (San Diego, CA: Harcourt Brace Jovanovich, 1988); and Joseph Berger and David Wagner, "Do Sociological Theories Grow?" *American Journal of Sociology* 90 (1985). Opposing the program of scientific theory is a strong program of grand theory, though both share a longing for certainty, foundations, and conceptual unity. With regard to the latter trend, I have referred to the work of Jeffrey Alexander, *Theoretical Logic in Sociology*, 4 vols. (Berkeley: University of California Press, 1982–1984) and Anthony Giddens, *The Constitution of Society* (Berkeley: University of California Press, 1984), *The Consequences of Modernity* (Stanford: Stanford University Press, 1990), and *Modernity and Self-Identity* (Stanford: Stanford University Press, 1991).

Chapter 5

In his short life, C. Wright Mills wrote a series of important works in sociology and social criticism. His 'trilogy' remains the core: *The New Men of Power* (New York: Harcourt, Brace, & Co., 1948), *White Collar* (Oxford: Oxford University Press, 1951), and *The Power Elite* (Oxford: Oxford University Press, 1956). His major statement on sociology as a critical public discourse is *The Sociological Imagination* (Oxford: Oxford University Press, 1960). His critical relation to Marxism is to be found in *The Marxists* (New York: Dell Publishing Co., 1962). Many of his key theoretical and empirical essays are collected in the volume *Power, Politics, and People* (New York: Oxford University Press, 1963).

Mills's social ideas were heavily influenced by European classical sociology and American pragmatism. We recall that his dissertation was on pragmatism, posthumously published as *Sociology and Pragmatism* (New York: Paine-Whitman, 1964). Bruce Kuklick's *Rise of American Philosophy* (New Haven: Yale University Press, 1977) provides a fine overview of the intellectual context and meaning of pragmatic thinking. The reader should consult Irving Louis Horowitz, *C. Wright Mills* (New York: Free Press, 1983) for an overview of Mills's life and work. A general portrait of Mills from a radical social perspective is offered by Joseph Scimecca, *The Sociological Theory of C. Wright Mills* (Port Washington, NY: Kennikat Press, 1977).

Mills's social ideas generated a great deal of controversy. In particular, *The Power Elite* caused a public debate because it challenged both the traditions of American pluralism and Marxist class analysis. The reader who wishes a taste of the controversy should consult William Domhoff and Hoyt Balard, eds., *C. Wright Mills and The Power Elite* (Boston: Beacon, 1968). A volume that collects critical assessments of Mills's social ideas is Irving Louis Horowitz, ed., *The New Sociology* (London: Oxford University Press, 1964).

Jürgen Habermas is an enormously prolific theorist. His writings span philosophy, politics, and sociology. His most important social theoretical writings are *Knowledge and Human Interests* (Boston: Beacon Press, 1971), *Theory and Practice* (Boston: Beacon Press, 1973), *Toward a Rational Society* (Boston: Beacon Press, 1970), *Legitimation Crisis* (Boston: Beacon Press, 1975), *Communication and the Evolution of Society* (Boston: Beacon Press, 1979), *The Theory of Communicative Action*, 2 vols. (Boston: Beacon Press, 1984–1987). His early works, recently translated into English, *The Logic of the Social Sciences* and *The Decliner of the Public Sphere*, a historical and empirical social analysis, remain key works in social theory.

Habermas's work is connected to the evolution of the Frankfurt school of critical social theory. Its founding figures included Max Horkheimer, *Critical Theory* (New York: Herder and Herder, [1932–1934] 1972); Theodor Adorno (with Max Horkheimer) *The Dialectic of Enlightenment* (New York: Seabury, [1944] 1969); and Herbert Marcuse, *One-Dimensional Man* (Boston: Beacon Press, 1964). Excellent historical overviews of the Frankfurt school are provided by Martin Jay, *The Dialectical Imagination* (Boston: Little, Brown, 1973) and Helmut Dubiel, *Theory and Politics* (Cambridge: MIT Press, 1985). A fine succinct statement is Robert Antonio, "The Origin, Development, and Contemporary Status of Critical Theory," *The Sociological Quarterly* 24 (Summer 1983). Although influenced by many other intellectual currents and traditions, Habermas's work is very much an effort to rethink critical theory in late twentieth century. In this regard, see Albrecht Wellmer's *The Critical Theory of Society* (New York: Herder and Herder, 1971). There are quite a few excellent overviews of Habermas. In particular, I recommend Thomas McCarthy, *The Critical Theory of Jürgen Habermas* (Cambridge: MIT Press, 1978) and David Held, *An Introduction to Critical Theory* (Berkeley: University of California Press, 1980).

Habermas's work has been the object of much critical discussion. For critical analyses of his work through the 1970s, see John Thompson and David Held, eds., *Habermas* (London: Macmillan, 1982) and Richard Bernstein, ed., *Habermas and Modernity* (Cambridge, Mass.: MIT Press, 1985). For discussions of *The Theory of Communicative Action* in relation to Habermas's oeuvre, I recommend Seyla Benhabib, *Critique, Norm, and Utopia* (New York: Columbia University Press, 1986); David Ingram, *Habermas and the Dialectic of Reason* (New Haven: Yale University Press, 1987); and Rick Roderick, *Habermas and the Foundations of Critical Theory* (London: Macmillan, 1986).

Chapter 6

There is surprisingly little written by way of overviews of French poststructural social theory in English. I cannot point to any one volume that offers a comprehensive historical and interpretive analysis. However, the recent volume by Steven Best and Douglas Kellner, *Postmodern Theory* (New York: The Guilford Press, 1991) provides a serious critical analysis of many of the leading (male) French poststructuralists. For perspectives on the broader intellectual context of postwar France, the reader should consult Mark Poster, *Existential Marxism in Postwar France* (NJ: Princeton University Press, 1975); Edith Kurzweil, *The Age of Structuralism* (New York:

Columbia University Press, 1980); and Jim Miller, *History and Human Existence* (Berkeley: University of California Press, 1979). An excellent overview of French poststructuralism is provided by Jonathan Culler, *On Deconstruction* (Ithaca: Cornell University Press, 1982).

Jean-Francois Lyotard is a prolific author. His major statements in English include *The Postmodern Condition* (Minneapolis: University of Minnesota Press, 1984), *Driftworks* (New York: Semiotext(e), 1984), *The Differend* (Minneapolis: University of Minnesota Press, 1988), (with Jean-Loup Thebaud) *Postmodernism Explained* (Minneapolis: University of Minnesota Press, 1993), and *Just Gaming* (Minneapolis: University of Minnesota Press, 1985). Selections of Lyotard's writings are available in Andrew Benjamin, ed., *The Lyotard Reader* (Oxford: Basil Blackwell, 1989). For critical discussions of Lyotard's work, I recommend Steven Best and Douglas Kellner, *Postmodern Theory*; Geoffrey Bennington, *Lyotard* (New York: Columbia University Press, 1988); Seyla Benhabib, "Epistemologies of Postmodernism: A Rejoinder to Jean-Francois Lyotard," in *New German Critique* 22 (1984); and Richard Rorty, "Habermas and Lyotard on Post-Modernity," *Praxis International* 4 (1984).

Jean Baudrillard's work can be divided between his early writings which fuse semiotics and Marxism and his later statements which might be characterized as social poststructuralism. With regard to the early writings available in English, the reader should consult *The Mirror of Production* (St Louis: Telos Press, 1975) and *For a Critique of the Political Economy of the Sign* (St. Louis: Telos Press, 1981). The chief statements of his "social poststructuralism" are *Simulations* (New York: Semiotext(e), 1981), *In The Shadow of the Silent Majorities* (New York: Semiotext(e), 1983), *Fatal Strategies* (New York: Semiotext(e) 1990), *Forget Foucault* (New York: Semiotext(e), 1987), *America* (London: Verso, 1988), and *Seduction* (New York: St. Martin's Press, 1990). A useful, though somewhat limited, anthology is Mark Poster, ed., *Jean Baudrillard* (Stanford: Stanford University Press, 1988). Useful critical discussions of Baudrillard as a social theorist include Douglas Kellner, *Jean Baudrillard* (Cambridge: Polity Press, 1989); Mike Gane, *Baudrillard* (New York: Routledge, 1991); and William Bogard, "Closing Down the Social: Baudrillard's Challenge to Contemporary Sociology," *Sociological Theory* 8 (1990).

Michel Foucault authored a series of books that are central to debates over social theory and society. His early writings were deeply influenced by structuralism, especially *The Order of Things* (New York: Vintage, 1973) and *Madness and Civilization* (New York: Vintage, 1973). Although Foucault retains a focus on structural analysis, his subsequent writings highlight a concern with institutional practices and power. His major "social poststructural" statements are *Discipline and Punish* (New York:

Vintage, 1979), and *The History of Sexuality*, Vols. 1–3 (New York: Vintage, 1980–1988). Questions of knowledge, theory, and politics are discussed in several key essays collected in *Power/Knowledge* (New York: Pantheon, 1980). A fine anthology has been compiled by Paul Rabinow, ed., *The Foucault Reader* (New York: Pantheon, 1984). Interviews with Foucault are an accessible way to his basic ideas. The reader should consult James Bernauer and David Rasmussen, eds., *Power/Knowledge, The Final Foucault* (Cambridge: MIT Press, 1988); Lawrence Kritzman, *Michel Foucault* (New York: Routledge, 1988), "Final Interview," *Raritan* 5 (1985). Two biographies on Foucault have been written: Didier Eribon, *Michel Foucault* (Cambridge: Harvard University Press, 1991) and James Miller, *The Passion of Michel Foucault* (New York: Simon & Schuster, 1993). There are many fine critical overviews of Foucault's ideas. Among the more useful and accessible interpretations are Alan Sheridan, *Foucault* (New York: Tavistock, 1980); Barry Smart, *Michel Foucault* (New York: Tavistock, 1985); David Shumway, *Michel Foucault* (Boston: Twayne Publishers, 1989). There is a wide-ranging critical debate around Foucault's ideas. A useful overview in this regard is David Couzens Hoy, ed., *Foucault*, (Oxford: Basil Blackwell, 1986); also see Mark Poster, *Foucault, Marxism and History* (Oxford: Polity Press, 1984); Barry Smart, *Foucault, Marxism and Critique* (London: Routledge, 1983); Hubert Dreyfus and Paul Rabinow, *Michel Foucault* (Chicago: University of Chicago Press, 1982); Jana Sawicki, *Disciplining Foucault* (New York: Routledge, 1991); John Rajchman, *Michel Foucault* (New York: Columbia University Press, 1985).

Chapter 7

The term "new social movements" is intended to contrast with working class movements on the one side and single-interest group organizations such as the Teamsters union or the National Firearm Association on the other side. These movements are said to be concerned centrally with quality-of-life issues – the environment, health care, education, personal well-being – in contrast to the focus on economic issues and institutional aspects of politics. For useful and accessible overview discussions of the new social movements, the reader should consult Jean Cohen, "Strategy or Identity: New Theoretical Paradigms and Contemporary Social Movements," *Social Research* 52 (Winter 1985); Klaus Eder, "The New Social Movements: Moral Crusades, Political Pressure Groups or Social Movements," *Social Research* 52 (Winter 1985); Alberto Melucci, "The New Social Movements," *Social Science Information* 19 (1980).

Feminism preceded the 1960s in the United States. Useful overviews of the history of feminism in the United States can be found in Ellen Carol Dubois, *Feminism and Suffrage* (Ithaca: Cornell University Press, 1978); Eleanor Flexner, *Century of Struggle* (Cambridge: Harvard University Press, 1975); and William O'Neill, *The Rise and Fall of Feminism in America* (Chicago: Quadrangle, 1969). For analyses of the women's movement in the postwar period, I recommend Sara Evans, *Personal Politics* (New York: Knopf, 1979); Judith Hole and Ellen Levine, *Rebirth of Feminism* (New York: New York Times Books, 1971); and Jo Freeman, *The Politics of Women's Liberation* (New York: David MacKay, 1975). There are several excellent overviews of contemporary feminist theory. The reader should consult the following: Alison Jagger, *Feminist Politics and Human Nature* (Totawa, NJ: Rowman and Allenheld, 1983); and Josephine Donavan, *Feminist Theory* (New York: Frederick Ungar Publishing Co., 1985). For feminist theory from the perspective of women of color, see the classic text Cherrie Moraga and Gloria Anzuldua, eds., *This Bridge Called My Back* (New York: Kitchen Table; Women of Color Press, 1981). The classic statement of lesbian feminism is "Woman Identified Woman" in Anne Koedt et al., eds., *Radical Feminism* (New York: Quadrangle Books, 1973); also see the statements collected in Nancy Myron and Charlotte Bunch, eds., *Lesbianism and the Women's Movement* (Baltimore, MD: Diana Press, 1974). A critical discussion of lesbian feminism is available in the fine volume by Shane Phelan, *Identity Politics* (Philadelphia: Temple University Press, 1989). Overviews of the feminist sexuality debates can be found in Ann Ferguson, *Blood at the Root* (London: Pandora, 1989) and Steven Seidman, *Embattled Eros* (New York: Routledge, 1992).

A self-conscious postmodern feminism did not surface until the late 1980s. Donna Haraway has been a key figure. Her "A Manifesto for Cyborgs: Science, Technology, and Socialist Feminism in the 1980s," framed the discussion between feminism and postmodernism. Her writings, collected in *Primate Visions* (New York: Routledge, 1989) and *Simians, Cyborgs, and Women* (New York: Routledge, 1991), are crucial to this debate. Haraway's work appeared simultaneously with other key texts rethinking feminism from a postmodern point of view. In particular, Sandra Harding, *The Science Question in Feminism* (Ithaca, New York: Cornell University Press, 1986), Nancy Fraser and Linda Nicholson, "Social Criticism without Philosophy: An Encounter between Feminism and Postmodernism," in Linda Nicholson, ed., *Feminism/Postmodernism* (New York: Routledge, 1990); and Jane Flax, "Postmodernism and Gender Relations in Feminist Theory," in *Feminism/Postmodernism* were important efforts in imagining a postmodern feminism. Judith Butler's *Gender Trouble* (New York: Routledge, 1991) has brought French poststructuralism to bear on feminist theory and politics. There are several excellent volumes exhibiting the postmodern turn of feminism. The reader should begin with Linda Nicholson's *Feminism/Postmodernism*, which contains many major statements for and against postmodern feminism. In addition, I recommend Chris Weedon, *Feminist Practice and Poststructuralist Theory* (Oxford: Basil Blackwell, 1987); Judith Butler and Joan Scott, eds., *Feminists Theorize the Political* (New York: Routledge, 1992); and Michele Barrett and Anne Phillips, eds., *Destabilizing Theory* (Stanford: Stanford University Press, 1992).

A broad overview of African-American thought and politics in the twentieth century is available in Harold Cruse, *The Crisis of the Negro Intellectual* (New York: William Morrow and Co., 1967). The rise of a Black power movement and ideology is surveyed in John McCartney, *Black Power Ideologies* (Philadelphia: Temple University Press, 1992). Also see Edward Green, ed., *Black Liberation Politics* (Boston: Allyn and Bacon, 1971) and Stokely Carmichael and Charles Hamilton, *Black Power* (New York: Vintage, 1967). A broad overview of postwar Black politics is provided by Manning Marable, *Black American Politics* (London: Verso, 1985).

Molefi Kete Asante is the major figure in fashioning an Afrocentric social theory. His key works are *Afrocentrity* (Buffalo: Amulefi, 1980) and *The Afrocentric Idea* (Philadelphia: Temple University Press, 1987).

Patricia Hill Collins's *Black Feminist Thought* is an important effort to fuse Afrocentrism and Western feminism. Her work should be grasped in relation to the development of a powerful tradition of Black feminism. In this regard, I recommend Bell Hooks, *Ain't I a Woman* (Boston: South End Press, 1981), *Feminist Theory* (Boston: South End Press, 1984), and *Yearning* (Boston: South End Press, 1990); Barbara Smith, ed., *Home Girls* (New York: Kitchen Table, Women of Color Press, 1983); Gloria Anzuldua and Cherrie Moraga eds. *This Bridge Called My Back* (New York: Watertown, Persephone, 1981); Audre Lorde, *Zami, A New Spelling of My Name* (Trumansberg, NY: Crossing, 1983) and *Sister Outsider* (Trumansberg, NY: Crossing, 1984).

Kwame Anthony Appiah's *In My Father's House* (Oxford: Oxford University Press, 1992) is a critical challenge to Afrocentrism without abandoning a critical perspective on Eurocentrism. His work should be seen as part of a broader movement among people of color to craft a critical perspective on Eurocentrism that draws heavily on postmodern assumptions. In this regard, see Cornell West, "The New Politics of Difference," *October* 53 (1990); Kobena Mercer, "Welcome to the Jungle: Identity and Diversity in Postmodern Politics," in Jonathan Rutherford, ed., *Identity, Community, Culture, Difference* (London: Lawrence & Wishart, 1990); Henry Louis Gates, Jr., ed., *'Race,' Writing, and Difference* (Chicago: University of

Chicago Press, 1986); Gloria Anzuldua, *Borderlands/La Frontera* (San Francisco: Spinsters/Aunt Lute, 1987); Gayatri Spivak, *In Other Worlds* (New York: Routledge, 1987); Minh-ha Trinh, *Woman, Native, Other* (Bloomington: Indiana University Press, 1989); and Homi Bhahba, "The Other Question – The Stereotype and Colonial Discourse," *Screen* 24 (1983).

There are several fine overviews of the lesbian and gay movement and social thought available, in particular, Barry Adam, *The Rise of a Gay and Lesbian Movement* (Boston: G.K. Hall, 1987); Dennis Altman, *Homosexual Liberation and Oppression* (New York: Outerbridge & Dienstfrey, 1971); John D'Emilio, *Sexual Politics, Sexual Communities* (Chicago: University of Chicago Press, 1983); and Margaret Cruikshank, *The Gay and Lesbian Liberation Movement* (New York: Routledge, 1992).

The new history and theory of homosexuality and sexuality is much indebted to Michel Foucault's effort to theorize sexuality as a social and political event. Foucault's efforts were paralleled by the work of Jeffrey Weeks. His major statements include *Coming Out* (London: Quartet, 1977), *Sex, Politics, and Society* (London: Longman, 1981), *Sexuality and Its Discontents* (London: Routledge, 1985), and *Sexuality* (New York: Tavistock, 1986), and *Against Nature* (London: Rivers Oram Press, 1991). Weeks is part of a broad movement of thinking prominent in the late seventies through the eighties called "social constructionism." Key texts include Jonathan Katz, *Gay American History* (New York: Thomas Y. Crowell, 1976) and *Gay/Lesbian Almanac* (New York: Harper & Row, 1983); Carroll Smith-Rosenberg, "The Female World of Love and Ritual: Relations Between Women in Nineteenth-Century America," *Signs* 9 (1975); Kenneth Plummer, ed., *The Making of the Modern Homosexual* (London: Hutchinson, 1981); John D'Emilio, *Sexual Politics, Sexual Communities* (Chicago: University of Chicago Press, 1983); Lillian Faderman, *Surpassing The Love of Men* (New York: Morrow, 1981); Gayle Rubin, "Thinking Sex," in Carole Vance, ed., *Pleasure and Danger* (New York: Routledge, 1984). A useful anthology of social constructionist writings is Martin Duberman et al., eds., *Hidden From History* (New York: Penguin, 1989). For critical discussions of social constructionism, see Edward Stein, ed., *Forms of Desire* (New York: Routledge, 1992) and Dennis Altman, ed., *Homosexuality, Which Homosexuality?* (London: Gay Men's Press, 1989).

The tradition of lesbian feminism offers an alternative social and political approach to sexuality and homosexuality. Central to lesbian feminism is the link of gender and sexuality. The classic statement is Radicalesbians, "The Woman-idenified Woman," in Anne Koedt et al., eds., *Radical Feminism* (New York: Quadrangle, 1973). Many of the best earlier statements of lesbian feminism can be found in Nancy Myron and Charlotte Bunch, eds., *Lesbianism and the Women's Movement* (Baltimore, MD: Diana Press, 1975). Adrienne Rich has been central to this tradition; her "Compulsory Heterosexuality and Lesbian Existence," *Signs* 5 (1980) is a key statement. Lesbian feminist themes are evident in the work of Kathleen Barry, *Female Sexual Slavery* (New York: New York University Press, 1978); Susan Griffin, *Woman and Nature* (New York: Harper & Row, 1978); Mary Daly, *Gyn/Ecology* (Boston: Beacon Press, 1978); Andrew Dworkin, *Our Blood* (New York: Harper & Row, 1976); and Catherine MacKinnon, *Towards a Feminist Theory of the State* (Cambridge: Harvard University Press, 1989).

New strains of lesbian and gay thinking that draw heavily on French poststructuralism have been prominent in the late 1980s and early 1990s. Eve Sedgwick's *The Epistemology of the Closet* (Berkeley: University of California Press, 1991) is a key text. Diana Fuss, ed., *Inside/Out* (New York: Routledge, 1991) includes both major theoretical statements and exemplary statements of the new "Queer theory." Other key texts include Teresa De Lauretis, ed., Special Issue: "Queer Theory: Lesbian and Gay Sexualities," *Differences* 3 (1991), Michael Warner, ed., *Fear of a Queer Planet* (Minneapolis: University of Minnesota Press, 1993), and the Special Issue: "Theorizing Lesbian Experience," *Signs* 18 (Summer 1993).

Chapter 8

The period roughly between the mid-1980s and the present is one of enormous turmoil and change in the intellectual culture of Western societies. Disciplinary knowledges have been challenged by both European intellectual movements and American pragmatic and radical traditions of social critique. Central to these critical social knowledges is an emphasis on cultural analysis. In intellectual currents as varied as semiotics, poststructuralism, feminism, Queer Theory, and Afrocentrism, the analysis of cultural meanings, rituals, symbolic orders, and discourses has moved into the center of social analysis. This cultural centering of the human studies has been further encouraged by the prominence of cultural anthropologists such as Clifford Geertz, *The Interpretation of Cultures* (New York: Basic Books, 1973); Mary Douglas, *Purity and Danger* (London: Routledge, 1966); James Clifford, *The Predicament of Culture* (Cambridge: Harvard University Press, 1988); and Renato Rosaldo, *Culture and Truth* (Boston: Beacon Press, 1989).

The cultural centering of social analysis has been paralleled by the cultural framing of much recent literary and film criticism. Indeed, I observe a broad-based movement of cultural studies anchored primarily in the humanities. Its roots are in the Centre for Contemporary Cultural Studies at Birmingham, England. Stuart Hall has been its leading light; see Hall's statement on cultural studies, "Cultural Studies and the Centre: Some Problematics and Problems," in Stuart Hall, ed., *Culture, Media, Language* (London: Hutchinson-CCCS, 1980) and, more recently, "The Emergence of Cultural Studies and the Crisis of the Humanities," *October* 53 (1990). Cultural studies in the United States has been significantly influenced by poststructuralism and the knowledges produced by the new social movements. For a statement of the American cultural studies movement, the reader should consult Lawrence Grossberg et al., *Cultural Studies* (New York: Routledge, 1992).

The cultural turn in social analysis has only recently begun to be absorbed in sociology which has been dominated by utilitarian traditions of social analysis (e.g., exchange theory, conflict theory, Marxism, structural sociology), all of which are relatively deaf to the nonrational and symbolic. Important statements of a culturally centered sociology include Jeffrey Alexander, *Action and Its Environments* (New York: Columbia University Press, 1988); Robert Wuthnow, *Meaning and Moral Order* (Berkeley: University of California Press, 1987); Ben Agger, *Cultural Studies as Critical Theory* (Washington, DC: Falmer Press, 1992); and Norman Denzin, *Imges of Postmodern Society* (Newbury Park, CA: Sage, 1991).

Robert Bellah and Zygmunt Bauman have been important figures in this cultural centering of sociology. Although Dorothy Smith situates her own work in the tradition of materialist feminism, she draws considerably on phenomenology and ethnomethodology and makes the analysis of discursive structures central to her sociology.

Robert Bellah's work is deeply rooted in the functionalist tradition. However one may characterize and assess functionalism, this tradition has insisted on the importance of cultural analysis. From Durkheim's analysis of religious-moral order and the ritual production of solidarity, to Parsons's centering on values, Lloyd Warner's analysis of rituals of death in America, and Edward Shils on the role of tradition, functionalism has been virtually the only macrosociological tradition to take culture seriously. Bellah has developed a culturally centered sociology. For example, his major early works, such as *Tokagawa Religion* (Glencoe, IL: Free Press, 1957), "Religious Evolution," *American Sociological Review* 29 (1964), and "Civil Religion in America," *Daedalus* (Winter 1967), integrate the cultural focus of the classical sociology of Weber and Durkheim with anthropological approaches through the lens of Parsonian functionalism. Although his later work departs from the Parsonian evolutionary perspective, Bellah does not surrender a cultural focus. His key works include *Beyond Belief* (New York: Harper & Row, 1970), *The Broken Covenant* (New York:

Seabury, 1975), *Habits of the Heart* (Berkeley: University of California Press, 1985), and *The Good Society* (New York: Alfred A. Knopf, 1991). Bellah articulates the concept of sociology as a public philosophy in "Social Science as Public Philosophy," in *Habits of the Heart*, "Social Science as Practical Reason," in Daniel Vallahan and Bruce Jennings, eds., *Ethics, The Social Sciences, and Policy Analysis* (New York: Plenum Press, 1983), and "The Ethical Aims of Social Inquiry, in Norma Haan et al., eds., *Social Science as Moral Inquiry* (New York: Columbia University Press, 1983). A terse autobiographical reflection is available in the Introduction to *Beyond Belief.* A wide-ranging critical discussion of *Habits of the Heart* can be found in Charles Reynolds and Ralph Norman, eds., *Community in America* (Berkeley: University of California Press, 1988).

Zygmunt Bauman's early writings combined the critical spirit of Marxism with interpretive or meaning-centered social approaches. The interested reader should consult *Culture as Praxis* (London: Routledge, 1973), *Hermeneutics and Social Science* (London: Hutchinson, 1978), and *Memories of Class* (London: Routledge, 1982). As Bauman's approach to the human studies shifted to a postmodern perspective, the emphasis on cultural analysis, in particular, the analysis of meaning and power, has remained central. His major writings since making a postmodern turn include *Legislators and Interpreters* (Ithaca: Cornell University Press, 1987), *Freedom* (Milton Keynes: Open University Press, 1988), *Modernity and the Holocaust* (Ithaca: Cornell University Press, 1989), and *Postmodern Ethics* (Oxford: Basil Blackwell, 1993). I recommend *Intimations of Postmodernity* (New York: Routledge, 1992) as an excellent introduction to Bauman's postmodern sociology and to the sociology of postmodernity. Provisional critical assessments of Bauman's work can be found in Dennis Smith, "Modernity, Postmodernity and the New Middle Ages," *The Sociological Review* 40 (1992) and Andrew Travers, "Mobilizing Postmodernity," *Reviewing Sociology* 8 (1992).

Dorothy Smith has sought to fuse Marxism, interpretive sociology (phenomenology and ethnomethodology), and feminism. Her essays have been collected into three volumes: *The Everyday World as Problematic* (Boston: Northeastern University Press, 1987), *Texts, Facts, and Femininity* (London: Routledge, 1990), and *The Conceptual Practices of Power* (Boston: Northeastern University Press, 1990). For critical responses to Dorothy Smith's sociology, see the symposium on her work in *Sociological Theory* 10 (Spring 1992); Patricia Clough, "On the Brink of Deconstructing Sociology: Critical Reading of Dorothy Smith's Standpoint Epistemology," *Sociological Quarterly* 34 (Spring 1993) provides a deconstructive reading of Dorothy Smith.

Epilogue

I have cautiously linked the surfacing of post-Enlightenment paradigms of knowledge and society to broader social changes which I've described by the term "postmodernity." As we have seen, theorists such as Jean-Francois Lyotard, Donna Haraway, and Zygmunt Bauman have argued in some detail that Western societies have entered a postmodern phase of social development, one aspect of which is a basic alteration in the structure of knowledge. The question of whether Western societies are entering a postmodern era has become a major area of contestation. Some of the key texts not mentioned previously that mark out this debate include: Fredric Jameson, *Postmodernism, or The Cultural Logic of Late Capitalism* (Durham, NC: Duke University Press, 1991); Andreas Huyssen, *After the Great Divide* (Bloomington: Indiana University Press, 1986); David Harvey, *The Condition of Postmodernity* (New York: Blackwell, 1989); Scott Lash, *Sociology of Postmodernity* (New York: Routledge, 1990), and Scott Lash and Jonathan Friedman, eds., *Modernity & Identity* (Oxford: Blackwell, 1991). Critics of the claim that the West has moved into an era of postmodernity include: Alex Callinicos, *Against Postmodernism* (New York: St. Martin's Press, 1990) and Jürgen Habermas, "Modernity versus Postmodernity," *New German Critique* 22 (1981). Barry Smart's *Modern Conditions, Postmodern Controversies* (New York: Routledge, 1991) and *Postmodernity* (New York: Routledge, 1993) provide accessible introductions to this debate.

Finally, for the reader who wishes to follow this debate over postmodernism as it pertains to questions of social knowledge, I recommend the following texts: Linda Nicholson, ed., *Feminism/Postmodernism* (New York: Routledge, 1990); Judith Butler and Joan Scott, eds., *Feminists Theorize the Political* (New York: Routledge, 1993); Steven Seidman and David Wagner, eds., *Postmodernism and Social Theory* (Oxford: Blackwell, 1991); Steven Seidman, ed., *The Postmodern Turn* (Cambridge: Cambridge University Press, 1994); and Steven Best and Douglas Kellner, *Postmodern Theory* (New York: Guilford Press, 1991).

Index